Call Of The Conch

THE HISTORY OF CHINMAYA MOVEMENT

Compiled by

SWAMI CHIDANANDA

RUKMANI RAMANI

CENTRAL CHINMAYA MISSION TRUST

Mumbai-400 072

First Edition - April 2001 - 3000 copies

Published by:
Central Chinmaya Mission Trust
Sandeepany Sadhanalaya
Saki Vihar Road
Mumbai-400 072
Tel.: 857 2367, 857 5806
Fax: 857 3065
Email: ccmt@vsnl.com
Website: www.chinmayamission.com

Distribution Centre in USA:
Chinmaya Mission West
Publications Division
560 Bridgetown Pike
Langhorne, PA 19053, USA
Tel.: (215) 396-0390
Fax: (215) 396-9710
Email: publications@chinmaya.org
Website: www.chinmayapublications.org

Printed by:
Sagar Unlimited
28-B, Nand-Deep Industrial Estate
Kondivita Lane, Andheri-Kurla Road
Mumbai-400 059
Tel.: 836 2777, 822 7699

Credit:
Cover design: Creative Minds
Kottayam, Kerala

ISBN - 81-7597-010-3

Dedicated

to

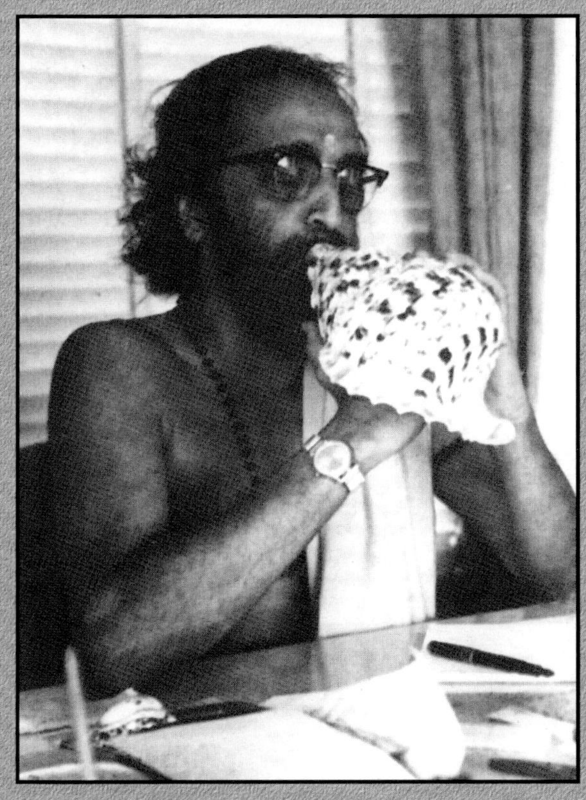

Parama Pujya Gurudev

Swami Chinmayananda

who made our lives meaningful.

FOREWORD

The saga of spiritual service that Pujya Gurudev Swami Chinmayanandaji did for more than four decades is colossal and awe-inspiring. Around him grew the Chinmaya Movement, which has showered benefits to millions of people. Generations to come will adore this mighty master who stood for strength, virtue and revival of goodness in all.

As the Movement reaches its fiftieth year, there is a need in the minds of both old-timers and recent members to know in great detail the wonderful story of this great work. Those who are part of the story enjoy the march down the memory lane. Others savor the new pieces of information that they gather here. Facts and figures, as well as amusing anecdotes, fill these pages.

Many souvenirs, and our own magazines like the *Tapovan Prasad*, have no doubt covered most of what you will find in this *Call of the Conch.* However, it is for the first time that the history of the Chinmaya Movement for fifty years is covered in a single publication.

The book, in the first place, is a record of history. Details here are drawn from reports received from New Delhi and New Zealand, Chennai and Chicago, Mumbai and Muscat, Jakarta and London, Bangalore and San Jose. The story pieces them all together to make a single interesting narration. In addition to the ever-delightful life story of Pujya Swamiji, we read here the enthusiastic work of many a dedicated devotee and disciple. Some of them gave their entire life to the master's service.

Secondly, this volume throws light on the activities of the Chinmaya Mission. Spiritual education, as well as social service are described here with some specific details of how it all happened. We see here how one man's indomitable urge to express his love for people led to thousands taking up the cause and working together for the good of humanity.

Thirdly, the *Call of the Conch* acts as a reference manual for research students to trace the journey of a historic phenomenon. They get authentic information for relating to any other historical record. In fact, this book can be a launch pad for many other works, acting as a source of vital facts and figures.

For the proud members of the Chinmaya Family, around the world, this will be a cherished possession, a special addition to their personal library. They can share the contents of this work with their children. This work is surely a valuable gift to posterity.

I compliment all those who worked on this sizable project, particularly Swami Chidananda and Rukmini Amma, and pray to Pujya Gurudev to accept this opus as a humble offering to him.

Tejomayananda

March 3, 2001 SWAMI TEJOMAYANANDA

CONTENTS

PREFACE

On December 31, 2001, the Chinmaya Movement completes fifty years. The renaissance Movement started by Swami Chinmayananda is celebrating its Golden Jubilee.

Swami Tejomayananda, the present head of Chinmaya Mission worldwide, applied thought to the coming of this momentous occasion and conceived many a plan to observe it in a fitting manner. As early as in 1996, he asked me to collect data and write a history of the Chinmaya Movement. I was then serving our centre in San Jose, California. I made a questionnaire and started sending it out to all the Mission centres. With some help from members of Chinmaya Mission San Jose, the work began in a small way. However, it was only when Mrs. Rukmani Ramani joined me in this project in late 1998 that progress was significant. I had moved to Mumbai as the Acharya of the eleventh Vedanta course in Sandeepany Sadhanalaya. Rookku, as her friends call her, sent out in my name a large number of letters, reminders and further reminders. A huge amount of text and photographs poured in, though it began as a trickle. All through the two years, she has worked very hard with dedication to the cause and, I am sure, with great love for me. Of course, I gave my time and talent when possible, and, as she would want me to say, "guided and led" the project all along.

This is indeed an offering to our Pujya Gurudev, Swami Chinmayananda. We have done research on the subject– collecting and studying the published records, accessing data from the archives of the Chinmaya Mission, interviewing senior swamis of the Mission, and meeting devotees of Gurudev. We assessed the effect of the Mission's social projects on the socio-economic life of the people of India. At the end of the assignment, we have come out with a book recording the history of the Chinmaya Movement, giving briefly the story of the Chinmaya Mission centres (200 in India and about 50 abroad) and listing the chronology of major events during the period 1951 to 2000.

We have taken help from many as need arose. Our project team has been able to collect voluminous data, thanks to the cooperation of the Chinmaya Family worldwide. The spontaneous response from most quarters has been very gratifying and has inspired us. The team would, however, like to make the following humble submissions to the readers of this book and also to the devotees of the Chinmaya Mission:

* This is the first time that the Mission embarked on such a mammoth project. The members of the team had no experience in writing books but took up this assignment as an offering to Gurudev Swami Chinmayananda. So any shortcomings of this book may be viewed with sympathy and kindness.
* Thousands of sincere devotees have played an important role in shaping the history of the Movement during the five decades. It has not been possible for us to record all the names. We place on record our gratitude to these devotees who have put the organization on a firm and stable footing.

* "Swamiji" refers to Swami Chinmayananda in this book.
* The book focuses attention on the Movement and its major events, and in that context only, reference is made to the founder of the Chinmaya Mission—Swami Chinmayananda. For an elaborate reading on the life and work of Swami Chinmayananda, there are other publications, which are given in the References.
* The history of the movement is covered until 2000 AD. In some cases, events have been covered only until 1999 as the Mission centres submitted reports in 1999. We have tried to update the information by calling for particulars. Any omission in reporting latest events may be viewed in this context.
* During the past 50 years, names of some cities and towns have changed in India e.g. Poona to Pune, Bombay to Mumbai, Madras to Chennai. For the sake of uniformity, we have used the current names of the cities.
* Some centres have submitted exhaustive history reports. However, we have been compelled to edit, very carefully, such reports to ensure that the book is compact in size. We have preserved, for posterity, the reports in their entirety in the "Archives Section" in CCMT.
* We have spelt Gyana Yagna as *Jnana-Yajna* in conformity with international standards of transliteration.
* This is a major project covering fifty years of history of an organization, which has spread to the nooks and corners of the world. It is possible that we may have missed reporting inadvertently some events. We seek your forbearance.

* We have tried to bring out an error-free book and taken the help of professionals for editing. If errors have crept in despite our best efforts, we trust you will take into account the human element and overlook the shortfall.

* For the meaning of Sanskrit words used in this book, please check with the "Glossary".

It has been a labour of love for the past two years working on this project–we have enjoyed it and hope you will enjoy the product too.

With Prem and Om,

Chidananda

March 12, 2001

Swami Chidananda
President
Chinmaya International Foundation
Veliyanad, Kerala, India

1

Call of the Conch

"Saints are born, not made," said Swami Tapovan Maharaj once. He himself was a saintly man. He was a precious gift to us from the land of Kerala that gave to our country the immortal Adi Shankara. Fondly called "Chippu Kutty," the future saint was not attracted to formal education. Tutored at home, he took great delight in reading books on his own. For some years he studied spiritual works and was deeply drawn to the philosophy of *Advaita*. When he was still quite young, he resolved to renounce the pleasures and possessions of the world. He left his hometown, went on many pilgrimages, enriched himself by reading widely, and acquired vast spiritual knowledge. He set out in quest of Truth; he always shared his *Vedantic* knowledge with other true seekers. He had tremendous compassion for humanity and left indelible impressions of his greatness on those he met. He took *sannyas* in a unique way. Standing on the banks of the river Narmada, he cast aside his householder's clothes and donned ochre robes. Traditionally, a guru gives *sannyas* to his disciple when he considers him ripe enough for it. This is called giving *deeksha*. But Swami Tapovanam did not follow this tradition. Following the rules of *vidvat sannyas*, with the visible sun for witness and initiating guru, he chanted an appropriate *mantra* and assumed *sannyas*. The name he gave himself was "Tyagananda". Later on, he did go through the prescribed rituals, from Shreemad Janardanagiri Swami of Kailas Mutt, who named him Swami Tapovanam.

For quite sometime, Swami Tapovanam moved about in the beautiful Himalayan region. During his wanderings he reached Mount Kailas, earning the admiration of his fellow monks for this remarkable feat. He became well-known not just for his austerities but for his sensitive poetry as well, written completely in tune with nature. *Himagiri Vihar* and *Ishwara Darshanam* are outstanding examples of his poetry.

The swami lived for many years in the Himalaya. So great was the holiness he radiated that the *sadhus* living in the Himalaya often referred to him as the "beacon light of the Himalayas". He loved solitude. It was in 1924 that he visited Uttarakashi for the first time. The higher reaches of the Himalaya seemed to beckon him, for he saw in them the Lord's special manifestation. He was a highly evolved soul who saw God in everything–whether a stone, or a stream, or a tree. Full of compassion, he taught his disciples and all those who came to his *kuti* in search of knowledge. *Sannyasis*, men and women householders, pilgrims and others would continuously throng for a *darshan* of this great saint. Such a person was the guru of Swami Chinmayananda, the architect of the Chinmaya Movement.

Swami Tapovanam chose Uttarakashi for his Ashram and acquired great fame as a sage. He spent the winter months in Uttarakashi, and the summer months in Gangotri. To quote his pupil Swami Chinmayananda, he was "the last representative of the ancient institution of traditional gurus... a God without Temple, a *Veda* without language...."

THE STUDENT ARRIVES

Balakrishna Menon, as Swami Chinmayananda was known before he became a *sannyasi*, was a law graduate from Kerala. Later he became a journalist and worked for the daily newspaper National Herald (Lucknow). In order to understand the kind of life led by *sadhus*, he visited the Sivananda Ashram at Rishikesh. So strongly was he drawn to the daily life of spirituality that he stayed on there. He was greatly impressed with the teachings of Swami Sivananda. Presently this led to an intense relationship between Menon and Swami Sivananda. Finally, on February 25, 1949, Swami Sivananda gave him *sannyas*. Thus did Swami Chinmayananda emerge. Sivananda suggested to Chinmayananda that he go to Uttarakashi to study under the great *mahatma* Swami Tapovanam.

Swami Chinmayananda soon became a disciple of Swami Tapovanam. He studied Vedanta at Uttarakashi, and went through the *Panchadashi* of Vidyaranya carefully. He spent several years in the constant company of his guru in the Himalaya–learning, imbibing, and growing in knowledge and wisdom.

The name "Himalaya" is made of two Sanskrit words–"hima", which means "snow", and "alaya" which denotes "home". The Himalaya is not merely a home of snows; it has always been a stronghold of yogic wisdom and spirituality. The snow-clad mountains symbolize purity; the peaks dazzling in the sun symbolize proximity to the Lord. They appear to be constantly singing the glory of the Lord. According to the *Puranas*, great *yogis* lived in the caves of the Himalaya mountains, in deep meditation, waiting to shuffle off their mortal coil. Apostrophizing the caves, Swami Tapovanam once exclaimed, "Which mountain will not be jealous of you? In the dark caves on other mountains, one finds only jackals and tigers; in you alone dwell enlightened hermits in peace and bliss!"

Thus, up in the solitary mountains of the Garhwal region, in the holy centres of Uttarakashi and Gangotri, Swami Chinmayananda was inspired to start a movement for the renaissance of the Hindu religion.

Swami Tapovanam has written a glorious description of Uttarakashi and Gangotri in his book *Wanderings in the Himalayas*. Today the ecology of these two places has undergone a vast change owing to mindless deforestation and urbanization. The roar of the Himalayan leopards has yielded place to the hooting of the power horns of the buses. The *pranava* (Om) sound emanating from the Bhageerathi in Uttarakashi is drowned in the perennial noise of labourers digging roads. The roots and fruits, which the *sadhus* used to live on, are being fast substituted by junk food and colas. Fifty years ago, to go to Gangotri, there was no alternative but to trudge the 105 kilometers from Uttarakashi; but today buses drive right up to the top, almost up to the gorges from where the Ganga issues forth. And yet, even today, one can see *sadhus* living peacefully there: they appear to be revelling in the peace which they have achieved. Writing about Uttarakashi, Swami Tapovanam said that it was a place ideally suited for a seeker. It had a temple of Lord Vishwanath among the peaks of the Himalaya, on the banks of the Ganga. It had a solitary forest resplendent with divine beauty. It was associated with memories of the great *rishis* – could there be a more suitable place for *sadhana* of a seeker.

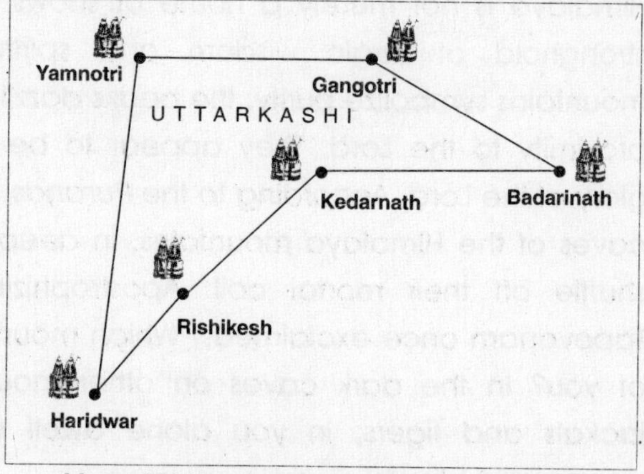

Map of Rishikesh, Uttarakashi and Gangotri

Uttarakashi is one hundred sixty kilometers from Rishikesh; even the lowest region there is 5,800 ft above sea-level. It is surrounded by a mountain range called Varanavata. The tributaries of the river Bhageerathi flow around the mountain tract like two hands hugging the plains. At the central point in the plain, almost like the lap of the mountain tract, is Ujeli. It is here that the Tapovan Kuti lies, the home of Swami Tapovan Maharaj. Built in 1936 by some of his devotees, its location is truly unique. The river Bhageerathi flows at the foot of the mountain giving out a soothing *pranava* sound that can be heard in the Tapovan Kuti. In the village is the temple of Vishwanath, the Lord of Uttarakashi. There is a *svayambhoo linga* in this temple, tilted slightly to the right side. This temple is also known as Sowmya Kashi. In fact, monks in the Himalaya referred to Swami Tapovanam himself as the Spiritual Bird of Sowmya Kashi– a bird possessed of the freedom and strength needed to reach great heights. He did reach great heights of spirituality, did he not?

Gangotri is at some 8,000 feet above sea-level. The road is long and winding, and is full of ups and downs. Looking out from the bus, one sees on one side the mighty mountains and, on the other, the Ganga--pure and white, as if it were a river of milk. One can see the snow-capped peaks of the mountains close to each other as if they were holding hands, as if they were determined to stand together unto eternity. Gangotri is the sacred place where Swami Tapovanam and Swami Chinmayananda spent four to five months of the summer together each year. There is a Tapovan Kuti at Gangotri too; the devotees of Swami Tapovanam built it for their guru.

During the summer months, Swami Tapovanam imparted Vedanta lessons to his disciples, with the *shishya* Swami Chinmayananda joyously performing *guru-seva*. The roaring sound of the Ganga provided background music, as it were, to the daily routine. Swami Chinmayananda was greatly inspired by the mighty flow and the roaring noise of the Ganga. It inspired him to trigger the Chinmaya Movement, which he then called the Gangotri Plan.

Thus Uttarakashi, to Swami Chinmayananda, was where he found the springboard of Vedanta. He found in Gangotri the very fountainhead of inspiration.

THE GANGOTRI PLAN

During the months when the climate was cold and chilly in Gangotri, the *sadhus* sat out in the sun and discussed a variety of subjects bearing on Vedanta. They used to call this *fakirstan* (place of the wise). Swami Chinmayananda used to listen to the arguments of the senior sages but differed with them on subjects relating to the preaching of Vedanta to the masses. Specifically no mention is made anywhere as to what made him unhappy about the discussions of the senior sages. Perhaps he did not agree with their orthodoxy as to who should be taught Vedanta; for he believed that anyone who was interested should be taught. Perhaps he did not approve of their view that Vedanta should be taught only in holy places and exclusively by the learned *pundits* (*brahmanas*). Listening to their discussions, Swami Chinmayananda used to be very concerned about what they should teach the people on the plains when they conducted *satsangs*. He was convinced that there was a crying need to change the approach so as to extend spiritual knowledge to the common man. Swamiji's anxiety was threefold. How best could he impart the knowledge he had gained to the people on the plains? How was he to focus on the target audience, i.e. the educated class? And, finally, which language should he use while communicating with the educated class, seeing that it was this class which in its turn influenced others?

It was the summer of 1951. Swami Chinmayananda strongly felt a tremendous urge to take up all these questions and solve them once for all. At the same time he was not sure if he would be able to carry out this momentous task without help. Sitting on the banks of the Ganga, in Gangotri, he asked himself: "Can I face the educated class and bring to their faithless hearts a ray at least of the understanding of our wondrous culture?" The answer, surprisingly, came from Mother Ganga herself. To quote the oft-repeated lines of Swami Chinmayananda, Mother Ganga seemed to say to him: "Son, don't you see me? Born here in the Himalaya, I rush down to the plains taking with me both life and nourishment. Fulfilment of any possession consists in sharing it with others." That clinched the whole issue. Mother Ganga served humanity by bringing the cool, fresh water of the Himalaya in abundance to the people on the plains with no bias towards any caste, creed or religion. She did not trickle down; she gushed forth roaring, making her presence felt by one and all. She did not restrict her flow to any specified geographical region but flowed from Gomukh to the Bay of Bengal. Her tributaries also contributed to the prosperity and fertility of the regions over which they flowed. These secondary sources supplemented the main one. All this had to be understood in relation to the Chinmaya Movement.

Swamiji's Gangotri Plan came to him in a flash. The knowledge of Vedanta, in its pristine glory, must be taken from the Himalayan heights to the plains below for the enrichment of humanity. Knowledge had to be spread with no bias towards any caste or creed. It had to cascade down to the whole of India that was Bharat, not flow down in a trickle. It must come down in all its splendour, roaring forth for all to hear. The main source for *prachar* work had to be supplemented by secondary sources, through training more and more people for the purpose. (In later years, Swamiji referred to these as the "arsenals of my rearmament"). He must reach out to these people and expose them to the fundamentals of Vedanta.

Thus, the work that lay ahead of him was now clear to Swamiji. But he had to convince his Master first, in order to make his dream come true. He called the Gangotri Plan an "afternoon dream". Swami Tapovan Maharaj, however, was a person who had very orthodox views on how to spread the knowledge of the *Upanishads* and other scriptures. He felt that it "is useless to carry Vedanta to the market place. Some may understand it. Many may not even listen to it. A few alone will be converted by it. And almost none will be benefited by it." He was of the firm view that the Almighty Himself would guide true seekers of knowledge to a guru and help them in acquiring the knowledge of truth and reality. For some time, Swamiji balked at confronting his guru and asking him for permission to descend to the plains. Knowing his guru's views, he let the matter lie for some time. But the thoughts kept on coming up and demanded an answer. Indeed, it became a compulsive urge, almost an obsession. Soon he approached his guru and sought his permission. The guru, as had been expected, held to his conviction that the plan, as Chinmayananda had conceived it, was not the right thing to be pursued. Nevertheless, his compassion for his pupil made him suggest an alternative: he asked him to make a reconnoitering tour of the plains and make his own assessment.

Accordingly, in May 1951, Swami Chinmayananda walked from Gangotri to Rishikesh, a distance of some two hundred sixty kilometres, and thence to Delhi. From Delhi he set out on a visit to important places, with their temples and *mutts* all over India. He travelled along the railway route and visited many cities including

Pune. (It was in Pune that he later–in December–conducted his first *jnana-yajna*). He returned to Uttarakashi in October 1951.

During his five-month sojourn, between May and October 1951, Swamiji was more than convinced that the people on the plains needed a qualitatively better exposure to our culture, religion and traditions. He saw how people were not even aware of our rich cultural heritage. If they were, they were going through the motions mechanically without understanding the inner meaning. The panacea for such a situation was, according to him, to conduct *jnana-yajnas* and spread the knowledge of the rich Hindu scriptures. He was determined to go ahead with his plan and without delay.

Swamiji conveyed to his guru his intention to execute the Gangotri Plan. He said that he would be conducting his first *yajna* for a hundred days beginning December 31, 1951 at Pune, at the Vinayak Temple at Rasta Peth. His guru did not want to discourage him but was not sure if there would be even fifteen people to listen to him. Swamiji was not discouraged. On the first day there were eighteen people. Soon the number swelled, the audience occupying not only the temple precincts but also overflowing into the nearby lanes.

WHAT IS A JNANA-YAJNA?

Swamiji had not drawn out a clear outline of such *yajnas* for that would need some experiments to be made and a structure to be framed on the basis of feedback he would get from them. He was, however, clear that the *yajna* would necessarily entail a detailed daily discourse on a selected *Upanishad*. The programme would last for a hundred days. Swamiji also meant to use the ancient method of developing concentration of the mind through meditation and *Akhandanama Sankeertan* (unbroken repetition of the names of God). He would also conduct a *'Havan'* or fire sacrifice and explain to people the meaning and special significance of the elaborate rituals involved. Then, at the end of the *yajna*, there would be a spiritual picnic to make the people understand the need for community living on an austere scale. Finally there would be an *Avabhrita-snana* (bath to mark the end of the undertaking). This was the bare outline of the *jnana-yajna*. The word *'jnana-yajna'* was a newly coined word, as Swamiji admitted before the Jagadguru Shri Shankaracharya of Shringeri Shri Abhinav Vidya Teertha Swami, during an audience with him in April 1958 after his fortieth *jnana-yajna*, at Bangalore.

THE MOVEMENT BEGINS

Swamiji had already chosen the centre for conducting the first *jnana-yajna*: it was Pune. He himself did not know why he had chosen that place except that he had met a young boy there, who was very enthusiastic and positive, eager to assume responsibility for organizational work. He was the personal assistant to the manager of an aided primary school in Pune. The boy had a daring spirit, and willingly took up the preparatory work for the *yajna*. Besides Swamiji had met Ms. Sushila Mudaliar of Pune at Uttarakashi during her visit to that place to meet Swami Tapovan Maharaj. This contact ultimately became very valuable as she willingly took up the *yajna* work at Pune. Indeed she agreed to do the same kind of work for the second *yajna* at Chennai. While coming to Pune, Swamiji had come via Hyderabad where he met one G.S. Reddy. Swami Sivananda had given a letter of introduction to Reddy. The Reddy family was thrilled to get a letter from their guru introducing a young swami. They arranged a *satsang* at Hyderabad and bought him a railway ticket to reach

Pune. Swamiji had only a four-anna coin in his pocket when he landed in Pune, but, undaunted he managed to conduct a hundred days' *yajna*!

Thus the first *jnana-yajna* was conducted at the Vinayak Temple in Rasta Peth, Pune from December 31, 1951 to April 8, 1952. Swamiji himself inaugurated the *yajna* because, in his words, "no one else was prepared to do so." During this *yajna*, Swamiji took up the texts of Kathopanishad and Kenopanishad. Some residents of Pune still recall how Swamiji took 60 days out of the 100 days to give them an introduction to the two *Upanishads*. Madhukar Veeraswami Naidu of Chinchwad, Pune, who attended, recalls even now, how he felt compelled to attend the discourse. He had been a regular visitor to the Vinayak temple, solely interested in taking the *prasad*, which was distributed in the evening. He was much drawn towards this young swami there holding forth so eloquently on the scriptures. Day by day the crowd increased, army officers of the Southern Command came cycling to listen to the swami, and the audience overflowed into the lanes near the temple. "My mission is to convert Hindus into Hinduism," said Swamiji. These words still ring in Naidu's ears. Here was a swami, a stranger to Pune, living in the Madras Dharamshala, dyeing ochre the cloth given to him by some devotees, speaking impeccable English, wearing a unique head-dress, and working with missionary zeal. All these traits appealed to the residents of Pune. Even today, the Chinmaya Mission, Pune, holds a *Geeta jnana-yajna* on December 31, every year to commemorate the event of 1951.

SAFFRON OM FLAG

Swamiji thus sounded the auspicious conch of the Chinmaya Movement on December 31, 1951 at Pune. A saffron flag with the mystic syllable 'ॐ' inscribed on it was first hoisted there.

The *jnana-yajna* movement was launched at a time when Hinduism was passing through a decadent phase. India had achieved independence in 1947 after a prolonged rule by a foreign power. This had left the masses without any sense of direction or goal. The ethical and moral fibre of the country had undergone severe strain. Conditions were thus ripe for a revivalist movement.

Swamiji's renaissance movement was ushered in with symbols that were already familiar to the public at large, as Hindu symbols. He especially adopted the most sacred Hindu symbol 'ॐ' (OM).

ॐ is the most significant (graphic) symbol recognized in Hindu tradition. The syllable is recited as part of thousands of *mantras*. ॐ is the sound with which creation of this universe began.

The colour of the flag is saffron–an auspicious colour representing fire. The Chinmaya Movement is deeply committed to the spread of the Fire of Knowledge so it was most appropriate. Thus the saffron ॐ flag became the standard flag of the Chinmaya Movement. Swamiji would arrive exactly at the appointed time and his car would have the flag fluttering.

Drawing inspiration from Mother Ganga, Swami Chinmayananda took the knowledge that he imbibed in the Himalaya to the plains. The first *jnana-yajna* was a great success. Swamiji thus translated his inspiration into action.

The auspicious sound of the conch that he blew beckons spiritual seekers even today.

Suggested Reading for some biographical details of Swami Chinmayananda:

1. The Journey of a Master by Nancy Patchen, republished by CCMT, 1996.
2. Swami Chinmayananda (A Life of Inspiration and Service) by Rudite Emir, published by CCMT, 1998.
3. Ageless Guru by Radhika Krishnakumar, published by CCMT, 1999.

View from Tapovan Kuti -
The mountain ranges and the river Bhageerathi

Swami Tapovan Maharaj with his disciple Swami Chinmayananda

At Ananda Ashram, Rishikesh

Swamiji with Swami Sivananda - 1949

Enter the Arena - 31st December, 1951
Jnana Yajna at Ganapati Temple,
Rasta Peth, Pune

The Presiding Deity - the First Worshipped

Swamiji with the "First Host Family"

Uttarakashi - A View of Kailas Ashram and Tapovan Kuti

2

The Message Resounds Nationwide

"It was an afternoon dream that took me to more than a hundred cities in India to address about 50,000 devotees in twenty-five jnana-yajnas."

Swami Chinmayananda

On December 31, 1951, the first day of the first *jnana-yajna* in Pune, just eighteen people attended Swamiji's discourse. Five years later, in December 1956, that number had swelled to 50,000 devotees. During the twenty-five *yajnas* between 1951 and 1956, Swamiji covered eight out of the ten major *Upanishads* and the first fifteen chapters of the *Bhagavad Geeta*. His *yajnas* lasted from a minimum of eighteen to a maximum of a hundred days.

Swamiji completed his first *yajna* at Pune on April 8, 1952. Thereafter he proceeded to Mumbai to recoup after an attack of typhoid. He also needed to rest after a hundred days of the *yajna* routine. He stayed with one of his friends, who was a devotee of Bhagavan Ramana Maharshi. There was a group of Ramana devotees who were planning to bring out a monthly magazine in

Mumbai, and Swamiji joined them in planning and editing the magazine. *Call Divine*, as the magazine was called, was to publish articles on Bhagavan Ramana and also on other saintly persons. The first issue of *Call Divine* was published in September 1952, with Swami Rajeshwarananda and Swami Chinmayananda as joint editors. In the first two articles credits were given to Swamiji as "Swami Chinmayananda M.A. (Eng.)". Thereafter the suffix seems to have been dropped. Swami Rajeshwarananda wrote all the editorials but for two. Swamiji wrote these two: the first in October 1952 and the other in January 1953. Swamiji did a series, "Talks with Aspirants." Outlining the objective of *Call Divine*, Swamiji said in the course of an editorial:

> There is many a great true soul who imbibed from the Master streaks of the Eternal Light of Wisdom. To harness all these flying sparks and shooting meteors of Spiritual Wisdom would be the main duty of this magazine.

Swamiji continued to be on the editorial board of *Call Divine* till December 1957. Thereafter Swami Yogiraj Shuddhananda took charge.

Swamiji often sought advice from his gurus, Swami Sivananda and Swami Tapovan Maharaj, on his plans as to his future *jnana-yajnas*. After waiting for a year, his second *yajna* was organized in Chennai to commence on April 28, 1953.

The conch that was thus sounded at Pune in 1951 with great hopes was at last well-heard; the message indeed spread to the four corners of the country. It looked as if Swamiji was determined to establish Chinmaya flag-posts in all directions–one *yajna* each in the east (Kolkata), west (Pune), and central India (Rewa), eight in the north (Delhi), and as many as fourteen in the south (Chennai, Madurai, Udagamandalam, Coimbatore, Palakkad, Bangalore,

Kozhikode, Kochi etc.). Swamiji believed that the success of any undertaking lay in meticulous planning. His choice of *yajna* centres shows that he meant each part of the country to receive his message.

THE SECRET OF SUCCESS

What made the *jnana-yajnas* so popular? Why did thousands of people come to listen to a former law student from Kerala expound on the tenets of a religion often regarded as a bundle of superstitions and rituals? How did Swamiji build in local communities the support that was necessary to conduct a *yajna*? How did he overcome the perception of the English language as a colonialist tool and skilfully use the very language to express ideas that were thousands of years old? Answers to these questions lie in the three essential qualities of Swamiji--reasoning, oratory, and progressive thinking.

The period from December 1951 to December 1956 witnessed the moulding of the *jnana-yajna* concept Indeed, out of this constant moulding emerged the final shape of the concept. After the completion of the *yajna* at Pune, Swamiji went back to his gurus, Swami Tapovanam and Swami Sivananda, discussed the conduct of the *yajnas* and the lessons he had learnt from them. They gave him advice and suggestions on how to deepen the impact of a *yajna* on new seekers. Thus by learning from his gurus and through trial and error, Swamiji was able to structure a format for the *jnana-yajna*, which, he was satisfied, would meet the expectations of his varied audience. To quote him, "The *yajna* scheme was not fully clear to me then. It became more and more revealed as I worked ahead with my daily lecture programmes. Some of the programmes which I then went through were later on rejected, and new schemes envisaged and incorporated into it from time to time, expanding, enlarging, widening, and deepening the *yajna* technique."

TWENTY-FIVE JNANA-YAJNAS IN FIVE YEARS

To ensure the success of a *yajna*, the *yajna* committee had to network with influential local persons. Swamiji was yet to establish his credentials: he was locally known just as the swami of Uttarakashi. His second *yajna* held in Chennai in 1953 became possible only because of the help received there from his uncle, Kuttikrishna Menon. The uncle found a Muslim family friend who had agreed to let the *yajna* be performed in his vacant estate. Once the *yajna* was organized, Swamiji would pull unprecedented crowds thanks to local enterprise but mainly because of his masterly exposition of the priceless teachings to be found in the *Upanishads* and the *Bhagavad Geeta*, combined with his sparkling humour and impeccable oratory in English.

The twenty-five *jnana-yajnas* conducted during this period reveal some interesting trends of the movement in the initial years. The stronghold of the Chinmaya Movement, during this period, was in the South. There are obvious reasons for this: Swamiji was from Kerala, and he had valuable contacts in Kerala and in the neighbouring State of Tamil Nadu.

An important factor, which contributed to laying a strong foundation for the Chinmaya Movement, was the choice of the English language for the discourses. Even though India had just gained independence, the English language was still the common bond between the educated classes in cities like Delhi, Chennai, Madurai, Bangalore, and Kolkata where the *yajnas* took place. Swamiji was facing an audience that already had a preconceived notion that the *Upanishads* and other scriptures were dry subjects written in an obscure language, Sanskrit. Justifying his choice of the English language, he said, "I have assessed the mood of the educated classes in these cities and found that they have, in their ignorance, an aversion to Sanskrit, a great language." He introduced the intelligentsia to Sanskrit by adopting a subtle method of quoting important *Upanishadic* statements in their original form but giving their meaning in English. At the end of a *yajna*, lots of people got interested in learning Sanskrit; so much so that on many occasions, after the *yajna* was over, the organizers found it necessary to arrange regular classes for teaching Sanskrit. In fact, when Swamiji met the Jagadguru Shankaracharya of Shringeri in April 1959, he justified his teaching the *Upanishads* in English. He admitted that he purposely cultivated English because his mission was to contact the English-educated masses that had no appreciation of the Hindu religion and scriptures.

One of the important aspects of a *jnana-yajna* was the performance of a *havan*, with the entire audience chanting *mantras* and *shlokas*. There was strong opposition to this chanting of *mantras* and *shlokas* by all and sundry, so much so that Swamiji once confessed: "I have been finding it rather hard to conduct *havans* because the perverted orthodoxy is shocked, outraged at this new limb of the *yajna*." At these *yajnas*, he faced audiences, which believed that Hinduism was nothing but a bundle of superstitions and rituals. Religious *yajnas* consisted quite often of elaborate rituals performed by pundits droning *mantras*, which made no sense to the common man. Through his novel idea of *jnana-yajna*, Swamiji was able to change the perception of the public. This was a revolutionary event in the history of Hinduism. People welcomed his liberal approach, especially as women were permitted, for the first time, to chant *Vedic mantras*.

The *Upanishadic* truths were given in a lucid manner in the market place with homely analogies. Knowledge of Sanskrit was no longer a must to understand the principles of Vedanta as expounded in the *jnana-yajna-shalas*.

Swamiji did not decry ritualistic, religious observances of the *bhakti-margis*. Indeed he absorbed them in his *jnana-yajnas* by introducing pure Vedanta in the mornings, practical Vedanta in his *Geeta* discourses in the evenings, *bhakti* in the *Akanda-nama-sankeertanas*, *Vedic* worship in his *havans* and, lastly, piety through visits to centres of pilgrimage. These features evoked a spontaneous response from the masses.

Swamiji's discourses were totally without bias towards any caste, creed or religion. His devotees included even Muslims, Jews and Christians. A Muslim teacher, Ms. Rahilla Ansari, in Delhi, who attended the seventh *yajna* for sixty-one days wrote: "Hinduism as expounded by Swamiji was a religion based, not on old wives' tales, but on a practical and highly developed code of morality... I found to my great joy that the essence of Hinduism and the essence of Islam were identical." Mosser, a Jewish resident of Delhi, working in All India Radio, attended Swamiji's discourses on *Kathopanishad* and was spellbound. He said: "I discovered in Vedanta the spirit of Persia. My own Persian literature became a live philosophy to me."

Swamiji's initiation of his listeners into elementary lessons of meditation and concentration was another popular component of a *jnana-yajna*. Most people who attended his *yajnas* were benefited by his practical lessons on meditation. He was able to convince people that regular and systematic practice of meditation would lead to spiritual evolvement and speed up their progress towards self-realization.

MOBILE YAJNAS: AN INNOVATION

Swamiji also innovated mobile *yajnas*. Lectures were arranged in different localities in the same town. During this period the seekers observed a week of *sadhana*. The twelfth *jnana-yajna* held in Chennai in June 1955 was a mobile *yajna*. It covered three localities–Egmore, Saidapet, and T. Nagar. In eighteen days Swamiji covered portions of Vivekachoodamani. Like a marketing expert, he literally took the product to everybody's doorstep. He did not hesitate to try out new approaches to reach out to people.

His commitment and desire to spread *Upanishadic* knowledge among the common people was often compared with the spirit of Swami Vivekananda, Shri Aurobindo, Bhagavan Ramana Maharshi and Mahatma Gandhi. Atheists and agnostics who came in contact with him changed overnight into deeply religious men because Swamiji could lucidly explain the Hindu religion and the truths contained in the *Upanishads*. Logical presentation and practical insights into daily life were his main scoring-points.

DISCIPLINE

The masses were most impressed with the discipline maintained in the *yajna-shalas*. The punctuality, the orderliness and the silence impressed them most–accustomed as they were to noisy discourses in temples. Devotees who came to the railway station to receive Swamiji were required to stand in a straight line on the platform and not crowd around him. Outside *yajna-shalas*, footwear once removed had to be arranged in a neat row. In *Akanda-nama-sankirtanas*, the chanting was done round the clock, each volunteer being allotted a time-slot. All devotees had to be present at the appointed time. Once there was a delay of an hour for a volunteer to report, whose allotted time was midnight.

The next evening Swamiji roared in his discourse, "Do you people want the *japa* or not? If this happens again the *japa* will be stopped." No latecomer to the *yajna* would dare enter the *pandal* as Swamiji would immediately stop his lecture and make his displeasure plain by means of some remark or other. Latecomers had to take a seat at the rear so as not to disturb those who were intently listening.

BIRTH OF THE CHINMAYA MISSION

In June 1953 the second *jnana-yajna*, the first to be held in Chennai, ended. Some devotees wanted to form a forum for study and discussion on *Vedantic* subjects. They got together to create an organization. Their idea was to name it the Chinmaya Mission. Accordingly they wrote to Swamiji at Uttarakashi. In his reply Swamiji said, "Don't start any organization in my name. I have not come here to be institutionalized. I have come here to give the message of our ancient sages, which has benefited me. If it has benefited you also, pass it on." They replied to Swamiji that the word "Chinmaya" only meant true knowledge and that, as seekers of Truth, they were naming the organization the Chinmaya Mission. The word "Chinmaya" need not be understood as connoting Swamiji's name. Swamiji relented at last. Thus was born the Chinmaya Mission on August 8, 1953.

The main architects of this forum were Rangaswami, Natarajan Iyer (later Swami Dayananda), and Kanti Iyer (later Swami Shantananda).

The constitution of the Chinmaya Mission, inter alia, mentioned that the membership of the Mission was open to all Hindus. One of the devotees, Professor Vidyadhar Sharma of Allahabad, raised an objection, stating that the Mission was promoting a separatist tendency by stipulating "Hindus". That was contrary to the precept of the *Advaita* or non-dualistic philosophy. In defence, Swamiji said: "I have a definite reason for putting in that word "Hindu"... One of the techniques for training the heart is to visit temples. At such times we cannot debar some members, saying that they cannot enter temples, which would be painful. Non-Hindus are welcome to join our study classes or weekly prayer meetings." Thus did he resolve a thorny question.

TYAGI: THE FIRST PUBLICATION OF THE CHINMAYA MOVEMENT

In September 1955 the first publication of the Chinmaya Movement, *Tyagi*, was released. The seed of this publication lay in the *yajna-prasad* that was distributed right from the time of the first *yajna* at Pune. Each of Swamiji's talks at the *yajna* was recorded in shorthand, typed, edited, and printed, all in twenty-four hours. Four or five of these were combined to make a booklet, which was mailed to 12000 addressees–those who attended the *yajna*, and their relatives and also those who sent requests therefor by mail. This distribution of *yajna-prasad* was soon found to be a heavy financial burden. Many organizers were reluctant to take up this additional responsibility while organizing *yajnas*. At this time a group of devotees in Chennai decided to bring out a journal that would publish Swamiji's discourses and also articles written by great saints like Swami Sivananda, Shri Aurobindo and others. The group offered to place this publication at Swamiji's disposal. He accepted it whole-heartedly and promised that all his talks at the *yajna-shalas* would be sent to them for publication. That was the genesis of *Tyagi*. He wrote, "May *Tyagi* hold the torch high so that our generation may walk out of the jungle into which they have wandered unwittingly." After seeing the inaugural issue of *Tyagi*, Swami Tapovan Maharaj wrote, "I am glad to say that *Tyagi* deserves its great name because it looks like a *tyagi* itself with no extra ornamentation about it. Such a journal is entitled to preach *tyaga*, *vairagya* and *jnana* to others. May it protect and follow the greatness of its name." The magazine was published from Chennai and the editor of *Tyagi* was G. Natarajan Iyer.

PUBLICATION OF HAIL RENAISSANCE-VOLUME ONE

The publication of the first issue of Hail Renaissance was released in December 1956, on the occasion of the twenty-fifth *jnana-yajna* at Hyderabad. It is an outstanding contribution made by devotees and was sponsored by Mrs. Sheila Puri, an ardent devotee of Swamiji in Delhi. It is a historical record of the *yajnas* conducted between 1951 and 1956, with contributions from people who had been drawn to Swamiji during this period. For the first time ever, as the records would show, Swamiji used an emblem of the Chinmaya Mission in a letter found in this publication. He called himself Chief *Sevak*. Dated December 20, 1956, this epistle addressed Swamiji's glorious vision of a Hindu renaissance. As the years passed by, the Mission had many more emblems designed to symbolize the activities of the different units within the Chinmaya fold. Under the title "The Genesis", Swamiji himself wrote an article about how the whole movement started, how he had only a hazy concept of *jnana-yajna* in the beginning, how there was opposition to the movement, and how it had been surmounted.

This publication has amazing data on the *jnana-yajnas*, their dates, the centres, the coordinators, and, above all, a graphical representation through bar charts showing the attendance at each *yajna*. The highest attendance was at the eighteenth *yajna*, at Bangalore, numbering 4,500 a day. Next came the sixteenth *yajna*, at Mylapore (Chennai) with 3,200 a day, followed by the twenty-first *yajna*, at Madurai with 3,000 a day.

The first volume of Hail Renaissance was followed by a series of three similar publications from time to time covering the Chinmaya Mission activities up to the year 1987. But for the foresight manifested in recording the activities of the Chinmaya Mission in this manner and in such detail, it would have been impossible for us to record the history of the Chinmaya Movement later with accuracy. This was again a masterly idea of Swami Chinmayananda's to ensure benefit to posterity.

Going through the Movement's early history, one cannot but wonder at the Master's management-oriented approach. He set the parameter for measuring the success of a *yajna*, in terms of the strength of the crowd it attracted. The organizers had to assess the attendance meticulously. He himself kept a log of the miles he travelled, the mode of transport, the cities visited, and the places where *yajnas* were held. All these data were presented in a graphic form so that the average man could get an idea of the impact that the Chinmaya Movement was making all over the country. To implement the management principle of motivation through participation, he introduced the *akhanda-nama-sankirtanas* and *havans*, which required full audience participation. Periodical feedback from the *yajna-shalas* was received and corrective action taken whenever necessary. Thus for a religious movement in its infancy, the Chinmaya Movement was founded on remarkably sound principles indeed.

MAHASAMADHI OF REVERED GURU SWAMI TAPOVAN MAHARAJ

In November 1956 the twenty-third *jnana-yajna* concluded at Kashmere Gate, Delhi. Meanwhile news reached Swami

Chinmayananda that his guru's health was fast deteriorating. He went to Uttarakashi in December to meet his ailing guru. He burst into tears upon seeing his Master who consoled him saying, "Death is born with us when we are born." This was his last meeting with his guru.

On Full Moon Day in January 1957, Swami Tapovan Maharaj breathed his last. At that time Swami Chinmayananda was conducting a *jnana-yajna* at Palakkad. Visibly shaken on hearing the news, he went into retreat at Rishikesh and observed a period of silence and meditation.

The Chinmaya Mission began to observe the Full Moon Day of the month of *Pausha* every year (Full Moon Day of a month nearer to January of the Gregorian calendar) as Tapovan Day. Later, in the 1980s, a change was made. Under directions from Swamiji, the Chinmaya Family now observes Tapovan Day on the saint's birthday. It is the same as the *Geeta Jayanti* (*Margashirsha Shukla Ekadashi*, the eleventh day of the bright fortnight of the lunar month *Margashirsha*).

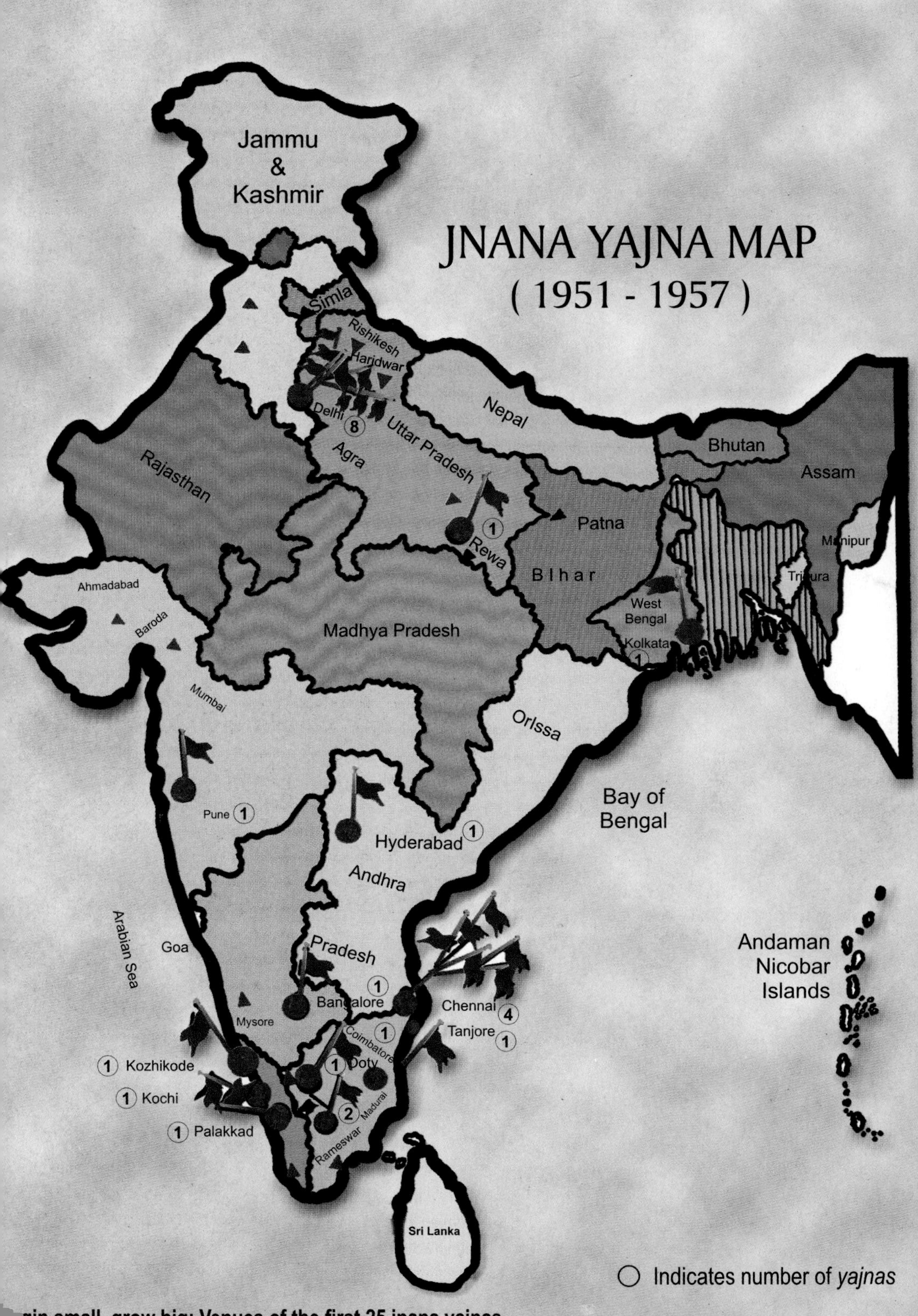

gin small, grow big: Venues of the first 25 jnana yajnas

Ernakulam Railway Station: Return of the prodigal son?

Breathing new life into old rituals: *A Havan*

Body gets a holy bath,
Mind is soaked in devotion:
Avabhrita snanam

A visit to a temple:
Offer everything to the Lord

e vibrant Chinmaya:
Time to wake up
a nation?

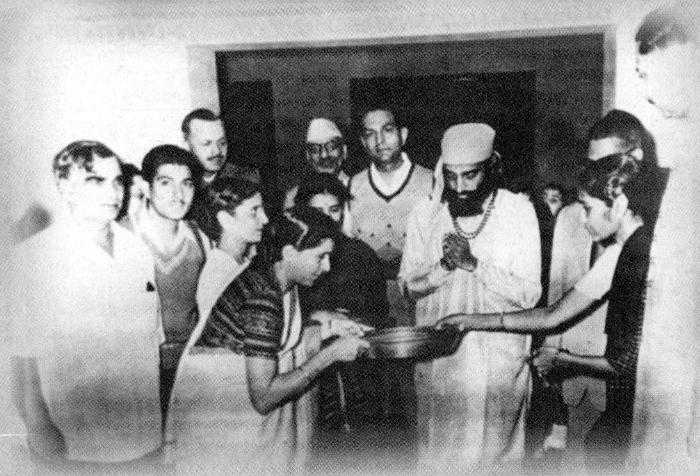

An ardent devotee and the young Swami: Sheila Puri of Delhi receives the master

The President presides: Swamiji's 23rd yajna at Delhi, was presided over by the President of India, Shri Rajendra Prasad

Uttarakashi : Maha-Samadh of Swami Tapovan Maharaj, January, 1957.

3

Om Sweet Home

The Om flag was now fluttering across the length and breadth of the country. The Chinmaya Movement had touched the hearts of the people. More and more spiritual, creative activities were taken up as a part of it; thanks to their success, the effulgence of Om spread farther. Between 1951 and 1967, Swami Chinmayananda conducted as many as 150 *yajnas*. He now strengthened the foundation of Study groups and gave shape to his dream of a Vedanta institute. He ushered in the publication of another journal, a monthly called *Usha*, to invoke the dawn of the revival of Hinduism. He did all this and more to make the Chinmaya Movement a force to be reckoned with.

The year 1957 was a watershed for the Chinmaya Movement; for Swamiji knew that in the years that followed, he had to do without the guidance and direction of his beloved guru, Swami Tapovan Maharaj. He was emotionally shaken after the *samadhi* of his guru; as stated already, he proceeded to Rishikesh for a short retreat lasting a few weeks. None the less he kept up his commitment to conduct a *jnana-yajna* at Kolkata in February 1957. In fact this *yajna* and the *yajnas* that followed were carried out without any change of plan. One of the unique programmes during 1957 was the holding of twin *yajnas* in the same city–Kochi. The subject of the twenty-eighth *yajna* held at Mattancheri, Kerala, was the *Bhagavad Geeta*, Chapters XII and XIII, between 6 p.m. and 7.30 p.m. On the same days the twenty-ninth *yajna* was under way at Ernakulam on Shankaracharya's Vivekachoodamani, from 8.30 p.m. to 10 p.m. In order to enable devotees to reach the venue of the second *yajna* in good time he asked the organizers to arrange for motorboats to take them through the backwaters from Ernakulam to Mattancheri. Also, the daily *Bhagavad Geeta* discourses were translated from English to Malayalam the same day; they were delivered, and distributed to devotees at 5 p.m. the next day. The Mission workers were so efficient that he could get things to work the way he wanted them.

After the thirtieth *yajna* at Bangalore in May 1957, Swamiji took devotees on a pilgrimage to a place near Mysore. In the course of his return journey to Bangalore he visited the Manoranjan Palace and the Maharaja's Choultry, which the Maharaja of Mysore had offered to Swamiji for the purpose of setting up a college–the Sandeepany College. The records available on this period in fact carry, references to the 'Sandeepany College at Mysore'. The original plan thus appears to have been to set up the Vedanta institute at Mysore. It was decided later to set up the Sandeepany Sadhanalaya at Mumbai in the light of certain events that took place in 1958-59. Indeed, in one of the *yajnas* Swamiji announced that he was not setting a date for any *yajna* after October 1958, as he was preoccupied with establishing the Sandeepany College.

The great disciplinarian that he was, Swamiji had the unpleasant duty in 1957, of dismissing from the Chinmaya Mission a devotee who had enjoyed his trust and confidence. He was enraged at the indiscipline of the devotee in leaving him without informing him for Rishikesh and in meeting Swami Sivananda there. The devotee did come back to Swamiji after taking *sannyas*, but orders of dismissal had been issued in the meantime. This action had a salutary effect on the conduct of other workers who realized that indiscipline would not be tolerated.

As stated already, the establishment of the Vedanta institute was now the primary concern of Swamiji. He was also making an all-out effort to stabilize the publication of the then official journals, *Tyagi* and *Usha*.

During the period 1955–59 the location of the editorial office of *Tyagi* changed several times. The printers in Chennai were not able to print the journal in time every fortnight. In fact there was soon a huge backlog of issues to be printed. So, when Swamiji found another printer at Bangalore who was willing to take up the work, the *Tyagi* office was shifted to that city. Again in 1960, Swamiji shifted the editorial office to Chittoor, where he had an ardent devotee ready to take up that responsibility.

As *Tyagi* regularly published Swamiji's discourses on the *Bhagavad Geeta*, Swamiji was keen to ensure that the publication of that magazine was kept up at least until all the eighteen chapters of the scripture were covered. The idea was to publish those discourses later in book form as the Holy *Geeta*. Swamiji completed his commentary on all the eighteen chapters in 1960, giving the meaning of each *shloka* word for word and expatiating on its purport at length. The Editor of *Tyagi* observed in the March 1960 issue of that journal: "Notwithstanding the hurricane–like *yajna* movement, Swamiji managed to dictate and prepare manuscripts and thus finish the colossal task in as short a period as four and a half years." Now it was only a matter time before the curtain was rung down on *Tyagi*. In 1962, when *Tapovan Prasad* started coming out from Mumbai, *Tyagi* ceased to be.

It was Swamiji's vision and compassion that made him go through tremendous stress and strain and make sure that the *Bhagavad Geeta* in its entirety was covered in one publication. Today, the Chinmaya Movement can take justifiable pride in the great contribution that this book has made, and is still making, to the dissemination of the message of the *Geeta*.

At least one *jnana-yajna* was being held every month at this time. Sometimes there were even two in a month, and there was an unprecedented increase in the number of devotees. Now the main concern was to sustain the interest kindled by the *yajnas*. Right after the first *yajna* at Pune, and the second at Chennai, Swamiji had been appealing to seekers to form small groups to be known as Study groups. According to him, the *yajna-shala* lectures had the effect of awakening the people. He did not want their interest in the subject of Vedanta to sag once they returned to the humdrum of their daily lives. He, therefore, told seekers to carry the torch of knowledge lit up at *yajna-shalas* to *mohallas* and form Mission groups or Study groups so that they might meet every week and study and discuss the subject and keep up their interest in it.

SUSTAINING THE ENTHUSIASM

Swamiji was happy with the enthusiasm shown by devotees in the formation and conduct of Study groups. Natarajan Iyer led the first Study group in Chennai. A. Parthasarathy was the leader of the first Study group formed in Mumbai. Swamiji's instructions were that when the number of members in a Study group increased beyond ten, they should split into two groups; it would be better to have compact groups in different parts of a city. Thus Swamiji laid down the organization structure: *yajnas* would lead to the formation of Study groups in different localities, and there would be a leader in each Study group. As time passed, more and more refinements were made such as appointment of a Study group coordinator for the formulation and implementation of Swamiji's scheme of study. Swamiji drew up a dynamic study scheme with suggestions for discussion in the Study groups. More about Study groups can be found in Chapter Eight, "Touching the Lives of Millions".

Swamiji himself observed, quite closely, the activities of the Study groups set up in some centres. He laid emphasis on punctuality and regularity in attendance to enhance the effectiveness of a Study group. A devotee in Delhi, associated with the Mission since 1960, vividly recalls how, at a Study group meeting in Shimla, Swamiji insisted upon punctuality. Swamiji wanted members to be punctual. For instance he did not want members to enter when the *mangalacharan* (invocation) preceding discussions was being chanted. The devotee asked him why he was giving so much importance to the invocation as against attendance at the discussion on the main text. Swamiji replied that unless a seeker came in time and made his mind quiet, he would not be able to follow the main text when it was taught. Seekers should come in time; they should not open their books till after the invocation was over. Laying stern emphasis on punctuality and regularity in attendance, Swamiji added: "You are not coming to hear a swami; you are coming because you have an appointment with the Lord."

USHA

In September 1958, Swamiji introduced a second publication, a monthly called *Usha*. It was to come out from Hyderabad.

According to Swamiji, *Usha* would be coordinating, monitoring activities of the Mission and crystallizing the thoughts first given utterance in *yajna-shalas*. Typically, an issue of *Usha* should contain a letter to children too, stressing and highlighting moral and ethical values; there should, further, be reports on the *satsangs* attended by members, as also Study group reports and photographs and reports on spiritual picnics. All contributions should invariably be from members of the Chinmaya Mission. The material submitted for publication should be signed and endorsed by their Group leader. Swamiji also made it mandatory for each *yajna* committee to publish in *Usha* an account of the *yajna* held under its auspices, giving details, inter alia, of the money collected and the expenses incurred. He thus laid down the foundation for the ethical governance of the *yajna* committee more than four decades ago.

Usha played an important role as a messenger to all Study groups in that it published reports on happenings elsewhere and informed the members from time to time of Swamiji's expectations. *Tyagi* continued to play its role as an organ for the publication of articles on serious texts and of Swamiji's commentaries on texts like the *Bhagavad Geeta*, *Vivekachoodamani*, etc. Thus *Usha* and *Tyagi* were complementary publications of the Chinmaya Movement, one covering the administrative aspects of the Mission and the second catering to the thirst of the seekers of true knowledge.

The First All India Conference of the Chinmaya Mission was held at Chennai at the Ambassador Hotel there, from August 30 to September 1, 1958. More than four hundred delegates from all over India attended it. The theme of the conference was "Dynamic, Integrated Hinduism". Eminent speakers like K.S. Ramaswami Sastri, Dr. T.M.P. Mahadevan, and Dr. Anantaraman of the Indian Institute of Science, Bangalore, took part in the various sessions. Swamiji stressed the fact that divinity was man's true nature and that he should always live like God at all levels. Endorsing this view, Sastri observed: "Our attempt should be to humanize God and divinize man". According to him, once we realised the Truth, we should express divinity through pure action, emotions and thoughts.

The significance of the conference for the Mission workers lay in the closed-door meetings that Swamiji held with Study group leaders. He told them that they should so conduct themselves, as to inspire others. They should emphasize the need for regular *sadhana*. The study of Sanskrit should not be made compulsory. Money should not be collected, but, if collected, it should be accounted for in detail. Study group leaders should be well trained and be capable of chanting the *Geeta*. Swamiji laid down such exacting standards for Study group leaders as to facilitate the grooming of other workers and seekers for the hard work that lay ahead of them.

In order to give women their due place in the work of the Mission an institution called the Devi Group was inaugurated at Chennai on November 2, 1958. In his message on the occasion Swamiji said: "Women of the country mould the future. The calibre of the children now in the laps of the mothers will be determined by the upbringing given by their mothers". *Devi* groups soon sprang up all over the country. Even today they are found to be foremost in inculcating proper values in the youth of the country.

WOMEN'S CONFERENCE

The Akhila Bharateeya Chinmaya Devi Sammelan (ABCD Sammelan as it was called) was held at Kollengode from

January 23 to 25, 1960. Kollengode is a small town in southern Malabar (in Kerala).

Swamiji said that the *Devi Sammelan* flag was unique. He explained its significance by saying that the lighted lamp signified the ignition of spiritual light in the heart of the *Devis*. The musical instrument *Veena* signified the acquisition of true knowledge by each individual and the spread of that knowledge all round, as also harmony. The objective of holding the *Sammelan* was to revive Hinduism and guide the younger generation to take up the right path. Thanks to the *Sammelan*, the enthusiasm and zest of women members in the Mission were redoubled.

The work of the Balavihars set up by the Mission also gathered momentum as more and more children came into the fold of the Chinmaya Movement. Enthusiastic and committed *sevaks* and *sevikas* were organizing these Balavihars. There was a *Balamahotsava* at Kollengode in 1961. This unique programme showed how our dreams of a better tomorrow could be realized through a proper moulding of our children. There was another *Balamahotsava* at Chennai. Swamiji took a group of children to Guruvayoor on a spiritual picnic. People of Guruvayoor were amazed at the *Vedic* chanting by children, and the *bhajans* they sang, as they marched down the street leading to the famous Krishna temple. Thus the Chinmaya Movement, which was barely ten years old in 1961, attracted people of all ages across the country. Its aim was to revive Hinduism, and a one-man army–Swami Chinmayananda himself—led it.

Swamiji did not stop at preaching to the seekers and children: he even rewarded talent and sincere, dedicated work. During the year 1958 and thereafter, he presented gold medallions from time to time in token of his appreciation. This made workers redouble their efforts towards the growth and development of the Mission. To receive gold medallions was good enough; to receive them from Swamiji himself was heavanly!

FIRST INITIATION

Swamiji added one more to the galaxy of Hindu *sannyasis* by conferring *sannyas deeksha* on a devotee named Dr. Ekambaram on *Shivaratri* Day in 1961 at Kaikalur (near Chennai city). This was Swamiji's first initiation. Dr. Ekambaram was a doctor who had retired after many years of service at a hospital at Chennai. He had also been a long-time *sevak* of Swamiji. He had always been seen selling Swamiji's books and other Vedanta literature at *yajna-shalas*, travelling with Swamiji from *yajna-shala* to *yajna-shala*, and taking care of not only the books but also the personal belongings of Swamiji. As a *sannyasi* he was known as Swami Premananda. He attained *maha-samadhi* on June 29, 1981 after living a life of unique selfless service to the Mission.

On March 8, 1961, Swamiji formed the Chinmaya Publication Trust (Regd), Chennai. He gave away all his works to it for future publication. In all, the Trust received fifty-nine books from Swamiji, which constituted its nucleus as it were. It had eminent citizens of Chennai like V.N. Subbaroyan, M. Ct. M. Petachi, Govardhandas Parekh, V. Sethuraman and P.V. Parthasarathi (of the Tamil magazine *Kumudam*) on its Board of Trustees. This Trust was the forerunner of the Books Division of the Central Chinmaya Mission Trust (CCMT). The trustees of the Chinmaya Publication Trust promptly flew to Mumbai to hand over their resignations, when the CCMT was formed in 1964.

Adding another unique activity to the Mission centre at Madurai, Swamiji opened, on June 8, 1961, a Meditation Centre in the Nagamalai Hills. These hills are about seven-and-a-half miles from Madurai. This centre known as Chinmaya Tapovanam is open to all seekers–Hindus, Muslims and Christians–to meditate undisturbed in its calm and serene environment.

The activity of the Mission was branching off into areas of social service. In December 1962 an organization called the Chinmaya Mission Nursing Home was launched at Bangalore. More details of this project are given in Chapter Eight, titled "Touching the Lives of Millions".

A CENTURY SCORE

The crowning glory of the end of the first decade of the Chinmaya Movement was the hundredth *yajna* held at Chennai in February 1962. The All-Women Centenary Committee brought out a beautiful souvenir on the occasion. It carried a profound message from Swamiji, which said, interalia:

> From December 1952 to February 1962, a hundred and ten months or three thousand and three hundred days, we have conducted a hundred Chinmaya *yajnas*. From a paltry audience of eighteen at Pune in 1952 the numbers increased to 11,000 at the ninety-seventh *yajna* in Mumbai in 1962.

Swamiji said that the Mission was now changing from the slow metre-gauge to broad-gauge:

> I propose to raise the tempo, speed and efficiency of our activities from now onwards... Let us surrender totally to

Him who has guided us so far and pray that He may make use of us in ever-greater fields and for the purpose of fulfilling ampler programmes.

The Karya Alochana Sabha of the Chinmaya Mission, Chennai, held a conference in 1962, where the constitution of the organization was drafted. There were eighty delegates. The deliberations were held over two days. Swamiji bade the participants farewell. His important message was: "The real *sadhana* for all of you is to learn to work in a cooperative way. Practise, live and preach the religious truths." Needless to say that even today this message is very relevant and valid for the workers of the Mission.

Yet another event to take place in December 1962 was the creation of the Tara Cultural Trust, Mumbai, which soon commenced publication of a monthly magazine called *Tapovan Prasad*. *Usha*, which was being published from Hyderabad, merged in Tapovan Prasad in October 1963. *Tyagi* from Chittoor followed suit in February 1965 to ensure that the Mission had only one voice from now on—*Tapovan Prasad*. It is so even today. The Editorial Offices were however, shifted from Mumbai to Chennai in 1968. The ownership was also transferred to the Chinmaya Mission, Chennai eventually. The magazine took, for its motto, the line from the *Bhagavad Geeta*, "O *Kaunteya*, know for certain: My devotee will never perish." (Chapter IX, verse 31)

The years 1961 and 1962 were a period of hectic activity for Swamiji, who was torn between *yajnas* and supervision of the upcoming college, the Sandeepany Sadhanalaya, at Mumbai. He was also concerned with the political danger to the country arising out of the Chinese aggression on India's borders. He gave a clarion call to the nation in his speech broadcast over All-India

Radio, Mumbai, and said: "This is the time for action. Here is an occasion for sacrifice. Get up, my countrymen, determined to fight, to die if need be, for our Motherland, the sacred Bharat." The Chinmaya Mission has always been in the forefront calling for action from its members whenever the security of our sacred country is threatened. For instance, most recently, in October 1999, Swami Tejomayananda, Head of the Chinmaya Mission worldwide, gave a purse of Rs. 63,00,000 to our present Prime Minister, Shri Atal Behari Vajpayee, in the wake of the Kargil crisis. This contribution made by him to the Army Central Welfare Fund was in appreciation of the heroism demonstrated and the sacrifices willingly made by Indian soldiers who fought Pakistan. As is well known, Pakistan army had illegally entered and occupied parts of Indian territory around Kargil.

THE DREAM INSTITUTE OPENS

In January 1963, the Sandeepany Sadhanalaya, the first institute set up for the pursuit of Vedanta studies, was inaugurated at Mumbai. The birth of this premier institution and of the other institutions that followed is discussed in Chapter Four, titled "Rishiputras of Sandeepany".

On 14 July 1963 the *deeksha guru* of Swamiji (the guru who had given him *sannyas*), Swami Sivananda Maharaj of the Divine Life Society, attained *maha-samadhi*. Swamiji had been ordained to *sannyas ashram* by Swami Sivananda in 1949. It was under his guidance and direction that Swamiji had sought out Swami Tapovan Maharaj at Uttarakashi and settled down there for a few years to pursue his scriptural studies and to perform spiritual *sadhana*. In the wake of the *maha-samadhi* of his *deeksha guru* Swamiji took up special austerities for a year.

The year 1964 saw a major restructuring in the Chinmaya Mission. The apex body of the organization, the CCMT, was registered at Mumbai in July 1964. The main objective of the Trust, amongst others, is to promote and spread Indian Culture and Education and enlightenment among the masses. This is the main thrust area of the Chinmaya Movement. To this end, CCMT co-ordinates the activities of many wings of the Trust such as Publications, Balvihar–International Monthly magzine, Tapovan Prasad (the Mission's monthly magazine), Chinmaya Video Dham for audio and video recording, CCMT Educational Cell based in Coimbatore, Chinmaya Vision Programme, and Chinmaya International Residential School.

The Third All-India Chinmaya Mission Conference was held at Mumbai under the presidentship of B.M. Kamdar. At this conference the delegates took a pledge, known as the Chinmaya Mission Pledge, which epitomizes the vision of Swamiji for the conduct of the workers of the Mission. The words "We stand as one family, bound to each other with love and respect" and so on inspired all. Recalling the impact of the pledge, K. C. Bhatia, one of the ardent devotees of Swamiji in Delhi, said: "Under Swamiji's direction, we took turns in nursing an ailing fellow-devotee who was in hospital as though we were members of his family." The spirit of camaraderie and sharing, implicit in the pledge is deeply ingrained in the hearts of all devotees. They share the joys and sorrows of life as members of one family.

In April 1964 the foundation stone was laid of the Jagadeeswara Temple on the premises of the Sandeepany Sadhanalaya at Mumbai. This was the first temple to be built by the Chinmaya Mission. It was consecrated on November 10, 1968.

VISHWA HINDU PARISHAD

B.M. Kamdar of Mumbai, who was a pillar of strength to the Chinmaya Movement, was also closely associated with the founding of the Vishwa Hindu Parishad (VHP). The involvement of the Chinmaya Mission in the VHP was no doubt due to Kamdar's close association with M.S. Golvalkar of the Rashtriya Swayamsevak Sangh (RSS), who was supporting the Hindutva movement. Swamiji had been getting letters from disciples and admirers everywhere, especially from those settled in foreign countries, alleging that the second-generation immigrants in those countries had no exposure to India's heritage; Golvalkar too held the same view. Swamiji and Golvalkar, therefore, joined hands in founding the VHP. The Sikh leader Master Tara Singh and Kulapati K.M. Munshi of the Bharatiya Vidya Bhavan were among those who supported them in this venture.

The inaugural meeting of the VHP was held at the Sandeepany Sadhanalaya in August 1964. The main objective of the VHP was to consolidate and strengthen the Hindutva movement. Swamiji headed the committee that drew up the Memorandum of Association for the Parishad.

The VHP had as its identity a saffron flag with five tips representing all the religions in India– Buddhism, Jainism, Sikhism, the Sanatanist Hindu religion, and all others. During his global tours, Swamiji participated in the functions organized by the VHP.

As the years rolled by, the VHP became more and more politicized. Swamiji found it increasingly difficult to associate with it although he sympathized with the objectives of the organization. When Swamiji had applied for a visa to visit Jakarta in 1968, he was refused one because of his association with the VHP. Swamiji made no fuss about the refusal, but jocularly remarked, "How can a country of Muslims be afraid of one Hindu Swami?"

FIRST GLOBAL TOUR

In March 1965 Swamiji went on a global tour–a *digvijaya*–covering thirty-nine cities spread over three continents. The tour lasted nearly four months and was very successful. It paved the way for the laying of firm foundations for the Chinmaya Movement in those continents. More is said about this in Chapter Five, titled "Meru Vidhi: Global Tours and Global Flag Posts".

CHINMAYA PRADEEP

The first Hindi monthly of the Chinmaya Mission was published from Mumbai in May 1965. The objective was to create a separate organ in the national language in recognition of a popular demand from Swamiji's followers. Sada Jivatlal, who was a sincere devotee and at the same time a keen follower of the VHP, was the publisher. Unfortunately the life of this publication was short. In fact it soon folded up.

As stated already, the publication of *Tyagi* was stopped in February 1965. In fact it stood merged in *Tapovan Prasad*. For twelve years Tyagi had played an important role in spite of great odds like not having a good infrastructure such as space, staff, and funds. In the 1950s, which witnessed the emergence of the Hindu Renaissance, the Chinmaya Movement needed an official organ to spread the message of scriptural texts such as the *Bhagavad Geeta*, the *Upanishads*, etc.; these precisely were the areas covered in the articles published in *Tyagi*. When one compares the articles published in *Tyagi* with those being published today in *Tapovan Prasad*, one can see that *Tyagi's* focus was largely on serious subjects like *Vedanta*; *Tapovan Prasad* is a mixed bag, the articles being published in it being concerned with in-house information on the Chinmaya Mission, as well as on *Vedanta*. *Tyagi* had an niche market, consisting of serious seekers; *Tapovan Prasad* has to cater to seekers at various levels of spiritual growth. *Tapovan Prasad* is an important communicator, in fact the only communicator, from the apex body, the CCMT, with the members of the Mission.

With the Indo-Pakistani War in September 1965, Swamiji turned his efforts to promoting service to the nation and preserving its culture. The Mission showed its concern for the nation's security when the head of the Mission, Swami Chinmayananda, met soldiers on the war front to obtain first-hand information on their conditions. In the same year the Government of India came out with a scheme of Gold Bonds to protect the exchange value of the rupee, which was facing a serious onslaught on the Foreign Exchange Market. The members of the Chinmaya Mission once again rose to the occasion. At the *yajna-shala* at Mumbai, the State Bank of India received 13,050 grams of gold in exchange for Gold Bonds. Thus, under Swamiji's leadership his devotees, being steeped in patriotism and exhibiting national pride, exemplified the culture of the members of the Chinmaya family – to put the cause of the nation above that of the organization, the cause of the organization above that of the individual.

The year 1966 is historically an important year as, for the first time, Swamiji conducted a *jnana-yajna* beyond the shores of India. He had a *yajna* performed at Kuala Lumpur, Malaysia, which was a great success in spite of inclement weather conditions. Although Kuala Lumpur has not developed into a full-fledged foreign centre, the impact of the Movement in Southeast Asian centres such as Jakarta and Singapore has been significant. Of course Kuala Lumpur continues to be an important place for spiritual discourses.

CHINMAYA LESSON COURSE

The concept of distance learning has been a part of the Chinmaya Movement since 1967. Swamiji was constantly travelling from place to place in India for his *jnana-yajnas*; he also undertook foreign tours from time to time to address both Indians and foreign nationals living abroad, on the *Bhagavad Geeta*, the *Upanishads*, and other *Vedanta* texts. Swamiji's first tour abroad came off in 1965. The discourses that Swamiji delivered at foreign centres were an instant success, bringing him more and more invitations. At that time there were very few swamis in the Mission capable of giving discourses on spiritual subjects.

To meet the large demand from seekers in foreign countries Swamiji introduced a correspondence course, called the Chinmaya Lesson Course in 1966. It was initially restricted to foreign students only. In its latest format it consists of twenty-four lessons and twelve questionnaires. The lessons are divided into four parts. After studying the monthly lessons students are required to answer a questionnaire in their own words, on the basis of their understanding of the ideas presented in the lessons. Their answers are later verified by *sevaks* and returned to them. Students can convey their doubts separately; these doubts are then answered by the examiners. Till his *maha-samadhi* Swamiji himself used to answer the doubts. This work has now been made over to the senior *sevaks* of the Mission.

At the end of his lecture or Chalk Talk at the visiting centres, Swamiji would collect registration forms for the lesson course, along with the course fee. He would then write a letter to Mumbai, giving a full list of the names and addresses of those who had registered for the lesson course, along with details of the money collected, which would include not only fees for the lesson course but also subscriptions to *Tapovan Prasad*. On his return to Mumbai he would check meticulously if the course material had been dispatched to applicants. He was very thorough in keeping the records, and his follow-up was without blemish. These are lessons which some of the devotees have learnt from him while working with him in the Mission.

After several global tours by Swamiji, a number of Chinmaya Mission centres were opened in various countries. With the opening of these centres, and the posting of regular teachers/Acharyas at these centres, the demand for the lesson courses saw a decline. However, a new trend was developing in India. Spiritual seekers were requesting Swamiji to keep the lesson courses open to Indian students as well. Consequently, in 1967, the lesson courses were thrown open to seekers in India. With its focus firmly set on value-based education, the Chinmaya Mission entered the field of education in 1965 with the opening of Chinmaya Nursery Schools and Chinmaya Vidyalayas. The teachers of these schools were encouraged to take up the lesson courses in order to acquaint themselves with the basic background of Swamiji's spiritual teaching. The *Vedanta* Home Study Lesson Course as designed by Swamiji caters to different types of students for the development of their personality, leading them to the highest state of perfection without interfering with their official, social or domestic commitments. Seekers have appreciated this method of learning; for it makes the learning process easy and simple with the help of structured lessons.

When the lesson courses started in 1966, they were administered and supervised by one of the very able devotees of Swamiji, Hamirbhai Vissanji. After ten years of careful administration and supervision, the responsibility was handed over to the CCMT at

Powai. The CCMT administers the course under the supervision of a senior brahmachari of the Mission.

The period 1957-67 was thus a decade of exponential growth for the Mission both in India and in foreign countries. In this short period Swamiji completed 152 *Geeta jnana-yajnas* and undertook three world tours.

CHINMAYA MISSION PLEDGE

We stand *as one family*
bound to each other, with love and respect.

We serve *as an army,*
courageous and disciplined,
ever ready to fight against,
all low tendencies and false values,
within and without us.

We live *honestly,*
the noble life of sacrifice and service,
producing more than what we consume
and giving more than what we take.

We seek *the Lord's grace*
to keep us on the path of virtue,
courage and wisdom.

May thy *grace and blessings,*
flow through us,
to the world around us.

We believe *that the service of our country,*
is the service of the Lord of Lords
and devotion to the people,
is the devotion to the Supreme Self.

We know *our responsibilties,*
Give us the ability and courage to fulfil them.

Om Tat Sat

Yajna-shala entrance

Mumbai: Swamiji on the dias.
On his left is Ms. Tara Sarup. B.M. Kamdar welcomes.

A typical stage design

Swamiji being taken in a procession

Tyagi Office

Chittoor :
With Dwaraknath Reddy

Mulund : Balavihar

Orlando : Balavihar Kids

Devi Group

Bhawanipatna : A Yuva Kendra programme
Br. Atul Chaitanya at extreme left.

Study Group: In progress

Yajna Audience

Fund-Raising Stamp : at 25 paise.each

Swamiji with Jamnadas Moorjani

Chinmaya Tapovan, A retreat near Madurai

Swamiji - *Fragrant as a Flower, Radiant as a Saint*

4

The Torchbearers

The Rishiputras of Sandeepany

Sandeepany, sam-deepany, according to Swami Chinmayananda meant perfect kindling or kindling of perfection in the hearts of men. Long years ago there was a great sage called Maharshi Sandeepany who ran a *gurukula* for imparting spiritual knowledge. He had acquired that knowledge himself in the *gurukulas* maintained by earlier rishis. In his own *gurukula* a number of boys received their training, one of them being no less a person than Lord Krishna himself. It had been one of Swamiji's dreams, since 1957, to found an academy to train young students in the study of Vedanta and to prepare them to be the torch-bearers of spiritual knowledge.

Swamiji selected the name 'Sandeepany' for the institute of Vedanta that he proposed to start at Mumbai and it would train over a hundred students at a time. Later, this name 'Sandeepany' became a generic one for all the teaching institutes of Vedanta that Swamiji launched under the banner of the Chinmaya Movement – Sandeepany West at Piercy, California, Sandeepany

Himalaya at Sidhbari, Himachal Pradesh, Sandeepany Tamil Nadu at Coimbatore, Sandeepany Karnataka at Bangalore, Sandeepany Andhra Pradesh at Trikoota, Sandeepany Prayag at Allahabad, and Sandeepany Kerala in Kasargod/Veliyanad. Students were carefully selected to undergo intensive training in Vedic literature for over a period of two-and-a-half years and to pass on to the next generation the fire of knowledge kindled by Swamiji at the *jnana-yajna-shalas*. The visionary thinking of the Master made it possible to draw up a meticulous plan for the training of field workers. It was an impressive show made possible by donations from a large number of Swamiji's devotees who contributed unflinchingly to the sacred cause so dear to the heart of their guru. Many students have walked through the portals of the Sandeepany institutes and have fulfilled the wishes of the Master by spreading the message of the *Bhagavad Geeta* and the *Upanishads*. Many have become Swamis/Swaminis. One of them, Swami Tejomayananda, now heads the Chinmaya Mission worldwide.

The land required for the setting up of the Sandeepany Sadhanalaya at Mumbai dropped, as it were, into Swamiji's lap when having finished his fifty-first *yajna* at Bangalore in February 1959, he was proceeding to Hyderabad for his fifty-second *yajna*. *Usha* of February 1959 reported: "At Bombay on the Powai lakes, a devoted and enthusiastic lady has offered a portion of her fourteen acre plot for setting up the Sandeepany Sadhanalaya. She is willing to put up for us our required accommodation also. We must now register and finalize the college work for which Swamiji will be in Bombay." Swamiji was at Mumbai from February 18 to February 20, 1959. The Tara Cultural Trust that was to run the Sandeepany Sadhanalaya–was registered at Mumbai on January 19, 1960.

The devoted and enthusiastic lady was Ms Tara Sarup, who donated the land and who is still happily a Managing Trustee of the Tara Cultural Trust, giving valuable guidance and direction to the Trust in the administration of Sandeepany Sadhanalaya. Recalling the circumstances in which the land was donated to the Mission, Ms Sarup told Swami Chidananda in a recent interview: "I had gone to listen to a talk by Swami Chinmayananda at the K.C. College, Mumbai. I was very inspired by his talk and went to meet him personally. His hostess Mrs. Jaimini Diwan, was a friend of mine. Swamiji said, in the course of a conversation in the Diwan house, that many people were promising to gift land to him for a Vedanta institute but that in the end they were backing out of the commitment." There was a distinct note of disappointment in Swamiji's voice. She immediately offered to give three acres of land from her estate in Powai and added firmly and with a ring of finality: "I will not back out of my commitment." Within a few days Swamiji visited the site and approved of it. It was thus that the Sandeepany of his dreams was born at Powai, Mumbai. A few years later, he received four more acres of land as a donation to the Trust, so that the Sandeepany Sadhanalaya stands today on a seven-acre plot of land.

The members of the Chinmaya Mission, Chennai, framed the rules and regulations required to run the college as a Vedanta institute. These rules and regulations were published in Hail Renaissance Volume I in the year 1957. Swamiji used to appeal for donations from time to time for the college in the issues of *Tyagi*. The aim of starting the college was to train a hundred young men and women in the study of Vedanta through a six-year course. Foreign students were also to be admitted as the spread of knowledge was not to be confined to the geographical frontiers of India but was intended to embrace the whole world.

On completion of his training every trainee was to go to his own region to do *prachar* work and train ten more students for similar work. Keeping this idea in mind, Swamiji often used to say that the institute would close down after training the first batch of a hundred students. However, his plans changed from time to time as the demand for *prachar* workers was on the increase. It was found that there was need for more and more trained workers. So the training of *prachar* workers went on from one batch to the next in an almost endless chain.

SANDEEPANY SADHANALAYA, POWAI, MUMBAI, 1963

This was the first institute of Vedanta to be started by Swami Chinmayananda: it was started with Swamiji himself as the Acharya. As stated already, Swamiji had been dreaming of such an institute since 1957, as he felt that there was a need for more and more trained workers to handle the increasing demand for *yajnas*. An institute of the kind he was dreaming of required many things – a generous and unceasing flow of donations, for instance. More important, there was need for suitable land on which to locate the institute. And then there was the need for time, precious time, for the administrative work related to the starting of the institute. Swamiji moved around like a hurricane from *yajna-shala* to *yajna-shala*, for the *yajnas* not only spread the message of Vedanta but also generated donations for the dream project.

Swamiji wrote: "When I was anxious to start the Sadhanalaya as early as in the year 1957, all I got was nothing save a few knocks of disappointment. And in sheer despair I shed my anxiety, letting Lord Narayana to shape things in His own inscrutable ways." Lo and behold! In the years that followed, there was a miracle as it were, men volunteered, money poured in, and the Sadhanalaya sprang up. On January 9, 1963, which was Tapovan Day, the Sandeepany Sadhanalaya was inaugurated but in a sober, low-key manner. The manner was low key because the nation was yet to recover from the Chinese aggression on its northern borders. Swamiji said: "If He has chosen the present veil of sadness to serve as a fit back-ground for the inauguration of this institution, dedicated to live and spread His own glories, there lies indeed a meaning in His move." This was how he reasoned and consoled himself and others.

About this very time, Swamiji's cottage, an offering from B.M. Kamdar, was also getting ready. Swamiji moved into a temporary accommodation at the site in November 1962 so as to be able to supervise the construction work, appointment of staff, etc.

The number of applications received for joining the Vedanta course was overwhelming. Swamiji scrutinized the applications meticulously and approved only sixty of them. Enquiries were still pouring in, and Swamiji was confident of getting qualitatively good students to reach his target of a hundred.

On January 7, 1963, true to the *gurukula* tradition, the students admitted to the course were initiated into *brahmacharyashrama*. To that end they went through a ceremony called *upanayana*. Kamdar and his wife took the *sankalpa*. Swamiji explained the significance of the *upanayana* to those assembled there on the occasion. The next day was devoted to the recitation of the *Gayatri mantra*. On January 9, the Sadhanalaya was formally inaugurated. Swami Chinmayananda, as the Acharya, took the first class.

Swamiji always looked upon the Sandeepany Sadhanalaya, which was opened on Tapovan Day, as a *prasad* from his guru,

Swami Tapovan Maharaj. It was in recognition of the relentless work he had put in towards the revival of Hinduism and the pains he had taken to spread the spiritual knowledge of the Vedas and the *Upanishads*.

From 1963 to 2000 there were eleven batches of trainees. These were all taught by Acharyas of eminence beginning with Swami Chinmayananda himself and followed by Swami Dayananda, Br. Swaroop Chaitanya (now Swami Viditatmananda, no longer in the Mission), Swami Tejomayananda, Swami Purushottamananda, Swami Chidananda and Swami Anubhavananda.

TABLE I

Vedanta Courses Conducted, 1963-2000

Course No.	Year	Acharya	No. of Students
1	1963-68	Swami Chinmayananda	16
2	1972-75	Swami Dayananda*	62
3	1976-78	Swami Dayananda*	70**
4	1980-82	Br. Swaroop Chaitanya*	33
5	1984-86	Swami Tejomayananda	22
6	1986-88	Swami Tejomayananda	35
7	1989-91	Swami Purushottamananda	20
8	1991-93	Swami Chidananda	35
9	1994-96	Swami Anubhavananda*	30
10	1996-98	Swami Anubhavananda*	28
11	1998-2000	Swami Chidananda	34
		TOTAL:	385

*No longer with the Chinmaya Mission.

**25 Students from the West.

DHARMA-SEVAK COURSES

Swamiji introduced Dharma Sevak courses in Sandeepany Mumbai in 1991. This was following his appreciating the Dharma Veer courses offered in Andhra Pradesh by Swamini Saradapriyananda. Thirty young people of below thirty years of age took part in the Dharma Sevak Lower (DSL) course that was launched in November 1991. It was just for two months. Fully residential, it consisted of the study of selected spiritual texts. As an attractive feature, it also comprised classes on Indian insights to management, music, etc. Following this immediately, the Dharma Sevak Higher (DSH) course was offered. It was a four months course. Participants were from the age group thirty to seventy years. Some visiting swamis and brahmacharis assisted the Acharya in conducting these courses. Sanskrit also was a part of the syllabus. Subsequently the DSL and DSH were merged together and the duration reduced to two months. Several such courses were offered. They may be revived in the years ahead.

SANDEEPANY WEST, 1979

Sandeepany West was the second of the Vedanta institutes established at the instance of Swamiji. The Chinmaya Mission West (CMW) founded it at Piercy, California, in 1979. Piercy is in the heart of Humboldt County, two hundred miles north of San Francisco. It is a place of natural beauty abounding in dense forests of redwood trees and conifers; and then there are the mighty oak trees too. The river Eel flows by the Sandeepany, making the location of the institute quite a scenic spot. Swamiji chose Piercy because of the scenic surroundings and majestic redwood trees. He had conducted several camps in the Napa Valley and in the Humboldt County before. It had brought back to him memories of the Himalaya during his earlier period of *sadhana*. In 1991 and 1992, when he revisited Piercy, he remarked that Piercy was the Sidhbari of the West. The tall redwood trees seemed as old as Vedic teaching itself. Students were greatly inspired by the trees, the river, and the green meadows. The *gurukula* was thus set up in the midst of a very inspiring scenario, the river almost reflecting the human mood-sometimes calm and at other times turbulent, and sometimes slow and at other times hurrying.

Piercy has a pride of place in the Chinmaya Movement, being the first property acquired by the Chinmaya Mission on American soil.

Sandeepany West was inaugurated on November 7, 1979. Most of the students there had earlier listened to lectures on Vedanta and had joined the course to make an in-depth study of the subject. On the occasion of the first anniversary of the institution, Swamiji said in a message to the students:

> Time runs out when the vision is steady and we enthusiastically work to reach out and attain a specific inspiring goal. With our meagre resources we, with faith in Narayana, dashed into this expensive and extremely exhausting programme of Sandeepany West. And we are justified–help came from everywhere, support reached us from all sides, and appreciation gushed out from all levels.... May success pile upon success, and may the Acharyas and brahmacharis live and serve the world around us with kindliness and love.

Many students passed out of this institute. They hailed generally from America and Europe, including immigrant Indians living in different parts of the world. The Acharya of this course was Swami Dayananda. A fair number of students graduated from here in

1981. Some of them are doing *prachar* work, possibly under different banners. Two of the outstanding students of this batch are Gaurangbhai and Darshanaben Nanavaty. They relocated themselves from Seattle, Washington State to Houston, Texas, in 1982. They have contributed to the spectacular growth of the Chinmaya Movement in the United States, in general, and in Houston, in particular.

At the end of the course, describing its teachings, one of the trainees at Piercy wrote, among other things:

> At first our insights were glimpses, quickly obscured like the redwoods by fog. As our preconceptions wore off, the glimpses began to hold their clarity, and, finally, we came to realize that what we were seeing was indeed what we were supposed to see–and that was more perfect than anything that could fit our preconceptions.

The first course at Sandeepany West ended in 1981, and no further courses were conducted. Instead, the centre at Piercy is being used as a retreat where camps are held year after year for children, youth and families.

SANDEEPANY HIMALAYAS, 1981

Sandeepany (Himalayas) is the second of the institutes of Vedanta started in India and also the third in the line of the Sandeepanys unveiled by Swamiji. The administration of this institute is vested in the Chinmaya Tapovan Trust. It fulfilled Swamiji's vision of setting up Sandeepanys to train students to do *prachar* work in various regional languages. It trains students to teach in Hindi, the official language of India. It was Br.Vivek Chaitanya who mooted the idea of starting a course for the Hindi-speaking people. Br. Vivek Chaitanya was the first Acharya of Sandeepany (HIM). Now he is well known as Swami Tejomayananda. He was at that time doing *prachar* work in the Hindi belt of India (in Allahabad, Kanpur, Lucknow and other places).

It was some time in 1969 that Swamiji, driving around in the Kangra Valley, was inspired by the striking beauty of Himachal Pradesh. He felt that it would be a grand idea to start a Vedanta institute under such an idyllic setting. Col. L.S. Pathania, Justice Mahajan and others took him to various sites. Swamini Saradapriyananda also made a tour of the Kangra Valley to select an ideal location for the institute. It was only at the end of 1977 that the present site at Sidhbari was selected. While Col. Pathania was driving Swamiji around, Swamiji spotted a hillock that was barren and which had no pine trees growing on it. When asked by Swamiji why this was so, Col. Pathania said that the wind was very strong, so no trees grew there. Almost at once Swamiji decided that this was the spot where he would have his Vedanta institute. Swamiji did not like cutting down trees, and here was some land actually without trees. However, by the grace of Swamiji, the Sidhbari Ashram now abounds in tall poplars reaching to the skies.

Writing about Sidhbari, R. S. Nathan, an ardent devotee of Swamiji's and a prolific writer contributing interesting articles to *Tyagi* and *Tapovan Prasad*, said: "Sidhbari means the abode of the *Siddhas*." (Nathan later became Swami Nityananda.) *Siddhas* are those who have acquired one or more of the eight spiritual powers defined by Maharshi Patanjali. It is said that several *siddhas* had their hermitages around this place in the distant past, which is how this place got its name. Sidhbari is six kilometres from the famous Dharamsala. It is adjacent to the Yol cantonment. The towering Dhauladhar peaks of the Himalaya present a perfect setting for this scenic place. Not far away is McLeod Ganj, where the Dalai Lama now lives in exile.

Although the land was identified in 1977, permission from various authorities to start construction work took a long time in coming. The foundation was laid on Guru Poornima Day in July 1979, and work started in September 1979. The progress of the work was rather slow. On November 7, 1979 Swamiji handed over charge of all his administrative work and organizational duties in the CCMT to Swami Dayananda. He then went abroad for a bypass surgery, which was performed in September 1980. On his return to India in December 1980, he decided that he would resume the exacting work at Sidhbari. He decided to move to the Himalaya and turn his full attention to serve the poor and the people living in the interior regions. He was also keen to develop a band of workers capable of teaching aspirants in Hindi. Thus was born Sandeepany (HIM) with a campus large enough to accommodate forty brahmacharis to preach in the Hindi-speaking areas, and twenty brahmacharis to teach in the upper and interior areas of the Himalaya.

Sandeepany (HIM) had a two-day programme for the inauguration, on April 25 and 26, 1981. Many dignitaries such as Ramlal, the then Chief Minister of Himachal Pradesh, Justice Mahajan, Col. L.S. Pathania and Dr. Karan Singh attended it. There were many delegates/devotees from the foreign centres of the Chinmaya Mission. The first Acharya was Br. Vivek Chaitanya. Those who toiled to complete all the work for the inauguration included Jagdish Prasad, who was the Managing Trustee of Chinmaya Tapovan Trust, his wife, and Swami Vajreshwarananda. Swamiji was closely monitoring the progress of the work. One of the foreign devotees, who was then at the site, described Swamiji as "a straight, vividly shining orange flame against a sky of the deepest and the most brilliant Krishna-blue."

For Swamiji, the starting of Sandeepany (HIM) was a dream come true. His guru, Swami Tapovan Maharaj, had told him in

1950s, to stay back in the Himalaya and to teach the *pahadis* (mountain folk). But in 1951 the cities had beckoned to him. Now was the time for Swamiji to repay his debt to the Himalaya for enabling him to attain the highest knowledge available to man.

The local inhabitants of Sidhbari regarded the advent of the institute at first with caution. An interesting episode is said to have made them change their outlook. Owing to acute scarcity of water, the land at Sidhbari was excavated in preparation for an underground tank. Then there fell torrential rain. But the rainwater from the hillock came down and flowed to the right and left of the excavation, causing no damage to the area earmarked for the proposed water tank. The local people noticed this phenomenon with awe. They felt convinced that this was thanks to the influence of a great *mahatma*. Thereafter they gave their full support–which continues even today.

The Vedanta courses started in earnest and several batches of students completed their studies and went out for *prachar* work. Six batches of students have so far passed out and the seventh batch will pass out around May 2001.

TABLE 2

Vedanta Courses Conducted, 1981-2001

Batch No.	Year	Acharya	No. of students
1	1981-83	Br. Vivek Chaitanya	9
2	1984-86	Br. Nirvan Chaitanya*	2
3	1987-89	Br.Vishal Chaitanya	7
4	1990-92	Swami Subodhananda	14
5	1993-95	Swami Subodhananda	15
6	1996-98	Br. Sumitra Chaitanya	7
7	1999-2001	Br. Sumitra Chaitanya	16
		TOTAL:	70

* No longer with the Chinmaya Mission.

The trained brahmacharis and brahmacharinis are out in the field doing *prachar* work. There are more than twenty-two centres in this region, which comprises of centres in the States of Haryana, Himachal Pradesh, Madhya Pradesh, Chattisgarh, Punjab, Rajasthan, Uttaranchal and Uttar Pradesh.

SANDEEPANY ANDHRA PRADESH, 1982

Sandeepany Andhra Pradesh is different from the other training centres in that it functioned in an informal manner in the initial years. Swamini Saradapriyananda started teaching Vedanta to selected brahmacharis and brahmacharinis, according to the syllabus formed for Sandeepany Mumbai. The regular functioning of Sandeepany began in 1982 after the Ashram at Chinmayaranyam was fully operational. The teaching was carried out in two languages–in English for some students and in Telugu for those who did not know that language. There was no clear-cut division of students into batches. Students were taken as and when they came, and the earlier texts were taken separately. This was the tradition set up by Swamiji himself in the initial years at Sandeepany, Mumbai, which was later on changed to clear-cut batches.

Sandeepany Andhra Pradesh had no formal inauguration or function to mark the start of an institute for the study of Vedanta. No single person was appointed Acharya. All the Swamis and Swaminis took classes as and when they found that they had enough time to spare. It was an informal arrangement, but it worked out. Swamini Saradapriyananda played the leading role and involved others in the work such as Swamini Bodhananda, Swamini Seelananda and Swami Prasannatmananda. For the first three batches of students, *brahmacharya deeksha* was given at the start of the course. The trainees were given yellow robes to wear. Subsequently this system was changed: *deeksha* was given after completion of the course. The *upanayana* for students was performed at the beginning of the course itself, as the brahmacharis were required to do duty sometimes in the temples. The brahmacharies also guided children in and about the Ashram to perform the *sandhya-vandana* ritual.

Sandeepany Andhra Pradesh did not stipulate any minimum educational qualifications for those who wished to join. Even those who were illiterate were accepted. Importance was given rather to the spirit of service (*seva*) and to dispassion (*vairagya*). Those who did not have adequate educational qualifications were asked to do '*shramadan*' in the kitchen and to participate in occasional rituals etc. The multifarious activities at Chinmayaranyam enabled the absorption of students in carrying out of tasks that they were fit to carry out.

Apart from the teaching of the Vedanta texts, Sandeepany Andhra Pradesh organizes annual *Geeta* chanting competitions at the institutional, State and district levels. The brahmacharis and the students go round and teach *shlokas* from the chapter selected for that year for the competition. The number of children participating in the competition from the three levels has steadily increased, and it is estimated that in the year 2000, about 29,000 participated in the competition.

Since the year 1996 Sandeepany Andhra Pradesh has organized Brahmasadas, which is a State-level conference of the representatives from all Mission centres along with the *pracharaks*. The duration of a *sadas* varies from seven days to one month. Many important texts have been taken up at these conferences and explained to delegates. The *sadas* is similar to a refresher course in the *Upanishads*. It serves as a retreat for those who want to spend time exclusively on study, reflection and meditation.

Sandeepany Andhra Pradesh conducted a course known as the Dharma Veera course. It was an eleven-month course covering important Vedanta texts, Vedic chanting, *poojas* and *homas*, as well as the chanting of the *Geeta*. It was a programme which harmonized with Swamiji's vision to involve more and more *grihasthas* in *prachar* work. In 1990, after witnessing a function at Chinmayaranyam-Trikoota, where certificates were awarded to candidates from the first batch, Swamiji applauded this programme. He replicated it in Sandeepany Mumbai as the Dharma Sevak Course. At Sandeepany, Andhra Pradesh, fifty-four candidates have completed the Dharma Veera course between 1990 and 2000. This course has had a very good impact on the spread of the Chinmaya Movement. In the village of Takumatla in the Warangal District, a Dharma Veer has created a lot of enthusiasm in the local people. These people have even contributed a building to the Mission.

The number of *rishiputras* who have completed the Vedanta course at Sandeepany Andhra Pradesh, doing *prachar* work and/or shouldering administrative responsibilities in their respective Ashrams is given in detail below:

TABLE 3

Vedanta Courses Conducted, 1982-2000

Medium of Instruction: English

Batch No.	Year	No. of students	No. of students	No. of students
		Joined	Completed	Continuing
1	1982-85	2	2	Nil
2	1985-90	10	3	1
3	1991-94	3	2	-
4	1994-97	2	2	-
5	1998-to date	4	Course continues	-

Medium of Instruction: Telugu

Batch No.	Year	No. of students Joined	No. of students Completed	No. of students Continuing
1	1982-85	3	1* *(Left the Mission)	
2	1985-89	5	1	
3	1991-95	15	10	5
4	1995-99	12	10	
5	1998-to date	7	Course continues	

SANDEEPANY PRAYAG, 1985

As announced by Swamiji, a Vedanta institute to impart education in Hindi was inaugurated on April 14, 1985 at Prayag. This was facilitated because Br. Vishal Chaitanya (now Swami Subodhananda), who had just completed the first Hindi course in Sandeepany Himalayas, was posted at Allahabad. He was appointed the first Acharya.

Seven students joined the course, which concluded on March 31, 1987. There was no second course thereafter as it was felt that there was no need to run two simultaneous courses in Hindi: one at Sidhbari and the other at Prayag. In consequence Br. Vishal Chaitanya was transferred to Pitamah Sadan in Kanpur.

SANDEEPANY TAMIL NADU, 1988

As the years rolled by, several batches of students passed out of Sandeepany Sadhanalaya, Mumbai. Presently Swamiji felt the need to train students so as to enable them to give discourses in various regional languages. His vision was to have a garland of similar academies all over India. He often said, "Plan out your work and work out your plan." His plan to set up institutes of Vedanta all over India was beautifully executed with the founding of Sandeepany Himalayas in 1981 and a string of similar institutions in the South–Sandeepany Kerala in April 1988, Sandeepany Tamil Nadu in May 1988, and Sandeepany Karnataka also in May 1988.

The institute of Vedanta planned for Tamil Nadu was to be run on the same lines as the Sandeepany Sadhanalaya, Mumbai, except that students would be trained to give discourses in Tamil, the language of the State. The medium of instruction, however, was to be English. Swami Sahajananda (now no longer in the Mission) did the preliminary work of locating a plot of land suitable for it – at Siruvani, Coimbatore, in the year 1986.

Sandeepany Tamil Nadu is run under the auspices of the Chinmaya Garden Trust, Coimbatore. The inauguration of the institute, the sixth Vedanta institute in India, came off on May 9, 1988. Dignitaries present at the inaugural function included Sundara Swami of the Kaumara Mutt and Santhanalinga Swami of the Perur Mutt. Swami Tejomayananda, Swami Purushottamananda and Swami Subodhananda represented the Chinmaya Mission. Br. Atma Chaitanya, the first Acharya of the institute, was also present. (Swami Sahajananda had earlier given Vedanta training to inmates and others at this site in an informal manner.)

From May 1988 to March 1999 the institute ran four courses. The institute was shifted from Coimbatore to Chennai in 1993 according to Swamiji's directions. In a letter he said, "Sandeepany Tamil Nadu is in a jolt. Why not shift it to Chennai?" In 1993, two courses were conducted simultaneously in Coimbatore and Chennai. However, the institute was shifted back again to Coimbatore in the year 2000.

TABLE 4

Vedanta Courses Conducted, 1988-2000

Batch No.	Acharya	No. of Students	Year
At Coimbatore			
1	Br. Atma Chaitanya	1	1988-1990
2	Br. Dharmesh Chaitanya	2	1991-1993
At Chennai			
3	Br. Praveen Chaitanya	7	1993-1995
4	Swami Shridharananda	5	1996-1999
At Coimbatore			
5	Br. Samahita Chaitanya	20	Started on 31 August 2000

There are eleven brahmacharis/brahmacharinis of this institute now, engaged in *prachar* work in Tamil Nadu. One brahmachari is engaged in looking after Tamil publications, also takes classes for villagers. The *prachar* work has spread far and wide, covering centres like Chennai, Kodaikanal, Coimbatore, Madurai, Tamaraipakkam, Tiruchirapalli, Tirunelveli, and Tiruvallore.

Swami Tejomayananda inaugurated the fifth course on August 31, 2000 at the Sandeepany Vidyamandir, Coimbatore. Br. Samahita Chaitanya is the Acharya. Swami Tejomayananda observed that those who had joined the course were lucky as they would be able to make a systematic study of Vedanta. He added that we had to be thankful to Swami Chinmayananda; for it was Swami Chinmayananda who had thought it all out and made it possible for them all to acquire spiritual knowledge almost at their doorstep. Swami Chinmayananda was still present, he averred. He himself was teaching–through the Acharyas.

SANDEEPANY KERALA, 1988

On Maha Shivaratri Day, February 16, 1988, Sandeepany Kerala formally came into existence. On that day it was inaugurated at Kasaragod, at the northern tip of Kerala. This was the fifth Vedanta institute to be opened in India by Swami Chinmayananda, the other four being located at Mumbai, Sidhbari, Chinmayaranyam and Prayag.

In a seven-acre plot of land in the Vidyanagar area of Kasargod, the seminary stands side by side with the Chinmaya Vidyalaya. It received guidance from Swami Bodhananda, the chief Acharya at the Ashram. Chinmaya Seva Trust, Kerala managed the institute. At the time of the inauguration, in February 1988, there were *poojas* and other rituals. In the evening of February 16, Swamiji arrived at Kasargod to a grand ceremonial welcome with the traditional Kerala *panchavadyam* and *talpoli* (a welcome dance) by the children of the Chimaya Vidyalaya. The Om flag fluttered all over the town.

Swami Vishwesh Teertha of the Pejavar Mutt, Udupi, did the formal inauguration in the evening. In his address he said, "The sun of knowledge should rise so that the lotus of your heart may blossom." The function was held in the presence of dignitaries like the District Collector, the representative of Kasargod in the Kerala Legislative Assembly, and A.S. Menon, the Chief Sevak and Trustee of the Chinmaya Seva Trust, Kerala. Swamiji in his keynote address said that it was not that he had come to bless the Sandeepany Sadhanalaya there, but that the devotees who had gathered on the occasion had to bless the institution and lend a helping hand by making donations in cash and kind. Swamiji compared the invisible thread that carried all the flowers together in a garland with Sandeepany. Sandeepany, he added, would bind the people together within the Hindu culture and tradition.

Sandeepany Kerala is to cater to the students who need Malayalam as the medium of instruction. There were twenty students in the first course. It was conducted between 1988 and

1990. The Acharya was Swami Bodhananda. In 1994 Sandeepany Kerala was shifted to the Chinmaya International Foundation (CIF) at the Adi Sankara Nilayam, Kochi. The Acharya was Br. Atma Chaitanya. The second course was conducted from 1994 to 1997.

Sandeepany Kerala contributed quite a few *brahmacharis* from out of the two batches.

TABLE 5

Vedanta Courses Conducted, 1988-2000

Batch No.	Location	Year	Acharya	No. of Students
1	Kasargod	1988-90	Swami Bodhananda	3
2	CIF Cochin	1994-97	Br. Atma Chaitanya	5

The *bramacharies* are engaged in *prachar* work in Kerala. There has been no course after 1997. Plans for the future are yet to be drawn up.

SANDEEPANY KARNATAKA, 1988

Sandeepany Karnataka is the seventh Vedanta institute to be opened in India by Swamiji. At this institute the teaching was done in the regional language, namely Kannada. Swamiji wanted to open Vedanta institutes all over India, so that teaching work might be done in the relevant regional language at each place. He knew that the regional languages were going to play a greater role in the years ahead. Sandeepany Karnataka was the sixth institute to take up teaching in a regional language.

Sandeepany Karnataka came to be known as Chinmaya Sandeepany. Academic work started there in 1988 on the premises of the Deenabandhu Devasthanam at Bangalore. It was placed under the management of the Karnataka Chinmaya Seva Trust. Tiruchi Swami of the Kailas Ashram, Kenchanhalli, inaugurated the institute in the presence of Swami Chinmayananda and Swami Tejomayananda on May 10, 1988. After Tiruchi Swami had bestowed his blessings, Swami Chinmayananda spoke. He said that the Mission was opening more and more Sandeepanys in order to train brahmacharis and propagate spiritual knowledge in the regional languages. Swami Tejomayananda, who spoke in Hindi, said that, under the guidance of Swamiji, the Mission was spreading Vedic culture in the interior of every State.

Ten students were on the rolls for the first course, which was conducted from May 1988 to June 1990. The Acharya was Swami Brahmananda. Br. Lokanatha Chaitanya and Br. Suresh Chaitanya ably assisted him in the work.

Br. Suresh Chaitanya gave lessons on Yoga also. Lanka Krishnamurti taught Sanskrit. N.S. Anantarangachar gave many valuable guest lectures on different philosophies (*darshanas*).

TABLE 6

Vedanta Course Conducted, 1988-90

Batch No.	Year	Acharya	No. of Students
1	1988-1990	Swami Brahmananda	10

No course has been conducted at the seminary since 1990. Future plans are not yet finalized, but Sandeepany Karnataka is expected to function from Chokkahalli in future. This beautiful retreat comprising ten acres is near Kolar, about seventy kilometers from Bangalore.

Swamiji's expectation from Sandeepany Karnataka was to promote discipline and to instil spiritual values. He was keen to inculcate simple living and high thinking upon the brahmacharis. In fact this is to be the goal for all the future courses.

OTHER SANDEEPANYS

Two more Sandeepanys were on the anvil at the time of the *maha-samadhi* of Swami Chinmayananda in 1993. One was at Kolhapur, Maharashtra with plans to teach Vedanta in Marathi. This institute opened on August 24, 1997 for a brief period. The Ashram at Kolhapur has turned meanwhile into a retreat for holding spiritual camps. The second one is to be in Sri Lanka to be called Sandeepany Sri Lanka. There was demand for such an institution there, one that would cater to the needs of the sizable Tamil-speaking population there. Although preliminary work such as acquiring land was completed, further work has been suspended owing to the political turmoil there. The place has nonetheless come up nicely as an Ashram with a temple and other facilities.

Swamiji's dream of weaving a garland of Sandeepanys has thus become a reality. Bringing up trained workers and setting them to prachar work is the largest contribution that the Chinmaya Movement has made since 1963.

Swami Chinmayananda used to proudly call the Sandeepanys "arsenals of cultural rearmament."

SPARKS FROM THE FIRE

On August 3, 2000 at Chicago and on August 15, 2000 at Sandeepany, Mumbai, Swami Tejomayananda released a CCMT publication, titled *Sparks from the Fire*. It was a compilation of the bio-data of all Swamis and Swaminis of the Chinmaya Mission all over the world. The Swamis and Swaminis represent the sparks shooting out from the blazing fire that was Swami Chinmayananda. The Chinmaya Mission's monastic order today consists of forty Swamis and twenty-five Swaminis with a high level of scholastic and practical achievements. Barring a few, these monks have all gone through the Vedanta course in one Sandeepany or the other.

Details of the roles that they are playing today in carrying forward the missionary work begun by Swamiji are given in the book. The book brings out the specialization of each of the Swamis, Swaminis and specifies the areas in which they are doing their *prachar* work. Each has given a "Message for the Millennium" to the devotees, readers and all others who may glance through the book. The book pays homage to all the Swamis and Swaminis who have attained *samadhi* while serving the Mission; it has a special write-up on each of them. This is the first time in the history of the Chinmaya Movement that an attempt has been made to record the historical data in a systematic manner and make the record a useful book of reference. This effort is along the path laid out by Swamiji, due attention is given, from time to time, to record the events of the Mission so as to ensure that posterity has easy and ready access to the historical data.

BRAHMACHARIS AND BRAHMACHARINIS

Students who have completed the Vedanta course, accepted *deeksha* and chosen a life of renunciation are out in the field doing *prachar* work. There are ninety-three brahmacharis and forty-nine brahmacharinis in the field. They work under the guidance of the CCMT, the regional heads of various regions, and co-ordinate with the members of the local committees at the different centres.

They ensure that the activities of the Mission are conducted regularly and effectively at the grass-root level. A few of the *brahmacharis/brahmacharinis* have taken up administrative jobs; some others are engaged in doing creative work for the Mission.

Photographs and bio-data of the brahmacharis and brahmacharinis of the Chinmaya Mission are published in a separate roster titled *More Sparks from the Fire*.

Jaya Jaya Shankara Vijaya Pataake
Jaya Jaya Chinmaya Darshaka Range
Jaya Jaya Shashwata Dharma Sumoorte
Jaya Jaya Nirmala Keerti Vilase.
Hail ! Hail ! Oh, the flag of Victory
Proclaim the message of Shankara and Chinmaya
Hail ! Hail ! Oh, the flag of Glory
Uphold the fame of our sustaining dharma.

A poem composed and sung at the Sandeepany Sadhanalaya, Mumbai, while hoisting the flag, in the early years.

Prapya varan nibodhata: Know the Truth from wise teachers.
Rishi Sandeepany instructs Shri Krishna and Sudhama.

Sandeepany Sadhanalaya Acharyas

*1.*Swami Chinmayananda, *2.* Swami Dayananda,
*3.*Swami Purushottamananda, *4.* Br. Swaroop Chaitanya,
5. Swami Anubhavananda, *6.*Swami Chidananda,
7. Swami Tejomayananda

Sandeepany's Acharyas

Centre : **H.H. Swami Chinmayananda.**
Clockwise Starting from the top : **Swami Tejomayananda, Swami Subodhananda, Br. Sumitra Chaitanya, Swami Brahmananda, Swamini Saradapriyananda, Swami Bodhananda, Br. Atma Chaitanya, Swami Shridharananda, Br. Samahita Chaitanya, Swami Vageesananda**

Powai : Swami Chinmayananda's Pratima

Piercy : Students at Sandeepany (West).

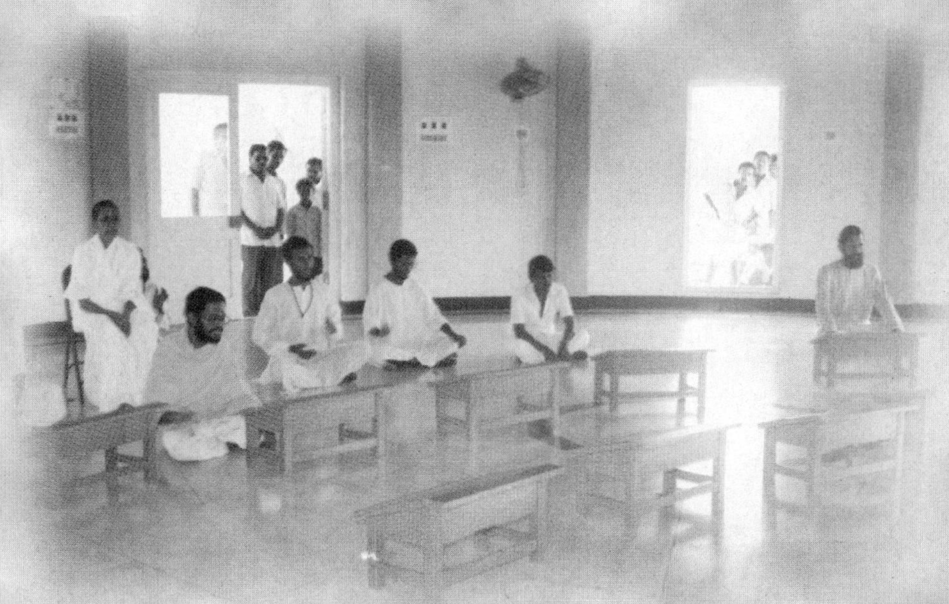

Tamaraipakkam : Sandeepany (Tamil Nadu)
Students with Acharya (extreme right).

Trikoota : Students at Sandeepany, Andhra Pradesh

Sidhbari : Sandeepany (Himalayas), a Class in Progress

Brahmacharis at Sandeepany, Kerala
with Acharya Br. Atma Chaitanya and Swami Gabheerananda

Bangalore: Inaugural function of Sandeepany Karnataka, May 1988
Shri Tiruchi Swamigal and Swami Chinmayananda bless the institute.

Coimbatore: Sandeepany Vidyamandir
Br. Samahita Chaitanya speaks.

Mumbai: Brahmacharinis at a devotional *satsang* at Jagadeeswara Temple - March, 2000

In a lighter vein: Vedanta class in progress, eleventh batch at Sandeepany Sadhanalaya - March, 2000.

5

Meruvidhi
Global Tours & Global Flag Posts

In Vedic literature there is a significant reference to *parivraja*. Elaborating on this, Swami Chinmayananda said:

> The job of the *mahatmas* (great souls) is to tour from place to place at all times. The *mahatmas* renounce all things. They give up love and hatred for worldly things in order to move about in the world from village to village, spreading the great culture, inspiring others, and themselves getting inspired. This has been the function and duty of all *mahatmas*.

Describing a unique pilgrimage known as *Meruvidhi*, Swamiji said that this was considered the greatest *tapasya* that a *mahatma* can perform. *Meru* is associated with the North Pole. Many *mahatmas* have undertaken this journey, crossing jungles, travelling over continents, reaching *Meru*, and, finally, returning, after completing the pilgrimage.

Swamiji undertook his first global tour, symbolically a *Meruvidhi*, on March 7, 1965 from Mumbai. He returned from it on July 5, 1965, after corvering thirty-nine cities spread over three continents.

During this tour, he delivered four lectures a day and a minimum of one television interview. This global tour, along with many more that followed, laid the foundation for Chinmaya centres all over the world—centres which today are playing a key role in the spiritual enlightenment of all seekers everywhere—regardless of age, caste, creed, and nationality.

In 1963, Swamiji's dream of a Vedanta institute was fulfilled with the opening of the Sandeepany Sadhanalaya at Powai, Mumbai. In fact he was anxious to involve people all over the world in his Renaissance movement. He decided to undertake a global tour and make a first-hand assessment of the situation in the industrialized countries of the world. Said he: "I am going not as a philosopher or champion of any particular religion but as a humble disciple of Mother Shruti to advocate certain values of life as enshrined in the *Upanishads* and other ancient scriptures." A global tour calls for detailed planning; it also requires experience of travelling extensively all over the world. Swamiji was, as we all know, an excellent judge of men, of the skills of the people around him; he also possessed the uncanny knack of spotting the right person for the right job. And he identified a very ardent devotee from a British corporate house at Chennai, B.V. Reddy by name. Reddy accompanied him on this tour as his Overseas Organizer. In fact it was Reddy who had planted the thought of a global tour in Swamiji's mind in 1962. Once, while alighting from a train at the Victoria Terminus (now called Chhatrapati Shivaji Terminus) at Mumbai, Swamiji first heard from Reddy of the great need for him to travel to countries in the West. Reddy took several steps to plan this tour. He also handled the vast correspondence that a foreign tour entailed. Swamiji made special mention of this work by Reddy while paying a glowing tribute to his contribution. He wrote a letter on the subject to the Hindi monthly of the Chinmaya Mission, *Chinmaya Pradeep*. He called Reddy a *karma-yoga-veera*, pointing out that Reddy had sent out 18,967 letters and received 15,740 replies! Reddy handled the tour with equanimity. He kept his cool; he never lost his patience even when Swamiji was in a temper.

In a message to devotees, prior to his departure on March 6, 1965, Swamiji said:

> The Lord, who has sustained the outer efficiencies and inner poise in me so far, will continue to do so in my ardent faith. In this faith, I leave the shores of this country to meet the world outside and to discuss with them the Hindu way of life and the eternal philosophy of this great culture.

Swamiji felt a great urge to share with the world the inner peace and tranquillity arising out of the experience of the Truth. He declared: "With a heart full of love for all mankind, we undertake this pilgrimage to see Him in all and to show Him to all Who is in everyone."

There was a mammoth public meeting at the Oval Maidan in Mumbai; it was attended by not less than 30,000 devotees to bid Swamiji a fond farewell. Various religious organizations—Hindu, Jain, Sikh, Buddhist, Parsi—felicitated Swamiji on his global spiritual tour. Many recalled and drew a parallel to the farewell given at Chennai, seventy-two years earlier, by a group of schoolmasters to Swami Vivekananda when he was about to embark for America. Both the Masters–Vivekananda and Chinmayananda–addressed the materialistic world of the West and hammered home the essence of Hindu philosophy. Swami Chinmayananda declared: "Hinduism is not a form of thought; it is a way of life." His plan was to organize a group with a view to ensuring that study was continuous and that seekers were consistent in their search. Seekers should be encouraged to come to the Sandeepany Sadhanalaya at Mumbai as *sadhaks*. He said he would bring children, youth, and women–and in fact all seekers of spiritual growth–into the fold of the Mission.

The history of the Chinmaya Mission abroad can be recorded even if we merely trace the route taken by Swamiji during his first global tour. Swamiji left the shores of India from Kolkata (then Calcutta), his first halt being Bangkok. From there he went on to Hong Kong.

HONG KONG

Often called the treasure chest of the East, Hong Kong gave Swamiji a warm welcome when he arrived on March 10, 1965. Swamiji held the first *Geeta jnana-yajna* there five years later, in 1970. The Hemrajanis were the dynamic force behind the activities of the Mission there. In 1972, K.P. Daswani took over, and he still continues to play an active role. He is a trustee of the Hong Kong Chinmaya Foundation. With the return of Br. Susheel Chaitanya (now Swami Swaroopananda) in 1986, the centre became a beehive of activity. At present there are three Study groups, ten Balavihars, and weekly classes on meditation, the *Bhagavad Geeta*, and the *Upanishads*. There are video classes also. Twice a month the centre has programmes under the title *Ghar Ghar mein Geeta*. Swami Chinmayananda used to visit Hong Kong regularly from 1988 to 1993 and conduct *yajnas*. Two significant events managed by this centre are Swamiji's visit to Beijing in 1982 and the hosting of the First Asia Pacific Hindu Conference in 1988. The Hong Kong centre also arranged for *yajnas* at Kuala Lumpur, Bangkok, Penang, Manila and Jakarta. The Chinmaya Seva

Ashram, as the centre is called, organizes week-end seminars and workshops for youth, retreats for families, etc. Many distinguished people have visited the centre. They include especially Sant Asaram Bapu (1991), Swami Chidananda of the Divine Life Society (1995), and Swami Govindananda of the Gangeshwara Veda Dham (1992). Swami Tejomayananda paid his first visit in 1989. He has paid regular visits every year since 1993. The Hong Kong centre publishes its own in-house newsletter *Seva* that covers all its activities. The centre brought out in 1990 a souvenir, titled *Inspirations*, which has over seventy pages of inspiring quotations from various sources.

Swami Sacchidananda took charge as Acharya in 1994. Brni. Nishita Chaitanya has taken charge as Acharya since November 2000.

SOUTHEAST ASIA

MANILA

The seed for a full-fledged centre for Manila was sown during the *Geeta jnana-yajnas* of Swami Chinmayananda. Swamiji had visited Manila several times prior to 1981 and had been a guest of a devotee, Dr. Pradhan. The first Study group was started in 1981; the first Balavihar, in 1989. The speedy growth of the centre after 1981 is largely attributed to the dynamic role played by Br. Susheel Chaitanya. His frequent visits to Manila in the company of Swami Chinmayananda and Swami Tejomayananda had created tremendous enthusiasm, particularly among the youth. In 1990 the Chinmaya Seva Group was formed with five couples joining the group as members. Initially the *yajnas* attracted a crowd of fifty people or so and were held in the house of some devotee or other. Later, as interest increased, the *yajnas* were shifted to halls and auditoriums. Over the years Manila devotees have taken part in major Chinmaya events like the *Swarna Tulabhara* at Mumbai (1991), the first International Spiritual Camp at Jakarta (1995), and the International Camp at Sidhbari (1998). The Manila centre continues to grow, thanks to the encouragement being given by Swami Tejomayananda, the spiritual head of the Chinmaya Mission Worldwide and by Swami Swaroopananda.

JAKARTA

This centre came into existence because of the initiatives taken by the Hong Kong centre. Swami Swaroopananda was keenly interested in developing a new centre in Indonesia and visited Jakarta frequently to prepare the ground therefor. Swami Chinmayananda visited Jakarta for the first time in 1987. As Indonesia is a predominantly Muslim country, the authorities there refused to give permission to Swamiji to hold public discourses because of his association with,the Vishwa Hindu Parishad. Swamiji then went to Bali and held some talks there. Bali has a rich heritage of Hindu culture. So far we have had two students from Bali in the Ashram in Mumbai for the residential Vedanta course.

In February 1993, the local devotees finally managed to persuade the authorities in Jakarta to allow Swamiji to give a public discourse. The talk was on Chapter Seven of the *Bhagavad Geeta*. Swamiji was very happy at his success in wearing down Indonesian reluctance to allow him to speak to Indonesian audience.

Among local people, Radha and Madhan Krishnan (along with other followers) were the pioneers of the Chinmaya family at Jakarta. They took guidance from the visiting Acharyas and arranged various discourses. Many visiting *sevaks* helped the

Indonesian centre to grow and stabilize by conducting *yajnas*, Balavihar classes, etc. Mention must be made of Gaurang Nanavaty and Ms. Darshnaben Nanavaty who paid a visit in 1987. Uncle Mani of the CCMT arrived in 1989 to conduct classes on *Valmiki Ramayana*.

The Jakarta centre conducted the First International Chinmaya Spiritual Family Camp in Southeast Asia in 1995 at Puncak. The theme was: "Win the Mind, Win the World." Over 200 people from all over the world attended the five-day retreat.

Swami Tejomayananda visited Jakarta in 1997, 1998 and 1999. Ms. Lakshmi Lasmana has been patronizing and volunterring with dedication. The Jakarta centre has rendered selfless service to schools and temples and to people in need of help in times of crisis. It deserves credit for translating into the Indonesian language Swami Chinmayananda's book *Art of Living*.

UNITED STATES OF AMERICA

SAN FRANCISCO, CALIFORNIA

Swami Chinmayananda continued his global tour from Hong Kong through Japan and Hawaii (Honolulu), meeting people and giving talks at important places. He set foot on American soil when he reached San Francisco on March 20, 1965. Little did he know at that time that thirty-five years later, California would attract a large Indian immigrant population that would also be in search of spiritual knowledge. Today there are Chinmaya Mission centres at Piercy, San Jose, Los Angeles, San Diego and Bakersfield–all in California. These centres play an important role in keeping Indians in touch with their rich heritage.

The day that Swamiji arrived in the United States, an incident occurred that typically illustrates his obsession for perfection.

Swamiji was scheduled to speak the same evening at 8 p.m. at the Metaphysical Town Hall Library. The topic was, "How to Realize God?" A large audience had gathered. Walking into the hall and casting a look around, Swamiji declared that he would not speak because the hall was not congenial for a spiritually inspirational talk. He added that he would instead have a question-and-answer session. It was true that the hall was not suitable, but how many would have the courage of conviction to say "no" in a foreign country on the day of arrival? The twin qualities of fearlessness and determination in Swamiji were what set him apart from others. In India, Swamiji would visit the *yajna-shala* prior to the commencement of a *yajna* along with the organizers and supervise the arrangements. Nothing would deter Swamiji from getting what was rightly due to him. To mention another incident–A few days after his visit to San Francisco, he was to visit Mexico to deliver a series of talks, but the Mexican embassy at San Francisco refused to give him a visa. Yet he landed in Mexico without a visa and fulfilled his engagements. Officials of the Indian embassy in Mexico came to his rescue. Who would venture to enter a foreign country when the authorities there have refused to give a visa? Once again it was his courage of conviction, that made him do what he did. His behaviour always reflected the maxim, "Truth and Truth alone will take you to victory–*Satyam eva jayate*."

While at San Francisco, Swamiji visited the University of California at Berkeley to deliver a talk to students there. Professor Michael Nagler, who is still with Berkeley, recalls the visit. Swamiji arrived a few minutes late for the talk and the organizers were trying to take the blame upon themselves, saying that they had notified the time wrongly. When Swamiji rose to speak, he said that the time notified had been correct and that it was he who was late for the appointment. He apologized to the audience but applauded the organizers for their gentlemanly attempt to protect his image.

Swamiji made an indelible impression on the people in Califonia. There were always requests for more visits by him. During his first visit, Swamiji met Ms. Nalini Browning, who later became his Personal Secretary. An American by birth, she did a lot of selfless service to promote the Chinmaya Mission in the San Francisco Bay Area. Bill Browing, her husband, took over the printing of *Mananam*, a speciality journal aimed at a select readership deeply committed to the pursuit of self-knowledge. Ms. Browning arranged several talks in the Redwood County, which Swamiji loved. The scenic surroundings and the redwood trees inspired him. It brought back to him memories of the days he had spent in the Himalaya. Swamini Saradapriyananda, impressed and inspired, used to comment that the large redwood trees were none but the *rishis* of yore, providing an awesome backdrop to Sandeepany West (as Piercy was known earlier).

PIERCY, CALIFORNIA

Piercy has a pride of place in the Chinmaya Movement. This is an Ashram rather than a centre. The first Vedanta course (1979–81) outside India was held at Piercy. The Ashram there was then named Sandeepany West. It was there that in 1978 the Chinmaya Mission acquired property on American soil for the first time. Swami Chinmayananda chose Piercy as the headquarters of Chinmaya Mission West. After the completion of the Vedanta course in 1981, organizational changes took place in India. It was decided to drop the idea of setting up an Institute of Vedanta at Piercy. So there was a period of lull at Piercy for about eight years.

Swami Chinmayananda visited Piercy again in 1989 and decided to turn Piercy into a spiritual retreat. He formally inaugurated it as a spiritual retreat in 1990. Simultaneously the name Sandeepany West was dropped. Swamiji wanted to rename the place Shivalaya, but somehow orders for a Shiva idol were not carried out in time. However, there was an idol of Krishna already at the centre. In his inimitable style, Swamiji remarked: "Krishna has arrived before Shiva." And he renamed the centre Krishnalaya (However, as if with a vengeance, an idol of Shiva did arrive in 1999 and was installed outside the *kutia* of Swamiji). Krishnalaya now holds camps for children, youth, and parents. Chinmaya Mission West (CMW) also extends the centre's facilities for community meetings, *Dharmasevak* courses, and inter-faith meetings and provides retreat facilities to individuals. During the Thanksgiving week-end and other long weekends, the San Jose centre holds spiritual camps for devotees, which are very popular events at Piercy.

Swami Tejomayananda is a regular visitor to Piercy and holds camps, gives discourses, etc. there. Those who have visited the centre include Swamini Saradapriyananda, Swami Shantananda, Swami Dheerananda, Swami Chidananda, and Swami Sharanananda.

SAN JOSE, CALIFORNIA

After Swami Chinmayananda's first visit to San Francisco in 1965 and his subsequent tours in 1967 and 1971, the activities of the Mission at San Francisco increased manifold. Most of these activities were carried on at the residences of devotees at and around San Francisco. The Bay Area had a Sunday school, and the classes there were given a formal name–the India Cultural School.

Ms. Malti Prasad, Ms. Indra Advani, Ms. Rita Assisi, Francis Assisi and Tej Singh—all enthusiastic devotees, ran the classes. Ms. Malti Prasad, sister of one of Swamiji's school friends, organized a *yajna* by him at Stanford University campus, California, in February 1975. Later Swamiji asked devotees to shift their activities to Los Altos, California, about forty miles south of San Francisco. Uma Jeyarasasingam was at San Francisco originally. She shifted to Los Altos later in 1968. She is the very dedicated Secretary of the Chinmaya centre at San Jose and organizes the activities of the centre in tandem with the Acharya stationed at San Jose. As the years rolled by, the devotees started feeling the need for a place of their own. In fact it was a dream of theirs. The dream came true in 1988. Swami Chinmayananda inaugurated Sandeepany San Jose with a week-long *Geeta jnana yajna*. The San Jose centre, under the dynamic leadership of Swami Tejomayananda and, later, of Swami Chidananda, turned into a hub of spiritual activity. The Balavihar classes at the centre had only six children in 1981; now the strength is 500 children. There was just one Study group in 1971; there are as many as nine Study groups. These nine Study groups cover a number of places including, especially, Cupertino, Milpitas, Fremont, Pleasanton, Sunnyvale, Los Altos, and San Ramon. In 1991 the centre introduced a family sponsorship programme with a contribution of $500 from each family. Starting with twenty families in 1991, it now has 125 families as sponsors. The centre has fifty-five volunteer teachers and about eight teenagers to teach younger children in the Balavihar and Yuva Kendra classes. Besides spiritual and cultural studies, the centre has organized the teaching of Indian languages such as Hindi, Tamil, Kannada, Telugu, and Oriya to about 600 children. The San Jose centre has ably catered to the cultural and spiritual needs of almost all families living in the Bay Area—both young and old. Witness the successful Chinmaya youth camps, Memorial Day weekend camps, and Thanksgiving weekend camps held at Krishnalaya Piercy. The youth have formed a special bhajan choir–Chinmaya Dhvani—to sing bhajans etc. at the programmes of the Mission and other functions. The centre celebrates all important Hindu festivals. It publishes a bimonthly newsletter called *Chinmaya Tej*, which provides inspirational material to those who are not able to attend classes physically at the centre. It has, besides, brought out a few publications such as *Mukunda Mala*, *Hindu Culture*, *Stotra Mala* and *Gita's Words of Guidance*. There is a shrine, with an image of Lord Shiva as Jagadeeshvara at the altar. The shrine exudes vibrations ideally suited for meditation. Swami Nikhilananda was the third Acharya here.

The first two Acharyas at San Jose, Swami Tejomayananda and Swami Chidananda made significant contributions to develop Los Angeles also as a full-fledged centre.

LOS ANGELES, CALIFORNIA

Swami Chinmayananda visited Los Angeles for the first time on March 23, 1965. He delivered lectures then at several places, the titles of his lectures being "The Secret of Achievement", "Art of Self-Unfoldment", "How to Reach God", etc. He had enthusiastic audiences which generated lively question-and-answer sessions. Swamiji once took an opportunity to meet the famous Walt Disney and spent some time with him. He was shown around Disneyland, where he evinced keen interest in Marineland and witnessed trained sea animals.

Los Angeles took a longer time to generate enough activity to justify a separate centre. The Acharya at San Jose was asked to look after the spiritual and cultural needs of the people of Los Angeles.

The activities of the Mision at Los Angeles gathered momentum soon enough. In 1977 there was a Chinmaya Family Camp at the University of California, Santa Cruz campus. Balavihar classes and Study groups were formed. Brni. Kaivalya Chaitanya held Vedanta classes at the Anaheim Hills, California Yuva Kendra classes were started at Cerritos in 1987. Brni. Arpita Chaitanya, who edited Swami Tejomayananda's very useful book, titled *Hindu Culture*, served the Los Angeles centre for a couple of years. In 1992 the foundation was laid for a regular centre to be started on its own premises. Swami Chinmayananda named this centre Kasi. The first Acharya, Br. Someshwar Chaitanya (now Swami Ishwarananda) took charge in 1994. Since then the centre has been very active with Baiavihar classes at week-ends at Anaheim, Norwalk, Diamond Bar, Chatsworth, Agoura Hills, San Gabriel, and Irvine. A bhajan group called *Shruti*, which comprises largely young people, performs regularly. The Acharya takes classes in Vedanta, Vedic chanting, and Sanskrit. The centre has organized many camps between 1996 and 2000—Thanksgiving camps, Family camps, Teachers' conferences and weekend seminars. Visiting Swamis of the Chinmaya Mission from India and the United States and many guest speakers–from the Divine Life Society of Rishikesh, the Shankara Mutt at Shringeri, and other leading religious organizations – have delivered lectures at this centre. The centre has published many books; it has also released various cassettes on subjects useful to Balavihar classes and Study groups. It is now planning to conduct bi-monthly meetings of senior citizens for health education and spiritual guidance.

The centre is under the charge of Swami Ishwarananda, who is the Acharya there.

VISIT TO MEXICO

From Los Angeles, Swamiji went to Mexico on a lecture tour. He spent three days there. Mexico was a more difficult place for Swamiji to deal with and make an impact upon owing to the language barrier, Spanish being the language of the people there. Even so, with the help of interpreters, Swamiji carried through his programme of lectures.

BAKERSFIELD, CALIFORNIA

Swami Tejomayananda, who had frequently visited the centre to encourage devotees, inaugurated this centre in February 1992. He visited it again and again in 1995, 1997, and 1999. The main activities of the centre are Balavihar classes, Yuva Kendra classes, Study groups, Vedic chanting and *yajnas* by different Acharyas. Swami Ishwarananda, who is posted at Los Angeles, is the Acharya there.

CHICAGO, ILLINOIS

Swamiji arrived at Chicago on April 5, 1965. He spoke at a number of universities there, his focus being on the student population. Importantly he went to the place where the Parliament of World Religions had been held in 1893 and paid a silent tribute to Swami Vivekananda, who had made history by his participation in that Parliament. Swamiji visited Chicago again in 1978 and 1979. The first *Geeta jnana yajna* there was held in 1979. The factors responsible for the strong foundation of this centre were the presence of a large immigrant population, the active part played by Brni. Pavitra, and the services offered by Gaurangbhai and Ms. Darshanaben Nanavaty in carrying out various activities. In 1987 the Mission bought 6.5 acres of land and by August 1988 had its own premises. Swami Chinmayananda declared the building open. He called himself the first Acharya of the centre. In March 1989, Br. Sudhansu Chaitanya (now Swami Anubhavananda, no longer with the Mission) took charge as the second Acharya. He was followed by Ananthanarayanan (Uncle Mani) in March 1991. With the appointment of resident Acharyas, the centre grew from strength to strength, and more and more Indian families were attracted to it. At a convention held in August 1989 at Orlando, Swami Chinmayananda christened the Chinmaya Mission, Chicago, as the Chinmaya Mission Badri. Visiting *mahatmas* at Chinmaya Badri included Swami Tejomayananda, Swamini Saradapriyananda, and Ma Amritanandamayi (1992 and 1993). The construction of the Badri Narayan Temple commenced in August 1992; Swami Tejomayananda consecrated it on Vijayadashami Day in October 1993. Swami Chinmayananda paid his last visit to Chinmaya Badri on July 2, 1993. Looking around the place from his car, he said: "My *sankalpa* for an Ashram here has been fulfilled."

In July 1993 Swami Chinmayananda was unanimously elected President of Hindu Religion at the World Parliament, an honour that he accepted. He, however, attained *maha-samadhi* on August 3, 1993, before the convention. Swami Chidananda of the Divine Life Society visited Badri and gave a memorial talk in September 1993 on Swami Chinmayananda. Both Swami Chinmayananda and Swami Chidananda had received *sannyasa deeksha* at the hands of Swami Sivananda Maharaj of Rishikesh in 1949. They respected, even revered each other. The activities of the Mission continued to grow, including the training of "student teachers", a *Geeta* chanting competition for the entire Midwest Region, and the first-ever residential National University Camp (organized in 1999).

Shanker Pillai, Ashok Dholakia and Ravi Sansgiri are among the leading organizers.

The present Acharya, the fourth in a row, is Swami Sharanananda, who received his *sannyasa deeksha* from Swami Tejomayananda in August 1995 at Badri. He has established six satellite centres in the states of Ohio, Indiana and Illinois—the last one being at Libertyville.

GRAND RAPIDS, MICHIGAN

Uncle Mani, the then Acharya at Chicago, inaugurated the Chinmaya centre at Grand Rapids on September 21, 1991. Swami Chinmayananda visited the centre in July 1992. Swami Tejomayananda visited it in 1993-94 and conducted *satsang* programmes. Mithilesh J. Mishra and Jitendra M. Mishra are now in charge of the work at the centre. The main activities are the holding of Balavihar classes and the staging of cultural programmes.

DALLAS / FORTWORTH, TEXAS

The itinerary of Swami Chinmayananda during his global tour undertaken in 1965 included a visit to Dallas. However, from the records available in the archives, it would appear that he did not visit Dallas. He flew from Los Angeles to Mexico and from Mexico to St. Louis, thus bypassing Dallas. Swami Purushottamananda came to this city in September 1984. The initiative to start a Chinmaya centre at Dallas was taken by a couple of families, which had relocated themselves from Houston to Dallas. First they started an informal Study group (in 1984). Balavihar activity with seven children followed (in 1990), the classes being held in the garage of a devotee. The strength of the Balavihar grew rapidly to 125 children in 1999. The Dallas centre was formally recognized as a Chinmaya centre by Swami Tejomayananda in July 1994, when he came for a *yajna*. The centre received encouragement from Gaurangbhai and Ms. Darshanaben Nanavaty, both stalwarts of the Chinmaya Mission in the United States. The centre registered a rapid all-round growth, with increasing strength of membership in the Balavihar classes, adult classes, bhajan classes, and language classes. The uniqueness of this Dallas centre lies in that it organizes an annual inter-faith programme in co-operation with the Dallas North Unitarian Church. With many members like Ms. Asha Ghate working with great dedication, the Mission at Dallas/Fortworth has its own beautiful facility now–Chinmaya Saket. Swami Nikhilananda is the resident Acharya.

HOUSTON, TEXAS

Swamiji's first visit to Houston was in 1980 to undergo an open heart surgery. He came again in 1981 for a ten-day *yajna* at the University of Houston. An informal Study group was started in the northen part of Houston after the *yajna*.

It was in 1982 that Chinmaya Mission Houston was established in an apartment with a small group of two families and four children. This group quickly grew to fifteen families and thirty children. In 1983, Swamiji appointed Gaurangbhai and Ms. Darshanaben Nanavaty, who had earlier (1981) completed the Vedanta course at Piercy, California, as Acharyas. Since then the centre has been a beehive of activity. Today the Houston centre is one of the most active, spreading the message of the Master and accomplishing his vision for the Mission. It must be recorded that Gaurangbhai and Darshanaben have not only contributed to the astounding growth of the Houston centre but also played a key role in helping newly formed centres elsewhere to develop and grow. They visited the Jakarta centre in 1987, when the centre conducted its first *jnana-yajna*. They have conducted *yajnas* and given discourses in the United States as well as in India. The remarkable manner in which the centre conveyed the relevance of Swamiji's *maha-samadhi* to the Balavihar children and the youth of the Yuva Kendra speaks of their sensitivity and creativity. The Balavihar children and the youth were not ready to accept that Swamiji would not be back in physical form and that the mighty powerful engine had really broken down. Under the guidance of Darshanaben the centre developed a script and four oil paintings of "The Blue Little Engine Which Could". The play was most effective. All Balavihar children were little blue engines, and together they could go on pulling this choo-choo train forever. Tears rolled down the eyes of all children and teachers, but the meaning was indelibly impressed upon their minds.

In 1986 the *sankalpa* for a facility was made in Swami Purushottamananda's presence, and the search for a place began. By 1987 the centre had acquired a building of its own on 7.5 acres of land. Swami Chinmayananda named the Houston centre Chinmaya Prabha. The membership has now grown to 250 families and 300 children. Chinmaya Mission Houston (CMH) was formally incorporated as a non-profit religious organization in April 1990. Swami Chinmayananda performed the *bhoomi-pooja* for a hall and a Shiva temple in July 1991. Swami Tejomayananda consecrated the Shiva temple in the year 2000.

This centre is a classic example of an effective method of teaching children's classes. Darshanaben, who is Director of the Balavihar and Yuva Kendra programmes, has nurtured the growth of these two wings of the centre. Swami Chinmayananda appointed her Director of the Balavihar Programme of Chinmaya Mission West. The Balavihar and Yuva Kendra classes are taught "to learn with fun". The learning process includes, and has to do with, stories, games, plays, arts and crafts, discussions, debates and field trips. *Shlokathon* is a favourite activity of the Balavihar children. It is a collection of more than 250 *shlokas* from the Hindu scriptures. It is divided into fifteen sections. When a student masters all the *sholkas*, Acharya Gaurangbhai Nanavaty or one of the visiting swamis awards a large trophy to him (or her).

The centre conducts classes in spiritual and non-spiritual subjects such as Sanskrit, bhajans, languages, etc. They also train boys and girls for SAT and PSAT (college entrance examinations). Classes for adults cover the Vedanta, the *Bhagavad Geeta*, Vedic chanting, etc. Every Sunday there are adult *satsangs*, which include discourses on the scriptures as well as Vedic chanting, and meditation. Questions from members are also answered.

The Acharyas have helped Study groups to come up in neighbouring cities, such as Austin, College Station and Dallas/Fortworth–all in Texas.

The centre publishes a single-page newsletter every month. Longer newsletters are also published every quarter. Since its inception, the centre has published six books, which include a teacher's training manual and a *Shlokathon* book and tape. It has also released several bhajan audiocassettes and CDs.

AUSTIN, TEXAS

The centre has mainly Balavihar and Yuva Kendra classes, as also classes for adults. The Balavihar and Yuva Kendra classes are divided into two groups–Junior and Senior–according to age. Classes are conducted for adults on the *Bhagavad Geeta*.

The centre is under the constant guidance of Gaurangbhai Nanavaty, who visits it often and also conducts a yearly weekend camp. Swami Tejomayananda visited Austin in 1996.

TRI-STATE

. The Chinmaya Mission Tri-State Centre covers three States–New York, New Jersey, and Pennsylvania. Swami Chinmayananda inaugurated this centre on November 30, 1992. It has two resident Acharyas Swami Siddhananda and Swami Shantananda in addition to Br. Krishnamoorthy. The main activities are Balavihar classes, Study groups, and yoga classes. The centre also conducts dance classes and classes in Sanskrit. It has, besides, the responsibility of publishing books/audio tapes of the Mission. Books printed in India are kept in stock at this centre so that they may be supplied to other centres in Canada and the United States. The Acharyas visit other centres to conduct *yajnas* and camps. Swami Tejomayananda has been visiting the centre frequently since its inception.

BOSTON, MASSACHUSETTS

Swami Chinmayananda visited Boston in 1989. Balavihar classes were started in 1991 at the residence of one of the devotees. There were twelve children when the activity started. Gradually it picked up momentum along with classes for youth and adult groups. Swamiji paid his last visit in December 1992.

The strength of the membership is now about 225. The centre has bought land in the Andover area, north of Boston, with the help of generous contributions from the community, notably from Gururaj Deshpande, a successful Indian entrepreneur. The construction of the centre building has started. The building is expected to be ready by May 2001. The centre is to be named Chinmaya Maruti. There is no resident Acharya now in Boston, the activities being well supported by the Acharyas stationed in the Washington, San Jose, Los Angeles, and Tri-State centres. Gopal Sharma and Brni. Pavitra (later Swamini Pavitrananda) did much work in early years. Shashi and Dwarakanath have been warm hosts and dedicated workers. Swami Tejomayananda has visited Boston for *yajnas* and camps in 1988, 1992, 1993 and 1996.

NEW YORK

Swami Chinmayananda travelled through Michigan, Massachusetts, and Connecticut to arrive in New York on April 16, 1965. Enroute he fulfilled many lecture engagements. For instance, he addressed students at the Harvard, Columbia, and Yale universities. Having assessed the mood of his audience, he spoke on subjects like "The Light of Reason", "The Oneness of Religions", etc. He laid emphasis specially on the importance of *Upanishadic* truths. The New York centre is one of the oldest and has acted as a catalytic agent for the opening of numerous other centres in America. The Acharya there is Br.Krishnamoorthy, who had done the Vedanta course at the Sandeepany Sadhanalaya, Mumbai.

BUFFALO, NEW YORK

Swami Shantananda inaugurated this centre officially in 1994. The main activities of the centre are the conduct of *jnana-yajnas*, the holding of *satsangs*, the taking of Balavihar classes, etc. Swami Tejomayananda visited Buffalo several times, starting in 1988. Patricia Loganathan and Krishnaswamy are among the long-time students and organizers.

PITTSBURG, PENNSYLVANIA

The first *Geeta jnana-yajna* by Swami Chinmayananda at Pittsburgh was conducted in 1978. Pittsburgh is located in the green rolling hills of Western Pennsylvania, where two large rivers, the Allegheny and the Monangahela, join and become one. The city has a large immigrant Indian population. It has three famous temples besides—the Shri Venkateshwara Temple, the Hindu-Jain Temple, and the Shri Satya Sai Baba Temple. The Chinmaya centre here is closely associated with the Shri Venkateshwara Temple and the Hindu-Jain Temple. It has had Study group meetings since 1978. Swami Chinmayananda had, at one time, toyed with the idea of making Pittsburgh the headquarters of Chinmaya Mission West. However, the final choice fell on Piercy, California. Balavihar activities are in full swing at this centre. In fact, the two temples referred to above conduct children's activities based on books published by the Chinmaya Mission such as the *Bala Ramayana*, the *Bala Bhagavatam*, and *Geeta for Children* as also the *Tarangini* booklets. Senior swamis and swaminis, as also Br.Krishnamoorthy, have conducted several *jnana-yajnas* at Pittsburgh. The centre has plans to acquire a building of its own for work, which is now being done at the temples or at the Carnegie-Mellon University. The enthusiasm of the local devotees has kept the centre thriving. They fervently hope that a resident Brahmachari or Swami would soon be appointed at Pittsburgh.

WASHINGTON D.C.

Swamiji visited Washington for the first time in April 1965. He was taken there by one John Murěsan, a devotee, whom he had met in Hawaii. It was the German consul and his wife who received Swamiji in Washington. The Indians in the city were surprised to find the German embassy was arranging Swamiji's programmes. The Indian embassy was nowhere involved.

In 1978, Swamiji visited Washington again and conducted the first *yajna* there. Vilasini Balakrishnan had just returned after completing the Vedanta course at the Sandeepany Sadhanalaya, Mumbai. She and her mother made all the arrangements for the *yajna*. After the *yajna*, the first Study group was formed, which met regularly for several years. Encouraged by the response of the devotees, Swamiji visited Washington in the years 1985 and 1986. Study groups had started in Chevy Chase, Falls Church, and Fairfax. In 1988, the members of the Mission resolved to buy some property for the activities. This was accomplished on *Vijayadashami* day, October 1988. The papers relating thereto were signed in the presence of Swami Tejomayananda. The centre has plans now to construct a bigger hall, *Chinmayam*, to accommodate more people. This centre has many branches—Baltimore, Md, Richmond, Va, and Salisbury, Md. Balavihar and Yuva Kendra classes are regularly held. The resident Acharya is Swami Dheerananda. Along with Brni. Arpita Chaitanya and Ms. Vilasini, he holds regular classes on the Vedanta and other subjects. The most interesting activity is the summer camp held annually at this centre: forty children each week for ten weeks, are trained in the summer holidays to say. their prayers, recite *shlokas*, sing bhajans, dance, etc. These activities enhance the richness of their daily lives.

SEATTLE, WASHINGTON

There was in early years a core group of devotees who kept the Seattle centre busy. In 1975, Elizabeth Burrows, founder and teacher of a Centre of Christian Studies in Seattle, invited Swami Chinmayananda to give a series of talks. This core group consisted of Ms. Darshana Nanavaty, Gaurang Nanavaty and Arun Desai. Lee Schultz was another enthusiastic participant. This group held regular meettings. Again Swamiji was invited in 1978 to hold a *yajna* at the University of Washington. Travelling with Swamiji were Ms. Vilasini, Ms. Nalini Browning (Swamiji's Secretary in America), and her daughter. The *yajnas* of 1985 and 1988 attracted more people, with about twelve people from Seattle joining the first Vedanta course at Sandeepany West. After completion of the course they spread out across the country, with Gaurangbhai and Darshanaben actively working at the Houston centre. The Seattle centre has been fortunate in getting many Acharyas to visit it. Swami Tejomayananda came in 1990 for the first camp he conducted in the United States. Brni Arpita, and Brni. Robyn (of Vancouver, B.C.) conducted many classes here. Seattle continues to hold Study group meetings in the homes of devotees. Seekers like Bill Herguson have been long-time participants in Chinmaya programmes.

ANN ARBOR, MICHIGAN

The Ann Arbor centre owes its origin to the Balavihar classes conducted in Long Island, NY, by Ms. Sharada and her husband Kumar, ardent devotees of Swami Chinmayananda. When the couple moved to Ann Arbor, Swamiji blessed the Balavihar activity that was then being conducted in the basement of their home there. In 1994, the Ann Arbor centre was incorporated. From then on, many events took place, the centre manifesting all the characteristics of a vibrant Chinmaya centre. It has now a Yuva Kendra, *Geeta/Upanishad* classes for adults, Vedic chanting, Study groups, Karnatak music classes, Devi groups (where *shlokas* are taught), and bi-weekly bhajan classes. The centre also covers

Novi, Troy, and Canton areas. There are Balavihar classes in all the four centres; each centre has up to two hundred children. To begin with, although the Balavihar classes triggered off activity, it was the adult group accompanying the children, which made it possible to expand the range of activity. At first the adults were compulsorily required to attend the *Geeta* classes, and thereafter in the light of the keen interest shown by them, the centre gradually introduced various other activities. The centre observes almost all Hindu festivals, as also some American traditional celebrations like Mothers' Day, Fathers' Day, etc. By introducing such all-comprehensive activities, it has succeeded in involving all the members of a family. The centre has no newsletter but lists all its activities/programmes on their website: http://www.chinmaya-aa.org. The activities have recently moved into the centre's own facility *Avantika*.

FLINT, MICHIGAN

It is almost twenty-two years ago since the waves of the Chinmaya Movement first touched the shores of the Michigan, the land of the Great Lakes. Major credit for this goes to the dedicated Chinmaya families in Flint who have worked with devotion and sincerity in establishing and implementing Swamiji's spiritual ideologies. The five families who initiated the Chinmaya Movement here are Venkateswarans, Prathikanthis, Mukkamalas, Galis, and Nagarajus.

The first *jnana-yajna* by Swamiji was conducted in 1978. Several ten-day *yajnas* were conducted in the years 1980, 1984 and 1988. Chinmaya Mission Flint sponsored the Second International Spritual camp at Olivet, Michigan, which was attended by delegates from different countries of the world.

Dr. Apparao Mukkamala, an ardent devotee of Swami Chinmayananda, is ably guiding this centre. Dr. Mukkamala has been on the Board of Chinmaya Mission West (CMW) since 1981 and presently he is the President of the Executive Committee of the Board.

The first Acharya at this centre was Br. Shashwata Chaitanya, who joined in 1993. Br. Alok Chaitanya succeeded him in 1996 and served for a year. In the initial years the centre used to hold its meetings in the houses of the devotees. It was in 1990 that the centre acquired its own premises, which are equipped with a shrine. The centre is coming up quite well. It is busy with activities like the Balavihar classes, the meetings of the Devi group, *satsangs*, bhajans and adult classes every Sunday. It celebrates all Hindu festivals and arranges picnics for the Balavihar children. Reports of its activities also are published in a bi-monthly newsletter. Once a year a *maha-samadhi* issue is also published.

Chinmaya Seva Samiti was born in 1988 with the objective of fostering spiritual discussions and related activities. The centre, Chinmaya Tapovanam, was inaugurated by Swami Chinmayananda. The shrine here has a beautiful Krishna idol installed. Swamiji wanted Tapovanmam to be used as a sacred place of worship, a place for meditation and urged that it should "buzz with activity".

MIDDLE GEORGIA

This is a young centre that was started as recently as1994, with the Hindu Temple in Atlanta as its base. The initial response of the people was lukewarm. Just ten children were then attending Balavihar classes. In 1997 activity picked up. Currently the Balavihar programme has as many as 110 children. There are eight teachers. In 1996 Swami Tejomayananda conducted a camp at Atlanta, Ms. Darshanaben Nanavaty of Houston conducted a refresher course for the Balavihar teachers in March 1998. With the blessings of Swami Tejomayananda an adult Study group and a Devi group were started in Warner Robins, in September 1998. The centre started a Balavihar programme in Warner Robins in August 1999. There are twenty children now at this location. Its strength is growing as witnessed by the interest shown by local parents. Many spiritual programmes were held in 1999 at this centre, with the keen participation of Swami Tejomayananda, Swamini Saradapriyananda, and Swami Dheerananda.

ORLANDO, FLORIDA

The Orlando centre started on a small scale at the office of Dr. Shailaja Nadkarni, whom the children of the centre affectionately called "Shailaja Aunty". There were a few families, which wanted to learn more about the Indian heritage. The main inspiration to the devotees was the late Swamini Pavitrananda, an ardent devotee of Swami Chinmayananda. She had done her Vedanta course at the Sandeepany Sadhanalaya, Mumbai. Orlando devotees attended Swami Chinmayananda's *yajna* at Pittsburg. Eventually, in 1980, the centre conducted its spiritual activities at Tapovan, another location in Water Springs. Swamiji formally inaugurated the Orlando centre in 1990.

Nine years later in 1999, the centre had 282 children from the age of three to nineteen years participating in the children's and youth programmes. About fifty adults participate in the adult programmes. In 1992 the Orlando centre acquired ten acres of land adjacent to Tapovan. With the blessings of Swami Chinmayananda it built an Ashram there. Swamiji lovingly named the proposed Ashram *Kaivalya*, which means ultimate liberation.

On July 18, 1999, Swami Tejomayananda installed an idol of Shiva, Jagadeeshvara, at Kaivalya. He gave discourses on the *Kaivalya Upanishad* for five days following the ceremony. The centre conducts language classes in Hindi, Gujarati, and Marathi. The Yuva Kendra publishes a quarterly newsletter titled *Kaivalya* that covers all its activities. Vimal Desai is among those, who guide the Vedanta studies here. The Orlando centre aspires to have a Vedanta Institute on the eastern shores of America.

MIAMI, FLORIDA

Mission activity started in 1989 with Brni. Pavitra's *yajna* in a devotee's home. In 1990 Swami Chinmayananda stopped over at Miami briefly and met twenty-five families. In 1991 Balavihar classes started with five students. Swamini Gangananda conducted *satsangs* in various homes. In 1992 Swami Shantananda held a *yajna*, by 1993 the number of children in the Balavihar increased to forty. Swami Tejomayananda held his first *yajna* at Miami in 1993. Swami Chinmayananda's videotapes on the *Bhagavad Geeta* were also screened for the benefit of the adult group. Brni. Aparna returned in 1995 after completing the Vedanta course at the Sandeepany Sadhanalaya, Mumbai. Swami Tejomayananda held a *yajna* in 1996. It was attended by 150 families. Vedanta classes were started for adults. The number of children in the Balavihar and the Chyk group increased to sixty. The centre holds regularly annual camps for the Balavihar children and the members of the Chyk group. The visit of Swami Swaroopananda was a great success with about a hundred families attending the *yajna* he performed. The number of children in Balavihar and Chyk groups increased to 150 in two locations. In the year 2000, through the International Friendship Walk and thanks to individual donations, the Miami centre contributed over $30,000 to the Orissa cyclone relief fund.

THE WEST INDIES

TRINIDAD

After paying a brief visit to Miami, Swami Chinmayananda arrived in Trinidad on May 10, 1965. About 2000 Indians and an equal number of natives, were at the International Airport to give him a tumultuous welcome. The Sanatan Dharma Maha Sabha Inc., of Trinidad and Tobago, a powerful organization that ran about forty schools in the island, had striven hard to make this visit a great success. Swamiji applauded the workers of the Sabha for their ceaseless endeavour to educate Hindus on the right lines. Swamiji's three-day visit to Trinidad was a memorable one. The Caribbean Islands has a large immigrant Indian population, settled more than 200 years ago, with a nostalgic longing for their Motherland. The children in the schools run by the Sanatan Dharma Maha Sabha were being taught the immortal Hindu culture. When Swamiji visited the Tunapne Hindu School, there were 999 students there. They presented a guard of honour to him. Swamiji addressed a *Geeta* class, the only one of its kind run by Mrs. I. Kelkar, a devotee of Swamiji from Nagpur. She had turned into a devotee long before the country had heard of the Chinmaya Mission and its activities. Swamiji's first visit to Trinidad was thus a conspicuous success. Pleased with this welcome given him by people living thousands of miles away from the Motherland, Swamiji said, "There are no frontiers for Spiritual India."

Swamiji paid a second visit to Trinidad more by accident than by design. It was in 1966. Swamiji was to visit Honolulu for a talk but at the last minute this programme fell through owing to a hitch about who would meet the expenses. Meantime the people of Trinidad extended a warm welcome to him and also sent him a ticket to come to Trinidad. So, during the "*Geeta* Talk Fest" of 1966,

Swamiji visited Trinidad and conducted a *Geeta jnana-yajna* from November 10 to 22, 1966. He spoke not only on the *Geeta* but also on *Bhaja Govindam*, and the *Kenopanishad*. The talks were a great success and the people of Trinidad even now recall the Swami with a princely gait. His penetrating discourses elicited all round appreciation. In between the *yajna* talks, Swamiji took up other activities. He addressed Muslims in a mosque, opened a temple of the Divine Life Society, and spoke to the forty trainees at the Monastery of Mount St. Benedict, where Indian and native students had been initiated and were being trained to work as missionaries.

The people of Trinidad responded spontaneously to Swamiji's lectures. Hundreds of devotees signed up for the Chinmaya Lesson Course instituted by the Sandeepany Sadhanalaya, Mumbai. Swamiji expressed the hope that they would form the nucleus for the Missionary work in the years ahead.

Another interesting development was that Rev. Dr. Baldwin A. George of Trinidad returned to India along with Swamiji to take up Vedanta studies. He was placed under the tutelage of Parthasarathy, the then *Pradhan* of the Sandeepany Sadhanalaya, Mumbai. After completion of his studies, he was given the honoured status of a brahmachari. Swamiji ordained him a *sannyasi* in June 1969 and gave him the name of Swami Bhaskarananda. He went back to his homeland to serve in the Gandhi Tagore College at San Fernando. To date, his is the only case of *sannyasa* in the Chinmaya Mission of a non-Indian origin. He attained *samadhi* in August 1970.

The Chinmaya Mission, Trinidad, was inaugurated on October 2, 1997. The Mission has acquired two and a half acres of land; the construction of an Ashram on the site is expected to start shortly. The Acharya at the centre is Br.Prem Chaitanya, who was posted in 1997. He has been taking active interest in the activities at the Mission. He visits four different schools every week and conducts two Sanskrit classes twice a week. He also visits prisons and talks to prisoners. In a programme called "*Pratah Smaranam*" on the radio, the centre has an hour's programme every Saturday – they play all the bhajan and chanting cassettes recorded by the Mission. A discourse is also given during this programme. From the inception of the centre, Br. Prem has conducted over fifty *yajnas* on the *Ramayana*, the *Bhagavad Geeta*, *Bhaja Govindam* and the *Upanishads*.

The *yajnas* are conducted in nine different villages on the nine days of the first *navaratri* in March-April. At the time of the second *navaratri* in October, they move the *yajnas* from street to street in a village that has nine streets.

The centre conducted a six-month *pooja* course. (This is because *poojas* are very popular in Trinidad.) Forty students participated in the course and attended class from 5 a.m. to 6 a.m. for six months.

Br. Prem Chaitanya has been travelling to Guyana (South America) for *yajnas* and has found it a potentially good place for the activities of the Mission.

CANADA

During the first global tour, Swami Chinmayananda paid a very brief visit to Canada. He went to a university town called Windsor on April 12, 1965. He meant it to be just a reconnoitering tour to observe the people of Canada. It was only much later, in the 1970s, that he visited important towns and identified centres where the Chinmaya Mission could play a meaningful role in the spiritual life of the people.

TORONTO, ONTARIO

The first *yajna* to be held by Swamiji in Canada was the one he conducted in a local church in Toronto in 1973. The first Study group was also organized in 1973 at the residence of one of the devotees, Ms. Charlton Walman. Activity picked up at this centre after Br. Barry was posted at Toronto in 1978. Br. Barry took two classes every week at the University of Toronto. This attracted a mixed audience of Indians and Canadians. There was a keen demand for the books of the Mission but it was difficult to import books. So, in 1979, Chinmaya Publications, Canada was established to ensure availability of the books.

The Chinmaya Mission, Toronto was registered as a charitable organization in 1981. Swami Purushottamananda held a *yajna* in 1983. Brni. Sadhana, who had completed the Vedanta course at the Sandeepany Sadhanalaya, Mumbai, arrived in Toronto in 1987. The centre has buzzed ever since with activity. Swami Chinmayananda, Swami Tejomayananda, Swami Purshottamananda, Swami Chidananda and Swami Shantananda have held *yajnas* year after year. Swami Chinmayananda's last visit was in 1992. It was then decided that the Mananam series of publications should be shifted from Piercy, California, to Toronto. This work is being done even now at Toronto. Swami Tejomayananda inaugurated the Chinmaya Shivalaya in 1998. The resident Acharya Brni. Sadhana conducts Balavihar classes, Yuva Kendra classes, and seven Study groups. The centre feeds the poor regularly. This is done as part of the *sadhana*. The centre also has seminars, teaches the art of relaxation, and holds bhajan sessions.

OTTAWA, ONTARIO

Swamiji first visited Ottawa in the year 1973. During that visit he delivered two evening lectures at the National Library of Canada.

His next visit was in 1977, when he spent much time with the families that had settled there and explained to them the import of the wisdom of the Vedanta. He also conducted a lecture series on the *Bhagavad Geeta*. It was during this visit that some devotees from Flint, Michigan, came, including Dr. Mukkamala, and met Swamiji. They went back and started the Chinmaya Mission Flint. At Ottawa, under the guidance of Swamiji the centre organize Study groups. Initially the response of the people was lukewarm. It was only in 1991, after the *Geeta jnana-yajna* by Swamiji that the centre was galvanized into activity. The centre has a comprehensive package to offer to all devotees, whether adults or children. The Balavihar movement has thirty children, the youth group, about twenty-five; and the adult group, about twenty. The centre has successfully conducted innovative programmes to introduce India to teenagers and young adults–a programme covering talks on temple architecture, food, fashions, and cricket. The Ottawa centre has many visitors including swamis. Swami Dheerananda of the Washington Regional Centre is a frequent visitor. The centre's classes, *yajnas* and conferences are well attended. The centre has six *sevaks* and *sevikas*, all trained by Ms. Darshanaben Nanavaty, who has played the role of a guardian angel for many newly formed centres in North America and elsewhere.

HALTON REGION, ONTARIO

Activities of the Chinmaya Mission started in 1982 in Burlington, Ontatrio; but the official legal body was constituted only in 1990. Some of the active members are Ms. Sneha Chakraburtty, Bhaskar Reddy and his wife, Ravi Arora and his wife. The first camp was held in 1985 at Waterloo and another camp in 1998. Surmounting many obstacles, a centre was formed under the name "Chinmaya Mission Halton Regional Centre."

To finance social service projects in India like hospitals and nursing schools, members of Halton Region started raising funds. They raised funds from the Canadian Government for the Sidhbari Project in India for its Rural Health Centre. Similarly they raised funds for the Bangalore Hospital. The Halton centre inspired activities in Niagara also. Toronto and Niagara promote spiritual studies for the benefit of the members, Chinmaya Mission Halton Region on the other hand is more active in the field of fund-raising.

CALGARY, ALBERTA

This centre is affiliated to the Vancouver centre. Its membership is quite small. Even then these members are quite regular. Every year the centre organizes a yajna by a senior swami. For example, in the year 2000, Sharadamma Rao and other devotees organized a *yajna* by Swami Shantananda.

VANCOUVER, BRITISH COLUMBIA

Swami Chinmayananda visited Vancouver for the first time in 1972. He came to inaugurate a Hindu Temple, maintained by Vishwa Hindu Parishad, as also a recreation centre in South Burnaby. More than five hundred people sat barefoot in yoga posture to hear the visiting spiritual teacher. Swamiji expressed the hope that Vancouver would become a "mutual place" for cultural exchanges between the Indian community and the Canadians. Raj Kapahi and his wife, hosts for Swamiji when he came to deliver a series of lectures in the Simon Fraser University in Burnaby, became ardent devotees of Swamiji after their first meeting with him in 1972. They even attended the camps conducted by Swamiji in the United States of America. The first Study group was formed at Vancouver in 1976. The early teachers included Brni. Dhanya, Brni. Mary Anne Kniest and Br. Allen, and his wife Joan. Brni. Robyn Thompson came to Vancouver in 1986 after completing the Vedanta course at the Sandeepany Sadhanalaya, Mumbai. She presided over Study group sessions. Thanks to the encouragement given by Swami Tejomayananda, she started Balavihar classes in 1988, which soon became a Yuva Kendra group before it folded up in 1997. Brni. Robyn has been promoting satellite centres at Victoria, and visits Seattle, regularly. Currently the Vancouver centre is running two adult classes, two Balavihar classes, and a weekly video session for elders. It has plans to have a place of its own and expand its activities.

Swami Tejomayananda visited Vancouver for the first time in 1988 and conducted a *yajna* on Chapter Seven of *Bhagavad Geeta* and the *Ishavasyopanishad*. From 1995 to 1999 many visiting swamis/swaminis–Tejomayananda, Purushottamananda, Saradapriyananda and Chidananda–conducted *yajnas*. Swami Swaroopananda visited Vancouver for the first time in October 1999, and gave a discourse on *Hanuman Chalisa* for five days. It was a great success. He also gave talks on *Gayatri Mantra* and *Ek Omkaar*, which were also well received.

The centre publishes Chinmayam, a newsletter that covers all activities.

EUROPE

After covering the American continent, Swamiji went on to London on May 19, 1965. A reception committee headed by R. Parekh and the President of the Hindu Centre welcomed him. He fulfilled a number of engagements, giving talks on varied subjects to different groups—medical students, members of the Hindu Centre, Indian students living in the Young Men's Christian Association (YMCA), and the active workers of the Hindi Prachar Parishad. The highlight of his engagements in London was the meeting organized by the Hindu Centre at the Mahatma Gandhi Hall. The then High Commissioner for India, Dr. Jivaraj Mehta. presided. Swamiji spoke on the "Technique of Self-Development". He explained very vividly how all sciences sought to make the world better and better in order to promote man's happiness and how, religion was concerned about man himself rather than the world. There was a very large gathering and Swamiji's message went down very well with it.

LONDON, UNITED KINGDOM

The Chinmaya Movement in London took shape in 1986, when the First International Camp was organized by Laju and Kavita Chanrai at the Crystal Palace, South London. Devotees, mainly from Europe and the United States, and the general public attended this camp. Swamiji spoke on Chapter Three of the *Bhagavad Geeta*, his favourite chapter. He also took the *Kenopanishad*. There was consequently increased interest in Swamiji's interpretation of the scriptures. People became more aware of the Chinmaya literature. In 1988 the initiators of a Study group movement in London, Karia and Morjaria, organized a series of lectures on the Vedanta philosophy at the Kings' College, Chelsea. The third *yajna* came off in August 1991, when Swamiji discoursed on Chapter Seven of the *Bhagavad Geeta*. In 1992, when Swamiji was in London again for a *yajnã*, he was able to take only the evening classes owing to ill-health. This time he dealt with Chapter Two of the *Bhagavad Geeta*. Uncle Mani took the morning classes on the Valmiki Ramayana. In 1993 Swamiji, accompanied by Swami Swaroopananda, came to London for a *yajna*. The London devotees were then introduced to Swami Swaroopananda. His frequent visits to London thereafter inspired the adults and the youth. He conducted the third Chinmaya Yuva Kendra residential retreat in 1998, "Online with a Higher Power", which was a great success with 105 members participating in the retreat. The first Chyk retreat was held in London in 1996 with thirty-five youth and the second residential retreat was in 1997, with the participation of seventy-five. This annual event is now very popular. The London centre has been very active with a variety of programmes, initiated, boosted, and supported by visiting brahmacharis and swamis. A resident brahmachari was posted in 1998. Swami Sacchidananda was later posted to London, which gave a fillip to the activities there. The Acharya started additional classes on meditation, Vedic chanting, and the *Upanishads*. He also initiated the *Ghar Ghar mein Geeta* programme. Swami Tejomayananda visited London in June 1999 and conducted a *yajna* on Chapter 15 of the *Bhagavad Geeta*. The fourth Chyk residential retreat was conducted by Swami Swaroopananda, which is voted as one of the best so far. The subject was "A View of Perfection". The first Balavihar camp, titled "Krishna, My Friend" was staged in September 1999. It was well received both by the children and their parents. Chinmaya Mission, United Kingdom, became a registered charity in October 1999. At present there is a Yuva Kendra in addition to four Study groups for adults and five Balavihar classes. The centre has a regular newsletter; it was introduced in 2000 and has a pro-active committee comprising members, who are young, sincere and committed. It has comprehensive plans to develop a number of additional activities like a bookshop, daytime seminars, etc. It also plans to establish premises of its own for carrying on its activities.

PARIS, FRANCE

In the course of his first global tour Swamiji touched Paris as well. He addressed three groups. The most successful of his lectures was the one he delivered at L'Home et La Connaissance, an association which invites leading personalities to deliver their messages and discuss their thoughts. The first and second sessions went off very well indeed. The organizers feared that there might be thousands of people to listen to Swamiji if they went ahead with a third session. They, therefore, suggested that the third session be restricted to special invitees, as they would not be able to arrange a suitable hall for the session at such short notice. Swamiji brushed aside this suggestion on the ground that philosophy was not meant for a select gathering.

Swamiji visited Paris again in 1983 and 1985 in response to an invitation from a yoga centre. He conducted camps during these visits which were attended by more than two hundred people, and his talks made a deep impact on many in the audience. One such person was a young lady who joined the Vedanta Course in 1989 and received *brahmacharya deeksha* in October 1991. This was Brni. Bhakti (formerly Christiane Madeline), who is at present in charge of the Paris centre. Upon her return to Paris after her completion of the Vedanta course, others who were interested in the subject helped her in organizing the Chinmaya Mission as an official association. This was done in July 1992. The Paris centre extended an invitation to Swami Chinmayananda to visit Paris, which actually took place in June 1993. Swamiji was not too well then. His condition was a matter of serious concern and the centre made all medical arrangements to meet any emergency. Swamiji spoke on June 11, 1993 on the subject, "Why God?" Over 250 people attended this talk. Swamiji released the first book published by Chinmaya Mission, France, on this occasion. He was immensely pleased with the work done by the Paris centre. The enthusiasm of the devotees increased, and the first Study group was formed in October 1993, with about twelve people.

In November 1993 the Paris centre had a memorial *pooja* for Swami Chinmayananda. Swami Pranavananda came from Mauritius for the purpose. It was a moving function.

Membership is at a moderate level. There are several reasons for it, but the most important is that the centre does not get support from the local Indian population or from other spiritual organizations. In October 1994 the centre started publishing a bi-annual newsletter. Thanks to the missionary zeal of Brni. Bhakti, the centre has organized camps and weekend sessions since 1994. Swami Tejomayananda visited Paris in 1994, 1996 and 1998 and conducted camps that were three to five days' long. Brni. Bhakti conducted weekend camps in 1995 and 1997. Swami Pranavananda came in 1996 and conducted a five-day camp. The most creditable achievement of the centre is the publication of French translations of some selected books by Swami Chinmayananda. A French translation of the *Bhagavad Geeta* was published in 1998. Swami Pranavananda came to France to be present on the occasion.

MIDDLE EAST

On the last leg of his first global tour Swamiji visited Geneva, Rome and Athens. In all these famous cities Swamiji held informal meetings with Indians. In Athens he met the artists who formed the main strata of the society there. In spite of his crowded programme of meetings he managed to snatch some time to visit famous places.

In the Middle East Swamiji covered Beirut and Damascus. His programmes there were organized by the Indian Embassy. There was a *satsang* at the Indian Embassy in Damascus, which Swamiji enjoyed. He stopped over for a short while in the Lebanon; He addressed a public meeting there, which was well attended.

Thus ended Swamiji's tour—his first *digvijaya*. He returned to India on June 27, 1965. Devotees back home were happy to receive him: Many public receptions were held for him. They poured out their love for him and showed their devotion through twenty such public receptions. There were, besides, four formal recepitons by municipalities. Swamiji addressed a few press conferences too and gave interviews to journalists and others.

GLOBAL TOURS IN 1966 AND 1967

Swamiji received several invitations to visit foreign centres again. He was not content with undertaking tours and giving only general lectures or formal interviews to TV stations. He asked organizers to arrange for *yajnas* so he might expound the Hindu philosophy in depth. So in March 1966, he held his first *jnana-yajna* in a foreign country–at Kuala Lumpur and a "Talk Fest" in August–November of that year in America. (In keeping with modern jargon, he called his *yajnas* Talk Fest or Talk Festival). During this period the Chinmaya Movement got a firm foothold at San Francisco, at Los Angeles, and in Trinidad in the West Indies. The Chinmaya Movement had come to stay.

The *yajna* at Kuala Lumpur was a great success. Swamiji had asked two of his devotees—Jamnadas Moorjani and Prakash

Mehra—from Mumbai to join him so they could brief the organizers about setting up study classes. The two devotees had also brought with them booklets and aluminum plaques with *shlokas* from the *Geeta* inscribed, to be distributed as *yajna-prasad*.

SINGAPORE

Swamiji motored down from Kuala Lumpur to Singapore via Ipoh—almost three hundred miles and visited Singapore for the first time in March 1966.

Swamiji addressed his first meeting in Singapore at a hall near Perumal Koil. There was a crowd there of five hundred people. The subject was: "Do We Need Religion?" Before leaving Singapore, Swamiji gave a date for a *jnana-yajna* to be held in February 1967. His brilliant exposition fired the imagination of the audience. People clamoured for more talks and lectures. The *yajna* in 1967 too was a great success. On Swamiji's advice the devotees started Balavihar classes. The first Balavihar class was inaugurated in 1968. Subsequently, as the number of children increased, classes were held at the headquarters of the Ramakrishna Mission in Singapore. The Balavihar classes held by the Chinmaya Mission received spontaneous co-operation from Swami Siddhatmananda of the Ramakrishna Mission. Swami Chinmayananda appreciated the work done by the devotees in Singapore and in a letter made special mention of the Paran family, which had played an important role in promoting the work of the Mission there. By 1970 the number of Balavihar classes increased to nine, with nearly 270 children on the rolls. A youth group was also started with about thirty members. This group helped the Hindu Centre in organizing various activities for young men. The second *jnana-yajna* in Singapore was held in 1973. Swamiji held meditation classes in the morning and *Geeta jnana-yajna* in the evening. In 1976 there were as many as 250 children participating actively in the Balavihar. However, for want of dedicated workers, there was a setback, and by 1979 the Balavihar centres closed down. Swamiji sought to control the damage, as it would appear; for in 1987, he introduced Br. Susheel Chaitanya (now Swami Swaroopananda) to Singapore. This was a turning point in the history of the Chinmaya Movement in Singapore; for the activities at the centre were revived: Br. Susheel Chaitanya captured the hearts of the local people. He took then step by step on the path of self-unfoldment and created a group of dedicated workers.

In 1986 K.P. Daswani, a devotee from Hong Kong, came to Singapore and started *Geeta* classes there for women. Inspired by him and under his guidance, Jyoti Kundalia set up a *Geeta* Study group. In 1988 Swamiji inaugurated the First Asia-Pacific Hindu Conference that was attended by more than five hundred people from sixteen countries. In 1990 a camp was held on the subject "The Vedanta Intensive and Meditation Retreat" with Swamiji expounding the Yoga of Action and the *Kathopanishad*. Later the Singapore centre published the instructions given in this camp on medifation in book form. The title of the book is *Art of Contemplation*.

The *yajna* held by Swamiji in Singapore in April 1993 was Swamiji's last there; it was also his tenth. He gave dates for the next *yajna* to be held in February 1994, but his end intervened.

The history of the Chinmaya Movement in Singapore reveals that there has been a general awakening and enlightenment among the youth as well as the older generation of Hindus. It reminds us of Swamiji's oft-repeated goal of converting Hindus to Hinduism.

Swami Tejomayananda first visited Singapore in 1994. He has continued his annual visits since then. Swami Swaroopananda has had a tremendous impact on Singapore devotees, Swami Mitrananda has also been a frequent visitor since 1997. He carries the youth with him. Under his guidance the youth group consisting of thirty members in the age group of 16-28 has blossomed into a forceful group. The backbone of the Singapore centre is the Balavihar work. Hundreds of children attend the Balavihar classes with "Keep Smiling" as their motto. The Yuva Kendra has its own website and an orchestra made up of its own members; It actively participates in social service projects. The Study group consists of thirty regular members. It has been meeting regularly to study major texts like *Vivekachoodamani*. A bhajan group meets once a week to sing devotional songs and to learn how to chant. Some members of the centre take active part in social service. The key project for the celebrations due in 2001 is a vegetarian cookbook.

The centre has its own newsletter, which is published quarterly, called *Chinmaya Darshan*. The centre was registered in April 1996. Chances of the centre owning premises of its own appear difficult in view of the prohibitive cost of real estate in Singapore. The work of the Mission is conducted from the office of Chandru Bharwani; the classes are held at private homes.

FOREIGN TOUR OF 1971

In 1971 Swamiji undertook the longest tour of foreign countries for missionary activity. Starting in August, he toured round the world continuously for as many as 190 days, touching ten different countries, and visiting many Chinmaya centres, and addressing six different universities, This tour laid the foundation for Chinmaya centres in the Middle East, particularly Bahrain and Kuwait. There is a very large Indian population in the countries of the Middle East, particularly immigrants from Kerala. The local Indians took keen interest in organising Swamiji's talks. Swamiji visited Kuwait and Bahrain in April 1971 and again in August of the same year.

To briefly enumerate the success of this tour of 190 days: Swamiji visited seventeen Chinmaya centres. He came in contact with about 50,000 people. Books sold at the *yajnas* crossed the figure of Rs. 20,000 (Rupees twenty thousand only). Swamiji received about a thousand subscriptions for *Tapovan Prasad*, and for the Lesson Course. Eight hundred students signed up for the Lesson Course.

Again, in 1972, Swamiji made a global tour lasting 172 days. The achievements of this tour were: He held ten *Geeta jnana-yajnas*. He took eight *Upanishad* classes. He gave nine short talks. He participated in an inter-religious symposium. He visited eighteen world-famous Universities. Twenty thousand people brought their offerings to the Chinmaya Mission.

Out of the 172 days, as many as forty-one were spent in the Middle East. In January 1973, Swami Dayananda wrote:

> Highly conservative in their ways of thinking, the Arab countries were never in contact with any other culture or religion, save Islam. It is an amazing phenomenon in the history of the Arabs that they have taken such a serious interest in Swamiji. The seeds of Truth sown by the unfailing hands of Swamiji will sprout and grow to bless them.

During the tour of 1972, Swamiji went to Zurich for a health check up. His tours abroad became almost an annual affair—both to spread spiritual knowledge and to check up on his health.

KUWAIT

Swamiji visited Kuwait for the first time in April 1971. At that time there were about 12000 Indians living there working in the oil fields, employed in Government services, etc. Swamiji gave two talks at the Geeta Mandir, a newly opened hall.

This short visit was followed by a full fledged *Geeta jnana-yajna* in August 1971. This was well organized and successfully conducted. Unfortunately the books, which were shipped from India for the *yajna*, were over-shipped to the next port of call, and the organizers were obliged to lithograph Chapter Twelve of the *Bhagavad Geeta* and sell the lithographs to the people attending the *yajna*. Reporting about the *yajna*, the local Indian representative wrote that the majority of the people attending the yajna were Christians and Muslims. Hindus were conspicuous by their absence.

Another important engagement that Swamiji fulfilled was the installation of an 18-inch marble idol of Muralikrishna at the Geeta Mandir. This was a gift from the Mumbai Chinmaya Mission to the Kuwait's Geeta Mandir.

The Chinmaya family in Kuwait is registered with the Indian embassy, Kuwait, as Bharat Samskara Kender (Bhasker). Swamiji visited Kuwait eight times in all. His last *yajna* was in February 1989. The visits planned subsequently were cancelled on account of political unrest and Swamiji's own ill health.

Swami Tejomayananda visited Kuwait for the first time in 1988. After taking charge as the head of the Chinmaya Mission worldwide, he visited Kuwait for the first time in 1994.

The Kuwait centre has conducted ninteeen *yajnas* so far. These *yajnas* were conducted by either Swami Tejomayananda or Swami Swaroopananda. The centre has eight Study groups, and fourteen Balavihars. Then there are Devi groups. They have been successful in fund-raising programmes in which over 2000 Indians participated. It was like a festival.

The preponderance of the Indian population in Kuwait has helped in bringing families together. Although there is no Acharya there are a few trained *sevaks* and *sevikas* who carry out a variety of activities. Many families that have returned to India continue to be ardent devotees of the Mission and are rendering useful service.

BAHRAIN

In April 1971 Swamiji visited Bahrain on his way back to India from Switzerland, where he had gone for a health check-up. He inaugurated the Mission centre there on April 6, 1971. He paid a second visit in August of the same year. On his arrival, the Devi group of the Chinmaya Mission received him. Here Swamiji adopted a novel method for his lectures. He held what he called "chalk talks". He would, with the help of a blackboard and a piece of chalk, explain the basics of the Vedanta. He delivered three chalk talks at a local school auditorium in Manama. These three talks steadily took the listeners from an inquiry into the need of religion, to the logic of spiritual quest as expounded in the Hindu scriptures. The centre has grown since its inauguration by Swamiji. Every year it conducts a *Geeta jnana-yajna*, and invites a swami from India to conduct the *yajna*. The centre has six Balavihar classes and a Study group which meets weekly. Study group classes are conducted in English, Gujarati, and Hindi. The Devi group meets every Tuesday for *sahasranamarchana* and bhajans. The Friday *satsang* is well attended: it attracts from seventy to eighty members. The centre is registered as a society–Chinmaya Society–and carries out all its work with great enthusiasm. Swami Tejomayananda conducted a *Geeta jnana-yajna* there in September 1999; Swami Swaroopananda followed suit in February 2000.

DUBAI

Swamiji had a ten-day *yajna* at Dubai in 1979. The 750 strong audience was kept enthralled as Swamiji went through the depths of Vedanta. Again, he arrived in Dubai in May, 1981 accompanied by Chandrika Pradeep of Bangalore. He had a five-day lecture series on "Man of Perfection Downtown". The Indian Ambassador inaugurated the talks and for 5 days Swamiji captivated the audience with eloquence, humour and wisdom. The centre has been moderately active since then.

MUSCAT

Chinmaya Family Muscat (CFM) started a study class in 1984, thanks to initiative of one Mr. Pillai. Swamiji visited Muscat in 1989 and in 1993. The basic activities of this centre are Study groups, Balavihar classes, and prayer and meditation sessions. There are two Study groups and four Balavihar classes. Prayer and meditation sessions are held every week. The centre also conducts Sanskrit classes. The activities of the centre are carried out in the hall in one of the two temples in Muscat.

SRI LANKA

Swamiji had a large following in Sri Lanka; for many of his devotess had attended the *yajnas* that he had conducted at Chennai and other cities in India. Owing largely to their demand, a formal centre was opened on June 25, 1980. A resident brahmachari was posted in 1980. A plot of ten acres land, about 150 Kilometres from Colombo, was acquired with a plan to start

Sandeepany Sri Lanka. Owing, however, to the communal holocaust of 1983, all activities came to a standstill. In 1989 the centre was reactivated, and Study groups, Devi groups, etc. were recommenced. Representatives of the Chinmaya Mission have held discourses there from 1992 onwards. Swami Swaroopananda, Swamini Vimalananda, Swami Mitrananda, Swami Nikhilananda and Br. Samahita Chaitanya have visited the centre. Swami Tejomayananda visited Sri Lanka for the first time in 1996. In 1997 he laid the foundation stone for a Hanuman temple there. An Ashram complex has also come up. Swami Tejomayananda formally inaugurated the temple in October 1999.

The centre conducts Balavihar classes and Yuva Kendra classes regularly. It publishes a quarterly journal titled *Voice of Chinmaya*. It published a biography of Swami Chinmayananda in Tamil language. Tejomayananda released the book in October 1999.

The resident Acharya is Swami Shridharananda (Since January 2000), and the resident Brahmachari is Ramana Chaitanya (Since May 1998).

The original plan to set up an Institute of Vedanta—Sandeepany Sri Lanka—is now held in abeyance. The Mission has plans to start a centre at Kandy, in addition to the present locations of Colombo and Ramboda.

NEPAL

The centre at Kathmandu in Nepal is called Chinmaya Adhyatmic Seva Sangh. In April 1990 Swami Chinmayananda asked a devotee in Delhi (Ms. Durgi Singh) to organize a *Geeta jnana-yajna* at Kathmandu. Accordingly in June 1990, the *yajna* was held. Subsequently, the centre had several *yajnas*. These were held by visiting brahmacharis, swamis, and swaminis. The centre conducts four Balavihar classes. Its activities are conducted from two locations—Kathmandu and Patan.

In April 2000 there was a grand International Camp at Pokhara (Nepal), at the Fulbhari Resort in the Nepal Valley. About 350 delegates from thirty-three countries attended the camp. Swami Tejomayananda held discourses on *Yoga Vashishta*, the essence of Vedanta. Swami Swaroopananda gave inspiring talks on *Gopika Geet* and Swami Mitrananda handled the Yuva Kendra activities. Brahmacharinis–Sadhana, Bhakti and Arpita took care of Balavihar classes. The camp was a grand success. At the end of the camp, the participants left with "a true sense of belonging to a gigantic, dynamic, pulsating movement, a warm wonderful family bound together with love."

AUSTRALIA

Swami Chinmayananda was keen on carrying the message of the Mission to "Down Under". Recently many Indian professionals have moved down to Australia in view of the liberal approach of the Government of Australia towards immigration. One of Swamiji's devotees, Dr. (Mrs.) K.T. Ganapathy, moved to Melbourne in 1981.

MELBOURNE

The work of the Chinmaya Mission in Melbourne started in 1981 at the residence of Dr. Natteri Chandran on the birthday of Swamiji, May 8. Dr. Ganapathy was then taking Vedanta classes to a small group of sincere seekers. Swamiji visited Melbourne in 1984 and conducted a *yajna* at the University of Melbourne. By 1991, the Mission had over a hundred members. Vedanta classes were being conducted almost every day. Interest in the activities of the Mission was growing and the need was felt for a central place for holding classes. Swami Swaroopananda visited Melbourne in 1993; and Swami Tejomayananda in 1994. They urged members to go ahead and buy a place of their own—with some help from the devotees from Hong Kong. Accordingly the Mission took a loan and bought a property in 1994. This place is now named Chinmaya Dham. A full-time Acharya was posted in 1995 in Melbourne—Swami Swaroopananda. Since then the centre has been throbbing with activity—talks and lecture series at Melbourne, at Sydney and in several cities in New Zealand. The spread of knowledge, under the guidance of Swami Swaroopananda, was explosive. Four students came from Australia to the Sandeepany Sadhanalaya, Mumbai in 1996 for the Vedanta course. In 1998, the centre bought a bigger property so as to find room for the increasing number of its activities.

In 1998 three out of the four students who underwent training at Mumbai returned to Australia and took active part in nurturing the growth of the centres at Melbourne and Sydney. Meanwhile, one more student from Australia joined the Vedanta course at Mumbai. She is posted now in Hong Kong. The centres in Australia are running at full throttle. Within a short period of six years they are wholly engaged in the task of spreading spiritual knowledge.

SYDNEY

The Chinmaya Mission as it obtains today in Sydney really began with the visit of Swami Chinmayananda to Australia in 1984. Shanti (earlier Janetta Haim) was trained by Susan Wetner, a brahmacharini trained at Sandeepany Sadhanalaya, Mumbai. (Susan Wetner is no longer with the Chinmaya Mission). Shanti visited Melbourne to meet Swami Chinmayananda. She drew up a plan for a camp in Sydney and sought and obtained Swamiji's approval. Along with other committee members and with help from certain influential members of the Melbourne centre (as for instance Dr. Ganapathy and Ms. Christine Grimmer) organized a camp in 1987. A large contingent of devotees came from Melbourne to attend the camp. The camp was unique and turned out to be a turning point in the activities of the Mission in Sydney. Some of the newcomers there are even today staunch supporters of the Sydney centre. Ms. Christine Grimmer moved to Sydney from Melbourne and worked with Shanti. She organized Balavihars and Study groups in different areas. Swamiji came to Sydney once again in 1989 for a *yajna* and then again in 1993. Meawhile Hema Krishnamurthy, who was teaching at the Chinmaya Vidyalaya at Chennai and later at Mumbai too, moved to Sydney. This gave a boost to the growth of the work of the Mission. She was able to attract more children to the Balavihar classes. With her help, the centre was able to use the premises of a school in Strathfield for conducting classes during the weekend. Later in 1993, Manisha Khemlani from Mumbai moved to Sydney for higher studies. Her experience of the work of the Mission at Mumbai was of invaluable help. In 1993 Swamiji visited Sydney along with Swami Swaroopananda. This visit by Swamiji sowed the seeds for a unified Australian Mission. Soon enough, in 1995, Swami Swaroopananda was made the Resident Acharya for all Australia.

Swami Tejomayananda visited Australia in 1994 and 1996. He conducted two very successful *yajnas*.

NEW ZEALAND

NELSON

The work of the Chinmaya Mission at Nelson began soon after the arrival of Brni. Bhakti in July 1994. She started a Study group immediately on arrival as the neighbours were curious about the books being unpacked. It was at Nelson that the first Chinmaya Foundation came up in New Zealand. Study started with *Atma Bodh* and *Art of Manmaking*. Swami Swaroopananda held the first *yajna* in May 1995. This was followed by a second lecture series in November 1995. Next there was retreat to the beautiful Abel Tasman National Park. The theme chosen for discussion and meditation was "Finding joy in the midst of Life's Dilemmas". In April 1996, Swami Tejomayananda visited Nelson and his lectures, being clear and logical, were very well received. People were impressed with his humility. In May 1997, Swami Swaroopananda did a lecture tour—five lectures on "Facing Adversity in Life". These lectures were compiled by Maria Reckers and published in book form by the Nelson Chinmaya Foundation. In December 1977, Swami Swaroopananda again gave a lecture on the subject "Wise and the Otherwise" It was basically Chapter Two of the *Bhagavad Geeta*, *Karma Yoga*. There was also a weekend retreat; the theme of the camp was "*Dhyana-swaroopam*". The first newsletter of the centre, called the *Chinmaya Vision* was compiled and printed by a devotee named Sandii Daly. It contains reports of events, articles by members, and inspirational thoughts from Brni. Bhakti. In April 1998, a group travelled to Sidhbari and attended the International Camp. In July 1998 Swami Swaroopananda visited Nelson and gave a series of talks on "Success without Stress". The winter retreat was held at Onekaka in Golden Bay, where Swami Swaroopananda spoke on "Steps towards Inner Peace." Nelson is a lovely seaside city with a population of about 40,000–mainly European–and is ideal as a place for retreats and spiritual pursuits.

AUCKLAND

The Chinmaya Mission, Auckland came into prominence in 1999 with the arrival of Swami Swaroopananda there. The first centre in New Zealand was started at Nelson in the early 1990s. The second came up in 1999 in Auckland. This was followed by the commencement of Balavihars and Yuva Kendra groups. Swami Swaroopananda has conducted two *yajnas* in Auckland so far.

MAURITIUS & REUNION ISLANDS

Mauritius and Reunion Islands have a predominantly French-speaking population. The Mission must, therefore, have French-speaking Acharyas at these centres. Of course, the Acharyas have been trained at the Sandeepany Sadhanalaya, Mumbai.

After receiving his brahmachari-*deeksha* at the Sandeepany Sadhanalaya, Mumbai in 1975, Br. Pranava Chaitanya came back to his own country, Mauritius, and settled down at his parents' house. He wrote to Swamiji one morning, giving the details of the situation there and the conditions of the Hindu religion. He also invited Swamiji to visit the country. Br. Pranava Chaitanya started his work on Krishnajanmashtami, did *jayantipooja* at Shri Draupadee Amen Temple at Rose-Hill, and the very next day, he went to Reunion Island on an invitation from them and started work there too. He travelled from Mauritius to Reunion Island and back for many years, visiting temples and houses, smuggling the message of the *rishis* into the country! In the year 1977, Swami Chinmayananda paid his first visit to Mauritius. However, he was not keen to go to Reunion. He told Br. Pranava Chaitanya then: "I don't know the language; you know the language, so you go there!" Endlessly, Br. Pranava Chaitanya served the two countries. In neither country had the Mission its own premises. It was in 1982, after a few years of sacrifice and dedicated service that the Mauritius centre managed to save five hundred thousand rupees. With that money it bought one-and-a-half acres of land. Swami Chinmayananda was made aware of the property. He was, in fact, asked to give a name to it. So he named it "Parna-Kuti". Since the establishment of the Ashram, many *mahatmas* have blessed the place with their discourses. These *mahatmas* include Swami Nisshreyasananda and Swami Ranganathananda of the Ramakrishna Mission. Meanwhile, in 1986, Br. Pranava Chaitanya became a full-fledged monk. Swami Ranganathananda asked him if Swami Chinmayananda had ever visited the Ashram. The answer was negative. Thereupon the Swami requested Swami Pranavananda to write to Swami Chinmayananda and ask him to come and visit his Ashram in Mauritius. The letter was written, and the reply came: "OK, I'm coming." That was in 1987. Swamiji stopped over in Mauritius for twenty-four hours on his way from Singapore to South Africa. The theme of his evening lecture in the Ashram that day was "I want Happiness". Seeing the interest of the audience, Swamiji declared on the spot that he would come again. As promised, he returned in 1989. He came for the last time in 1990. During each of these visits he attracted large crowds—not less than five thousand people.

The activities of the Chinmaya Mission in Mauritius consist of week-end Balavihar and Chyk classes, daily *satsangs*, spiritual camps, celebrations of all Hindu festivals, and *jnana-yajnas* area-wise across the country. *Jnana-Yajnas* are also held in Reunion. It was after the *Geeta* marathon camp at Sidhbari that Swami Chinmayananda announced that he would give *sannyasa* to Br. Pranava Chaitanya and that it would take place at the Mumbai Ashram. As mentioned earlier, the *sannyasa-deeksha* was given in 1986. Other swamis to visit Mauritius were Swami Purushottamananda and Swamini Saradapriyananda. Swami Tejomayananda visited Mauritius in 1995 and in 2000. He visited Reunion Island in July

2000. Brni. Bhakti from the Chinmaya Mission, Paris, visited the island in April 2000.

In Reunion Island the Chinmaya Mission has bought a plot of land of about ten acres. The *Bhoomi-pooja* was performed in July 2000. They have plans to put up a small facility there.

In Mauritius, a great project is also on its way. The centre has commenced the construction of what is called the *Vijnana Nilayam* (Seat of Learning). The building will have an area of 14000 square feet and will be embellished with decorative work.

Swami Pranavananda has been travelling abroad for the past fifteen years, delivering spiritual discourses on all Hindu scriptures. He often visits Reunion. He was invited in 1995 for the World Hindu Conference held in South Africa. He goes regularly to France, to the Czech Republic, to French-speaking Canada, and to Rodrigues Island (Mauritius).

KENYA

NAIROBI

The first visit of Swami Chinmayananda to Kenya came off on May 27, 1986. Accompanying him were two devotees—Ms. Anjali Singh from Delhi and Ms. Usha Kumar from Darjeeling. Swamiji's hosts were Manubhai Patel and his wife. Their nephew, Dilip Patel, who used to be at Houston Texas, organized the *yajna* at Nairobi. The Hindu Council of Kenya at the Premier Club hosted the *yajna*. Swamiji spoke on the *Kenopanishad* in the mornings. He dealt with Chapter Twelve of the *Bhagavad Geeta* in the evenings. The Nairobi audience was hearing Swamiji for the first time so Swamiji gave an elaborate introductory lecture for three days on the fundamentals of the Vedanta. The *yajna* continued till June 3, 1986. During this brief stay Swamiji managed to visit some famous places of tourist attraction in Kenya like the Nukuru National Park, the Nairobi National Park, the Rift Valley and Lake Nukuru.

In 1992, the Nairobi centre organized a *Geeta jnana-yajna* under the aegis of the Hindu Council of Kenya. It did all the planning as well as the organizing of the *yajna*. Swami Swaroopananda arrived from Hong Kong via Mumbai for the purpose of conducting the *yajna*. The *yajna* was a great success. During this visit Swami Swaroopananda asked Ramesh Pattni to serve as the coordinator of the Chinmaya Mission in Kenya.

In 1993, the centre organized another *jnana-yajna* at Nairobi, with Swami Swaroopananda taking up Chapter Four of the *Bhagavad Geeta*. The *yajna* was cut short when news of Swami Chinmayananda's illness and subsequent *samadhi* reached Nairobi.

Meanwhile, Study group activity was picking up. There were ten to twelve dedicated workers. A three-day camp followed the *Geeta jnana-yajna* of 1994 for adults. Swami Swaroopananda conducted it.

In April 1995, Swami Tejomayananda visited Nairobi for the first time. He had *satsang* with the members, and they were delighted with his bhajans. In 1996 the centre organized a *Geeta jnana-yajna* in Gujarati by Swamini Vimalananda. East Africa, particularly Nairobi, has a strong presence of Indians from Gujarat. The *yajna* was an immediate success. This was the first visit by Swamini Vimalananda to Kenya. She covered not only Nairobi but also Mombasa and Kisumu.

In March 1997 the first international camp was organized at Nairobi under Swami Tejomayananda. Owing to the good fortune of the centre and the grace of the Lord, the organizers were able to locate an ideal setting for the camp. They decided to use the

Commercial Bank Training Centre at Karen. With 153 participants from different places–Tanzania, Bahrain, India, Australia, the United Kingdom, and the United States–it was a great success. There were discourses by Swami Tejomayananda on Chapter Fifteen of the *Bhagavad Geeta*, the *Vibhishana Geeta*, and *Maneesha Panchakam*. It was a treat to the listeners. Besides, there were his melodious bhajan sessions. The skits presented by Babubhai were thoroughly enjoyable. Food was prepared under the meticulous supervision of women like Ms. Hasuben, Ms. Lataben, and their group and was well appreciated.

In response to popular demand, Swamini Vimalananda visited Nairobi again in August 1997 and yet again in February 1999. Mission activity was in full swing. For Shivaratri in 1999 the centre organized *Shivasahasranamajapa*, the thousand hallowed names of Lord Shiva. Over two hundred people attended it.

In August 1999, Swami Tejomayananda conducted a *yajna* at Nairobi. In response to an invitaion he attended the opening ceremony of the Swaminarayan Temple. Devotees from other countries too visited the centre–Ms. Shivangi Bhatt from Chicago, Ms. Pratibha Jobanputra from Mumbai, and Ms. Shail Mehrotra from Kanpur–who took active part in all the events.

The year 2000 dawned with a *Geeta jnana-yajna* and a Chyk camp with forty students at Masai Mara. Swami Swaroopananda conducted it. A number of devotees from Nairobi attended the international camp at Nepal in April 2000.

SOUTH AFRICA

DURBAN

Swami Nirmalananda Saraswati is the founder and the spiritual head of the Chinmaya Mission of South Africa. He studied Vedanta at Sandeepany Sadhanalaya Mumbai from 1972 to 1975. Prior to that, he served the Divine Life Society of South Africa for a couple of years. After successfully completing the Vedanta course at Sandeepany Sadhanalaya, he returned back to South Africa. From 1975 to 1979, he toured the country holding *satsangs* at various places like Transvaal, Kwa-Zulu Natal, Port Elizabeth and Cape Town.

After evaluating the interest of the people, he formally established the Chinmaya Mission of South Africa. Once the Mission was formed, the need for a central establishment from where the activities of the Mission could be coordinated and carried out was felt. Efforts were made to find a suitable location.

In 1982, the actual site of the Ashram was identified and acquired. Very soon construction of the Ashram started and was almost completed by 1986 and was formally inaugurated by Swami Chinmayananda during his visit to the country in 1987.

The Ashram is a beautiful one. There is an imposing building housing a hall that can seat 500 to 800 people. There is a shrine for Swami Chinmayanananda in the hall. The building also has a well-equipped kitchen, a dining hall, a library hall, a small conference room and a few living rooms with bathrooms attached. There is also a small temple dedicated to Lord Jagadeeshwara outside the hall. *Arati* is performed twice a day at the temple.

It has been visited by many swamis and swaminis, including especially Swami Tejomayananda, Swami Pranavananda, Swamini Gangananda, Swamini Vimalananda, and Swami Swaroopananda. The centre plans to expand its work and attract the support of the local Indians in Durban. Br. Peetambar was posted here in July 1999.

Thus, the Chinmaya Movement has in the 35 years between 1965-2000 established 46 vibrant Mission centres around the globe.

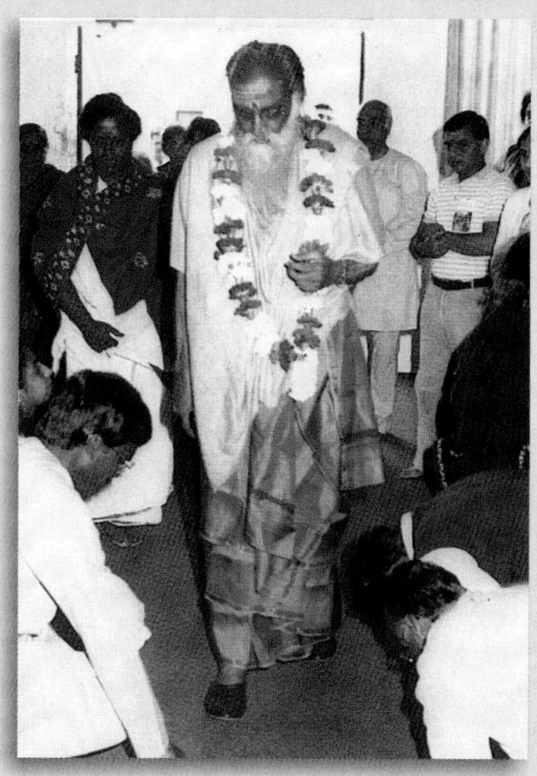

San Jose, CA: Swamiji entering the centre on Park Avenue

Toronto: Swamiji with devotees
Margaret Leuverink, editor of *Mananam,* is seen
(leaning against the wall).

Swamiji visits Trinidad 19
Shyam to his left and
Dr. Avtar to his right

Chicago : Badri *bhoomi Pujan*
done by Swamiji,
August 26, 1989

Mauritius:
The Mission Ce

Nairobi: Inspired devotees around
wami Tejomayananda

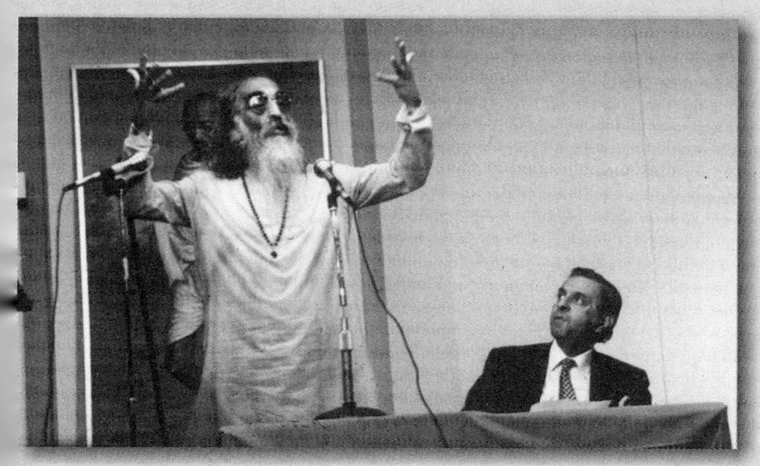

London : Swamiji addressing an audience at Bharatiya Vidya Bhavan 1986-1987.

Melbourne: Swamiji with
Mrs) K.T. Ganapati

Paris: Waiting to reach towering heights

Vancouver:
Kapahis host Swamiji

Piercy:
Entrance to Krishnalaya, CMW Headquarters

Swami Shantananda, Acharya Tri-State USA : At Brussels Yajna 1999.

Houston: The Choir Group

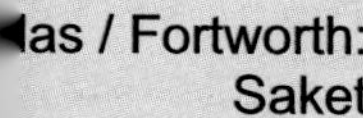

las / Fortworth: Saket

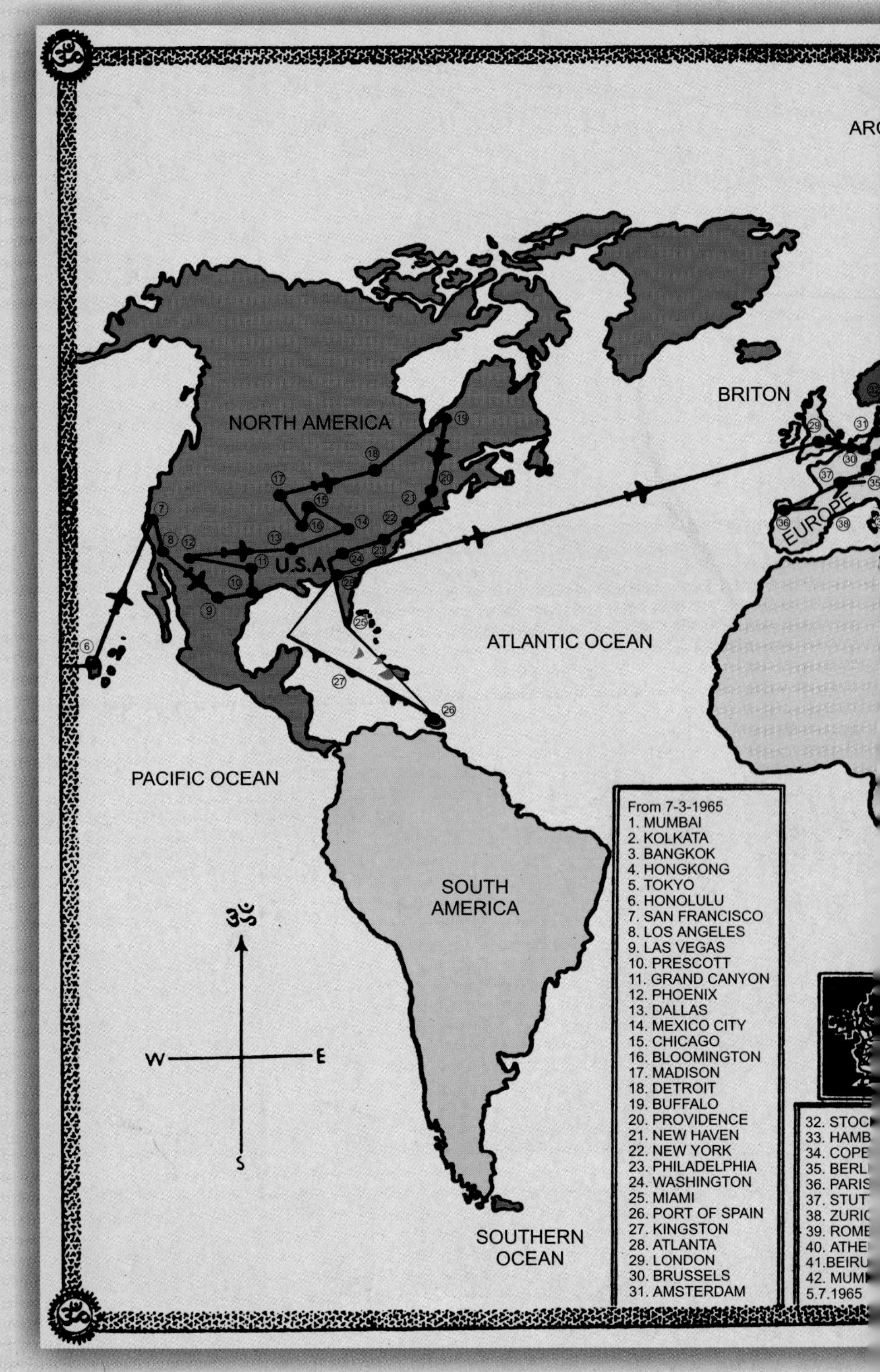
ARC
BRITON
NORTH AMERICA
U.S.A
EUROPE
ATLANTIC OCEAN
PACIFIC OCEAN
SOUTH AMERICA
SOUTHERN OCEAN
W
E
S
From 7-3-1965
1. MUMBAI
2. KOLKATA
3. BANGKOK
4. HONGKONG
5. TOKYO
6. HONOLULU
7. SAN FRANCISCO
8. LOS ANGELES
9. LAS VEGAS
10. PRESCOTT
11. GRAND CANYON
12. PHOENIX
13. DALLAS
14. MEXICO CITY
15. CHICAGO
16. BLOOMINGTON
17. MADISON
18. DETROIT
19. BUFFALO
20. PROVIDENCE
21. NEW HAVEN
22. NEW YORK
23. PHILADELPHIA
24. WASHINGTON
25. MIAMI
26. PORT OF SPAIN
27. KINGSTON
28. ATLANTA
29. LONDON
30. BRUSSELS
31. AMSTERDAM
32. STOC
33. HAMB
34. COPE
35. BERL
36. PARIS
37. STUT
38. ZURIC
39. ROME
40. ATHE
41.BEIRU
42. MUM
5.7.1965

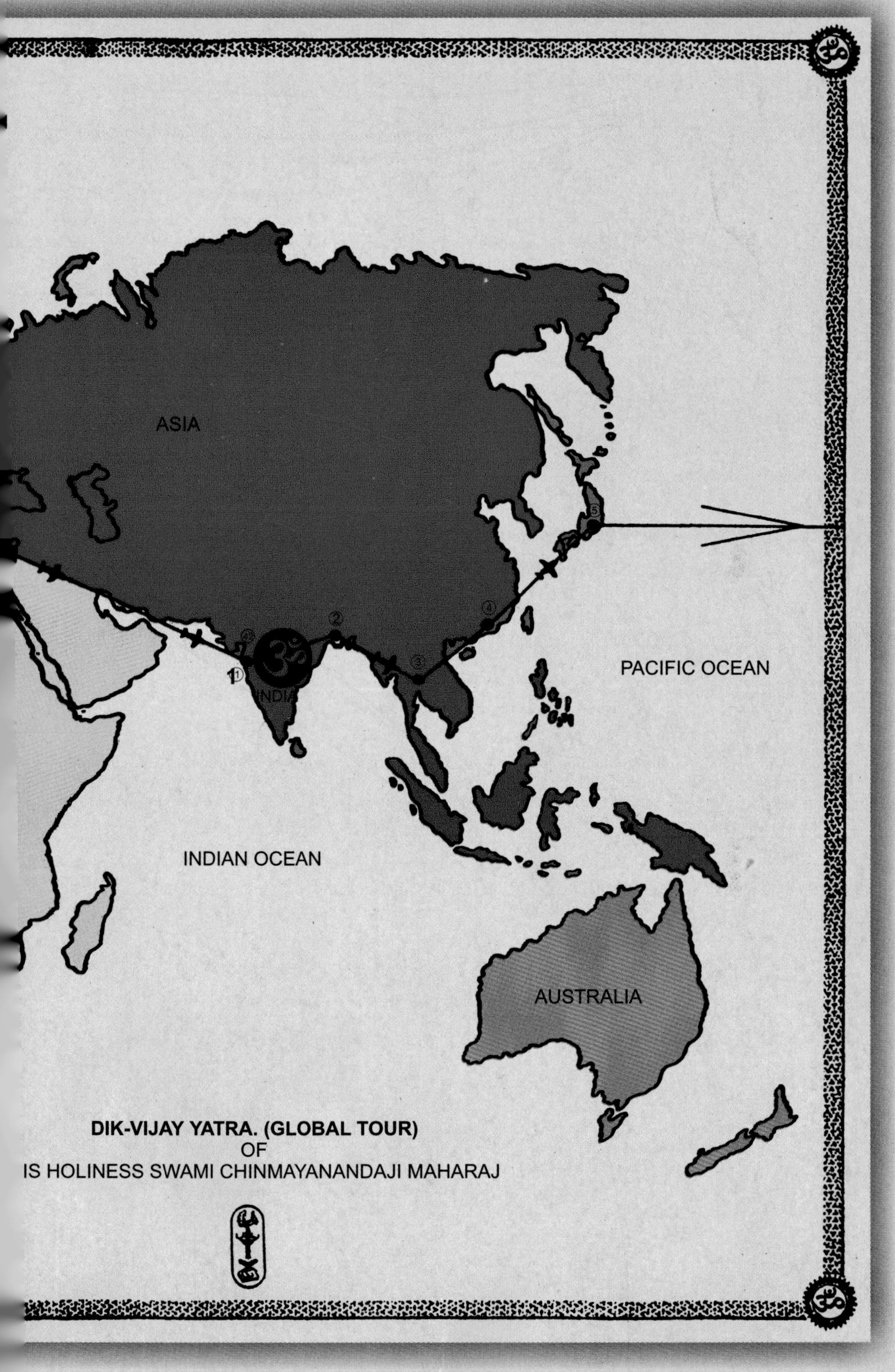
ASIA
PACIFIC OCEAN
INDIA
INDIAN OCEAN
AUSTRALIA
DIK-VIJAY YATRA. (GLOBAL TOUR)
OF
IS HOLINESS SWAMI CHINMAYANANDAJI MAHARAJ

San Jose : Sandeepany, The Mission Centre on Park Avenue

Vindu and K. P. Daswani
Singapore and Hongkong

Singapore:
Jyoti Kundalia with Swamij

Washington D.C. :
Acharya Swami Dheerananda
Between a Laptop
and the BMI Chart

London : Chyks with
wami Swaroopananda
Camp, 1999.

Washington D.C.: Vilasini Balakrishnan

Ann Arbor: Avantika

Houston: *Pratima* of
Swami Chinmayananda

Los Angeles:
Swami Ishwarananda with members of the Board.
Dr. D.V. Pillai and P. Mahadevan - third and fifth from right

San Jose : Uma Jeyarasasingam with Swamiji

Flint, MI: The Mission Centre

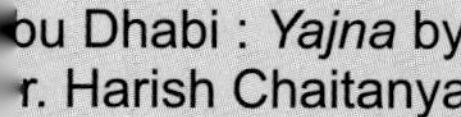

ou Dhabi : *Yajna* by
r. Harish Chaitanya

Indonesia:
Swami Tejomayananda
in front of a temple in Bali

Kathmandu : Madhu Sengupta
and Swami Tejomayananda
at the inaugration of the
International camp 2000.

Auckland, New Zealar
Mission members wit
Swami Swaroopananc

6

Harvest In Homeland

The Indian Network–200 Centres

The Chinmaya Movement spread its wings far and wide. After the *jnana-yajnas*, eager seekers met regularly in groups and pursued diligently a deeper study of the texts that Swamiji had dealt with at the *yajna*. They met at the residences of devotees or in a school and continued their studies. After sometime, the grass root level activities like Balavihar, Yuva Kendra, Study groups, Devi groups etc. took firm root and the need arose for a common forum to plan the Mission's activities. Thus the informal Mission centres came to be established. More than a decade passed by and in the sixties, a need was felt for formalizing the organizational structure. Swamiji was having his headquarters in Mumbai– overseeing the construction of the Ashram and the Sandeepany Sadhanalaya. It was then decided to establish an apex body in Mumbai, which would control and monitor the functioning of the various Mission centres in India. It would also lay down policy guidelines for the centres to follow. Thus was born Central Chinmaya Mission Trust (CCMT) in 1964, with headquarters at Mumbai. This Trust was registered as a charitable Trust with the main objective of promoting and spreading Indian Culture and Education among the masses.

At each centre, an Executive Committee was constituted by CCMT comprising persons of local standing and repute who would guide and direct the activity of the centre. The selection of members of the committee was based on the recommendations of the local Mission representative–a senior member of the Mission, a brahmachari or a swami. Once the Executive Committee was approved by CCMT, the centre would become an official one and was entitled to some privileges such as funding by the apex body for meeting regular expenses, finance for undertaking special or major projects, need-based posting of brahmacharis/ brahmacharinis to the centre etc. CCMT has introduced a management information system (MIS) whereby every centre reports every month details of membership, activities undertaken etc. so that a qualitative assessment can be made of the working of the centre. When the number of centres in a State increased significantly, Swamiji introduced the position of a Regional Head to look after the working of the centres in that State and sometimes including centres in other neighbouring States. This was first introduced in Karnataka and Kerala and later extended to other States or groups of States. As of the year 2000, the Mission has four Regional Heads, and the present incumbents are:

Swami Purushottamananda	:	Regional Head–Maharashtra, Goa and Gujarat.
Swami Jyotirmayananda	:	Regional Head–Delhi
Swami Brahmananda	:	Regional Head–Karnataka
Swami Subodhananda	:	Regional Head–Northern region

In addition, Swami Viviktananda is the Regional coordinator for Mission activities in Kerala.

The Chief Executive of CCMT is Narain Bhatia who is a longtime, devoted member of the Mission.

The CCMT also co-ordinates the activities of the Chinmaya Publications, the international magazine *Balvihar*, *Tapovan Prasad* a monthly magazine, Chinmaya Video Dham–an audio-video recording unit, the Educational Cell in Coimbatore which controls the various Chinmaya Vidyalayas, Chinmaya Vision Programme (CVP), CIRS–the Chinmaya International Residential School, Coimbatore, Chinmaya Diagnostic centres in Mumbai and Kolkata, Chinmaya Institute of Higher Learning (CIHL), Bangalore, and the Chinmaya Vibhuti Project, Pune.

The Tara Cultural Trust (TCT) registered on January 19, 1960 looks after the administration of Sandeepany Sadhanalaya, Mumbai. In addition it manages and administers the Powai Ashram. The TCT also supervises the temple activities and oversees the maintenance of the Jagadeeswara temple. The Chief Executive of TCT is Jairam Jaisinghani, an ardent devotee of Swamiji who has been serving the Mission for many years.

THE INDIAN NETWORK

During the fifty years of the Chinmaya Movement, the Mission has established 200 centres in India. These centres are spread over seventeen States of the Indian Union, the Union Territory of Andaman and Nicobar Islands and the National Territory of Delhi. The distribution of centres State-wise is given in a chart appended to this chapter.

Andaman and Nicobar Islands is a Union territory of the Indian Union. The Chinmaya Mission has one centre here at Port Blair. The Chinmaya Movement started in the islands in 1978 with the arrival of Br. Vishwa Chaitanya (now Swami Viviktananda). With much effort through *satsangs*, community meets, etc., the Mission acquired a building of its own, called Vijnana Mandir in 1981. This was later developed into a large complex. Swami Chinmayananda inaugurated the Ashram, which was named Chinmayalaya in July 1992, during the tenure of Br. Samartha Chaitanya (now Swami Visuddhananda). The first Acharya here was, as has already been noted, Br. Vishwa Chaitanya (1978-84); he was succeeded by Br. Pavan Chaitanya (1984-89). Br. Nandan Chaitanya (now Swami Chaitanyananda) also served here for some time. The present Acharya is Swami Vishuddhananda.

There are two satellite centres set up at Campbell Bay, the southern-most island in the group, and at Car Nicobar, which has a *satsang* group.

Andhra Pradesh with fifty-four centres has the largest number of centres. Swamini Saradapriyananda showed a great deal of enthusiasm and drive. She encouraged the local people to promote grass root level activities such as Balavihars, CHYKs, Study groups, Bhajan groups etc. This in turn made it necessary to have a formal centre, which would be able to guide the groups. Many of the centres were established and inaugurated by her. She took personal interest in the growth of the centres and she was ably assisted by Swamini Seelananda. She adopted innovative strategies to get the involvement of the local people—if there was an Ashram that was languishing for want of funds, she would take over the Ashram with the consent of Swamiji; if there was a dilapidated temple and the local people approached her for its renovation, she would do so, if she was convinced. Thus, she would get the adoration and love of the people. Her greatest achievement was the development of Chinmayaranyam–conversion of 24 acres of arid land into a place of plenty, a place of verdant forest–a project that has earned kudos for her and for the Chinmaya Movement from all quarters. (For more details, see Chapter Eight).

People used to call her Amma/Mataji (mother) and had great reverence for her. When she attained *maha-samadhi* on April 17, 2000, it was a moving scene when the villagers wept for her. She was a legend by herself in her lifetime.

By and large all the centres are active and regular in the conduct of Balavihar classes, Yuva Kendra classes and Study groups. Mention may be made of Nellore, Hyderabad, Proddatur, Adoni, Visakhapatnam, Kaikalur, Chittoor and Vijayawada for their special activities. The Yuva Kendra at **Vijayawada** did a remarkable job of collecting data for the project "Swami Chinmayananda as I know him" by interviewing twenty-six people. In social service also some centres have done innovative work—donating bed sheets to the pavement dwellers in winter. For most of the Mission workers selfless service is their *sadhana*.

While propagating the teachings of the scriptures, some of the centres have not only organized *Geeta jnana-yajnas* but also introduced a programme called *Grama Deepika*. Through this programme the *Bhagavad Geeta* is carried to the interior of distant rural villages. In the Cuddapah centre 100 *Grama Deepikas* have already been lit up and the goal now is to reach 1000 *Grama Deepikas* by the end of 2001. The Mission Centre at **Bapatla** is unique in that all its members are women who are very enthusiastic and committed. Social service at this centre includes poor feeding, distribution of clothes, books etc. to the poor. The **Vikarabad** centre has installed two drinking water units to provide water to the local residents. It is important to mention the **Nellore** centre which distributes free bed sheets and free homeopathic medicines to the poor; it also provides a *shmashanavahanam*—a vehicle to carry dead bodies to the burning ground. The members of the Nellore executive committee distribute bed sheets to the poor and the homeless by covering them with sheets whenever they find them sleeping under trees by the wayside in the cold winter months. Two thousand bed sheets were given away to the poor in the winter of 1998.

The outstanding performance of Andhra Pradesh is in its Ashrams–the **Chinmayaranyam**, about which exhaustive details are given in Chapter Eight, the **Gita Ashram** which was taken over from another organization in 1999, **Chinmaya Yoga Ashram**, Iruvaram, Chittoor, where it is proposed to have a retreat centre for the monks of the Mission. (There are several caves in this site where years ago Swamini Saradapriyananda did *sadhana* in a cave for two years.) **Chinmaya Sarada Tapovanam**, Kothapatnam was established with the original idea to set up a *Pitamaha Sadan* and a place of retreat for individuals. The inspiration for this Tapovanam is contained in the motto: "In the hushed silence of your heart, listen to the divine melody of the Lord".

Social service activities at **Adoni** centre include the planting of trees, blood donation camps, health camps, grant of scholarships to needy students, adult education, etc. The centre has the support of local spiritual organizations such as the Tirumala Seva Samstha, the Divine Life Society, and the Swami Vivekananda Seva Samstha. It has adopted an ancient Shiva temple named Shri Shanta Malleswara Swami Temple and renovated it. The reinstallation of the image was done in 1996. The **Hyderabad** centre has a special place in the history of the Chinmaya Movement, because Swamiji went to Hyderabad in 1951 before reaching Pune for his first *jnana-yajna*, with a letter of introduction from his *deeksha guru* Swami Sivananda. A special report on Hyderabad is included at the end of this Chapter. Swamiji first visited **Visakhapatnam** in 1959 to explore the possibility of opening a centre there. Local devotees had organized a talk at the Town Hall. Swamiji held his first *Geeta jnana-yajna* there in 1962. Ten *yajnas* were performed between 1962 and 1993 with the help of the generous financial support given by a local industrialist family–the House of Mittals. The **VSP Steel Township** is another important centre, which has a cosmopolitan group of white-collar workers who have shown keen interest in spiritual discourses. This centre is showing a steady growth in grass-root level activities.

At the **Rajupalem** Centre (Prakasam Dist.), following the *maha-samadhi* of Swami Chinmayananda on August 3, 1993, the centre observed extra austerity for a whole year. On the third of every month there was an *ashtottara-shata-nama archana*, as well as poor feeding. Clothes were distributed and the children of the poor given notebooks and books. On the seventieth birthday of Swamini Saradapriyananda, the centre held a *tulabhara* for the saint, weighing her against coins minted in India. Ms. Annapoorna of this centre has translated quite a few Chinmaya books into Telugu and has fulfilled a much-felt need in the State of Andhra Pradesh. Swamini Saradapriyananda too honoured her for this work. The **Cuddapah** centre implements a rural project called *Grama Deepika*. The goal is to introduce the *Bhagavad Geeta* to people in the remote villages. In the summer of 1999 there were a hundred *Grama Deepikas*–distant, obscure villages lit up by knowledge of the *Geeta*. The goal is to reach a thousand by the end of 2001. An *akhandajyoti* was lit and brought to Cuddapah by Br. Vishruta Chaitanya in acknowledgement by Swamini Saradapriyananda of the Cuddapah centre being recognized as an Ashram allied to Chinmayaranyam.

Proddatur is an old centre established in January 1979, when Swami Chinmayananda conducted the First All-Andhra Sadhana Camp. About 120 delegates attended the camp. Swamini Saradapriyananda and Br. Prasada Chaitanya had organized it.

This centre became a pioneer in the publication of books in Telugu, the regional language, under the banner of the Central Chinmaya Mission Trust (CCMT). J. Vemiah and D. Mohan Kumar started it all. Many other centres followed suit. Vemiah has been the President of Chinmayaranyam for over twelve years.

Chittoor is an old centre established in 1961 by the well-known industrialist, Dwarakanath Reddy. Swamiji conducted the first *yajna* in Chittoor in 1961 and took the town by storm. That was when activities started with great enthusiasm. Several *Geeta jnana-yajnas* have been conducted at Chittoor by senior swamis, swaminis, brahmacharis, and brahmacharinis, as well as by *pracharaks* like professor C.G. Vasudevan. Dwarakanath Reddy was a very devoted follower of Swamiji and has contributed in many ways for the growth of the Chinmaya Movement–he facilitated the publication of *Tyagi* from Chittoor for many years, written and published spiritual books, and had been a trusted devotee of Swamiji. **Guntur** has been a centre for many activities of the Chinmaya Movement. There were several *yajnas* by Swami Chinmayananda and Swamini Saradapriyananda. The Chinmaya Vidyalaya at Guntur City conducts classes from Lower Kindergarten to Class X, with English and Telugu as the two media of instruction, in separate streams. Till the year 1998, the Chinmayaranyam Publications in Telugu were published from Guntur. Under the guidance of Swamini Saradapriyananda, the **Vijayawada** centre has been associated with many important events of regional and national importance. The All-India Chyk Office-bearers' Conference was held here in 1990. The First Andhra Pradesh Regional Conference of Mission Workers, Brahmacharis, Swamis, and Swaminis was conducted here in 1995. At the National Book Exhibition in 1992, it put up a bookstall for the sale of books of the Chinmaya Mission. Similarly it put up a bookstall at Krishna during the Krishna Pushkaram festival in 1992. It hosted a Yuva Kendra activity, known as Cam-Tra-Con, in 1989 and 1999.

Aranya Spandana is an in-house publication giving details of activities at different centres in Andhra Pradesh. This is published from Vijayawada since 1987.

While concluding, it can be justifiably claimed that the fifty-four Chinmaya Mission centres in Andhra Pradesh have made incredible social and economic impact on the persons living in the areas covered by them. Indisputably the credit goes to Swamini Saradapriyananda and the committed workers of the Mission.

Assam has only one Chinmaya Mission centre at **Guwahati**. Owing to insurgency and political instability, not much development has taken place in the State. The interest in the Chinmaya Movement started in 1974 when the first *jnana-yajna* by Brni. Sarada Chaitanya (later Swamini Saradapriyananda) was held in Guwahati. Thereafter the interest in spiritual discourses increased and the people wanted to hear Swami Chinmayananda. This wish of theirs was fulfilled in September 1977 when Swamiji held his first *yajna* in Assam. During this visit he also inaugurated the Rama Lila function in the famous Nehru Stadium in the presence of about fifty thousand people; the Chief Minister of Assam also attended the function. Those who attended the *yajnas* came from far off places like Shillong, Sibsagar, Tezpur, and Tinsukia. In 1979 an Assamese translation of Swamiji's English commentary of *Narada Bhaktisutra* was released. The Mission activity at the centre is now picking up and a resident brahmachari Kailas Chaitanya has been posted at Guwahati.

Bihar has two Mission centres at Gaya and Patna, and Jharkhand has four—at Chas, Bokaro, Ranchi and Jamshedpur.

The establishment of the **Gaya** centre in 1982 is an awe-inspiring story. Shyam Nandan Prasad was an advocate at Gaya. He and his two friends were a group of spiritual seekers, fervently praying for a guru to lead them on the right spiritual path. One of them happened to attend Swami Chinmayananda's *jnana-yajna* at Jamshedpur, which greatly influenced him–he felt that he had found the *sadguru* he had been looking for. The three of them went to Sidhbari to prostrate before their guru. They found Swamiji profoundly inspiring. Following the guidance given by Swamiji, the centre at Gaya was established in 1982. The Chinmaya Vidyalaya and the Chinmaya Health Centre were the major projects that the centre took up in 1992 at the suggestion of Swamiji.

Jamshedpur is another important centre in Bihar. Swami Chinmayananda and other swamis have conducted several *jnana-yajnas* here. The outstanding contribution of this centre has been the souvenir it brings out at every major *yajna*. In 1974 the centre made an original contribution when it compiled a publication titled "How to Organize a National *Yajna*". The CCMT appreciated the publication and circulated it to all centres.

Ranchi centre was established in 1962 when Swamiji conducted a *yajna*. The construction of an Ashram is in progress. Grass root level activities are going on with good participation from children, youth and adults. There is an active Chinmaya Vanaprastha Sansthan at this centre. **Chas** centre was established in 1994 and the grass root level activities rake place at the residence of devotees. The Acharya is Br. Jaganmitra Chaitanya.

Goa has six Chinmaya Mission centres—at Ponda, Panaji, Margao, Vasco, Churchorem and Mapusa. Swamiji visited Goa in 1965 for the first time and this led to the establishment of a centre at **Vasco**. Swami Purushottamananda visited Goa and held his discourse in Marathi. This attracted many people to the Mission. Br. Manan Chaitanya (now Swami Nikhilananda) was posted in 1988 and this further strengthened the bond, as the brahmachari belonged to the State and was fluent in the local language. The group activities of the Mission like Balavihar, Study group, Yuva Kendra are being conducted regularly. Senior sevak Vivek and sevika Varsha are guiding the activities at the **Margao** centre.

Gujarat has six Chinmaya Mission centres of which four are relatively more active. So far the Chinmaya Movement has not had a great impact in the State. There are several other religious movements of Gujarati origin, which are fairly deep-rooted in the State. The Mission centres at Ahmedabad, Surat, Jamnagar, Vadodara, Rajkot, and Surendranagar are making efforts to attract more and more people towards the Chinmaya Movement. When Swamiji conducted his first *jnana-yajna* at **Vadodara**, he explained the importance of a *japa-mala*. He also demonstrated the technique of rolling the beads. It is said that people were so impressed with his talk that the *japa-malas* in the bazaar of Vadodara were sold out! The centres in Gujarat have been holding *jnana-yajnas* regularly. Swami Tejomayananda had his first *yajna* at Vadodara in 1994. A number of books of the Mission have been translated into Gujarati.

Ahmedabad centre was established in 1966 soon after the visit of Swamiji. Param Dham, the Ashram at Ahmedabad is the centre of all *adhyatmic* activity. It is built on a two-acre plot of land and is situated in Jodhpur Tekra. It was inaugurated in 1979 in the gracious presence of H.H. Akhandananda Maharaj. There is a temple of Lord Krishna in the Ashram where Swamiji did the *kalasha-prathista* in 1980. Deities of Hanuman and Ganesha adorn the two sides of the Dhyana Mandir. The centre is very active with Balavihar classes, CHYK, Study groups, Devi groups, *Geeta*-chanting, Bhajan groups, etc. Since 1997 yoga classes have been conducted daily by a member of the Mission. The centre has a library, which is well stocked with books, audio and video cassettes.

Karnataka has fourteen Chinmaya Mission centres and is under the overall charge of Swami Brahmananda, the Regional Head of Karnataka. **Bangalore** city has from the early years of the Movement extended a spontaneous response to the Mission's activities. More details about the centre are covered under the title, "Bangalore - the Garden City" at the end of this chapter. The twelve centres (outside Bangalore city) in the Karnataka State are active and vibrant. All the centres have the basic group activities of Balavihar, Yuva Kendra, Study group, Devi group etc., which are conducted regularly. It was in the early 1980's that an idea arose that Karnataka should have a Vedanta Institute with Kannada as medium of instruction. The first course was held in Bangalore. **Chokkahalli** in Kolar District is identified as the centre for holding future courses. There is a temple of Lord Omkareshwara here. A 45-feet tall Ganapati–Chinmaya Ganapati–has been installed here in 1998. This centre has been a place of attraction for pilgrims. The **Shimoga** centre celebrated the seventy-fifth birthday of Swami Chinmayananda in a novel way. Seventy-five wheelbarrow talks on the *Geeta* were organized in seventy-five houses. Swami Brahmananda gave the talks. He began on February 26, 1992 and ended them on February 17, 1993.

The concept of a wheelbarrow was drawn from the system of shopping in small villages where vendors took their ware in a barrow—vegetables, toys etc. from street to street hawking their wares at the very gate of the customer. Swamiji said, " To carry on our *Geeta* talks from house to house in seventy-five houses is a beautiful idea." The **Mangalore** centre of the Mission is one of the oldest, established in 1959. The centre has now acquired its own building. *Jnana-yajnas* are conducted regularly at this centre. Other important centres are **Mysore**, **Mandya**, **Hubli**, and **Tumkur**, where the Mission activities are pursued with enthusiasm.

Kerala has thirty Chinmaya Mission centres, the second largest number next to Andhra Pradesh which has fifty-four. The Movement took roots here more effectively, perhaps, because Swamiji hailed from Kerala and had good contacts here. In 1954 the first meeting of the Chinmaya Mission was held at **Ernakulam** in the presence of Swamiji. He explained to the large gathering the purpose of the Mission and he nominated the President and Secretary of the centre. In this State, the Chinmaya Movement has its stronghold in the Vidyalayas, which were started here. **Kollengode** has the honour of starting the first Chinmaya Vidyalaya, which it did in 1965, when the Chinmaya Nursery School was inaugurated. The Royal family of Kollengode had always extended its fullest support to the activities of the Mission. The Chinmaya Vidyalaya in **Ernakulam** developed into a premier educational institution. The Chinmaya Tailoring Institute was founded in 1969. The women were taught tailoring so that they could supplement the family income. In fact training women in tailoring became a common activity in many centres, and was offered to needy persons in Kerala.

On Kerala's soil stands the Chinmaya International Foundation (CIF), the prestigious research institution of the Chinmaya Movement.

Veliyanad, 30 kms to the south of Ernakulam, is the village where, on an eight-acre plot, this Adi Sankara Nilayam has Indological and Sanskrit studies going on. With a beautiful Ayyappa temple, a traditional large house (*illam*), a pond and a few other structures, this facility is also a venue for many spiritual camps.

The **Palakkad** centre has been one of the most active centres in the Chinmaya Movement. Hence, a special report on the Palakkad centre is given at the end of this Chapter.

On the spiritual side, Kerala centres have been conducting the group activities of Balavihar, Yuva Kendra and Study groups effectively. The first meeting of the Akhila Bharata Chinmaya Devi Sammelan (the ABCD sammelan) was held in Kollengode where Swamiji emphasized the important role that women had played in bringing up the youth of the country.

The **Kozhikode** centre has contributed a great deal to the spread of the teachings of our ancient scriptures. It conducted training of *sadhaks* at the Vijnana Mandir. Br. Atma Chaitanya was the Acharya from 1975 to 1977. Again he was the Acharya from 1979 to 1988. In 1979, ninety-three students attended the training course for *sadhaks* and were awarded certificates by Swamiji. Br. Prabuddha Chaitanya (Swami Adhyatmananda now), who was posted in 1992, gave a series of *Geeta* talks called *Geeta Sarani* in eighteen temples; this activity helped in spreading the message of the *Bhagavad Geeta* and attracted a number of people to the Mission. A 21-day *yajna* by Br. Atma Chaitanya (in connection with the 50th year of the Chinmaya Movement) also was a notable programme. *Sagara Samvad* (Dialogue with the sea), a monthly get together during summer months on the sea shore, with cultural programmes, *satsangs*, guided meditations etc. is held. Weeklong *sadhana* camps are held periodically. So far 5 camps have been held and all barring one were conducted outside Kerala. The Yuva Kendra has been very active at this centre. Members conduct seva projects, *yajnas*, camps, and study classes with guidance from Br. Prabuddha Chaitanya (now Swami Adhyatmananda). The Chyks won the award of "The Best Upcoming CHYK centre" in 1998 at the All India CHYK Conference. In the same year, they carried out a prestigious project called 'Chinmaya Pratibha–98.' In 1999, they also got the Best CHYK centre award for major cities. It has also organized a general programme for the public called *Oonjalu Venam* (want a swing). It was presented in an exclusive 2 day camp. As many as 150 Balavihar students took part in the camp (organized by CHYK). The theme was evolved metaphorically from the movements of a swing. Some 35 swings were provided for the students to entertain themselves first and then to listen to the enlightening and interesting lessons in life as the swinging unfolded.

The main activities of the **Kannur** centre are Balavihar classes, Study group, Devi group, bhajan groups, and CHYK groups. Swamiji's *jnana-yajna* in the sacred premises of Shri Sundareswara Temple in 1959 was the great beginning. A Vanitha Hostel for working women and a Bala Bhavan for children are special aspects of the facilities here. A Chinmaya Mission College and a Chinmaya Vidyalaya are run under the able guidance of K.K. Rajan. Training in Television Technology in colloboration with BPL is offered to unemployed youth by Chinmaya Academy of Education. Brni. Maitri Chaitanya was the first Acharya. She is now Swamini Apoorvananda and Br. M.K. Ramakrishnan also serves this centre. One of the unique programmes that this centre has, is conducting classes for prisoners in the Kannur Central Jail. Swamini Apoorvananda has ben doing this service for the last nine years. The centre has also given donation of essentials like fans, books, musical instuments etc. Swami Tejomayananda has visited the prisoners at the jail on three occasions. **Kasargod** has a sprawling area over which the Chinmaya Vidyalaya stands. A ten-and-a-half feet high statue of Swami Chinmayananda stands in the Vidyalaya campus. In **Kottayam** the centre runs three schools at different locations. **Nileshwar** centre has a Vidyalaya, which is running efficiently. But the pride of accomplishment is that the centre opened the first women's college of the district in 1984. However, later in 1999 due to change in the preferences of the local people for co-education, (amongst other reasons) this college had to be closed down. The other important centres like **Thrissur**, **Tripunithura**, **Thiruvananthapuram** etc. have typically a similar pattern of Mission activities such as Balavihar, Yuva Kendra and Study groups etc., as in other active centres.

Madhya Pradesh and **Chattisgarh** States have six Chinmaya Mission centres, the oldest being **Rewa**. The history of the Rewa centre is covered at the end of this chapter in a special report titled "*Rewa*" The other centres–**Indore**, **Jabalpur**, **Gwalior**, **Satna** and **Bhopal**–have all been active in conducting group activities like Balavihar, Yuva Kendra, Study group etc. Swamiji conducted *yajnas* at these centres. Swami Tejomayananda, as Sudhakar, a college student attended Swamiji's first *yajna* at **Bhopal** and was drawn to the Chinmaya Movement. After he completed the Vedanta course and received *deeksha*, he became Br.Vivek Chaitanya and was posted in Bhopal in 1971. According to local devotees, the most memorable *yajna* of Swamiji in Bhopal was in 1983—when Swamiji was welcomed to the *yajna-shala* by the Chief Minister, Shri Arjun Singh and Governor Sharma who were waiting for him at the entrance. The recognition for the **Jabalpur** centre came from Swamiji through a letter from CCMT dated

November 1991. Rao Ran Bahadur Singh inaugurated the centre in April 1992. Swami Purushottamananda conducted a *yajna* in September 992. Several *yajnas* that followed were conducted by Swami Bhaskarananda, Swami Subodhananda, Brni. Amrita Chaitanya and Rao Ran Bahadur Singh. Swami Chinmayananda visited Indore in 1985 for conducting a *jnana-yajna*. Prior to this, Swami Tejomayananda had conducted a *jnana-yajna* in 1984. The first Acharya of the centre was Br. Dhruv Chaitanya. Brni. Samta Chaitanya (now Swamini Geetananda) followed him in 1989. The centre has been organizing regular programmes. **Gwalior** centre was established in 1985, with Sushri Shakuntala Verma (who later became Swamini Samvidananda) as the President. The main activity at the centre is weekly *satsang* on Sundays. Swami Purushottamananda, Br. Abhaya Chaitanya, Swamini Samvidananda and several others have conducted *jnana-yajnas* in Gwalior.

Meghalaya has two Chinmaya Mission centres at **Shillong** and **Tezpur**. Swamiji's first *yajna* at Shillong was in 1972, arranged by the then Inspector General of Police, Shillong, Mr. Iyer and the then Chief Secretary to the Government, Mr Ramesh Chandra.

In June 1981, the Mission centre was officially opened. Mahant Singh was the first President of this centre. In 1982, Swamini Saradapriyananda conducted a *yajna* at Krishi Kendra. From then on Sudhakar Tamhan (later on Br. Sudhanshu Chaitanya and later Swami Anubhavananda) started looking after the Mission activities with a strong support of Suraj Loungani. In 1996 Swamini Purnananda conducted a *yajna* in Shillong and reactivated the centre. Her regular visits brought new enthusiasm to the devotees. There are regular Balavihar classes. *Swadhyaya Mandal* activities also go on at the centre. In March 2000, Shillong Hindu Dharma Sabha, invited Swamini Purnananda for a *jnana-yajna* in connection with the centenary celebration of their organization. She also onducted *satsangs* in Bengali at the temple of Lord Jagannath at Shillong.

In the beautiful state of Meghalaya, the Chinmaya Mission is becoming popular with the Bengali, Marwari and local communities.

Orissa State has eight Chinmaya Mission centres. The first one to be established was the Rourkela centre in 1966. Other centres are at Angul, Lathikata, Bhubaneswar, Cuttack, and Berhampore. The centre at Angul serves an industrial belt; the one at Lathikata caters to the needs of the tribal community and has been in existence since 1978. By and large, although the network is not very widespread in Orissa, it covers the vital segments of the population. Mission activities at these centres are in full swing and there is an ever-growing interest in the typical activities of the Mission. A super cyclone hit Orissa in 1999 and there was heavy loss of life and property. Swami Tejomayananda immediately addressed the Mission centres and asked them to send relief/aid for the victims. The response was spontaneous from the centres. Chyks from various States came and, in co-ordination with the Bhubaneswar centre, helped in carrying out the relief operations.

A commendable project in Orissa conceived and implemented by the Chinmaya Mission, is the Chinmaya Seva Project at the Lathikata centre. The project is being implemented under the guidance of Br. Vishwatma Chaitanya (now Swami Kevalananda) who was appointed in 1998 as the Project Director. The project has come up near the Chinmayanagar colony and the tribal villages are in the vicinity of Lathikata. The activities in progress are, to mention a few, a year's diploma course in sewing and embroidery, a ready-made garment unit, training programmes in collaboration with other voluntary organizations, self-help groups in different villages where women are trained to take some economically viable activity. At **Rourkela**, the *jnana-yajna* activity continued after the first *yajna* by Swami Chinmayananda in 1966. A Chinmaya Vidyalaya was opened in Rourkela in July 1979 with the help of K.C. Patnaik and S. Kabisathpathi who was the headmaster of the school. In 1991 a Chinmaya Vidyalaya was opened on the premises owned by the Mission at Chhend colony. The interesting story about the establishment of **Berhampur** (Brahmapur) centre is that it was opened after Swamini Saradapriyananda (at that time Brni. Sarada) initiated correspondence with one M. Bhimsen Rao who had just completed the Chinmaya Lesson Course. She congratulated him and added: " Don't you feel it is necessary that you should share your new vision with those around you? Don't you think it is a sacred duty to serve others with your newly discovered knowledge?" These two simple questions combined with some coaxing and persuasion, resulted in Bhimsen Rao and his friends establishing the Mission centre in July 1975. The **Bhawanipatna** centre was established in 1981. The present Acharya is Br. Atul Chaitanya.He motivated the people to form a centre by holding a *Geeta shravana-sadhana*.

Punjab has three Chinmaya Mission centres, including Chandigarh. The movement started quite late in this State–say in the 1990s. In **Chandigarh** the movement started in 1989, when a group of people who had met Swamiji during his brief visits decided to function as a centre. The members meet in the residence of the President, Ms. Promilla Chandra Mohan and have organized Study groups, Vedic chanting etc. *Jnana-yajnas* have also been conducted here. The Mission activity in **Patiala** started in 1998. The centre is in fact called Chinmaya Study Group, Patiala. It restricts its activities to Study group meetings on Sundays at the local Geeta Bhavan. The centre at **Amritsar** has been active since 1997, although it was formally inaugurated only in March 2000. It has conducted nine *jnana-yajnas* between 1997 and 2000. It publishes a monthly spiritual newsletter called *Chinmaya Amrit*. It also recently organized a *Vriddhavastha Samadhan Shibir* which was attended by more than a hundred delegates.

Rajasthan has only one centre in the State at **Jaipur**. Although the first *yajna* by Swamiji was conducted in 1976, the level of Mission activity was rather low. It was only in 1996 when Swami Shankarananda conducted a *yajna* that enthusiasm at the local level increased. Br. Abhaya Chaitanya took the initiative to revitalize Jaipur and he conducted three spiritual youth camps, which attracted many young boys and girls. *Jnana-yajnas* by Swami Tejomayananda and Swami Subodhananda were conducted in 1999. Balavihar and Study group activities are being conducted regularly.

Sikkim has its Mission centre in Gangtok, which flourishes mainly due to the patronage of Government officials. Ms. Tikachamlin (wife of the Chief Minister of Sikkim) and Justice M. L. Shrimal have played a key role in popularizing the Chinmaya Movement. As the grass root level activities gained momentum, in 1995, a resident brahmachari, Br. Vijaya Chaitanya, was posted in Sikkim. The centre received a generous donation of land from the Government of Sikkim and P.K. Basnet near Ranipool, Gangtok. Plans have been devised to have the Chinmaya Human Research and Development Institute (CHRDI) in Sikkim for the training of rural people in various skills, crafts and education in micro banking, and in yoga and Vedanta. The centre has been registered with the Government in November 1997 and Br. Hārish Chaitanya has been posted as the resident Acharya. Sikkim will also be made the headquarters of the Chinmaya Mission in Northeastern India. In August 1998 Br. Harish Chaitanya visited Nepal to strengthen the Chinmaya Movement there. Swami Tejomayananda visited Gangtok in November 1998 and held a *jnana-yajna* on the Ramayana. He also addressed the Sikkim Legislative Assembly and laid the foundation stone for the *Chinmaya Dham* near Ranipool. The centre has set a 15-point programme as its Action Plan, which includes conducting of *yajnas*, increasing the members of the Balavihar classes, enrolling more members for the Mission, translation of books in Nepali, live telecast of *Geeta* discourses, setting up of a new institute for rural welfare etc.

Tamil Nadu has Chennai as a very vibrant Mission centre. The history of the Chinmaya Movement is closely connected with the history of the **Chennai** centre. The devotees of this first centre perhaps did not dream that they were creating history for a Hindu Renaissance that swept the country like a storm. More details are given at the end of this chapter about the Chinmaya Movement in a special report titled, "Chennai – the Cradle City".

Chennai (South) centre was started in 1983 primarily to meet the needs of the devotees in the outskirts of the city like Guindy and Tambaram. While it was housed in a temporary thatched terrace in 1983, from 1995 it has its own building at Adambakkam. The centre has, in June 2000, two hundred and fifty members, eighteen Balavihars, eleven Study groups, one Devi group and one Vedic chanting group.

Hosur is a small centre started in 1995. It conducts two Balavihar classes and *satsangs* once in a week. On Saturdays members meet and chant *Vishnu Sahasranamam*. **Salem** centre made a start in August 1980 thanks to the collective effort of devotees in the town. Over the years, the range of its activities has widened. Brahmacharis like Shubha Chaitanya, Shuddha Chaitanya and Paramartha Chaitanya held a number of area *yajnas* between 1980 and 1982. Br. Chandramouli who came to Salem in 1982 was a great asset. He held various group activities like Balavihar, Devi group meetings and Sanskrit classes in different locations. Prof. C.G. Vasudevan with his erudite discourses captured the minds of the public. The year 1983 was an eventful year for Salem as Swamiji conducted a *Geeta jnana-yajna*. Br. Swabodh Chaitanya (now Swami Mitrananda) took care of the centre for two and a half years. Swami Tejomayananda inaugurated the owned premises of the Chinmaya Vidyalaya in October 1996. The Yuva Kendra activities expanded over the years and the centre conducted five Cam-Tra-Cons in 1989, 1990, 1993, 1995 and 1997.

At **Salem**, packed audience heard the discourses of Swami Mitrananda and Swamini Niranajanananda in the year 2000. To make an appeal for donations for the Sandeepany Vidyamandir at Siruvani, Coimbatore, Br. Gagan Chaitanya, Br. Samahita Chaitanya and Swami Mitrananda visited Salem.

Swamiji conducted his first *jnana-yajna* in **Tiruchirapalli** in 1979, which had a remarkable impact on the audience. Every alternate year after 1979, *yajnas* were held in this city. The books Kathopanishad, Meditation and Life etc., were translated into Tamil during this period. Br. Praveen Chaitanya (now Swami Shreedharananda) played an important role in the development of this centre. The centre opened a satellite branch at BHEL, Tiruvarambur. The Tiruchirapalli Chinmaya Seva Trust was formed in 1992. There is a Chinmaya Vidyalaya at Srirangam. These were due to the tireless efforts put in by Swami Shreedharananda, Br. Aniket Chaitanya and Br. Samahita Chaitanya. Their presence was highly inspiring. In 1981 Swami Brahmananda gave his first discourse in English at this centre, owing largely to the encouragement given by Swamiji. Br. Gagana Chaitanya and Br. Anirudh Chaitanya have been engaged in the *prachar* work in nearby towns like Tanjore, Nagapattinam, Namakkal and Theni.

The late Ms. Muthurkrishna Devadas donated two acres of prime property in **Kodaikanal** in 1980 to the Chinmaya Mission. Till 1993, this property was maintained by Prof. Sadashivam of Bharatiya Vidya Bhavan. Br. Samahita Chaitanya was posted at this centre. Study classes, a Yuva Kendra group, Devi group and Balavihars were started. After 1996 there was no resident brahmachari and so there was a lull in the activity. In 1999 Br. Dhruva Chaitanya has been posted and the activities have revived. In November 2000 Swami Tejomayananda did *bhoomi pooja* in the land complex for the construction of an office and residential quarters for the Acharya and for guests who might visit the centre. **Nagapattinam** centre was inaugurated in January 1997. The centre has organized several *yajnas* by brahmacharis. The Chinmaya Vidyalaya started in 1997 with classes up to Standard-I. In February 2000, the centre acquired three acres of land and plans are under way to construct a spacious building for the Vidyalaya. The centre has Study groups, Devi group, and classes for the teachers of the Vidyalaya. Br. Rishi Chaitanya has been posted as the resident Acharya.

Chinmaya Mission, **Pondicherry** owes its birth to the tireless efforts of Shri Ashok Kumar. Even before a proper committee was formed, he organized two *yajnas*, introducing the Mission to the Pondicherry public. Br. Avinash Chaitanya conducted the first *jnana-yajna* in January 1999 and Swami Mitrananda conducted the second *yajna* in September 1999.

Seeing the overwhelming response, Swami Mitrananda inaugurated the Chinmaya Mission, Pondicherry on the auspicious day of *Saraswati Pooja* on October 17, 1999. Col. S. Nagarajan, Smt. Pushpa Bhat and Divakar Bansal were the President, Secretary and Treasurer of the centre. Since its inception the centre has conducted many *jnana-yajnas* and a few three-day talks by swamis and brahmacharis. The *pracharaks* include Swami Mitrananda, Swamini Purnananda, Br. Avinash Chaitanya and Br. Gagana Chaitanya. Br. Rishi Chaitanya is rendering his service in Pondicherry for two days in a week conducting Balavihar, Yuva Kendra, Devi group and Study group classes. Classes for learning Sanskrit have also begun. All activities are conducted in the houses of devotees.

Swami Chinmayananda conducted his fifth *jnana-yajna* at **Madurai** in March 1964, this being the first one for Madurai. It was a major endeavour to organize a 41-day *yajna* at this ancient pilgrim town, which was well known for its orthodoxy. The initiative to hold this *yajna* came from two leading industrialists–Karimuthu Thiagaraja Chettiar of Madurai and P.A.C. Ramaswamy Raja of **Rajapalayam**. The *yajna* was very successful and created a record for daily attendance–about 1,500 people came daily. Mr. Chettiar in his article, contributed to Hail Renaissance Vol. I, wrote: "The *yajna* course of lectures was very helpful in enlivening the natural piety of the people of this place". Madurai continues to be a stronghold of the Chinmaya Movement. A large number of Study groups, Balavihar classes and Yuva Kendras came up. Area *yajnas* were on the increase with the active participation of Br. Sudheer Chaitanya, Br. Praveen Chaitanya and Br. Swabodh Chaitanya. Br. Dharmesh Chaitanya (later Swami Vageesananda) was posted in 1989 as resident Acharya and he served the centre till 1991.

The present Acharya is Br. Srinivasa Chaitanya. A unique facility at Madurai is the existence of a Meditation centre–Chinmaya Tapovanam–at Nagamalai Hills about 12 kms from Madurai. It is a place where silence and calmness reign supreme. The retreat is situated by the side of a perennial sulphur spring known as Puliuthu and was inaugurated by Swamiji.

The Madurai centre organized a *Geeta* chanting competition in the year 2000 where 5000 children participated. Swami Tejomayananda held his first *yajna* in 1996. A large audience attended the *yajna* held in September 2000. The centre holds two area *yajnas* per month. This is a very active centre with all grass root level activities like Balavihar, Yuva Kendra, Study group etc.

Coimbatore, the textile town of Tamil Nadu, has an important place in the history of the Chinmaya Movement. It has fostered the growth of many important projects of the Mission—The Mission centre and Chinmaya Vidyalaya at Thadagam Road, the Vidyalaya at Vadavalli, Sandeepany Vidyamandir at Chinmaya Gardens, and the prestigious Chinmaya International Residential School (CIRS) at Nallur Vayal. The Mission centre which functions from Thadagam Road has organized and conducted many an important spiritual event over the years. *Yajnas* by Swami Chinmayananda, Swami Tejomayananda, Swamini Saradapriyananda, Swami Swároopananda, Swamini Vimalananda, and by Brahmacharis—Santa Chaitanya, Subodh Chaitanya, and Sahaja Chaitanya have taken place here and drawn a big crowd. The first *jnana-yajna* of Swami Chinmayananda took place in 1954 and attracted an audience of over a thousand every day for twenty-one days. Leading industrialist of Coimbatore G. K. Sundaram took keen interest in organizing the first *yajna*. In 1984 the centre organized a Kumbhmela under the guidance of Swami Sahajananda.

In 1986 a unique programme was presented by the CHYK members titled, "Chinmayopanishad", which was a depiction of Swamiji's BMI (Body, Mind, Intellect) chart. Sandeepany Tamil Nadu was inaugurated in 1988 and the Acharya was Br. Atma Chaitanya.

An International Residential School, a dream project of Swami Chinmayananda, became a reality in 1996, thanks to the determined effort of Swami Tejomayananda. More details are given later in this section about the CIRS.

Br. Dharmesh Chaitanya who later became Swami Vageesananda attained *maha-samadhi* on January 25, 1994. He was greatly loved and respected by the devotees of the Mission.

In 1997, Ms. Chandramati Gopalakrishnan, Principal of the Vidyalaya was awarded the Dr. Radhakrishnan Award for the Best Teacher.

The brahmacharis and brahmacharinis attached to the Coimbatore centre and the CIRS have been actively participating in the *yajnas* in the city. Br. Praveen Chaitanya, Brni. Sumati Chaitanya, Br. Aniket Chaitanya, Br. Avinash Chaitanya and Br. Samahita Chaitanya have made significant contributions by their discourses at the *yajnas*.

Chinmaya International Residential School (CIRS) is really a *sankalpa* of Swamiji made in the year 1970 to provide a school for the children of Non-resident Indians so that the new generation could be brought up in an environment that derived its strength from Indian traditional values and culture. Some early events in connection with the school were *Vanabhojan* in March 1983 and *Bhoomipooja* in June the same year. Swamiji's *sankalpa* was fulfilled in 1996. The school was opened in June 1996. Swamini Vimalananda is a Director of the school. The motto of the school is

Jnanam seva cha Kaushalam–knowledge, service and efficiency. The school aims at imparting a holistic vision that will instill a spirit of service. The Central Board of Secondary Education (CBSE) in Delhi and also the International Baccalaureate (IB) in Switzerland recognize the school. The school is a testimony to the fusion of Western pragmatism and scientific skills with Oriental traditions and cultural values, which paves the way for a life with values. The school can justifiably boast of a dedicated and experienced faculty to teach and take care of the students' needs.

There is an old saying, which runs thus: "All can be done if there is God's touch." Sometimes destiny chooses a particular person who has a mission that has to be fulfilled, come what may. Swami Tejomayananda accomplished his Guru's dream for this school in 1996.

MAHARASHTRA

The most active centre in Maharashtra is the **Mumbai** centre. In order to give this centre a special place in the Indian network of Mission centres, a special report is given at the end of this chapter titled "O Mumbai".

Swami Purushottamananda, one of the most senior swamis of the Chinmaya Mission is the Regional Head of Goa, Gujarat, and Maharashtra. He oversees the activities of 41 centres. He is also a Trustee of the CCMT, Mumbai and CST, Nagpur. He heads the Ganadheesha Cultural Project, Kolhapur, and the Chinmaya Sadhana Kendra, Paunar, Wardha. He first heard Swami Chinmayananda in 1965. In 1966 he joined the Vedanta course and was initiated as a brahmachari. He became a *sannyasi* in 1977.

He initiated an important programme called the *shravana sadhana*. Each month for seven days a chapter of the *Geeta* is taken for evening discourse and in eighteen months the whole *Geeta* is completed. This programme thus facilitates the first two steps of the Vedantic *sadhana*, viz. *shravana* followed by *manana*. It gained rapid popularity wherever it was held. Swami Chinmayananda was very pleased with this method of teaching. One of the consequences of this programme was that the entire Geeta with Swamiji's commentary was translated into Marathi.

The Chinmaya Ganadheesha programme at Kolhapur proposes to install an idol of Lord Ganesha that would be the tallest in the world. There would be a meditation hall under the seat of the idol. The height of the Meditation hall would be 24 feet and that of the idol (including the hall) 85 feet.

A brief report on the history of some of the centres in Maharashtra is given below.

Pune centre has been covered under a special report at the end of this chapter, to highlight the important role it has played in the birth and fostering of the Chinmaya Movement. The special report is titled "Pune".

Chandrapur was registered as a Mission centre in November 1994. From 1991 to 1994 it was functioning informally with programmes such as *Bhagavat Saptah* followed by *jnana-yajnas* and *shravana sadhana* by various Acharyas. In 1997 on the occasion of the sixtieth birthday of Swami Purushottamananda, the centre held a *Tulabhara*, weighing him in coins, as an offering to him. The centre holds *satsang* every Sunday. The grass root level activities at this centre are conducted on a regular basis. There was a *jnana-yajna* of Swami Tejomayananda in February 2000.

Dahanu and **Bordi** was founded in 1977 soon after a *yajna* conducted by Swami Purushottamananda. It confines its activities to the town of Dahanu, the township of BSES Nagar and the villages of Bordi and Gholvad. The resident Acharya here is Br. Ashutosh Chaitanya. He has conducted *yajnas* at all these places and also in the village of Zai, near Bordi. Besides the Study group activity, the *Gayatri havan* is held every Sunday at Bordi. The centre is making efforts to spread its activities to cover more villages in the district.

Dombivali centre was established in 1985. They have the typical group activities of a Mission centre, which are being conducted regularly. Social services rendered by this centre include blood donation camps, planting of trees and collection of material and resources for the Orissa Super Cyclone Relief work.

Ichalkaranji was established as a Mission centre in 1973. Br. Ananta Chaitanya was sent to explore the potential of this place and a centre was formed with G. S. Satpute as President. Swami Chinmayananda visited the centre once and gave a talk. Swami Tejomayananda gave discourses on Tulasidas's *Rama Charita Manas*, which attracted more people to join the movement.

Swami Purushottamananda conducted his first *jnana-yajna* in **Kalyan** in 1981. From 1981 to 1994 the centre was conducting moderate activities at the grass root level. It was formally established in 1994. Bhagwat Kaka, the head *sevak* of Maharashtra and Goa zones gave a new thrust to the activities of this centre. Under the guidance of Br. Uttam Chaitanya (now Swami Sadananda) the centre established its presence even in Kalyan (East). Spiritual camps have been conducted every year for the last four years. Balavihar camps of the duration of 5 days have been organized every year by this centre. Bhagwat Kaka conducted seven training sessions in 1999 to meet the need for more *sevaks* and *sevikas*. A Yuva Kendra training camp was held in 1999.

Khopoli was established as a Mission centre in 1982 and had the benefit of many discourses by the visiting swamis and brahmacharis. Swami Chinmayananda, while appreciating the work done by some devotees, remarked that generally at other centres activities followed his *yajna*, but at Khopoli activities had preceded his *yajna*. In July 1980, Uncle Mani conducted a discourse on Valmiki Ramayana and sowed the seed for a centre. Br. Sahaja Chaitanya came to Khopoli on his *pada yatra* from Pune to Mumbai and the Yuva Kendra members accompanied him on this *yatra*. Swamini Gangananda held a discourse in 1984 followed by Br. Sudanshu Chaitanya in 1985 and 1986. S. Neelakantan of Zenith Pipes and many others from industries in that area worked with much enthusiasm. A medical aid centre was established in 1995. There is a temple in the Zenith complex which is often used for the centre's activities such as *satsangs*, discourses etc. This centre gets the support of industrialists and their workers as it has the advantage of being located in an industrial belt. The present Acharya is Br. Vijay Chaitanya.

The first *yajna* that heralded the advent of the Chinmaya Movement at **Kolhapur** was the *jnana-yajna* performed in 1980 by Swami Purushottamananda at the Radhakrishna Temple of Shahupuri area. This was followed by a visit by Swami Chinmayananda himself in 1982. Swamiji was in Sangli and came to Kolhapur for his first visit. The year 1985 is important in the history of Kolhapur as Swami Chinmayananda conducted his first and only *yajna* in March at this temple city. Swami Tejomayananda held his first *yajna* in Kolhapur in December 1985. In 1988, there was an audio-visual show by the Chyks, Pune, which attracted large crowds. The show was on the life of Swami Samartha Ramdas and it was an extravaganza with more than a hundred artistes. There were three performances and the funds raised during these shows really helped to fill the coffers of the centre. The Chinmaya Mission, Kolhapur was registered under the Bombay Public Trusts Act on February 10, 1989.

The centre published its first issue of a monthly newsletter in November 1989, with the blessings of Swami Purushottamananda. In 1990, thanks to a generous donation of an acre of land by S. K. Deshpande, the Kolhapur Ashram came up in Sambhapur, 15 kms away from the main city. On January 22, 1991 Swami Chinmayananda blessed the project of an Ashram at Kolhapur. The first camp at the Ashram was the All Maharashtra CHYK camp in November 1991 on the theme, "Secret of Success in Life".

On March 2, 1992, *Shivaratri* day, the Dakshineshwar Kailasnath Temple in the ashram was consecrated. Kolhapur is known as "Dakshina-Kashi". Swami Chinmayananda gave the name of "Kailasnath" to the *sphatika* (crystal) *linga*, which is placed in the temple. There is an interesting story about the *linga*. Swami Purushottamananda had seen an unusual *sphatika linga* at the Vana Rāma Temple in Sidhbari. He had a wish that such a *linga* should be in the temple at Kolhapur. One of the devotees in Rewa promised to get him a *sphatika linga* from abroad where crystal glass was famous. The *linga* arrived at the devotee's place, although of a smaller size. There was a camp at Sidhbari where Swami Purushottamananda had gone to meet Swamiji. The devotee from Rewa had also come to attend the camp and to hand over the *sphatika linga*. Swami Purushottamananda wanted the *linga* to be handed over to him by Swamiji. Swamiji saw the *linga* and, with all kindness and love, asked Swami Purushottamananda to take the bigger *linga* from the temple of Rama at Sidhbari. Swami Purushottamananda was thrilled. Thus the *sankalpa* of Swami Purushottamananda bore fruit. That speaks of the vision of *Mahatmas*. Swami Chinmayananda while conveying his blessings sent a message: "Go ahead! You will find me just beside the *Shiva-Linga*."

To provide a wider field of activity and to involve Chinmaya devotees from all over Maharashtra, a new trust named "Chinmaya Seva Trust Maharashtra" was formed on February 19, 1993. A symbolic silver Tulabhara of Swami Chinmayananda was performed on September 8, 1993, even though Swamiji had attained *maha-samadhi* on August 3. This event is of great historic importance as the Acharyas had decided to fulfill all commitments they had made to Swamiji prior to his *samadhi*. Devotees strongly believe that, though not in his physical form, the Guru is still around protecting all.

The 60th birthday of Swami Purushottamananda was celebrated on a grand scale in Mumbai in 1996. CSTM had mooted this idea. His Holiness Mahamandaleshwar Shri Vidyananda Giri Maharaj of Kailas Ashram (Rishikesh) graced the occasion by his presence.

On February 25, 1998 it was announced that the tallest Ganesh idol (85 ft. tall) in the world would be constructed in the Ashram. With this, other Seva projects would be taken under Chinmaya Ganadheesha Cultural Project.

The 5th anniversary of the Shiva Temple was celebrated with a *Panchadravya Abhisheka* on Mahshivaratri day, 1998. On January 1, 1999, Swami Purushottamananda inaugurated a *Shravan Sadhana* camp in Kolhapur.

Swami Tejomayananda visited in May 1999 and Swami Chidananda visited Kolhapur in March 1999. The people of Kolhapur had an opportunity to listen to their talks during their visits. Br. Ambarish Chaitanya conducted a Balavihar camp in May 1999. Sixty children from all over Maharashtra attended this camp.

The first Dharma Sevak course in Marathi was organized in Kolhapur Ashram from June 3 to July 18, 1999 and the Chief Acharya was Swami Purushottamananda. Br. Ambarish Chaitanya, and Brni. Tattvapriya Chaitanya assisted him. S.V. Bhagwat, a senior *sevak* who has done excellent service in Maharashtra for the Mission, also assisted Swamiji.

Kolhapur centre has been very active since its inception, with the focus on *yajnas*. Kolhapur is also concentrating on grass-root activities like Study groups, Devi groups, Chyks and Balavihars. But more stress is on spiritual camps and activities related to the Ashram in order that the ready-made infrastructure can be used to the maximum.

The activities in **Mulund** started with a Balavihar group. There was a spontaneous response from the spiritually inclined residents of Mulund to the Chinmaya call. In November 1980, Br. Vivek Chaitanya conducted a Geeta *jnana-yajna* and it was followed by visits of many other teachers. In 1982, the first Balamahotsav was conducted . The Chyks participated in the *Jnana Jyothi* march of Br. Sahaja Chaitanya. Swamiji conducted a *yajna* in Mulund in 1984. Impressed with the enthusiasm and commitment of the devotees, he approved of Mulund centre being an independent one. An apartment was bought in the area and the Mission office operated from there. Br. Sarvatma Chaitanya (now Swami Sacchidananda) was posted in Mulund in 1988 and worked vigorously to keep the centre active. There were several *yajnas*, talks at this centre by Br. Dharmesh Chaitanya, Br. Lokanatha Chaitanya (now Swami Chidananda), Br. Ashish Chaitanya (now Swami Asheeshananda) and others. There was Chyk Soul Song Nite in 1991, and Swami Tejomayananda held a *yajna* in 1993. Other swamis/swaminis who conducted *yajnas* were Swami Subodhananda, Swamini Gayananda, and Swami Chidananda. After the transfer of Br. Sarvatma Chaitanya, Brni. Dhruti Chaitanya, Br. Uttam Chaitanya, Vivek and Varsha served the centre for sometime. "Yugapurusha", a play on the life of Swami Chinmayananda was enacted in 1998 and Vivek Gonasgi played the title role. The year 1999 was busy with a *yajna* and a *Bhagawat Saptaha* by Swami Swaroopananda and Swami Subodhananda respectively.. The centre has an active *Vanaprastha Samsthan*. The centre has guided meditation classes by K.S. Rindani and Management talks by Swami Chidananda. It is extremely active and has a variety of programmes for its members at the grass root level.

Nashik has an interesting story behind the establishment of a centre. A chance meeting on a train of a devotee of Swami Chinmayananda and two industrialists of Nashik was the seed for the birth of the Nashik centre. Ajit Kapadia was a sincere and fervent devotee of Swami Chinmayananda, in the early years of the Chinmaya Movement. He was travelling to Nashik and his fellow travellers were Govind Tharani and Ramubhai Mehta, industrialists of Nashik. This journey ended with a determination to bring the Chinmaya Movement to Nashik. Br. Visuddha Chaitanya started a three-day talk at Nashik in September 1980, on the auspicious day of Ganesh Chaturthi. Immediately, thereafter, in December 1980, Swami Harinamananda, the then Acharya of Sandeepany Sadhanalaya, Powai, held a four-day discourse. These two programmes led to the formation of a Study group.

P.G. Ananthanarayan, popularly known as Uncle Mani, conducted in February 1981 discourses on the Valmiki Ramayan. In 1981 and 1982 Swami Purushottamananda conducted *jnana-yajnas*, which attracted a sizeable crowd. Swami Purushottamananda talked to a few of the zealous and enthusiastic listeners and floated the idea of having an independent centre at Nashik and thus was born Chinmaya Mission **Nashik** and **Deolali** in 1982. Encouraged by the response, the centre organized a *Geeta jnana-yajna* by Swami Chinmayananda. When the *yajna* was in progress, there was a national event at Nashik—*Bharatmata Rath Yatra* and *Kalash-yatra*. Swamiji, along with thousands of listeners, went to witness this and the people of Nashik were amazed at the discipline, which Swamiji had instilled in the crowd. It was a rare scene! In 1984 another *yajna* by Swamiji was conducted and a second Study group was formed. From 1983 to 1985, the resident Acharya was Br. Divya Chaitanya, who gave many discourses on various texts. An important event at this time was the staging of the Marathi play "Anand Vana Bhuvani" performed by 110 artistes from the Chinmaya Mission, Pune. All the four shows were running to packed houses. It created an awareness in the minds of the people of Nashik about the activities of the Chinmaya Yuva Kendra. Swami Purushottamananda performed *Shravana Sadhana* from January 1987 to October 1988, which brought the *sevaks* together and made the foundation of the centre stronger. The highlight of this *sadhana* was the presence of Swami Chinmayananda at Nashik when more than 500 participants performed *pada pooja*. People presented him with a silver chariot, which he held on his head and thereby made the crowd very happy. In 1992, Chinmaya Seva Trust, Nashik was formed. Through the good offices of Jamnadas Moorjani, a Trustee of CCMT, the centre got a donation of premises from Lachmibai Dwarakadas Jaising Trust. The resident brahmachari was given accommodation on the premises. The centre started a charitable dispensary for the people of nearby localities. Br. Ananta Chaitanya was the Acharya here, and Br. Ambarish Chaitanya later succeeded him. A Yuva Kendra was formed in 1997. Members have taken keen interest in social service activities like distributing fruits to patients in the civil hospital, educating hutment dwellers when there was a plague scare.

Since May 1997 the centre regularly brought out an official publication Chinmaya Prakash. The **Nashik Road** centre was formed in February 1995 and the erstwhile centre was named Chinmaya Mission Nashik. The new centre has been conducting the usual Mission activities and, in 1999 and 2000, the centre had *yajnas* by Swami Subodhananda. The centre has three Balavihar classes, two Yuva Kendra classes, one Bhajan group, one class by Acharya for youth, guided meditation, *satsang*, Vedic chanting class, Devi group, six study classes, and two Bhajan groups of devis. The centre proposes to reach out to more people in the future through performance of *Guru Paduka Poojan* in residential colonies, *Gayatri havan*, *Ishta devta poojan*, recital of *Vishnu Sahasranam* and *Geeta* chanting.

The first mission activity at the **Pimpri** centre was in 1970 when M.V. Naidu and his wife started a Balavihar. Yuva Kendra was established in 1981. Highlights of the Yuva Kendra activities were participation in the Torch March from Pune to Bombay covering a distance of 185 kms during the first International *Yajna* and Spiritual camp at Mumbai in 1983, the First Maharashtra CHYK conference and organizing various *yajnas* of Swami Purushottamananda. In April 1991, the centre was officially recognized with the appointment of an executive committee. The Naidu and

Deshmukh (Rajabhau and Ashatai) families did the pioneering work for the centre.

The **Pimpri-Chinchwad** centre has been holding *jnana-yajnas* regularly since 1983. Swami Tejomayananda, Swami Purushottamananda, Swami Anubhavananda, and many brahmacharis/brahmacharinis have conducted *yajnas*. This centre has also actively participated in *Vichar-yajnas* i.e. discussions between members of different Study groups after the completion of a text. Other activities are on a moderate key and they are trying to motivate the Chyks to take more interest in the Yuva Kendra activities. It is also taking steps to increase the membership by holding area *yajnas* to stimulate interest. The centre has also taken the responsibility of translating CCMT books into Marathi. They are also organizing *Geeta* chanting competition and as a variation they have also included in the competition verses from Marathi *Geeta*. The *sadhaks* from the centre have gone on pilgrimages to Alandi, Dehu, Pawas, Kolhapur, Sidhbari and Uttarakashi. Recitation of *Vishnu Sahasra Nama* is a regular feature on the first of every month.

Two novel activities of the Balavihar children are: children are taught and trained by an artist to make greetings cards and a *Vasantic Melawa* is held which is a programme of cultural activity followed by *samashti bhiksha*. These two programmes have been greatly appreciated by members.

The centre at **Sangli** was established in 1967. Swami Chinmayananda held his first *jnana-yajna* at Sangli in 1967, which was attended by over a thousand devotees. Thirty students accompanied Swamiji from Sandeepany Sadhanalaya. This was followed by *yajnas* in 1979 and 1982 by Swamiji. Since 1967, the centre has Study groups, Devi group and Balavihar classes.

They also took land from the Municipality in 1988 on lease and started construction of an Ashram. The initial donation of Rs. One Lakh came from a retired professor, Shridhar Raghunath Risbood and, thereafter, generous donations came in from different quarters. The building has been completed in 1990. The first Acharya was Br. Anant Chaitanya and presently Brni. Tattvapriya Chaitanya is holding the position. She has been keeping the centre very active since her coming over in 1993.

Chinmaya Mission has become a leading spiritual centre attracting a number of devotees from the city. There are six Study groups, one Devi group, one Balavihar, three Vedic chanting classes and two Bhajan groups. The centre has fifteen patrons, hundred and five life members and ninety associate members. The Acharya conducts study classes, Vedic chanting classes and classes for Chinmaya Vedanta Course. Brni. Tattvapriya Chaitanya has completed *Shravan sadhana* on the *Bhagavad Geeta*. The centre is conducting Sanskrit classes for the members. It has organised spiritual retreats, camps, family camps to Uttarakashi (1983 and 1999) and Sidhbari (1982 and 1997). They have also organized youth camps in 1994 and 1998. They have had *jnana-yajnas* by Swami Tejomayananda (1984), Swami Purushottamananda (from 1978 to 1999), Swami Bhaskarananda, Swamini Gayananda, and Swami Brahmananda (1997). Swami Chidananda visited in 1999 and conducted a couple of *satsangs*. The centre has published souvenirs on occasions like *Shrimad Bhagawad yajnas* and *Geeta jnana-yajnas*. It was also publishing a monthly magazine *Chinmaya Balvishwa*, during the period 1988-1992.

A centre was established in **Solapur** in 1982 and was inaugurated by Swamiji. It organizes *Geeta* competition every year and it holds *jnana-yajna*, *sadhana shibirs* etc. regularly. The centre conducts regular group activities like Balavihar, Study group, Devi group etc.

Tarapur is known for India's first Atomic Power Station. It was in early 1980 that the idea of starting a Chinmaya Mission centre here was mooted. The necessary guidance and motivation came from a young devoted sevak named C. Ramachandran from Khopoli. He had the background and the experience of setting up a Mission centre. With the help of N.M. Kokcha and other local persons the centre was established officially with an executive committee in 1983-84. Even earlier many activities were going on, the most effective ones being the Balavihar programme. The centre also organized several spiritual discourses by Swami Tejomayananda, Swami Purushottamananda, Br. Virakta Chaitanya, Br. Sudhansu Chaitanya, Brni. Gayatri Chaitanya, Br. Nikhila Chaitanya and Uncle Mani. Swamiji visited Tarapur again for a *jnana-yajna* from February-March 1990. The visits of Swamiji and other senior Swamis boosted the morale of the members of the Mission. Balavihar activity thrived with Balavihar groups in eight residential colonies with 300 children. *Yajnas* by Swami Chidananda in 1999 and Brni. Dhruti Chaitanya in 2000 are among the programmes in recent times.

Chinmaya Vidyalaya, Tarapur was inaugurated on June 18, 1995. C. Ramachandran conceived the idea. Swamiji welcomed the plan to start the school and made an initial contribution of a lakh of rupees. The Vidyalaya has adopted the syllabus of CBSE, Delhi. At present there are 710 students at the level where they have adopted the primary Chinmaya Vision Programme. Dr. N.S. Vartak as chairman and M.K.M. Menon as Secretary guide the Vidyalaya. The Vidyalaya has entered the second phase of expansion. Swami Tejomayananda laid the foundation stone on

February 18, 2000. They expect to complete this project by the year 2001.

On *Geeta Jayanti* Day, December 9, 1978, the **Thane** centre was inaugurated by Swami Chinmayananda in the presence of Swami Purushottamananda and some of the members of the Executive Committee. Swamiji gave them a written message. It read: "Organize, Plan, Act and Achieve for the Society." The activities were being conducted in different locations but now the centre has its own premises. Brni. Kirti Chaitanya is the resident Acharya.

This centre has all grass root level activities, like Study group, Balavihar, CHYK, Devi Group etc. It has eight Study groups, eight Devi Groups, fifteen Balavihar groups, and three CHYK groups. Other activities include *Bhagavad Geeta* in Hindi, *Bhagavata Purana* in Hindi, and Vedic chanting classes.

The key person for the founding of the Thane centre is P.R. Parashtekar. At his initiative, a Study group was started where Br. Prema Chaitanya conducted a group in English. This group lasted for eighteen years. A Balavihar was also started in December 1978 at the residence of one of the devotees. The Study group and the Balavihar group came together and organized a *Geeta jnana-yajna* in Marathi by Swami Purushottamananda in November 1978.

The first Study group for adults in Marathi medium was started in December 1978. The first Balavihar group for children was started in July 1974. The Chinmaya Yuva Kendra was established in December 1978. The monthly newsletter Self Effort (*Atmakripa*) was launched on August 1, 1979 with communication partially in Marathi and partially in English. In October 1981, a "*shravana sadhana satra*" was conducted by Swami Purushottamananda which went till May 1983. During this period he conducted discourses on the nine major *Upanishads* and all the chapters of the *Bhagavad Geeta* and Swami Chinmayananda came for the concluding function. A souvenir was brought out on this occasion called *Samaras*. In the year 1987 Swami Chinmayananda gave a talk on "Nature Reflects Man". On August 15, 1994 there was a Balavihar programme in which the children and *sevaks/sevikas* participated. Swami Tejomayananda's first *jnana-yajna* in Thane was conducted in October 1984 and the text was Tulsi Ramayana. This was followed by his second *yajna* in March 1996. When he did a third *yajna*, the centre gave Rs.1,11,111/- as *guru-dakshina*. Swami Brahmananda conducted the first *jnana-yajna* of the year 2000. He gave away the entire *guru-dakshina* and *bhiksha* amount to the Thane centre.

Wardha centre was established in 1984 and the first *yajna* was organized in December that year on the *Bhagavad Geeta* and *Isavasya Upanishad*. They have been holding *yajnas* every year and sub-centres have been started at **Paunar** and **Bhugaon**. Swami Tejomayananda inaugurated the office of the Wardha centre in February 2000. The centre has been conducting regular group activities like Balavihar, Study groups etc.

Swami Chinmayananda established the **Akola** centre soon after the first *jnana-yajna* in 1964. Thereafter Mission activities like Balavihar continued by the enthusiasm shown by the committee members. However, from 1983 to 1989 the activity slowed down and they did not organize any programme worth mentioning. It was only when the mother of Brni. Aditi Chaitanya (now Swamini Mangalananda), Parvatibai S. Joshi became the President that the activity picked up. Brni. Smriti Chaitanya (now Swamini Vimalananda) conducted a *Geeta jnana-yajna* in Hindi. She influenced the Hindi and Gujarati speaking devotees during this *yajna*. In 1991, Brni. Aditi Chaitanya was placed in charge of Akola centre. She conducted two *shravan sadhanas* and this gave an opportunity to the people of Akola to be exposed to Vedantic literature. During this period Study groups, Devi groups and Balavihar groups were started in different areas. In 1993 the Chinmaya Seva Trust was formed. In 1993, land was donated to the Mission by a devotee couple where two rooms have been constructed. A pre-primary school with nursery was started in 1994.

On February 7, 2000 Swami Tejomayananda and Swami Purushottamananda installed an idol of Shri Bhagavan Vishnu in the newly constructed Chinmaya Kripa Ashram. Brni. Dhruti Chaitanya conducted Swamiji's *paduka pooja* programme at Akola in ten different places. On December 25, 1999, the Yuva Kendra had a *shibir* conducted by Br. Ishan Chaitanya from Jalgaon, which was well attended.

Swami Chinmayananda came to **Nagpur** in 1956-57. The city was agog with the news of a *sannyasi* delivering discourses on the *Bhagavad Geeta*, that too in English. This attracted a large number of people from the educated class. One devotee recalls the late Dr. G. T. Khare, telling others how, at the end of each lecture, Swamiji would stand at the door requesting people to put something in his '*joli*' (a shoulder bag)! The Nagpur centre was formed in 1962 due to the initiative taken by a devotee, Shri Saran, who had been close to Swamiji and had invited him for *yajnas* in 1960, 1961 and 1962. The first Study group was formed in 1963 in Sadar area with fifteen members. The Study group activity continued with the active involvement of *sevaks* like Shri Radhakrishnanan and Dr. G. T. Khare.

Balavihar classes started in 1964 at National Environment Engineering Research Institute (NEERI) and continued under able guidance of a devotee, Srinivasan. Swamini Gayananda, as Dr. Vijaya Hege in her *poorvashram*, used to conduct Balavihar classes at her residence. Another devotee Smt. Mangalatai Desai conducted Balavihar classes in different localities. Ashatai Yete, Kunda Deshkar are some of the senior *sevikas* and are conducting classes since 1964.

Brni. Gayatri Chatiranya (now Swamini Gayananda) started a Yuva Kendra in 1984. During the seventy-fifth birthday of Swami Chinmayananda the Chyks arranged 75 programmes. One of the programmes was a discourse by Swamini Saradapriyananda on *Shikshavalli* of the *Taittiriya Upanishad*. In *Geeta* chanting competition, 'Chant *Geeta* Land Washington' Kumari Iyer of Nagpur centre won the all-India first prize and visited Washington. At present there are no activities by the CHYK group at Nagpur.

There are two Vedanta classes at the centre. Swamini Gayananda and Ms. Aruna Kulkarni conduct a group in Marathi and the second group is by Swamini Geetananda where the classes are conducted in English. Senior *sevaks* also take classes. They follow the guidelines laid down by Swami Tejomayananda in 1997.

Jnana-yajnas are an annual feature. Swamiji, Swami Dayananda, Swami Purushottamananda, Swamini Gangananda, and Swamini Saradapriyananda conducted *yajnas* during the period 1963 to 1984. Swami Chinmayananda held a *jnana-yajna* in 1988. He made the membership of Chinmaya Mission compulsory and this helped in the membership drive. Swami Tejomayananda has come to Nagpur several times. His visits were intermittent from 1985 to 1989 for *jnana-yajnas*, mostly on Tulsidas's

Ramcharitmanas. In 1989 he inaugurated the *yajna* of Brni. Gayatri Chaitanya (now Swamini Gayananda). In November 1993 Swami Tejomayananda was in Nagpur for a series of talks and during this visit, he inaugurated "*Chinmaya Sadan*," the office of the Chinmaya Mission centre. In the evening of the same day, the Satsang Hall in Chinmaya Sadan was inaugurated by unveiling a picture of Swami Chinmayananda. During the visit of Swami Tejomayananda for a *jnana-yajna*, he released a book called *Chatuh-shloki Bhagawat* translated into Marathi by Swamini Gayananda. During this visit to Nagpur, he also visited Paunar and had *satsang* with the workers at the famous Ashram of Vinoba Bhave.

The first Acharya was Br. Vishuddha Chaitanya who built up the centre in a systematic manner. He conducted *Geeta yajnas*, Balavihar classes, and Study classes. Swamini Gayananda and Swamini Geetananda have been serving this centre with dedication, offering many classes and guiding the devotees in all ways.

Chinmaya Seva Trust, Nagpur (CST Nagpur) came into being in 1990 as per the instructions of Swami Chinmayananda.

The centre has organized many medical diagnostic camps at Bhayur in Bhandara District. The centre has collected donations for the Kargil Relief fund, and for the Orissa Cyclone fund.

Swamini Gayananda has translated several books in English to Marathi e.g. *Upadesa Sara*, *Drig-Drishya Vivek*, and *Chatuh-shloki Bhagawat*. Swamini Geetananda has given notations to Bhajans and *stotras* and this collection was released in the form of a book '*Chinmaya-Swar-Malika*' and was released by CCMT, Mumbai.

Chinmaya Mission Centre of Nagpur has received Swami Chinmayananda's *padukas* as a *prasad*. The centre plans to do

108 *Paduka Poojas* by the year 2001. Before the *maha-samadhi* of Swami Chinmayananda, Harish Deshmukh (of Aurangabad) and his family donated to the Mission a piece of land of three acres at Paunar near Wardha. An Ashram is to be built upon this land in phases for conducting spiritual camps.

Swami Chinmayananda inaugurated Chinmaya Mission **Solapur** in April 1982, where Swami Purushottamananda conducted the first *jnana-yajna*. The centre organizes a *Geeta* chanting competition every year. It also holds *jnana-yajnas* and *sadhana-shibirs*. There are one Devi group, two Balavihar groups and four Study groups.

Uttar Pradesh and **Uttaranchal** have fifteen Chinmaya Mission centres. Swami Subodhananda is the Regional Head. As Br. Vishal Chaitanya, he was posted to Prayag and was the Acharya at Sandeepany Prayag, which trained a batch of seven students in the Vedanta Course between 1985 and 1987. He has handled various important assignments e.g. in-charge of *Pitamah Sadan* at **Mandhana**, Kanpur and Acharya of Sandeepany (Him). He gained rich experience from all these, he is now guiding the centres in seven States including Uttar Pradesh.

Bulandshahr centre was established in April 1996 and was inaugurated by Swami Shankarananda. Swami Shankarananda was also the first Acharya. Since 1996, the centre has held a *Geeta jnana-yajna* every year. Every Sunday members meet at the Swadhyaya-mandal for *satsang*.

In September 1989, Dibyasingha Deb and G.S. Bhatnagar of **Dehra Dun** met at Sandeepany (Himalaya), Sidhbari, to attend a spiritual camp. The camp over, they met Swami Chinmayananda and sought his blessings to pursue their studies with other *sadhaks* at Dehra Dun. On their return to Dehra Dun they identified a group of ardent seekers and formed the Chinmaya Study Group. Brni. Soumya Chaitanya initiated the Study group.

Swamiji held his first *jnana-yajna* at Dehra Dun in 1991. Br. Sudhansu Chaitanya accompanied him. Swami Amarmuni Maharaj, head of the Swami Ram Thirth Mission, Dehra Dun, received Swamiji at the *yajna-shala*. The *yajna*, according to Swamiji, "roared to a very satisfying success." He came again in 1992 to conduct his second *yajna* there. Swami Tejomayananda conducted his first *yajna* at Dehra Dun in 1995. Other senior swamis and swaminis of the Mission have also held *yajnas* there both before and after 1995. This centre functions under the control of Chinmaya Tapovan Trust (CTT) Sidhbari. Swami Subodhananda guides the centre and approves of the annual action plan, which is drawn up by the executive committee.

Dr. Ashok Kumar Rastogi from Canada donated a building in a central locality in the city to the Mission. This building now houses the Mission centre. Swami Tejomayananda named it *Chinmaya Ganga*. There are plans to extend the building by providing more rooms to render for more facilities.

The Acharya at this centre is Br. Hitesh Chaitanya who conducts programmes to cater to the needs of all devotees.

Balavihar activity, which started in 1993 under the guidance of Ms. S. Radhika, has become very popular. There are now four Balavihars. This centre has a novel programme called "*Geeta in Schools*". Under this programme the *sevikas* go to schools to teach *Geeta* chanting and this is followed by lectures on moral education and personality development. Br. Sumitra Chaitanya of Sidhbari held two *Bhakti Satsangs* in 1998. Br. Hitesh Chaitanya at the Ashram and *sevaks* elsewhere in the district, conduct Study groups. With the active support of Ms. Loveleena Modi and other members of society, the centre provided relief to families affected by the Rudra Prayag landslides.

Taking part in functions of other organizations like the Divine Life Society, Rishikesh, the Ramakrishna Mission, and the Swami Ram Tirth Mission, the centre has demonstrated the principle of respecting other faiths and missions. Swami Subodhananda once addressed the Sikh community on the subject of martyrdom of Guru Teg Bahadur. The functioning of the centre is impressive with remarkable growth all-round.

The Chinmaya Mission **Kanpur**, began functioning in April 1967, when Swami Chinmayananda conducted his first *yajna* there. It was organized at the instance of the then administrator K. K. Sharma, of the Indian Administrative Service. During this visit by Swamiji the Mission Centre was also established and an Executive Committee formed. Swamiji visited Kanpur again in October 1969. This visit accelerated all the activities of the Kanpur centre, and at the IIT Campus in particular. It was in 1983 that he paid his most memorable visit, for during this visit a proposal was made to him to take over the Bankhandeshwar Temple and the surrounding area at Mandhana for establishing a *Pitamah Sadan*. In the year 1981, the CCMT opened a Hindi Publications Division at Kanpur. Its first publication was *Jeevan Jyoti*, a Hindi translation of Swamiji's *Kindle Life*. Br. Vivek Chaitanya, during his posting at Kanpur from 1976 to 1980, translated Swamiji's English commentary on the *Bhagavad Geeta* into Hindi, and had it published through the Kanpur centre. Writings by Swami Shankarananda have also been published from here.

Swami Shankarananda conducted Vedanta classes at the B.N.S.D. Shiksha Niketan regularly from December 1989 onwards. The course lasted about two-and-a-half years. On successful completion of the course, Swami Chinmayananda awarded certificates of competency to participants during his visit to Kanpur in October 1991. On this occasion members of the Balavihar at Kanpur also received certificates of competency.

Since July 1997 Br. Vishwesh Chaitanya has been the Acharya at Kanpur. Many swamis have conducted *yajnas* at Kanpur at different times. A landmark project of the Chinmaya Mission, Kanpur, was the publication of *Geeta Vatika*. This was the electronic version of *The Holy Geeta* by Swamiji, made by harnessing modern computer technology so as to make our ancient wisdom accessible to the modern world. The whole commentary was put on a floppy; the software employed 'hypertext' that was high-tech then. Made ready in 1993, it was the result of loving labour by Br. Vineet Chaitanya and Dr. T.V. Prabhakar of the I.I.T.

Swamiji conducted three *yajnas* at **Prayag** in the 1950s and the 1960s but no centre was established there till 1975. Swamini Saradapriyananda conducted a *Geeta jnana-yajna* there in 1975 and established a Study group consisting of five persons. This small Study group invited Br. Vivek Chaitanya from Kanpur to conduct a *yajna* and this humble beginning brought more devotees to the Chinmaya fold. Br. Vivek Chaitanya paid a few more visits of one to three days' duration and delivered discourses on Vedantic texts. He was instrumental in getting the Prayag centre formally approved as a Chinmaya Mission centre.

Sandeepany Prayag was inaugurated in April 1985 and Br. Vishal Chaitanya (now Swami Subodhananda) was the first Acharya. Seven students joined the course and completed in 1987. Swamiji decided that since the Mission already had a Hindi

Vedanta Institute in Sidhbari there was no need for another institute at Prayag and hence no further courses were held.

The nucleus for the Chinmaya Vidyalaya at **Samesi** was a school that was being run by the Navin Seva Trust. This school was brought in line with the teaching standards at the Chinmaya Vidyalayas elsewhere. It has classes today up to Standard VIII. There are three hundred children studying at the school. The Chinmaya Vision Programme is being conducted here in a phased manner.

The Chinmaya *Vanaprastha Sansthan*, which focuses on service to senior citizens, was formed in 1996. The work of the *Sansthan* is being well appreciated. In view of the potential of the institution, Swami Tejomayananda decided to extend the scope of the *Sansthan* to all India. This scheme is a notable contribution made by the Prayag centre to the Chinmaya Movement. Swami Tejomayananda inaugurated the *Central Chinmaya Vanprasth Sansthan* (CCVS) as a wing of the CCMT in March 1998.

The first Acharya at the centre was Br. Vivek Chaitanya and the current Acharya is Swami Chaitanyananda.

Shri Ifkaruddin, the Collector, inaugurated the centre in **Sultanpur** in October 1994. The first Acharya at this centre was Swami Shankarananda. Every year the centre organizes two *yajnas–Geeta jnana-yajna* and *Ram Charit Manas yajna*. There is a group of young people who are all members of the Yuva Kendra attached to the centre. The Yuva Kendra has been functioning for the last two years. Two members of the centre participated in the World Workers' Conference held at Sidhbari in 1998. Members participated in the meditation camps organized at Mirzapur and Uttarakashi. In February 1998 the centre organized a *vriddhavastha samadhan shibir*. This *shibir* was a great success.

Two *swadhyaya mandals* have been started in the city. These meet regularly on Sundays for ninety minutes.

The national Union Territory of **Delhi** has been included in our list of special reports on important centres and is titled "Delhi, the Portal to Divinity", the portal through which one has to reach—Uttarakashi, Gangotri and Sidhbari—places sacred to the Chinmaya Movement.

Similarly, **Kolkata** which is the only Mission centre in West Bengal is included in the Special reports and is titled "Kolkata Calling".

Thus, in this chapter, we have had glimpses of the missionary activities going on at the 198 Chinmaya Mission centres nationwide. The details of the work at all these centres are too large for this volume to cover. We have touched upon the essentials in many instances. A separate volume will cover many interesting details of the network of centres in India and abroad.

NAVARATNA (NINE GEMS)

We have chosen nine centres, out of the many, in the country, which have made a significant contribution to the stability and growth of the Chinmaya Movement. Special reports on these centres are given below. The criterion for selection of the centres has been, by and large, the important role they played in moulding and supporting the Chinmaya Movement in its infancy.

1. PUNE

In the history of the Chinmaya Movement, Pune (formerly known as Poona) holds a pride of place. It at Pune in 1951, that Swami Chinmayananda held his first *jnana-yajna*. He held it at Rastha Peth's Ganapati Temple. This was a 100-day *yajna*. Swamiji himself did the canvassing. He moved on a bicycle from house to house around Rastha Peth and invited people to the discourse. After this maiden *yajna* there was a big gap. The next *yajna* by Swamiji at Pune was in 1965 at Dehu Road, a suburb of Pune. There were *yajnas* again in 1968, 1969,1976,1978,1981 and 1986. Swamiji's last visit to Pune was in May 1986.

Pune had the pleasure and privilege of listening to a number of Brahmacharis and Swamis–Swami Purushottamananda, Swamini Saradapriayananda, Swami Harinamananda, Swami Tejomayananda, Br. Anant Chaitanya, and Br. Sarwaatma Chaitanya. During these *yajnas*, Yuva Kendra and Study group activities took root. Brni Karuna Chaitanya and Br. Shailesh Chaitanya are posted at Pune. Swami Purushottamananda is the guiding force. Sunil Prayagi also conducts classes, and K.P. Daswani helps in many ways.

We may now sketch some of the important events taking place at Pune.

In August 1978, the centre organized a *shravana sadhana* series, as also two *jnana-yajnas* on *Vivekachoodamani*. Swami Purushottamananda had the lion's share in these monthly discourses: he did as many as sixteen out of the twenty organized. The series concluded in May 1980 with a spiritual camp. A spectacular souvenir titled *samarpan* was brought out on the occasion. In a message published in this souvenir, Swami Chinmayananda commended the effort. He praised Swami Purushottamananda's innovative genius and said: "Swami Purushottamananda can do wonders. He has the natural flair to make others understand the message of the *rishis*".

The Chinmaya Mission Pune was registered in 1978 as a public trust, with many leading citizens as founder members. The late Atur Sangtani was the founder Patron. In December of that year,

Swamiji conducted his 278th yajna at Pune. At his instance, the Yuva Kendra arranged for a *Bhajan Rajani* and a *Dindi* programme. A *Dindi* programme means a march to a holy place, carrying the Lord's idol in a palanquin, singing bhajans on the way From out of the funds collected during the march the Yuva Kendra donated Rs. 5000 (Rupees five thousand only) to the Chinmaya Hospital at Bangalore.

Vijnan Mandir activity began in 1979, with regular Vedanta classes with regular Vedanta classes held at two locations. The centre took up the work of translating Swamiji's commentaries into Marathi. A translation Committee was formed, with Mr. Telang as the President. This committee was known as the Chinmaya Publications, Marathi Division. To make the books available to people at affordable prices, the first edition was sponsored by donation. Swami Purushottamananda diverted all his *bhiksha* offerings to this work with the kind permission and blessings of Swami Chinmayananda. Swamiji applauded this effort too while releasing the Marathi version of Chapter five of the Geeta at one of the Mumbai *yajnas*. He said "I have received a lakh for the Gujarathi translation but no book has come up even after two years; and here the Marathi Division is bringing out a chapter every month by collecting donations and with the help of Swami Purushottamananda's *bhiksha* offerings; wonderful effort!!" The Translation Committee has translated almost all the books and Swami Purushottamananda examines all translations with the help of a team of *sevaks*.

Swami Chinmayananda visited Pune in November 1981. He inspired the Mission centre to stage a show on the life and work of Samartha Ramdas on the occasion of the saint's 300th death anniversary. He said, "We cannot afford to forget our saints so easily". Thus was born the majestic "Anand Vana Bhuwani"–a sound and light show on the life and works of Swami Samartha Ramdas. About 100 artistes participated on five stages, enacting all the important events, from childhood to *samadhi* of the saint, depicting the historical and social background that had been then prevalent. This show was first staged in Pune in the presence of Swami Chinmayananda in December 1982. It was a moment of great achievement for the Pune centre in general and to Mr. & Mrs. Sharadrao Deshpande in particular, who played a key role in the Ramdas Project. The show was repeated in many cities in Maharashtra. The late Setu Madhavrao Pagdi from Hyderabad, who was the fist to speak about Ramdas in the lecture series arranged by the Pune mission to create the right atmosphere and setting for the project, observed, "It is a *Mani-kanchan yoga* that a modern saint like Swami Chinmayananda has asked you to stage Swami Samartha Ramdas who left this world three hundred years ago. This is most wonderful, this is unique."

During the first international *yajna* that was being organized at Mumbai, the Yuva Kendra of Pune organized a *Jnana Jyoti* (Torch March) from Rastha Peth Ganapathi Temple at Pune to the venue of the international *yajna* at Andheri, Mumbai. The Yuva Kendra boys from Pune carried the torch to the *yajna-shala*. Swami Chinmayananda received the Torch in the outskirts of Mumbai. A local devotee, Kanitkar from Chinchwad, organized an exhibition titled "From Seed to Tree" that was very spectacular.

The last visit of Swami Chinmayananda to Pune was in May 1986, when a national *yajna* and a spiritual camp were organized. About 250 delegates from other centres too attended the camp. Swamiji's further trips, though planned, did not materialize.

The members of Pune Mission centre recall the 1986 visit with nostalgia.

The Mission centre has a place of its own in Ganesh Nagar. Many activities are held in premises offered by devotees. A large hall in the camp area offered by Swamiji's devotee from Hong Kong, K.P. Daswani, is often the venue of the Mission's get-togethers.

Regular Balavihar classes are being conducted by *sevikas*. Camps are organized during the vacation.

Chinmaya Vanaprastha Sansthan: Since June 1998 a new wing has been started at the centre for the senior members. This activity is organised by the Central Chinmaya Vanaprastha Sansthan in Allahabad under the guidance of Swami Shankarananda and his team. This activity is greatly appreciated by senior citizens. This group took part in the International Gerontology Conference held at Pune in December 1999.

Chinmaya Mission Pune is now preparing for the December 2001 Golden Jubilee Celebration. Meantime, the centre is also taking action to strengthen and consolidate its activities.

2. *CHENNAI—THE CRADLE CITY*

The history of the Chinmaya Mission, Chennai, is closely connected with the history of the Movement itself. The Chinmaya Mission was born here.

After his first *yajna* at Pune in 1951, Swamiji planned the second at Chennai. Hurdles galore faced him. Orthodoxy opposed it; the priestly class did not cooperate; no place seemed to be available. At last, while he was feeling dejected, a Muslim friend of his uncle's offered his place. The *yajna* was arranged at Arni Palace, Egmore (where the Children's Hospital is located at present). Swamiji spoke on the *Mundaka Upanishad*, from April 25 to June 5, 1953. Starting with a modest crowd of just ten, the crowd swelled as the days passed by. On some evenings, power failed; but the discourse just went on, uninterrupted, in the light of petromax lights. The crowd wanted to hear more. Chennai hosted as many as twenty-five *yajnas* for Swamiji in the decades that followed.

THE BIRTH

Some devotees were keen on continuing their study of the Vedanta even after the *yajna*. They desired to form an organization and conserve the spiritual fervour generated in them by this great master. Rangaswami Iyer, W. M. Naidu (owning a chemists shop), Sundaresa Iyer (owning a firewood shop), Srinivasa Rao, and Kanthi Iyer (working in Voltas) were among the first to approach Swamiji, seeking his permission to start a mission at Chennai. So the Chinmaya Mission Chennai, was born, with Swamiji's blessings on August 8, 1953. It was a *sankalpa* made by them at Saketa Nilayam, a *mandapam* attached to the Perumal Temple at Egmore.

Organizational work moved equally fast. The byelaws for the organization were drafted and approved by Swamiji. The membership fee was fixed at four annas (25 paise at present) to meet the cost of the flowers needed for *pooja*. Swamiji wrote to the organizers:

> This is my dream of the Chinmaya Mission. It must instil into Hinduism the spirit of brotherhood, missionary zeal, and urge to live each day a more perfect life of love and self-control, of freedom and intelligence, of purity and meekness..... All conscious dreams come true always.

Sundaresa Iyer, known widely as the Firewood Iyer, became the first President of the Mission; and Rangasamy Iyer, the first Secretary.

GROWING UP

The Mission started with a great burst of energy bang with six branches in different areas in the city. The immediate activity was the work of the weekly *satsang* groups meeting at these six places by rotation. Saketa Nilayam was the common venue used for the meetings. The venue was later changed to the Presidency Girls High School, Egmore.

Swamiji did his second *yajna* at Chennai from December 16, 1954 to January 21, 1955 in T. Nagar. The text was the *Taittireeya Upanishad*. Thereafter, the *yajnas* year after year went on with vigour attracting larger and larger crowds. Each *yajna*, was marked by the publication of a souvenir. A seminar would sometimes accompany a *yajna*. The first symposium was held on September 23, 1959, in which Muslim and Christian speakers also participated. The topic was "Faith in God Gives Meaning and Purpose to Human Life."

Swamiji also took the devotees on family tours. These were picnics really and were designed as a "limb" of the yajna ritual to encourage community living. At the end of the first *yajna* they went in six buses to Dhanushkoti and Rameshwaram a distance of two hundred miles.

A novel experiment that Swamiji tried at Chennai during his third *yajna*, in 1955, was to make it mobile. Lectures were arranged in different localities in order to create an awareness at those places, and Swamiji would move around and address the public. It was during one of these addresses that Swamiji announced his idea of a residential *gurukula* to train spiritual teachers. He called such a *gurukula* Sandeepany, after the famous Maharshi Sandeepany of the Dwapara Age. Lord Krishna himself, studied as a boy in the *gurukula* he headed.

In 1975 a *yajna* was conducted for the first time in an open area—the playgrounds of the Ramakrishna Mission School. Stalls were arranged on one side of the ground, exhibiting the activities of the Mission. This became the model for all *yajna-shalas*.

The sixth national *yajna* in January 1978 was a special occasion, as it was the Silver Jubilee year of starting the Chennai centre. The last *yajna* in this city was held in November 1992.

In 1976 Chennai played host to Swami Dayananda's one hundredth *yajna*. Swami Tejomayananda as Br. Vivek Chaitanya visited Chennai for the first time in 1977 and spoke on Chapter 4 of the *Geeta*. His talks later, in 1982 on the Tulasi Ramayana enthralled the audience. The citizens of Chennai had for the first time the taste of a *Bhagawat Saptah* by Swami Tejomayananda. It was held when he came in 1994 as the Head of the Mission.

Initially Swamiji's home at Chennai was the residence of his uncle, Kutti Krishna Menon. Later he chose Ma Sundaram's house, on Harrington Road, Chetpet. Recalling the days, M. Ct. Petachi, an ardent devotee and President of the Mission from 1960 to 1980, said: "Swamiji was fond of swimming. He would come early in the morning to my house near the beach for a swim." From 1962 onwards and till his last days, Swamiji used to stay at the residence of the Nambiars' on College Road. Ms Leela Nambiar named it Guruniketan.

As the Chinmaya Mission, Chennai, had no formal office, each President or Secretary attended to the work from his own house. It was only in 1959 that a portion of the first floor of the Paramanand Das and Chota Das Dharmashala on Rasappa Chetty Street, became available to the Mission. Book sales took place there; notices were sent to members from that address. Ma Sundaram's house was also used for office work.

It was only in 1966 that a building was bought on Harrington Road at Chetpet. Swamiji called it Vijnana Mandir and said that it would function as a spiritual rest house. Since 1968 the Mission office has been at Chetpet.

Swamiji was preoccupied, in those days, with the idea of a housing complex for the members of the Mission. And so the Chennai Housing Scheme was inaugurated in 1968. Today the township, called *Chinmaya Gram* at Virugambakkam, is a sprawling 35-acre complex consisting of two stages. Besides houses, there are a Kalyana Mandapam (Community Hall), a Vinayaka Temple, a Harihara Temple, a free medical centre, and a Chinmaya Vidyalaya.

In 1983 Vijay Mehta and K.C. Kothari donated 7.1 acres of land to Chinmaya Mission, Chennai at Tamaraipakkam, about thirty-five kilometeres. from the city. The Shri Sarveswara Dhyana Nilayam was set up there in October 1989. A *Geeta Satsang* Hall, a home for the aged (*Pitamaha Sadan*), a free dispensary, and a school for the local children are located in the same complex. The Tamil Sandeepany also functioned there, and two Vedanta courses were completed. The Shiva Temple, Sarveshwara Dhyana Nilayam consecrated on October 15, 1989 has a *sphatika linga* two feet high. Swamiji had personally brought it from abroad. There is also a traditional *linga* for daily worship. The temple itself is a unique architectural structure in the form of a Shiva *Linga*, sixty feet tall and has an imposing visibility from quite a distance. It is constructed in such a manner that the deity is on the first floor, while the meditation hall is below and is used for *satsang*.

In 1988 the Chinmaya Mission, Chennai, formed a trust in the name of the Madras Chinmaya Seva Trust (MCST) to take care of the properties and carry out big projects.

Ever since Swamiji's first *yajna*, the activities of the Mission had been growing. The Mission was spreading its wings not only across the length and breadth of Chennai, but also among different sections of society.

In 1955, at the time of his third *yajna*, Swamiji started grouping children together and teaching them how to chant the *Geeta* before a discourse. He discussed children's programmes with members in May 1956. This was the starting point of the Balavihar Movement at Chennai. Balavihar classes were started in different areas of the city. Balamahotsavas, Culture India Quiz, "Chant *Geeta*, Land Washington", etc. were some of the other programmes of the Balavihar. The public evinced keen interest in them all. The Balavihar Kala Mandir, a new activity announced by Swamiji in 1970, trained children in arts like painting, drawing, light music, dancing, etc.

CHINMAYA YUVA KENDRA (CHYK)

The Chyk movement in Chennai took off in 1976. Prof. C.G. Vasudevan was nominated its Organizing Secretary. It grew fast and hosted the first All India Yuva Kendra meet in 1977. This gave a fillip to the Yuva Kendra Movement in the city. The youngsters launched a variety of programmes so they might express their energies in a meaningful manner. These programmes included social service programmes, seminars the debates, oratorical contests, training camps, excursions, cultural programmes like the staging of plays, etc. By 1977 they had made their mark. Impressed with them, Swamiji even directed Chyk representatives from Chennai to visit Visakhapatnam, Ernakulam, and Thiruvannamalai and help organize Chinmaya Yuva Kendras at those places. They hosted a Yuva *Mahotsava* in 1985. At this *mahotsava*, Chennai proposed a rolling trophy for the

Best Yuva Kendra in the country—which they themselves won in 1994 and 1998.

Their best show was yet to come. In February 1981, the Chyksters put up a light and sound show on the Ramayana, titled 'Kamban Tharum Katchi' (It might be translated into English as, "The Vision of Kamban". Kamban was a celebrated poet who wrote Lord Rama'a great story in Tamil.) The response from the public was overwhelming. Its success has been repeated many times. The maiden performance was held on the Congress grounds at, Teynampet in the distinguished presence of Swamiji and many dignitaries. On seeing the show in 1982, the then Governor invited the Chyksters to a party at Raj Bhavan (his official residence). The programme not only entertained the crowds, but also garnered funds for various activities of the Mission. Today several performances are being organized at different places in aid of different causes. A show was put up in Sri Lanka where a staggering sum of rupees thirty lakhs was the collection. The Sri Lanka Chinmaya Mission utilized it for the construction of a Hanuman temple there.

Swamiji suggested to young men that they spread the Vedanta through a bicycle *yatra*. Promptly the Chyksters organized just such a *yatra* to Ernakulam on the occasion the Third International Spiritual Camp in 1988. Participants fondly recollect their journey through Kaladi (birthplace of Shankara) and Kuzhalmannan (birthplace of Swami Tapovanam) before finally reaching Ernakulam (birthplace of Swamiji).

The same year, Chyk dynamism reached another milestone–the Chyks opned a free dispensary at Tamaraipakkam, under a banyan tree. It later developed into the Ananth Free Medical Centre.

The Chyks of Chennai have also brought out four volumes of *Hari Om Bhajan* cassettes. These have been very well received by the public.

STUDY GROUPS

Study Groups took birth at Chennai in 1960. A. Parthasarathy (former Pradhan of the Sandeepany, Mumbai) G. Natarajan Iyer (later Swami Dayananda), and almost all the secretaries who held the reins of the Mission later were members of these early Study groups. Several groups started functioning in different areas under the care of dedicated *sevaks*. Many of them have completed the schedules given to them. Today there are as many as forty Study groups.

In 1967 Chennai adopted a scheme called *Prachara Yajna* and distributed pamphlets, titled "Points to Ponder", to create an awareness among the public. In 1968 members started *Swadhyaya Yajna* sessions. At these sessions they would read selected spiritual text to the public. Swamiji described it as "divine courting to make the uninitiated interested".

In 1974 what were called area *yajnas* were started. The first one took place in Integral Coach Factory. The idea was to benefit local areas. Thus *yajnas* by brahmacharis and senior members in different areas and in different languages became the routine activity of the Chennai Mission all through the year.

In 1967 a Bhajan Group was formed. It started giving performances at the Mission centre and also at various public places.

CHINMAYA MISSION (SOUTH)

In 1983 members belonging to the southern parts of Chennai formed an organization called the Chinmaya Mission South to help promote activity in and around those areas. They even acquired a building at Adambakkam for housing their unit. Br. Sarveswara Chaitanya is posted there as Acharya.

In 1997 Swami Tejomayananda held a *yajna* at Chennai. He said that the Mission activities should reach every district headquarters. Meanwhile there was a request from Nagapattinam. Parents of a student of the Chinmaya Vidyalaya, Annanagar, transferred to Nagapattinam, saw the conditions there, and felt that there was need there for a school of the kind of Chinmaya Vidyalaya in the area. The MCST pursued the idea. It began conducting *yajnas* there. Soon an ad hoc committee of the locals came into being. The Chinmaya Vidyalaya is today a reality at Nagapattinam. It started functioning with effect from April 1999.

LEADING THE WAY

Chennai is the first centre of the Chinmaya Mission. It has many more "firsts" to its credit. The melodious tune for chanting the *Geeta* that the Mission uses the world over was first set at Chennai. This was thanks to many members who were good at singing and chanting. G. Rangaswamy, the founder Secretary, had two daughters. Swamiji called them the nightingales of *Geeta*. (One of them eventually became Swamini Pavitrananda, who attained *samadhi* in 1991.) There were also the Sanskrit Professor Lalitha of the University of Madras and P.A. Subramaniam, Professor of English at the Annamalai University, who helped members learn Sanskrit and chant *mantras* properly in accordance with the instructions of Swamiji.

The first person ever to be initiated into *sannyas* by Swamiji was also from Chennai. Dr. Ekambaram, a doctor from Egmore received the *deeksha* in 1961 and became Swami Premananda.

Chennai also takes credit for being the first to start publishing Swamiji's books, which it did in 1961 by forming the Chinmaya Publications Trust (CPT). Hoe & Co., owned by a devotee, and

V. Sethu, a member of the CPT designed a monogram for the purpose—a Kerala lamp enclosed in an ellipse. The trust functioned till 1981 when the CCMT took over the work. Many people participated in the activities of the trust. Special mention must be made of Govardandas Parekh who looked after it right from its inception onwards till he died. He earned much appreciation from Swamiji.

The First All-India Conference of Chinmaya Workers (1958) was hosted by the Chennai centre. So was the First All-India Chinmaya Balavihar Mahotsava. (1959).

The Chinmaya Mission pledge was born at Chennai. Swamiji gave it out in the All-India Workers' Conference held at Abbotsbury in 1964. Swamiji's famous address, 'True Worker' was given here.

Chennai has the distinction of being the first to start a Devi Group in 1958. The group formed the All Women *Yajna* Committee, which organized Swamiji's one hundredth *yajna* in 1962, the tenth year of the centre.

B. V. Reddy of Chennai conceived and organized Swamiji's first global tour, "Pilgrimage of Love and Serving". On his return in June 1965 Swamiji got a thumping reception at Chennai. He called Reddy a "*Karmayoga Veera*".

Chennai convened the First All-India Chinmaya Vidyalaya Conference in 1970. The decision to call every vidyalaya run by the Chinmaya centre by the name Chinmaya Vidyalaya was taken here.

In 1977 the First All-India Chyk Meet was held at Chennai. The keenly-sought after rolling trophy for the best Chyk centre in the country was introduced for the first time at Chennai in the year 1985.

Tyagi, the first magazine of the Chinmaya Mission, came out at Chennai in 1955.

PUBLICATIONS

Since May 1968 the Chennai centre has been handling the monthly journal *Tapovan Prasad*. From 1989 to 1995, Chennai ran *Balvihar*, the international children's monthly. The Mission started a monthly newsletter called *Chinmaya Dindima* in 1974.

Chennai published several souvenirs, one at each *yajna* and also to mark other events. On the occasion of Swamiji's 433rd *Geeta jnana-yajna* in September 1987, it took the privilege of publishing Hail Renaissance IV. This notable work records the progress of the Chinmaya Mission in the three realms of *bhakti* (devotion), *Jnana* (Knowledge), and *kama* (activity).

VIDYALAYA ACTIVITIES

Vidyalaya activity at Chennai started with the Chinmaya Nursery School; Swamiji inaugurated it in October 1968. On its site at Chetpet now stands a new, three-storied building with well-planned architectural features. A second building on the same road was brought later to accommodate the higher secondary classes Swamiji inaugurated the high school in 1974. In 1988, the Mission obtained a large piece of land in Kilpauk from the Government. In 1990 the Chinmaya Vidyalaya's higher sections moved from Chetpet to Kilpauk. The building is named Tapovanam.

The second Chinmaya Vidyalaya came up in October 1970 in the Chinmaya gram following reconstruction, it is today a beautiful facility, measuring 45,000 square feet, on three floors. Swamiji inaugurated it in 1986.

The third Chinmaya Vidyalaya came up at Annanagar. The Tamilnadu Government offered the land for a nominal sum. On January 1, 1990 Swamiji laid the foundation stone for the construction of the building and inaugurated two wings. Swami Tejomayananda later opened the third wing and the spacious auditorium.

A Board of Management, Vidyalayas, formed in 1989, manages the affairs of all the Chinmaya Vidyalayas at Chennai. Today the total strength of all the schools is over four thousand. The success rate has always been one hundred percent.

CHINMAYA FOUNDATION OF EDUCATION AND CULTURE (CHIFEC)

During a *yajna* in January 1976, the Chinmaya Foundation of Education and Culture (CHIFEC) was inaugurated at Chennai. Its objective was to provide comprehensive grounding in Hindu philosophy to the public by organizing educational and cultural programmes. It has thus become the venue for the Vijnana Mandir classes, it has special sessions to train Balavihar *sevaks/sevikas*. It has a library for children; it has also published two very popular books—*Bala Bhagavatam* for children and *A Manual of Self-Unfoldment* for youth.

PITAMAHA SADAN

The construction work of an Old Age Home began in 1986 at Tamaraipakkam under the scheme, "Own Your Cottage". The *Pitamaha Sadan* consists of five cottages, each containing two units. The construction was completed in 1989. The cottages are named after five rivers of India the Ganga, the Yamuna, the Godavari, the Krishna, and the Kaveri.

CHINMAYA ANANT FREE MEDICAL CENTRE

One day a village woman placed her sick child at Swamiji's feet for solace. Swamiji was moved. He then said that a free medical centre must be started on priority. The Chyksters had already been running a Chinmaya Free Medical Centre under a banyan tree since April 1988. Ms. Saraswathi Anant met Swamiji and gave a donation of Rs. 3,00,000 (Rupees three lacs only) for the project. A building of its own houses today the Chinmaya Anant Free Medical Centre. It caters to the basic medical needs of a number of villagers around the area.

HARIHARA SCHOOL

In 1990 Swamiji inaugurated the Harihara School at Tamaraipakkam. The school provides free education, free food, and free medical care to poor children. Many poor families are being benefited. It receives donations under the scheme, 'One Meal a Day for One Child for One Year/One Month"

The Chennai centre celebrated its silver jubilee on a fitting scale during the sixth national *yajna* in 1978. It brought out a souvenir, titled, "Saga of Service", in tune with the theme of the year. Swamiji had called 1978 the *Sadhana* Year.

TAMIL SANDEEPANY

On January 14, 1993, the auspicious Pongal Day, Swamiji inaugurated the Tamil Sandeepany in the Tamaraipakkam complex. Swami Shridharananda was appointed the Acharya. Two batches, each consisting of twelve brahmacharis, have completed their training there. They are serving different areas in Tamil Nadu.

CHINMAYA HERITAGE CENTRE

After the *maha-samadhi* of Swamiji in August 1993, the idea arose of constructing a Chinmaya Heritage Centre as an expression of love and gratitude and as a befitting tribute to the

Master. The objective was to promote and propagate the message of Swamiji, and also to sustain and enlarge the activities of the Chinmaya Mission in pursuit of human excellence, universal brotherhood, and world integration.

Swami Tejomayananda laid the foundation stone on August 31, 1994. A broad-based Committee was formed under the chairmanship of Bharat Ratna C. Subramaniam.

E.P.G. Nambiar is the Secretary-General of the project. Construction is currently going on in full swing.

CAVE

A special project called the Chinmaya Assisted Value Education (CAVE) was conceived in 1995 to reach more and more children beyond balavihars, and give them values in life. Ms. Radhika Krishnakumar took the lead. She prepared a series of manuals called Garden of Life. Published and marketed by Macmillans, the series is in great demand. Chinmaya Vision Project (CVP) is also a success.

LEADING LIGHTS

From the beginning Chennai has had the good fortune of having learned brahmacharis being posted there to carry on the function of *prachar* with full vigour. It was in 1976 that Br. Shuddha Chaitanya started taking classes at Krishnalaya, Santhome. On the administrative side, Br. Siddha Chaitanya (now Swami Siddhananda, in Pennsylvania) came in 1977. He helped in the publication of *Tapovan Prasad* and *Dindima*, was concerned in numerous aspects of organizing. Br. Gopinath and Br. Vinaya Chaitanya assisted in the work of *Tapovan Prasad*.

Br. Siddha Chaitanya and, later, Br. Prasanna Chaitanya conducted regular Vedanta classes every week. These classes were held at the Vijnana Mandir. Br. Paramartha Chaitanya arrived in August 1978. He took his classes on the *Geeta*, the *Upanishads*, and other texts, as well as his Sanskrit classes at Nungambakkam. Br. Prasanna Chaitanya continued to function at Santhome. He, as Swami Prasannatmananda later, taught at Chennai for many years. He is now at Chinmayaranyam, Andhra Pradesh. He made valuable contributions to the *Geeta Vatika* project, a sophisticated software containing hypertext *Geeta* on a floppy disk with navigational features (that were high-tech then). Br. Vineet Chaitanya who had conceived it; Dr Prabhakar of the Indian Institute of Technology Kanpur got it made. The response to the *Geeta Vatika* waned as new developments in computers overtook its technology.

Br. Sudheer Chaitanya (now Swami Dheerananda, Washington, D.C.) served the Chennai centre for about three years beginning 1986. Brni. Tapasya Chaitanya came in 1993 and offered a number of Area *Yajnas* and classes. As Swamini Niranjanananda, she is now the Editor of *Tapovan Prasad*. Her classes cover the teachers of the three Chinmaya Vidyalayas also.

Br. Swabodh Chaitanya (now Swami Mitrananda) completed his studies at the Sandeepany Mumbai in 1989. He first served Salem and later, in 1993 arrived at Chennai. Very popular with Chyks, he conducts many classes. He also travels to Sri Lanka, as also to countries in the Far East like Singapore. Br. Aniket Chaitanya also served Chennai for a while. He now operates from Coimbatore.

Chari Amma studied at the Sandeepany Mumbai (1986 – 88), she looked after the Harihara School at Tamaraipakkam till it was wound up in 1996 and did much *prachar* for the Mission at

Chennai for some time. As Swamini Sumedhananda, she is back at Tamaraipakkam now. Br. Jagdish Chaitanya, Br. Amaresh Chaitanya and Br. Sadasiva Chaitanya take care of all Tamil publications and carry out rural service at and around Tamaraipakkam. Br. Sarveswara Chaitanya serves the Mission in the city.

LENDING A HELPING HAND

The Chennai Chinmaya Mission has always kept an eye on the society around it, responding well to its needs. Members visit patients in hospitals and give them *prasad*.

In 1965-66 the country faced Pakistan's aggression on its northern borders. The Government declared a state of emergency. Swamiji collected lots of grain from Chennai following the *yajna* held there and handed it over to the Chief Minister. He sent donations to the Guruvayur Temple for its renovation in 1970, as also help to flood and cyclone victims of Tamil Nadu in 1976-77. He also provided cash and clothes to Uttarakashi when it was hit by an earthquake in 1991.

Chennai sent clothes, blankets and medicines to the Andhra Pradesh Chief Minister's Cyclone Fund, routing it through Chinmayaranyam in 1996 and through the centre at Vijayawada in 1997.

TAPOVAN PRASAD SILVER JUBILEE

The silver jubilee of the journal of the Chinmaya Mission, *Tapovan Prasad*, was celebrated in the year 1987. It coincided with the seventieth birthday of the Master. On this occasion the centre brought out a commemorative souvenir. In his message on the occasion, Swamiji said: "This is an age of publicity–Missionaries have to take up preaching, issuing pamphlets, organizing conferences, symposia, speak, talk, publish, prepare audio cassettes and video tapes etc. In fact we have to make use of all means of publicity, mass media." He concluded by saying, "I prostrate myself at Gurudev Tapovan Maharaj's sacred feet, fully recognizing that it is only His grace that has made this celebration possible."

LOOKING AHEAD

Chennai, the cradle city, is poised to take many more strides on the road to the spiritual renaissance heralded by Swamiji.

3. DELHI—PORTAL TO DIVINITY

Delhi was the third city, the first being Pune and the second Chennai, to have responded to the divine call of *jnana-yajna* by Swami Chinmayananda on September 12, 1953. These first steps taken by Swamiji became giant leaps in the unique historical process of spiritual awakening set going by the Chinmaya Movement.

The history of the Delhi Chinmaya Mission centre, in chronological order, is recorded below.

1953: The third *jnana-yajna* by Swamiji ran for ninety-one days in 1953. The subject was the *Mandukya Karika*, one of the highest spiritual texts. The commentary on the *Mandukya Karika* in English, available with the Chinmaya Mission today, is the result of those first discourses, taken down in shorthand and typed by Pathak. Swamiji edited them himself. During the *yajna*, Swamiji's *guru*, Swami Tapovanji Maharaj, sent a handwritten message, which was printed in the "Foreword" to the book.

About 500 to 700 people attended the *yajna*. It was quite remarkable in that Swamiji had imposed certain restrictions upon those who came to listen to him. People were advised to eat only one meal a day and to keep all sense organs in perfect control so that they might become worthy of listening to the holy text. This too for ninety-one days! Half-an-hour of intense meditation followed one-and-a-half hours of discourse. There were no morning talks. For eleven days there was a *havan* each morning of the *Maha-mrityunjaya mantra*. Each day, for twenty-one days, Swamiji organized twenty-four hours of *akhandakirtan*. After the evening meditation, Swamiji would go into his room and bolt the door from inside. No one could meet him after that. His dinner used to be just a glass of milk. Such austerity did Swamiji practise; not many people were aware of it. In his interaction with the world, he was like anyone else; otherwise people would not have opened up to him, especially the younger generation.

Ms. Sheela Puri and Ms. Shakuntala Bindra helped in the work. Swamiji showed them how to fold and wrap the *yajna-prasad* (which were booklets containing the texts of the previous discourses). He himself maintained a register and posted the booklets to all those who had participated in the previous *yajna*. He maintained great efficiency, even without the aid of our present-day computer system.

The wife of the President of India, Dr Rajendra Prasad, used to attend the *havan* each morning. One day Swamiji and a few other devotees were invited to spend the day at Rashtrapati Bhavan and to have lunch with the President and his family.

1954: The second *yajna* in Delhi was on the *Kathopanishad* and was held at the site of the General Post Office. It was a 61-day-long spiritual effort. Ms. Sheela Puri, Ms Shakuntala Bindra, and

Ms. Rani Bhan organized it. There was *akhandakirtan* for twenty-one days but no *havan*. There used to be meditation after each discourse. About a thousand people attended the *yajna*.

1955: Two *yajnas* were organized in 1955—from September 8 to October 28 and from October 30 to November 30. The listeners were increasing every day. Ms Sheela Sharma, who later organized Swamiji's *yajnas* in Allahabad and Rewa, and Ms Latika Sen Gupta (Lily Amma), along with her husband, met Swamiji during this time. Lily Amma, who is now at Sidhbari, donated her house at Chittaranjan Park to the Mission when she moved to Sidhbari in the late 1980s. Ms K. Vaidyanathan and her husband (who later served the Mission as President in the late 1970s) also met Swamiji about this time.

1956: There were three *yajnas* in Delhi. One was held on the grounds of the Modern School; the President of India, Dr. Rajendra Prasad, inaugurated it. The other two were held at Rajinder Nagar. Swamiji stayed with Choudhary Raghavendra Singh and also with Mr. Dua.

1957: In January, Swami Tapovanaji Maharaj attained *maha-samadhi*. When Swamiji passed through Delhi, he was looking very sad. Ms Sheila Dewan of Mumbai innocently asked him whether the swamis also felt sad; he replied, "I am also human".

1958: On the occasion of the first anniversary of Swami Tapovanam's *maha-samadhi*, Swamiji took devotees from Hyderabad and Delhi to Uttarakashi.

1959: A *yajna* was held between October 3 and October 23. The *yajnas* were now shortened to twenty days each as more and more people had started inviting Swamiji. Many people met Swamiji during the late 1950s and the early 1960s. They served the Mission in different capacities later.

1960: A *yajna* was held from March 2 to March 20.

1961: A *yajna* on Chapter Sixteen of the *Bhagawad Geeta* was held in the Community Hall at Panchkuin Road.

1962: Anjali, who had been greatly inspired by the previous *yajna*, taped the talks on the Chapter Eighteen of the *Bhagavad Geeta* on spools in March. Another *yajna* was held in July 1962.

1963: During the *yajna* that started in September, Swamiji explained the concept of happiness with great humour. "Joy is only an equation between two changeable phenomena. Not only the object in the world outside changes (flowers fade) but our mind and intellect also change (the second cup of coffee does not give the same pleasure as the first). The fading out of joy is the birth of sorrow. An ever-changing mind in an ever-changing world is trying to find a balance between the two. It is impossible! Take two wild horses, one is the mind, and the other the object. It is like trying to bridge the two with the help of a charpai (bed) and resting on it!"

1968: Swamiji came for a *yajna* in March. Jagdish Prasad, Director of Post and Telegraphs and Chairman of Delton Cables, had met Swamiji in 1962 and become an ardent devotee. He and his wife were involved in a lot of Mission activity. They played host to Swamiji in their house during the many *yajnas* that were held from the mid 1960s till 1972. It was only when they moved to Sidhbari that Swamiji started staying elsewhere. Swamiji also stayed with Ms. Rani Bhan a few times in the 1950s and the 1960s.

1970: Swamiji held a *yajna* at Windsor Place in March. He then proceeded to Mysore, where he suffered a massive heart attack. For two years he did not hold any *yajna* anywhere.

1972: Swami Jyotirmayananda (then Br. Radhakrishnan) was stationed in Delhi. There was an increase in activities of the Study Groups. There were thirty-six such groups functioning at the time.

Swami Jyotirmayananda was taking classes for as many as twenty-two of them.

1973: From this year onwards, Swamiji stayed with Ms. Padmini Nambiar and her husband, O.P. Nambiar, at their various residences. They kept an open house. Many members of the Mission enjoyed their generous hospitality.

1974: Swami Jyotirmayananda worked very hard and managed to get a highly prestigious site alloted to the Mission on Lodhi Road, where the Chinmaya Centre of World Understanding (CCWU) now stands. In 1991, Swamiji modified the architectural plans. He combined simple contemporary lines with a traditional centre-form of a sun window, representing the light of knowledge.

1975: Swami Jyotirmayananda started a New Delhi News Bulletin. He was also its editor for a year. Anjali succeeded him and held the office for ten years.

The Chinmaya Foundation (Vijnan Mandir) classes, organized by Ms Padma Narsimhan, were started in the basement of O.P. Nambiar's office. Br. Yajna Chaitanya was the first Acharya. He taught for six years under the Chinmaya Mission on the premises of the Ramana Kendra and the Bharatiya Vidya Bhawan. He has since left the Mission.

1976: One day Swamiji was scheduled to come to Delhi for a *yajna*. When he did not arrive at the *yajna-shala* even by 6.29 p.m., everyone concluded that something was wrong. The chief guest Dr Karan Singh walked towards the dais at 6.30 p.m. People were told that Swamiji had arrived in Delhi, but that he was running a temperature of 103°F. Instead of Swamiji, Dr. Karan Singh gave a discourse that evening. Nervous organizers got Br. Vivek Chaitanya (now Swami Tejomayananda) to hold the fort. The young brahmachari spoke quite well, having prayed to Swamiji earlier and besought him to speak through him! One never imagined at that time that one was listening to the future head of the Chinmaya Mission! Swami Dayananda arrived from Mumbai as Swamiji's condition got worse. Swamiji was flown in a serious condition to Mumbai and was taken directly to a hospital. He convalesced for some time in Mumbai before going on to Coimbatore for three months to undergo *ayurvedic* treatment at the hands of the Varier family who were famous for the skills.

1977: Swamiji came back for a *yajna* in September and delivered a series of such excellent discourses on Chapter Eleven of the *Bhagavad Geeta*, which describes the *Vishvaroopa* (cosmic form) of the Lord. If ever language revelled in the heights of poetry, wisdom, inspiration, and bliss for a period of ten days without coming down even an inch, it was during this *yajna*. Luckily these lectures were taped professionally and are still available for those who want to listen.

1978: Swamiji came officially only for a day when he spoke to business executives at the auditorium of the Federation of Indian Chambers of Commerce and Industry on October 6. The Mission produced a souvenir on the occasion, titled, "Poise in Action".

1979: Swamiji's younger sister, Kannakam Amma, came as a camp delegate to the national *yajna*. She was so shy that one could not catch her anywhere near Swamiji! It was only when group photos were being taken that she was forced to sit near him! Two eminent *mahatmas* of the century were on the dais during this *yajna*. One of them, our Swamiji, asked the other Swami Akhandanandaji of Brindavan to speak in Hindi. Swami Akhandanandaji complied, much to the joy of the audience.

During this year, Anjali Singh started taking Swamiji's photographs. She took about ten thousand photographs of

Swamiji around the world. She took another five to ten thousand photographs after his *maha-samadhi*.

On May 6, Swamiji blessed the inauguration of a Chinmaya Vidyalaya. Indira Bharadwaj, the first Principal, has been serving the school in that capacity with great dedication.

1980: The Chinmaya Vidyalaya celebrated the first anniversary of its founding. Swamiji graced the occasion by his presence.

1982: Swami Jyotirmayananda got some land allotted on the top of a hill in Vasant Vihar for the purpose of starting a school there. A national *yajna* in March and the *Bhoomipuja* in the Vidyalaya in May were the highlights of the year.

Br. Bodha Chaitanya came as Acharya and served the institution in that capacity till 1990.

1983: There was a sitar recital by Bharat Ratna Pandit Ravi Shankar, arranged by General and Ms Narinder Singh at the Siri Fort Auditorium. Sita Juneja decorated the stage with elegant floral swans. Swamiji conducted a *jnana-yajna* in November.

1984: The Chinmaya Vidyalaya was shifted in phases to Vasant Vihar.

1985: During the twelfth national camp in November, the Vidyalaya housed delegates from all over India. Swamiji stayed at Vasant Continental, in Vasant Vihar. He held his evening classes for the public at the very place where the CCWU now stands.

1987: There was a soul-stirring offering of classical bhajans by Padmashri Bhimsen Joshi as also a *yajna*. Anjali put up a special stall of thousands of Swamiji's pictures. Swamiji came especially to see the photograps.

1988: Dr M.S Subbalakshmi gave a very moving performance for the Chinmaya Mission at the Siri Fort Auditorium. She came to Swamiji's residence as well to meet him. Swamiji had great respect for her devotion.

1989: The twenty-third national camp held at the Chinmaya Vidyalaya was very meditational in character. After an early morning meditation session, Swamiji asked all the delegates to recite the *Tapovan Shatkam*. Most faltered. Very few knew it by heart. Swamiji said:, "Those who do not know the *Tapovan Shatkam* are not members of Chinmaya Mission!"

Ms. Sarita Kumar emerged as an inspired volunteer in this *yajna*. Her hospitality is well known to all.

1990: Br. Sudhanshu Chaitanya was appointed Acharya from 1990 to May 1993.

1991: Swamiji was weighed in silver (rajata-tulabhar) during the *yajna* in February. This was the Platinum Jubilee Year of Swamiji's birth.

This was the last *yajna* in Delhi by Swamiji—exactly thirty-eight years after his first. In all, between 1953 and 1991, Delhi hosted twenty *yajnas* by Swamiji.

In February, during a programme (*Bhakti Sandhya*) by Purushottam Jalota and his son Anup Jalota, Swamiji released Anjali's book, "On Wings and Wheels". This book drew on tape-recorded conversations with Swamiji in cars, trains and planes–the only places where Swamiji had free time!

1992: In spite of ill health, Swamiji graced the occasion of the *bhoomi-pooja* of the CCWU building on March 22.

1993: Swamiji paid his last official visit on March 14 to grace a dance performance. He did pass through the city on May 24, on his way to Sidhbari for his last camp there, but he was very ill. He stayed in a hotel near the airport.

Swamiji's last stopover in Delhi was on June 7, when he was at Delhi Airport for two hours en route from Sidhbari to Mumbai. He shared the snacks that some devotees had brought him with all those present in the room. It was like the Last Supper. His last words, before being wheeled away into security, were in reply to a question by Anjali. He said: "You will have rare photographs to take". (He was clearly hinting at his impending *maha-samadhi*).

On August 3, at San Diego, Swamiji shed his body and laid down for ever the responsibilities of the Mission.

On August 7, Swamiji's mortal remains were brought to Delhi and placed at the very place where a Statue of him now stands. Rare photos indeed were taken of his last journey through the capital city. Thousands queued up to pay their last tearful homage.

AFTER THE MAHASAMADHI

Swami Chidananda, who was briefly the Acharya in Delhi, took charge of the *yajna* that Swamiji was originally scheduled to take in October 1993. Swami Chidananda moved to San Jose soon after, Br. Manan Chaitanya (now Swami Nikhilananda) took his place. He served the Mission for six years before being sent out in 1999 to the Chinmaya Mission, San Jose, USA.

1994: On February 12, Swami Tejomayananda laid the foundation stone of the CCWU. He held a *yajna* at the All India Fine Arts and Crafts theatre in October.

1995: The audience swelled to beyond five hundred; the capacity of the hall was just three hundred at Swami Swaroopananda's first *yajna* (on the *Japji Sahib*). This *yajna* was an eye-opener. In view of its great success, bigger halls were hired for the *yajnas* both to be conducted by Swami Tejomayananda and Swami Swaroopananda.

The Delhi Chinmaya Seva Trust organized a seminar on "Indian Ethos and Global Competitiveness". The deliberations there were highly appreciated. Anil Sachdev, known for seminars to promote ethics and efficiency in business, led the organizing work.

A *Geeta jnana-yajna* by Swami Tejomayananda was arranged at the Federation of the Indian Chambers and Industry auditorium from September 9, onwards.

1996: Discourses by Swami Swaroopananda on the *Nauvan Mahalla* verses from the *Guru Granth Sahib* were again very well received.

Br. Manan Chaitanya received *sannyas* on *Maha-shivaratri* Day in Mumbai from Swami Tejomayananda. He is now Swami Nikhilananda.

1997: Discourses by Swami Swaroopananda on the Sikh scriptures were once more a resounding success. The Yuva Kendra did a 4-day residential camp, titled "Jagriti 97", at the Logicstat Farm.

On May 4, Swami Tejomayananda inaugurated the CCWU. Swamiji had insisted on this name for the Delhi centre because for one thing it was located in the capital of India. It was also the portal through which everyone passed in order to go to Uttarakashi, Sidhbari, Nepal, and other pilgrim centres. It had been hosting groups coming from all over India on pilgrimages. Swamiji had looked upon the Delhi centre as the one best suited to promote man's greater understanding of himself, of the world, and of his role in it. Lack of this understanding was the fundamental cause of all the world's problems and conflicts.

A *yajna* by Swami Tejomayananda in October and a youth camp, "Chetana 97" were the highlights of this year.

1998. Swami Tejomayananda conferred the Chinmaya Rasraj Award on Padma Bhushan Pandit Jasraj at a performance by the latter in February. The head of the Mission gave three talks in May on "Satyam, Shivam, Sundaram" at the CCWU. A statue of Swamiji made of five metals–gold, silver, copper, tin and zinc–was unveiled on May 16. Swami Brahmananda gave a bhajan *satsang* on *Mukunda-Mala* on July 24.

1999: The Chinmaya Yuva Kendra, Bangalore, presented a classical dance drama, "*Prakriti*", in February. Swami Gokulananda of the Ramakrishna Mission inaugurated the 4-day *Vanaprastha Sanstha* Programme in February. The senior citizens' group is doing very well: it meets regularly for discussions and *satsangs*. Swami Tejomayananda did a *yajna* in October at the CCWU. He gave the Prime Minister of India, Atal Behari Vajpayee, a cheque for Rs.63,00,000/- (Rupees sixty-three lacs) for the Kargil Relief Fund. The sum had been collected from members of the Mission all over the world. Later, the Mission also took up relief work to mitigate the suffering of those affected by the cyclone in Orissa.

The Director of the Chinmaya International Foundation (CIF), Dr. Ramaswamy Iyengar, coordinated two seminars on Indology in November. Dr L M Singhvi, M.P., showed great interest and lent a helping hand.

2000: A play by the Chennai Chyks, "LOC (Line of Control)", a *yajna* by Swami Mitrananda and the arrival of Swamini Purnananda as Acharya of the centre were the highlights of January. Swami Swaroopananda spent twenty days in the centre in February and gave a number of high value programmes.

A *yajna* and a *Bhakti Sandhya* programme by Swami Tejomayananda himself took place at the CCWU on May 16. Swamiji thrilled the audience with his devotional bhajans.

The contribution of the regional head, Swami Jyotirmayananda, to the progress of the centre through the years has been extraordinary. Many stalwarts have supported the growth. One of them, B.D. Kapoor, was the distinguished President of the Mission for seventeen years. He died in the year 2000.

Swamini Purnananda, the present Acharya, is spearheading the *prachar* work. Her dynamism is truly remarkable.

NOIDA

A Chapter of the Delhi Mission was started at Noida when Swamiji went there for a day in 1992 to be with Brig. Sanyam Vir Singh and Ms Sita Juneja. A meeting of Col. Ramanand's Study group was on and Swamiji blessed him. The Mission gained momentum in 1993. Ms. Indu Narinder Singh arranged regular classes. They even housed a brahmachari for a year. In the meantime Ms. Sahai worked hard to get land in a prestigious locality. Swami Tejomayananda laid the foundation stone on September 27, 1995. The centre was inaugurated on October 16, 1997. Brni. Dharmapriya served the centre for some time. Br. Vinayak Chaitanya is the present Acharya.

HARDWAR, SOLAN AND UNCHAHAR

The Delhi Chinmaya Seva Trust is running a postgraduate science college in the BHEL complex in Hardwar. Swamiji inaugurated the college in 1989. It is said that it is the best college under the Meerut University, getting 99.8% success results. As many as 980 students are studying there. Senior secondary schools are being run at Solan (with 300 students) and at Unchahar in the Rai Bareilly District (with 700 students). The Chinmaya Vidyalaya in Delhi has 1,300 students at present.

4. PALAKKAD, KERALA

This is one of the active centres in Kerala. Swami Chinmayananda chose Palakkad for his first *yajna* in Kerala, probably because of the association of the place with his guru, Swami Tapovan Maharaj. His guru used to live in Palakkad as a young lad and was engaged in social and literary activities. Swami Tapovanam, as "Chippu Kutty" in his *poorvashram*, was publishing a Malayalam literary magazine from Palakkad, besides observing spiritual pursuits. The first *yajna* for Palakkad and the fourth for Swami Chinmayananda was conducted from January 7,1954 to January 27,1954 and the text that he took was *Isavasyopanishad*. Swamiji had conducted ten *Geeta jnana-yajnas* at Palakkad between 1954 and 1990. After the second *yajna* by him between January 3, 1957 and January 12, 1957, the Chinmaya Mission centre was formed in Palakkad. The centre purchased land with an old building and constructed its own premises in 1975 and started all activities in the new location called *Chinmaya Tapovanam*. These premises are sacred as Swami Tapovanam used to reside here prior to his monastic days. Presently this is the hub of all Mission activities.

The first Acharya of the centre was Br. Yoga Chaitanya. From the very inception a number of devotees joined the Mission as members, and conducted Study classes in the residences of the members. This practice still continues, in addition to the Study classes conducted at *Chinmaya Tapovanam*. Swami Tejomayananda has conducted three *Geeta jnana-yajnas* at Palakkad. The centre has a Prayer Hall for which the foundation stone was laid by Swami Chinmayananda on January 3,1991. This hall is used for conducting study classes, mini-*yajnas* and *satsangs*. Balavihar classes are conducted in the houses of members in the town. Yuva Kendra classes, Youth Bhajan Group, Music classes, classes for youth are all conducted in *Chinmaya Tapovanam*.

The present Acharya at the centre is Swami Asheshananda. The Acharya conducts classes on Guided Meditation, *Bhagavad Geeta*, and *Upanishads* and also leads inter-active discussion group. Every year from May 1 to May 8 he conducts *Shrimad Bhagawat Saptah* in remembrance of Swami Chinmayananda's Birth Anniversary. The centre also invites swamis/swaminis/ brahmacharis/brahmacharinis of nearby centres to hold discourses.

Community service is rendered by free distribution of 1kg of rice to the poor on the 3rd of every month (Swami Chinmayananda's *samadhi* date is 3rd August). Free service and medicines are given to the poor every week.

The centre runs a bookstall in the Mission's premises '*Chinmaya Tapovanam*'.

Palakkad has another reason for being so fresh in the memory of Swamiji's devotees. In January 1957, when Swamiji was conducting a *yajna* at Palakkad, the news of Swami Tapovanam's *maha-samadhi* reached him.

Swamiji travelled often through Palakkad to reach other destinations in Kerala, particularly Kollengode. The royal family of Kollengode had great faith in and love for Swamiji. Whenever Swamiji wanted to launch a new activity he would use Kollengode as the testing ground – if the experiment succeeded in Kollengode it is bound to succeed in any other location. The First Akhila Bharatha Chinmaya Devi Conference was held here in January 1960. The first All Kerala Balavihar competition was held here. The centre has the honour of starting the First Chinmaya Vidyalaya in May 1965 when the Chinmaya Nursery School was inaugurated. The royal family at Kollengode had always extended their support to the activities of the Chinmaya Mission. Kollengode centre offered to its members the Chinmaya Kalamandir, started in 1999, for conducting music and dance classes; Chinmaya Tailoring Institute started in 1969, Chinmaya Commercial Institute started in 1973 and Chinmaya Institute of Computer Technology started in 1998.

5. KOLKATA CALLING

Swami Chinmayananda held the first *Geeta jnana-yajna* at Kolkata from December 3 to 21, 1955. It was Swamiji's fifteenth.

R.S. Nathan was a corporate executive serving in the city. He was drawn to the Chinmaya Movement and became the pioneering spirit behind the establishment of the Kolkata centre. He served the centre with such rare dedication and skill that his name became synonymous with the Chinmaya Mission. He made several literary contributions on serious texts; these were published in the Mission's fortnightly magazine *Tyagi*. He was a veritable treasure of knowledge ever ready to share it with anyone that asked for it. He was the first Acharya in charge of the centre since its inception in the 1950s. He later became Swami Nityananda and was appointed the regional head. He shed his mortal body on June 27, 1996. Several brahmacharis and brahmacharinis (including Br. Sudhanshu, Br. Someshwar, Br. Aniket, Brni. Pragnya and Br. Turya) were stationed at Kolkata to assist Swami Nityananda in promoting the activities of the Mission.

Sangit Kala Mandir (SKM) and Chinmaya Mission jointly sponsored a programme of Swamiji at Kolkata in 1966. SKM is an institution which was sponsored, amongst others, by Birla, Somany, Kothari and Jhawar families. Prominent local citizens supported the activities of the Chinmaya Mission. Shri G.D. Birla inaugurated the Fourth National Camp held in Kolkata in 1975. Swamiji had a large following in Kolkata. Some of the ardent devotees have been B.K. Birla and his wife, Kheruka family, Dr. V.N. Chaddha, Mahesh Shah, the Sahays, and the Mahindra Swaroops.

The activities of the Mission were conducted in the early years from South Kolkata; the devotees were predominantly South Indians. The centre rented the first floor of a three-storeyed building on Sarat Bose Road. In 1984, the rear of the same building was bought. Over the years the tenants on the ground and on the second floor left, so that the Chinmaya Mission is now using the entire building.

Brni. Punyaja arrived in 1993 and became Swamini Purnananda in 1996. She was the regional head for some time. In an interview she gave in 1997, she expressed the view that the Kolkata centre was fortunate in having good workers and in receiving encouraging response from the public, but that it suffered from paucity of funds. She hoped that the affluent sections and the Government could be persuaded to finance the activities of the Mission at the grassroots level. She moved to Delhi eventually. At present Br. Sakshi Chaitanya (now Swami Madhavananda) is in charge of the centre.

The Kolkata centre has hosted two national *Geeta jnana-yajnas*. The first, by Swami Chinmayananda was held in December 1975. Every year thereafter a *yajna* by Swamiji was held. Now the tradition continues with Swami Tejomayananda visiting Kolkata every year. He conducted the Second national *Geeta jnana-yajna* in December 1998. An audience of over a thousand attended this programme. *Tulsidas*, a presentation by Sekhar Sen, kept the participants spellbound one evening. The Calcutta centre invites other swamis for *yajnas* from time to time.

BALAVIHAR

The Kolkata Balavihar was started in February 1965 with twenty children. Today it has twenty centres catering to more than 250 children. Of course this strength varies from year to year. There was a time when the number of children attending was about 500.

Ms. Mohana Iyer, a Balavihar child in 1966 and a *sevika* today, is the live wire behind the Balavihar. She formed a Balavihar in 1999; and she has not looked back. She started a Balavihar class in New York when she was there on a dancing assignment. Similarly we have Ms. R. Kalyani and Ms. Subhashree Chandra, who are actively associated with the Mission, although not as *sevikas*; they have ever been ready to help in all Balavihar activities.

T.V. Narayanaswamy took over as Secretary, Balavihar, in the early 1970s. His association lasted for about twenty years–till 1989. In this period the centre had nearly 45 classes running at different places. Along with him was a dedicated *sevika*, Janaki Padmanabhan. The present Secretary is Ms. Gayathri, very versatile and popular. She won the third prize in the All India *Geeta* Chanting Competition held in 1995.

Again, Kolkata was lucky to have Gopal Bhaiya in the early 1970s as a Balavihar *sevak*. He was instrumental in inculcating a sense of discipline and a proper method of learning among the students of the Balavihar. Most of those who are associated with the Mission through the Balavihar have never looked back. Girls especially return even after their marriage to help children get the Balavihar training. Today the centre has, apart from the grassroots activities:

- Sit and draw competition
- Fancy dress competition.
- Art and craft competition
- On the spot essay competition.
- Extempore speech
- Prepared speech.

- Elocution competition • Shloka chanting.
- Bhajan competition (solo) • Bhajan competition (group).
- Geeta-chanting • Storytelling.
- Quiz competition (group).

Prizes are distributed to all winners. Those with all-round capabilities are awarded Bal Ratna shields, and the Best Child of the Year gets a cash award, a certificate and a shield for being the Chinmaya Child of the Year.

Besides, the centre conducts camps during the summer holidays, typically for ten days. Last year there was a five days' camp for the children of the Maheshwari Samaj under the aegis of the Dakshina Kalkatta Maheshwari Sabha during the *Pooja* Holidays.

A one-day camp in August and an annual picnic in January are held every year. Parents join their children in these outings.

The centre hopes to achieve the target of 20 Balavihar classes each week by the year 2001.

YUVA KENDRA CLASSES

Over twenty-five youngsters on the rolls, the Kolkata Chyks have to attend two classes; both are held on the Mission premises. *Sevaks* R. S. Kalra and R. Nandkishore conduct the senior and junior classes respectively. The texts are *Art of Man Making* and *Art of Living*. Earlier they used texts like *I Love You* and *Self-Unfoldment*. The Chyks organize the *Saraswati Pooja*, the *Guru Poornima Pooja*, the *Shivaratri Pooja*, *Shraddhanjali* (on August 3), and *Navaratri*, besides others. Several competitions like the competitions in making impromptu speeches, quiz competitions and talks on *Art of Man Making* are held. A drama on Swamiji's life for the *Shraddhanjali* programme, a symposium on education, and a workshop for teachers and students deserve special mention. The Chyks undertook newspaper collection drives tp help the Chinmaya Diagnostic and Research Centre (CDRC) project at Bansberia with much-needed funds.

Since 1998 we have had the *Vanaprasth Sansthan* (a senior citizens' programme). Under this programme regular weekly classes are held besides one-day camps, workshops, etc. by and for senior citizens. A 4-day camp held in May 1999 was well received. A pilgrimage to Tarakeshwar in August the same year added to the momentum. A day camp in October again kept elderly people active. There are twenty-five Vanaprastha members at present. Regular classes are held on Saturdays on yoga. Spiritual discourses are also given.

Sanskrit *shibirs* are organized from time to time under the tutorage of Suryanarayan Nanda, a teacher from the Sanskrit Lokbhasha Prachar Samiti, Puri.

Ms.Anuradha Jairaj holds music classes on the Mission premises every Sunday. About twelve children attend these classes regularly.

Br. Sakshi Chaitanya (now Swami Madhavananda) conducts guided meditation classes at the Tapovan Dhyana Mandir on the Mission premises; he also gives discourses on the *Bhagavad Geeta*, the *Upanishads* and other spiritual texts. He teaches Vedic chanting and holds special classes for the youth. Previously Swamini Purnananda used to take these classes. Study groups are meeting in areas like Salt Lake and Garia. Occasionally classes are held in chanting the *Geeta* and in singing bhajans, as also conducting Sanskrit classes.

All age groups enjoy a getaway when a spiritual picnic combines learning with games. A garden house or a jute mill, a little away from the city, is often the venue. Young and old sing bhajans together. This strengthens the Mission's one-family spirit.

Every year the Chinmaya Mission participates in the annual Calcutta Book Fair, which is the biggest book fair in Asia. The Fair covers an area of over rwo lakh square feet and is typically held in January-February. A lot of publicity, apart from sale of books, is an obvious benefit to the Mission. Volunteers man the stalls; they form good teams to take up many other challenges. New talents are often spotted.

Area *yajnas* are conducted throughout the year in different areas and in different languages.

Every Saturday Swamiji's video talks are played on the Mission premises.

Four doctors, assisted by a compounder, provide homoeopathic treatment on the Mission's premises. Called the Chinmaya Chikitsalaya, the project benefited thousands of people. At the same time, it has given the right field to many service-minded members to perform *sadhana*.

Every Sunday in the morning a *Gayatri Mantra Homa* is conducted. A short talk follows the *homa*. Large numbers participate and chant the holy *Gayatri Mantra*. Offerings are made into the sacrificial fire.

CHINMAYA DIAGNOSTIC AND RESEARCH CENTRE (CDRC)

Located at Bansbaria, about seventy kilometres away from Kolkata, the CDRC caters to the patients of that area. These patients have otherwise to take the trouble of going all the way to the metropolis for diagnostic services. Sonography, ECG, X-Ray, and pathological services also are offered.

Swamiji's books are being translated into Bengali. *Self Unfoldment*, *Meditation and Life*, *Bhaja Govindam*, and *Atma Bodh* have already been translated and published. Work on a translation of *Vishnu Sahasranama* is in progress.

6. BANGALORE—THE GARDEN CITY

Bangalore with its vast open spaces and beautiful parks is beloved of all lovers of nature. As flowers bloom and spread their fragrance, the Chinmaya Movement blossomed in this capital city of the State of Karnataka in the year 1956 when Swami Chinmayananda conducted his first *jnana-yajna*. The city and the fourteen Mission centres in the State are vibrant with spiritual activity today.

Like Chennai and Mumbai, Bangalore too responded instantly and enthusiastically to Swamiji. In the first twenty-five *yajnas* conducted by him, it was observed that the highest attendance per day at the *yajna* was at Bangalore at 4,300 people (Source: Hail Renaissance Vol. I). Even in the 1960s, when the Movement was in its infancy, so to speak, there were people like the N.V.R. Reddys, Neelaveni amma, the Purushottams and others, who worked with much zeal. At the time when Mumbai was preparing to build the Sandeepany Sadhanalaya, Bangalore was wholly involved in erecting the Chinmaya Mission Hospital at Indiranagar. By the year 1970 Swamiji had conducted twelve *yajnas* in this city. Study groups had been formed and were stable. People had expressed their faith in the Movement that was committed to the spread of Vedantic knowledge.

The Balavihar movement was also strong. Bangalore had the distinction of conducting the First All India Balamahotsav. Balavihar classes were very popular; there were many devoted *sevikas* like

Ms. Usha Bai and Ms.Vallabham Kalyanasundaram, who supported, strengthened and nourished that grass roots level activity meant for children.

Full credit should be given to Brni. Sarada (later Swamini Saradapriyananda) for creating the Chinmaya Mission Hospital. She also ensured that discourses were held on the Vedanta in the initial years without any hitch.

Swami Chinmayananda did not conduct any *yajna* at Bangalore from 1970 to 1977. This was when he suffered a major setback to his health because of a heart attack. Swamiji slowed down the pace of his activity in the *yajna* field. On the contrary, a new set of committed workers emerged who strengthened the Mission and helped with its various projects.

It was Br. Haridas who started the Vijnan Mandir classes (regular classes on *Vedantic* subjects over a long period) in 1973. These classes brought a number of serious seekers of knowledge into the fold. The classes became so popular that they brought about a change in the life style of people. What is more they proved that Vedanta could be taught effectively.

The same year a few members started a social service project called the Chinmaya Child Welfare centre at HAL Marath Halli with the help of private donations. The Chinmaya Child Welfare centre is truly a welfare centre and works for the benefit of the children in the slums and the children of construction workers by providing free pre-primary education and free midday meals. The mobile clinic of the Chinmaya Mission Hospital visits the school once a week and gives regular health care to the children and more important provides free medicine.

In 1975, Br. Brahma Chaitanya came out of the Sandeepany Sadhanalya, Mumbai and was posted to Bangalore.

His *yajnas* and Vijnana Mandir classes made a great impact on the seekers of knowledge. His Kannada oratory on Vedantic subjects was very well received. People adored him for his simplicity and his knowledge of rituals and Vedanta. He motivated the workers and knit them into a homogenous team.

The Deenabandhu Devasthanam, as also the temple complex, came into existence in 1978, Soon it attained prominence and became the centre of all attraction. The image of Lord Krishna dancing on the hood of the serpent Kaliya charmed people. Images of Anjaneya and Ganapathi were installed in 1989, Swami Harinamananda of the Bangalore centre, was called to Mumbai in 1978 to be the Acharya of the course at Sandeepany Sadhanalaya there. Brni. Pavitra Chaitanya, another dynamic worker, took his place. She was instrumental in starting the Chinmaya Vidyalaya at St. Johns Road. Swami Chinmayananda inaugurated it in 1981.

Bangalore hosted national *Geeta jnana-yajnas* and Spiritual camps in 1973, 1981 and 1984. The *yajna* of 1973 was graced by the presence of Puttaparthi Satya Sai Baba and Swaimi Vishwesha Teertha of Pejawar.

In 1975, the Chinmaya Yuva Kendra (Chyk) became an important means of activity of the Chinmaya Mission. It had its headquarters at Bangalore. (From October 2000 onwards, it is at Chennai). Br. Haridas was the architect of the Chyk movement. He was the live wire behind all youth activities. He especially guided Chyk Study groups.

The Golden Jubilee of the Chinmaya Yuva Kendra was celebrated on a grand scale at Bangalore in October 2000. About 800 members of the Chyk movement from all over India participated. Senior swamis, swaminis, brahmacharis and brahmacharinis participated in the programme.

In 1984, Br. Brahma Chaitanya received *sannyasa deeksha* from Swami Chinmayananda at Sidhbari. He then received the name of Swami Brahmananda.

Under Swami Brahmananda's able guidance, Bangalore organized in 1987 a spectacular event to celebrate the seventieth birthday of Swami Chinmayananda. Swamiji was weighed against silver in accordance with the tradition of the function *Rajata Tulabhara*, with traditional rituals. The function was a resounding success. It became the forerunner for many such *tulabharas* including the *Suvarna Tulabhara* (weighing in gold) in Mumbai in 1991.

In 1989-90 a Vedanta course, the first of its kind, was conducted in Sandeepany Karnataka at Indiranagar. The Acharya for the course was Swami Brahmananda. He conducted the course in Kannada. Five students completed the course and took *deeksha* and four of them are now serving the Mission.

In October 1991 the First National Youth Convention was held at Bangalore with 500 delegates from all over India taking part in the convention.

In May 1993, Swami Brahmananda inaugurated the *Satsang Bhavan* on the first floor of the Malleshwaram centre.

The Chinmaya Vidyalaya, Koramangala started working in June 1995. The first phase of construction was completed in January 1997. The Vidyalaya is also a venue for activities like Balavihars, Study groups etc.

In May 1997, the Vijayanagar branch was inaugurated and is now active.

Many swamis, swaminis, brahmacharis and brahmacharinis have rendered useful and devoted service to the centres in the Karnataka State. Special mention must be made of Swamini Darshaniananda (formerly Brni. Archana Chaitanya) who made a lasting contribution to the growth of the Chinmaya Movement in Bangalore and particularly in Malleshwaram. She attained *samadhi* in 1996. Two other names calling for mention are Swami Chidananda and Swami Ishwarananda. These made an impact as Secretaries of the Mission and teachers of the Vedanta.

The unique feature about the growth of the Chinmaya Movement at Bangalore is that it always took a project-oriented approach. Project after project has been conceived and executed with precision. Funds have been generated from within, from the devotees, to support the projects. To mention the major projects in progress there are the Chinmaya Mission Hospital (a 200 bed hospital), the Chinmaya Child Welfare centre, the Chinmaya Institute of Nursing, the Chinmaya Institute of Higher Learning (CIHL), and the Chinmaya Institute of Management (CIM). There are two Chinmaya Vidyalayas, besides.

All the centres in the Karnataka State are active and vibrant. In terms of membership of the Mission, Karnataka stands second only to Mumbai City. A strong foundation of loyal and devoted members has contributed to the stability and growth of the Chinmaya Movement. Bangalore City is going through an impressive phase of economic and technological growth. According to Swami Brahmananda, the spectacular growth in technology-oriented projects in the State and at Bangalore, in particular, has only increased the appetite for spiritual knowledge, belying the popular belief that materialistic progress tends to slow down or retard spiritual growth.

7. REWA, MADHYA PRADESH

Madhya Pradesh, formerly known as Vindhya Pradesh, is a State formed by merging 36 former kingdoms in the region. Rewa was one among the 36 kingdoms and was the capital of the former Vindhya Pradesh.

Rewa is one of the oldest Chinmaya Mission centres. It was informally established in 1954 when Swami Chinmayananda was invited by his former classmate K.K. Sharma, Indian Administrative Service, the then Chief Secretary of the Government of Vindhya Pradesh. This was the 19th *yajna* of Swamiji. Although in the Hindi speaking belt, this *yajna* was successful mainly because of the captive English speaking audience organized by Sharma–Swamiji's observation was that there was hardly any one in Rewa who understood English. There was no Chinmaya Mission activity in Rewa for the next 23 years. In 1977, a local person, Rao Rana Bahadur Singh went to Lucknow to meet Swamiji. He requested Swamiji to visit Rewa again. Swamiji directed him to Br. Vivek Chaitanya (now Swami Tejomayananda) and asked him to request the brahmachari to do a *yajna* in Hindi.

In March 1978, Br. Vivek Chaitanya conducted a *jnana-yajna* in Hindi at Rewa, which was the Mission's first *yajna* in Hindi. He visited Rewa again in the subsequent three years and conducted *yajnas* twice a year. The centre was officially formed in October 1978.

A devotee by the name of Bhagvati Singh donated some land to the Mission. The Mission could not utilize this land because the Government had acquired the land for an industrial complex. The authorities were prepared to allot any other land in lieu of the acquired plot or to pay a compensation. The search for an alternative site continued. In the meanwhile, another devotee Ran

Bahadur Singh (a name almost identical to Rao Rana Bahadur Singh, a devotee-cum-*sevak*) donated 2 acres of land on which, today, the Vanaprastha Chinmaya Ashram stands. The first Chinmaya Seva Trust was formed in Rewa in September 1982, to be followed by a number of such Trusts around the country. The Mission purchased an additional acre of land from the same donor. Swamiji gave funds to the centre to build a dispensary cum office cum library block in the new building. This was completed and Swamiji came in April 1983 to inaugurate the building. On this occasion he laid the foundation stone for the Shri Raghunathji Temple. It was at this time that Swamiji outlined his concept of *Pitamaha Sadan*–a home for the aged. He said, "Soon enough there shall be a dire need to provide a clean, quiet place for elders. The families shall no longer be of a joint nature. With the children gone away, the elders shall have lost all support of love and care. Such people will be welcome here." He wanted to provide all modern amenities of living in a clean and serene place where the elders would also be in touch with spiritual knowledge. Thus was born the institution of Pitamaha Sadans in the Chinmaya Mission.

The Raghunathji temple was ready in 1984 and Swamiji installed the idols of Ram, Sita and Laxman. The same sculptor who made the idols for Sidhbari, Kashinath of Shimoga, made these idols. Swamiji was sending funds from all over the world for more construction work to be carried out in Rewa. The additional construction included a dormitory, a dining hall, servants' room, water tank, garage etc.

During Swamiji's visit to Rewa in 1986, he was taken to an island on a lake for a question and answer session with devotees. He liked the scenic spot and asked the local people to look for land in the island, which he wanted to convert into a Retreat. A piece of land was identified and they went to the Maharaja of Rewa to whom it belonged to negotiate the purchase. The Maharaja was already the chairman of Chinmaya Seva Trust. He donated the 1.27 acres to the Trust and it was registered in November 1988. Swamiji proposed that the Retreat be named *Chinmaya Uparati*. The Maharaja laid the foundation stone in June 1992. Swamiji had planned to spend a few days in the Retreat in 1994 but unfortunately he attained *samadhi* in 1993. Swamini Vimalananda spent some time in *mauna* on two occasions at this Retreat. Thus the Rewa centre has a temple, a *Pitamah Sadan*, and an *Uparati*. The activities of the centre have continued to grow and expand. Constant efforts are being made through training, discourses etc. to enhance the quality of moral life of the society. One such camp was the Teachers Moral Education Orientation Camp that brought glowing tributes from the participants. Four such camps were held. Another camp was organized to bring home the logic of morality in the discharge of official duties by the Patwari (the lowest government official in the Revenue department), hoping that such training would improve the ethics of government servants. This camp was a surprising success but had to be discontinued for some sensitive reasons.

In September 1995 a free dispensary was started at the Ashram. A Non-Resident Indian from Birmingham, U.K, sponsors its expenses. A doctor visits the Ashram every day, monitors the health of the elders and then attends to the ailing villagers who come to the dispensary. He gives them free medicines and advice. Dr. Sajjan Singh, the Managing Trustee, has enhanced the services given by the centre by organizing a polio vaccine camp and arranging an eye camp jointly with the Red Cross. In 1997, Rewa and the adjoining areas experienced a cloudburst. Floodwaters entered the Rewa town and inundated 125 villages–the mission centre rose to the occasion and organized rescue work in the village of Silapri, allotted to the Mission by the Collector of Rewa. The centre arranged for clean drinking water, housed the homeless for 15 days in a community hall, provided them with food and rendered free medical service. Swami Tejomayananda made an appeal for help in the Tapovan Prasad, which brought funds and relief in material form from all over the country. The centre constructed a large tin shed in the village to take care of future emergencies. A temple of Hanumanji in that site has been renovated and consecrated.

The *Pitamaha Sadan* has eleven elders in permanent residence. Extra facilities like a post office in the campus, a library, and easy communication through intercoms in some of the *kutias* (residences) are some of the special features of the Ashram. The centre has conducted several *Geeta jnana-yajnas* through the ordained workers of the Chinmaya Mission and also through the services of Rana Bahadur Singh, a devotee-cum-*sevak* of the centre. Other important programmes held were mouna *sadhana* camps by Swami Shankarananda, Chinmaya Vision Programmes/ seminars, participation at national level workshops on Welfare awareness and the productive utilization of the aged component of human population etc. The contribution made by Dr. Sajjan Singh for the growth of the Chinmaya Mission centre in Rewa and for the care of the aged, is outstanding. This centre also helped in the setting up of the neighbouring centres at Satna, Jabalpur, Churhat, and Semaria. Presently there are 2 patron members, 119 Life members and two annual members.

8. HYDERABAD

It was sheer Providence that brought Swamiji to Hyderabad even before he reached Pune where he was to conduct his first *Geeta jnana-yajna* in December 1951. His *deeksha* guru Swami Shivananda of Rishikesh gave him a letter of introduction to C. Gopala Reddy of Hyderabad. Swamiji was on his way to Pune for his *yajna* but stopped at Hyderabad to meet Mr. Reddy.

Recalling the visit of the Master to the city, Lakshmi Reddy, a devotee of Swamiji and daughter of Gopala Reddy, who often rendered the chanting of the *Geeta* at Swamiji's *yajnas*, writes: "But why Hyderabad? This erstwhile Deccan kingdom was under the sway of the Muslim kings for almost seven to eight centuries. The Razakar movement, the communist upheaval after 1947 and its disturbances, turmoils, gave Hyderabad nightmares. In 1949, Hyderabad had the police action and the king was deposed. The educated masses were given another kind of an experiment–the Congress *mantra* of secularism and socialism. Only the Hindus adhered to this programme. The other religious groups ignored this call; they protected, practiced, and propagated their culture vehemently."

The city was going through a period of anguish and fear. At that opportune moment, Swamiji arrived in Hyderabad. Reddy's joy knew no bounds for here was this young statuesque Swami, his Guru's representative at his door. Swamiji himself suggested to the family that he would conduct a *satsang*. This was a new experience for the Hindus of Hyderabad who knew ritualistic *poojas* etc., but had imbibed, over the years, a Muslim-Urdu culture. They were awe-struck to see this ochre-robed young Swami with that mystic smile and half closed eyes chanting OM. God's presence was in the hall and the audience was transported into an unknown world of divinity. He gave a talk on *bhakti* and of the deep love of Shri Krishna and Sudhama. Thus started the divine bond between Swami Chinmayananda and the spiritual seekers of Hyderabad.

SOME DETAILS OF THE CENTRE

The Hyderabad centre was established in 1957, soon after the *yajna* (Twenty-fifth *yajna* of Swamiji) was concluded. Swamiji directed the centre to start a monthly magazine to chronicle the Chinmaya activities in the centres all over the country. Thus was born the second publication of the Mission, *Usha*. This magazine continued till 1968 when it merged with *Tapovan Prasad*.

At Kundan Bagh, Begumpet, Hyderabad, the Mission has its own centre and place for activities. Chinmaya Dhyana Nilayam, a temple-cum-meditation hall was consecrated by Swami Tejomayananda in February 1999. The presiding deity is Lord Parameswara. The *poojas* and rituals are observed meticulously. Meditation classes and Vedic Chanting classes are held. Several *yajnas* are conducted every year. There are over twenty Balavihar classes now in operation in the twin cities of Hyderabad and Secunderabad. Yuva Kendra meets regularly every Sunday. The Acharya, Swami Chidatmananda, takes many classes for the youth at regular intervals. A monthly magazine *Chinmaya Jyothi* acts as a news bulletin of all the local programmes of the Mission.

A Chinmaya Vidyalaya here, inaugurated by Swami Chinmayananda in 1993, is affiliated to CBSE. It sent out the first batch of students in March 1999. An earlier institution, Chinmaya High School on Chinmaya Marg in Malkajgiri, Secunderabad, has been active since 1968. This is run by a group of Swamiji's devotees in Malkajgiri.

Major Hindu Festivals, like Diwali, are celebrated at the centre regularly. Sports and picnic days are regularly arranged for the students of Chinmaya Vidyalaya. Annual programmes are a well-mixed choice. The Acharya has conducted spiritual retreats several times. His talks are covered on certain local and national TV channels.

Apart from regular grass root level activities like Balavihar, CHYK, and Study groups, the centre organizes Management talks to Government and Police department officials, on ethics and morals. Seva projects in operation are slum uplift and education programmes, free medical camps, and distribution of clothes, grains, and study material to the poor. Such benefits are given to the poor in the nearby Telangana area, which even today is an economically backward area. The centre is also planning to start a free Medicare centre.

In the year 1967, recording of Swamiji's talks was done at four centres–Mumbai, Chennai, Delhi and Hyderabad–and the longest recording was in Hyderabad. *Bhaja Govindam* was recorded in Mumbai on gramophone records. Chennai and Delhi recorded his one-day talks and at Hyderabad, All India Radio (AIR) recorded 52 talks. Every Tuesday before the English News, these talks on *Bhagavad Geeta* were aired for 52 weeks i.e. for one whole year. These talks were published later as a book, *The Art of Man-Making*.

Ms. Lakshmi Reddy had the good fortune of accompanying Swamiji on his tours in India and abroad. She had talent for singing, and offered beautiful chanting of the *Geeta* verses at many *jnana yajnas*.

Hyderabad can boast of a band of sincere workers who were fully with Swamiji in the early years, on his mission to revitalize Hinduism. Swamiji used to say, "*Yajna* is a co-operative endeavour", and thus motivate people to give their best in all the activities of the Chinmaya Mission. A mention may also be made of Janardan Rao, a civil engineer and an overseer in the Andhra Government, whose contributions to the building of Sandeepany Sadhanalaya in Mumbai, Sandeepany (Himalayas) in Sidhbari and Chinmaya Vidyalaya in Delhi are notable. He took two years of leave from his Government service and served the Mission.

9. O MUMBAI !

The history of the Mumbai centre has a somewhat hazy beginning. The Chinmaya Movement did not reach Mumbai till about 1957. Ms Sheila Dewan, a resident of South Mumbai, was in Delhi in 1956 to visit some relatives. At that time Swami Chinmayananda's twenty-fourth *jnana-yajna* was going on at the Modern School, New Delhi. Ms Dewan met Swamiji and requested him to visit Mumbai. In his characteristic manner Swamiji said, "Call me! Get a hall ! Do publicity! Contact Ms Sushila Mudaliar at Pune. She will help you." Swamiji came to Mumbai finally in May 1957 to give a series of talks at the K.C. College there.

This series of talks set off the Chinmaya Movement at Mumbai. The thirty-fifth *Jnana-yajna* was held at Mumbai from December 1, 1957 to December 22, 1957. Swamiji stayed with the Dewans; Ms. Sheila Dewan in fact organized the *yajna*. The evening talks were on the *Kenopanishad*; the morning *satsangs* were held at the residence of another devotee. At the end of the *yajna* a special picnic to Alandi was arranged; many devotees accompanied Swamiji on this picnic. The Movement was slowly picking up. Swamiji, again, consented to hold his fiftieth *jnana-yajna* at Mumbai, from December 25, 1958 to January 17, 1959. It took Mumbai by storm. This time Jaimani Dewan, husband of Ms. Sheila Dewan, served as the Secretary of the *yajna*-committee.

The Dewans were special to Swamiji. He kept in touch with them till the end–down to 1992, when he left for Sidhbari. In 1984 Swamiji gave *mantra deeksha* to Ms. Dewan, as we learn from Dr. Madhuri Sheth, who interviewed Ms. Dewan recently.

The fifty-fifth *yajna* (May 1959) and the seventy-fifth *yajna* (December 1960) were arranged at Matunga, Mumbai. Swamiji's activities at Mumbai were all organized by him directly: there was no need for a separate Mission centre to implement his plans and programmes. Perhaps that was why, in the initial years, the history of the Movement was entwined with the history of the Master. It was only when the organization assumed larger proportions, that the Mumbai centre came into being. Until then the Chinmaya Mission, Mumbai, was only an association of people who were dedicated and sincere followers of Swamiji. The Bombay Chinmaya Mission Trust (BCMT) came much later. It was registered as recently as 1989.

All activities of the Mission at Mumbai came under the umbrella of this trust once it came into being. Some enthusiastic devotees had earlier, in 1986, registered another trust, called the Chinmaya Seva Trust (CST), on their own initiative, in order to promote *seva* activities. In 1992 Swamiji directed all zones/centres to name all trusts uniformly as the Chinmaya Seva Trust. The chief executive of the CCMT advised that it would be easier to de-register the BCMT and to organize all activity under the auspices of the CST alone.

Long before the formation of the trust the Mission office had started functioning from 9 Wallace Street, Fort, Mumbai–the office premises of Vissanji brothers, Hamirbhai and Nalinbhai. In May 1978 a devotee leased his vacant office premises at Central Mumbai to the Mission so the office functioned from there. However, as the premises were not very large, the monthly meetings of the Executive Committee were held at the office of Ms Nirmal Gupta. In the mid 1980s Ms Kamla Chanrai donated the premises of the Kala Mandir to the Mission. This was not easily accessible. So it was sold with a view to buying a place at a more convenient location. It was only in 1991 that the new office at Panchsheel, Churchgate, was acquired. The inauguration took place on November 30, 1991. Besides acting as the office of the Mission it serves as the place of residence for the *brahmachari* assigned to Mumbai. This facilitates the taking up of activity such as *satsangs*, *pravachans*, Balavihars etc. on the Mission premises and in nearby areas.

BALAVIHARS

The first Balavihar was started in 1965 at the Reserve Bank of India Quarters, with Uncle Mani (Ananthanarayanan) as *sevak*. At meeting of all the *sevaks/sevikas* of the city in 1968, Mumbai was divided into eight sectors, and Ms. Nirmala Chellam was made the Balavihar-in-Charge. In December 1968, a *mahotsava* of Balavihars was held for children from all over Mumbai. Two hundred children attended. The Mission held a second *mahotsava* in 1969. That year, during the 205th *yajna* of Swamiji, there were sixty-three Balavihars, functioning with fifty-eight *sevaks/sevikas*; the number of children attending them was 2205. Sixty children went through the streets of Matunga doing *nagara sankeertan*. As many as seven hundred children took part in 1980, when a children's fair was conducted at Sandeepany Sadhanalaya, Mumbai, to boost the circulation of a magazine that was being published to publicize the activities of the Balavihars.

At present, there are about eighty-six Balavihars in sevemteen areas of Mumbai. Their activities includes orientation camps,

Geeta-chanting competitions, summer and winter camps, area-wise annual programmes, etc.

The Balavihar at Chembur was started in June 1966 with twenty children. They met on a Sunday afternoon at 2 o'clock. Most of them were children of the members of the Study groups. Classes were held initially at the residence of one Mr. Gupta on 14th Road. After some time members found it convenient to host classes by rotation in their houses. Ms. Nirmala Chellam (now serving at Chinmaya Gardens, Coimbatore) was the soul of the movement for over fifteen years. She was employed in a multinational company. She dedicated her week-ends completely to the children, running between one class and another, conducting a few, and observing others conducted by her own senior Balavihar students. Earlier, she had keenly attended, and observed, the Balavihars conducted by Uncle Mani for a period of two to three months.

Once in 1967 there was a *Vishnu sahasranama archana*. This was followed by a picnic to Fanaswadi. This in its turn led to regular annual picnics to the Powai Ashram. All this gave the children the feeling that their Balavihar was a second large home for them. Those who had attended a Balavihar for a few years were called upon to conduct Balavihars themselves. This again caused senior kids to remain deeply attached to the Mission even in their tumultuous teens!

Ms. Susheela Acharya selected a number of children with a good voice and opened a music class for them in 1968. This soon turned into a weekly bhajan class, equipping the prospective *sevaks* with what we might well call a bhajan bank.

Chembur alone had over five hundred children in its Balavihar by 1976. The completion of a decade was celebrated in January 1976. Swami Chinmayananda and Swami Dayananda sat right in the midst of hundreds of children to their utter joy and blessed the occasion. Ms. Pramodini Rao, who is now an ace singer in the Mission, recalls that great day. She remembers vividly how the children had gone from door to door and raised funds for the function!

Children acquired a number of qualities such as the ability to concentrate, outspokenness, eloquence, and discipline in the Balavihars. They cultivated these qualities. They had no television to distract them. Nor did they attend tuitions and other extra-curricular classes. Many children, being meritorious, later became doctors, engineers and other successful professionals. Every child in fact benefitted overall from attending a Balavihar. This fact was proved again and again. When a number of parents were asked why they were so keen on sending their children to a Balavihar, they explained how they themselves had benefited when they attended, and that it was the best part of their childhood.

CHINMAYA YUVA KENDRA (CHYK)

When the Balavihar children grew up and went to college, Uncle Mani started a "Teenager's Class" for them. In 1975 Br. Haridas started what he called the Chinmaya Youth Forum at Bangalore. Later the name was changed to Chinmaya Yuva Kendra (Chyk). During the fifth National *yajna* in 1976, Br. Haridas came to Mumbai to start Chyk activities there. The announcement was in fact made during the *yajna*. Those who showed interest in joining Chyk were invited to the inaugural meeting, which was held at the Sydenham College auditorium in May 1976. Within a month's time Chyk classes came up at five different places in Mumbai. The text taken up for study was *A Manual of Self-Unfoldment*. The second book prescribed was *Art of Man-Making*.

In 1977 the first annual Chyk programme was held at the Chhabildas High School, Dadar. The second annual programme, "*Bhakti Pravah*" was held in December 1978. The second All-India Chyk Camp came off at the Sandeepany Sadhanalaya from October 7 to 12, 1979.

In 1980, the Chyks organized a music concert by Dr. M.S. Subbalakshmi at the Shanmukhananda Hall. Although there was power failure, the celebrity continued with her recital as if nothing had happened. Without a microphone and in the light of a *diya* on stage she held the listeners spellbound. Even those seated in the last row of a 3000-seat auditorium heard her in hushed silence!

In 1981, Chyks presented a novel programme, called the "soul song nite." It was an audio-visual presentation of bhajans. They have so far held about ten such nights. After one such programme organized on the occasion of his seventieth birthday, Swamiji said: "If one gets an evening like this even after seventy years, it is still worth the waiting".

Once Swamiji saw an audiovisual presentation of Samarth Ramdas by the Chyks at Pune. He was so impressed that he asked the Chyks in Mumbai to work on a *son et lumie're* (night time entertainment where history is enacted with special lighting and sound effects) show based on the life of Shivaji. In the course of their preparation, the Chyks visited various forts of Shivaji like Lohgadh and Rajagarh under the guidance of G.N. Dandekar, an expert on Shivaji's forts. The Chyks later approached B. N. Purandare to write a script for them. He was at the time writing a script for a similar presentation himself. Later he staged it on a mammoth scale under the title "*Jaantaa Raajaa*", under the sponsorship of the Government of Maharashtra. However, the Chyks eventually, abandoned the idea of staging it themselves in view of the exorbitant costs entailed.

Before the first international *yajna* of December 1983, the Chyks organized a torch march from the Ganapati Temple in Rasta Peth, Pune, to the campus of the Bharatiya Vidya Bhavan at Andheri. Swamiji joined the torch march on the outskirts of Mumbai, accompanied by a cavalcade of cars.

In 1989 the Chyks held an elocution competition for college students. They called it "Podium". It soon became an annual feature. Later it was improved upon to include instrumental music and dramatics, the name being changed to "*Raag* Podium."

The Mumbai Chyks have on many an occasion won the Best Chyk Centre award. The year 2000 saw the Chyks celebrating their silver jubilee at Bangalore. The Mumbai Chyks made a significant contribution by compiling a national cultural quiz on the *Art of Man-Making* based on the *Geeta* for the youth of the country. In this they had the guidance of Swami Chidananda, Acharya, Sandeepany Sadhanalaya, Mumbai.

STUDY GROUPS

The Study group movement, the backbone of the Chinmaya Mission, struck root at Mumbai in the year 1962. As is well known, the idea of such a movement was in line with Swamiji's dream of a cadre of white-collared missionary workers, besides monks and brahmacharis.

In the initial stages five or six groups were formed in different areas. This number went up in course of time as the movement won increasing support from those who attended Swamiji's *jnana-yajnas*. At present there are over a hundred Study groups. From time to time the Mission organizes orientation camps for *sevaks* of the Study groups at the Powai Ashram to groom new *sevaks*. Any member who has completed the study of the first three books of the graded course viz *Kindle Life*, *Bhaja Govindam* and *Atma Bodha*—is eligible to be a *sevak*.

In the early 1960s Swamiji used to take *Vivekachoodamani* classes for brahmacharis and for members of the Study groups whenever he happened to stop over at Mumbai for a few days. He would hold an examination on the previous session first and embark upon continuing the next session thereafter. He would evaluate all the papers himself and then return them to the participants. Three hundred participants sat for the examination held in June 1964.

For administrative reasons Mumbai was divided in 1968 into several sectors. Today the city has seventeen areas, each area having a *sevak* to take care of the activities of the area.

During Swamiji's convalescence after his heart attack in 1970, there were daily *satsang* programmes at "Usha Kiran" on Carmichael Road. Swamiji had given twenty-five topics, both religious and secular, and asked members of Study groups to speak on one subject each for five minutes.

Swamiji declared 1980-90 as the Missionary Decade. In 1978. area *yajnas* by brahmacharis were started in different places. He also directed all brahmacharis to hold *yajnas* in regional languages. Br. Vivek Chaitanya (now Swami Tejomayananda) conducted the first area *yajna* in Hindi at Tardeo in September 1978. Br. Prem Chaitanya (now Swami Tadrupananda, no longer with the Mission) did it in Gujarati; and Swami Purushottamanda in Marathi. Uncle Mani began his Ramayana *yajnas* in January 1981.

In his New Year message Swamiji declared 1982 as the Year of Contact. All members of the Mission, including members of Study groups and Chyks, were asked personally to contact people and hand out literature regarding the Chinmaya Mission activities.

Swamiji said that we had only imbibed knowledge so far. The time had now come to share it with others. A *pracharak* training course was organized at Sandeepany under the guidance of the Acharya, Br. Swaroop Chaitanya, for *grihasthas* who were then to disseminate that knowledge. This camp ran for six weeks in the last quarter of 1981.

In 1988, Swami Tejomayananda conducted the first *Bhagawat Saptah* in the open-air auditorium at Sandeepany, which was a grand success. On popular demand, he conducted another *Saptah* at the Birla Kreeda Kendra.

In 1989 Swami Tapovan Maharaj's birth centenary was celebrated by holding an essay competition on *Ishwar Darshan*.

Members of the Mission participated in the *Swarna Tulabhara* of Swamiji in the year 1991.

In 1994, Swami Tejomayananda announced a *mahayajna* to be held in December that year covering all eighteen chapters of the *Geeta* in eighteen days. He said that it would be a homage to his guru. There was a *Bhajan Sandhya* earlier at Hinduja auditorium, Ms. Pramodini Rao and M.N.C. Saigal gripped the audience with their singing of devotional songs. Another programme was planned at this time was "*Ghar Ghar mein Geeta*" from June to December 1994. This programme was quite popular. It is even today a regular feature of the activities of the Mission in Mumbai. The host gets twenty to sixty people together and a senior member of a Study group gives a talk on the *Geeta*. This is followed by a question-answer session. Occasionally a brahmachari or swami is invited to speak.

The first issue of *Chinmaya Sandesh*, the monthly newsletter, was published in February 1972; and the first editor was the late G.H. Muni. *Sandesh* underwent a change in course of time: from being a mere calendar of events, it became first a newsletter and then a monthly magazine in order to cater to the tastes of the readers. Vipul Khanna served as editor from 1987 to 1994; he handed over the position to Ms. Sheela Chitnis in 1994. Maheshchandra Rao is the present editor, from February 2000 onwards. Circulation has now reached three thousand. The May and August issues every year are special in as much as they highlight the *Jayanti* and *Samadhi* of Swamiji.

CHINMAYA AROGYA SEVA

Some doctor devotees took up the Arogya Seva Project in October 1997: they looked upon it as their special way of *sadhana*. To start with, doctors and other members of the Mission went round and visited the hutments in the vicinity of the Ashram. They found that there was no medical help available in the colony at Filter Pada. When a municipal school offered to let them use its premises on Sundays, the doctors took the next step: they collected medical samples and also got pharmaceutical companies to donate some medicines. These doctors included physicians, gynecologists, surgeons, pediatricians, cardiologists, ENT specialists, ophthalmologists, and dentists. They saw hundreds of patients. They also carried out routine blood examination. Swami Tejomayananda visited one of the monthly camps. Soon, however, the doctors found, much to their disappointment, that the response of the patients dwindled as the general practitioners in the area in the vicinity refused to see the patients in between camps. Eventually, in view of this kind of attitude on the part of the medical practitioners, it was decided to give up the project–at least for some time.

Subsequently these doctors offered their services to needy people in distant places like Bordi, as also in tribal areas.

VIJNANA MANDIR

Under the Vijnana Mandir scheme a well-trained brahmachari gave weekly discourses on texts such as the *Geeta*, the *Upanishads*, etc. The idea in fact arose in 1978. The classes were launched in three venues, viz. Churchgate, Chembur, and Andheri. A nominal fee was charged for attending the classes. This fetched the Mission a monthly income of Rs. 5,000 (Rupees five thousand only). A convocation ceremony was also held, and Swamiji gave away certificates to all meritorious students. A flat in Santa Cruz was bought for the brahmachari to live in. The project ran quite successfully for four years. It was abandoned in 1982, when Br. Vishuddha Chaitanya, who was in charge, left the Mission.

RESTRUCTURING

Mumbai centre has been restructured from time to time. The area allotted to the centre has been divided into convenient blocks. As of the year 2000 there are 17 areas. The group activities in these areas are as follows: Balavihars–86; CHYKs–22; Study group–106. The membership at the Centre is as follows: Corpus Members–124; Patrons–103; Life members–2761; Associate members–298 and others–68.

CHRONOLOGICAL LIST OF ACTIVITIES AT THE CHINMAYA MISSION, MUMBAI

1969: Study group activity in full swing Brni. Sarada (later Swamini Saradapriyananda) was much impressed. She said to K. B. Shroff: "Like a factory, mass production of Study groups!"

1970: Seventy members of the Study groups took up the *akhandaparayan* of the *Geeta* as Swamiji suffered a heart attack. Later, while convalescing, Swamiji made Study group members speak on spiritual topics. He inaugurated a Kala Mandir on Warden Road on September 16, to encourage Balavihar children to learn and specialize in various arts such as drawing, painting, light music, folk dance, and play acting.

1972: As many as 150 people attended the *Sadhana* Camp held at Lonavala under the guidance of Swami Dayananda. First national *yajna* was held in South Mumbai.

1974: A public reception was given to Swamiji at Sunderbai Hall in January, upon his return from a global tour.

1976: Fifth national *yajna*. Evening talks by Swami Dayananda at Cross Maidan. Morning discourses by him at the Ashram.

1978: *Geeta Maha-yajna*, eighteen chapters in eighteen days by Swami Dayananda. Br. Vivek Chaitanya conducted first area *yajna*. A bust of Swami Tapovan Maharaj was unveiled in the Ashram on March 27.

1979: B.M. Kamdar, a trustee of the CCMT and a stalwart of the Chinmaya Mission, passed away in February. The 300th *Yajna* by Swamiji was held in November.

1980: Swamiji declared the new decade "The Missionary Decade". In December, Swamiji handed over all CCMT work in India to Swami Dayananda, who came from Sandeepany (West) once every four months till the course was completed.

1981: Uncle Mani joined the CCMT for organization and development. Swami Harinamananda, Acharya of Sandeepany, Mumbai, resigned. Ram Batra, Secretary of the Chinmaya Mission, passed away in August. He was a sincere and ardent worker. The *Ashtottara-shata-namavali* of Swamiji, compiled by Br. Vivek Chaitanya and others, was published.

1982: Swamiji declared it the year of contact in his New Year message. He asked each member to contact people and spread the message. 323rd *jnana-yajna* was held.

1983: First International *yajna* was held.

1986: The CST was formed.

1987: A Chyk Soul Song Nite was held at Shanmukhananda Hall in February to celebrate Swamiji's seventieth birthday. Swami Tejomayananda gave discourses upon the entire *Tulsi Ramayan* at Mulund.

1988: Swami Tejomayananda did the first *Bhagawat Saptah* at the Powai Ashram in April. Chyks did a second *Saptah* in *Sapta Swara* based on Chapter Sixteen of the *Geeta.* Following the great response that came forth to his first *Bhagawat Saptah*, Swami Tejomayananda conducted a second one at the Birla Kreeda Kendra in August.

1989: Swami Purushottamananda started the *Shravansadhana* series—monthly talks in Marathi on one chapter of the Gita every month. A Balavihar summer camp was organized by the Chyk in April. This became an annual feature. The Mulund Chinmaya Mission became an independent body.

1990: A balavihar summer camp, "Man to Superman", was held at Powai in May. An all Maharashtra Chyk Cam-tra-con (camp-training-conference) was held.

1991: Swamiji's last *yajna* in Mumbai, the 500th *jnana-yajna*, was held in October. Two shows of the all India Chyk Soul Song Nite were held at Mulund and Vile Parle, Chyks from all over the country participated in them. "Chant *Geeta*, Land Washington" competition's finals were held at the Ashram. Swamiji was weighed in gold. This Swarna Tulabhara was held in December at Hotel Leela Kempinski.

1992: National Balavihar Sevaks' Orientation Camp was held at Sandeepany. The Acharya was Swami Brahmananda; and the chief instructor Ms. Darshana Nanavaty (from Houston). Mumbai volunteers worked for this programme (and most other programmes) at the Ashram. "*Udaan*", a Balavihar summer camp, was held.

1993: Mumbai joined devotees all over the world in mourning Swamiji's *maha-samadhi*.

1994: The Balavihar summer camp, "Soul to Soul", was held in June. "*Ghar Ghar mein Geeta*" was launched in June. A winter camp was also held in November at Khandala, "We Want Fun". Swami Tejomayananda conducted the *maha-yajna* for eighteen days in December.

1995: Poojya Swami Chidanandaji of the Divine Life Society Rishikesh unveiled Swamiji's statue at Powai in February. Devotees celebrated the silver jubilee of the Sri Jagadeeshwara Temple. The National Balavihar Camp, "LOVE IS" was held at Khandala.

1996: Swami Swaroopananda did a *yajna* on a Sikh text–*Japji Saheb*. The theme of the Balavihar held camp held in the year was 'Loving Life Is Living Life." Devotees observed Swami Purushottamananda's *shastyabdhi–poorti* (completion of sixty years of life). A doctors' meet titled "Live Life Lightly", was well received.

1997: Swami Tejomayananda conducted a *yajna* in March. "Laugh It Away" was the theme of the Balavihar camp held in May at Khandala. Swami Tejomayananda did a youth camp at Powai in June. A second (winter) Balvihar camp was held in November on the theme, "Take It Easy." A music programme was presented; it was titled "*Chandrabhagechya Teeravarti*", being based on the lives of saints of Maharashtra.

1998: The Chinmaya Family Day was organized at the Ashram. It was a full day's programme, with suitable activities designed for children, youth, and adults. A spiritual picnic to Pune and a visit to the Ganapati Mandir "where it all began" and Alandi came off in February. A Balavihar camp on the theme "Welcome To Life," was held in April. Lectures in the Chinmaya Memorial Lecture series were held between May 6 and 8. There was a Chyk Camp in June, led by Swami Swaroopananda, titled "Ride The Roller Coaster Of Life." Ms. Jaya Bacchan inaugurated Swami Tejomayananda's *Geeta yajna* in Borivali in October.

1999: The Sevaks' Training and Enrichment Programme (STEP) for Chyks was launched. Swami Tejomayananda gave talks on "Ram Mahima" at Khar in March. A *Sevaks*' orientation camp was held at the Ashram in April-May for three days. A Balavihar camp by Swami Tejomayananda, titled, "Krishna My Friend" came off at the Ashram. Swami Brahmananda delivered the Chinmaya Memorial Lectures in May, on Guru *Geeta* for three evenings. Swami Tejomayananda gave a *Geeta jnana-yajna* at Chembur in June. Swami Chidananda spoke on meditation at Sydenham College for three evenings in June. Again, Swami Chidananda, Swami Swaroopananda. and Br. Someshwar Chaitanya (now Swami Ishwarananda) spoke on "Master the Mind through Meditation" at Jai Hind College in July Swami Swaroopananda conducted a youth camp at the Ashram on the theme "Win the World with Love". Swami Tejomayananda did a *yajna* on the *Geeta*, titled "Serve and Deserve". Smt. Sarla Birla inaugurated the discourse series.

2000: Swami Brahmananda conducted a *yajna* in February at the Powai Ashram. He also gave seven morning discourses in Vile Parle in August for seven days. On December 31, a Torch March was organized to herald the dawn of the Golden Jubilee year. Swami Chidananda and Swamini Premananda led the march. It started from Powai Lake and proceeded to Sandeepany Sadhanalaya. This was followed by a discourse by Swami Chidananda.

Thus, the Chinmaya Movement in 50 years has established 200 centres in India. Will the Movement maintain this pace or will it be accelerated in the years to come? In this context, we quote Swami Brahmananda, Regional Head of Karnataka who gave his view in a recent interview:

> Opening a new Mission centre cannot be compared with opening a new branch in a business plan in the commercial world. For opening a spiritual centre, the key ingredients are the interest of the local people in the pursuit of spiritual studies and identification of a dedicated and sincere worker or workers to establish the centre. The *sevaks* have to be committed to the cause. For establishing a centre one begins with a visit to the place to make an on-the-spot assessment of the needs. This may require a minimum of three visits to the place. To assess the potential of a centre one may conduct a *yajna* in that area. If the potential appears to be good, one must identify a person who is sincere and dedicated. He would be the catalytic agent who would generate interest at the grass root level for Study groups, Yuva Kendra activities, Balavihar classes, etc. Ideally he would be an energetic person with ability to work for a minimum of twenty years in the field.

Brahmacharis and brahmacharinis in the field are actively engaged in the work of creating awareness for spiritual studies. The Regional Heads of the various States are motivating the field level staff. With such positive signals, the Chinmaya Movement is bound to intensify its growth and strength.

The Indian Network

DISTRIBUTION OF CHINMAYA MISSION CENTRES STATEWISE

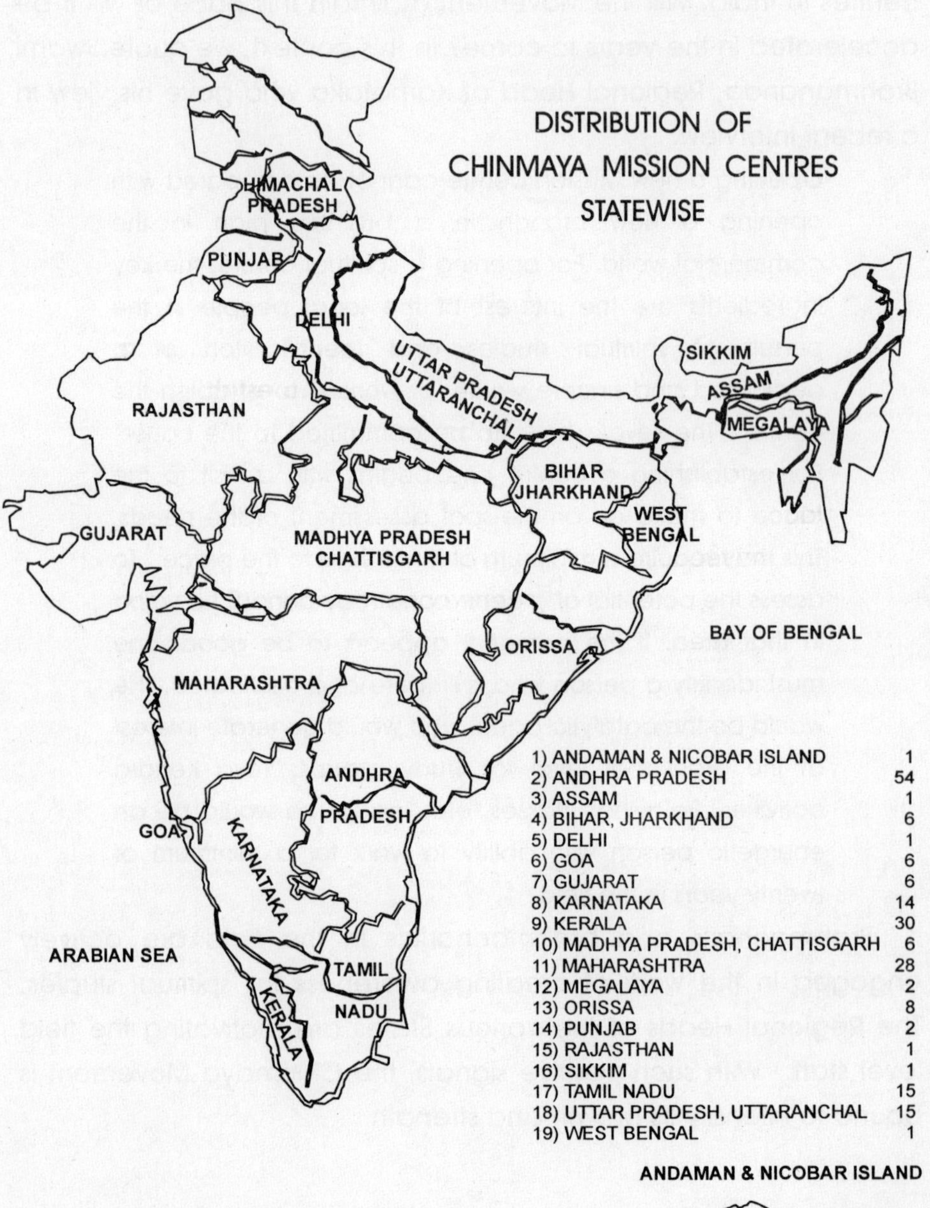

1) ANDAMAN & NICOBAR ISLAND	1
2) ANDHRA PRADESH	54
3) ASSAM	1
4) BIHAR, JHARKHAND	6
5) DELHI	1
6) GOA	6
7) GUJARAT	6
8) KARNATAKA	14
9) KERALA	30
10) MADHYA PRADESH, CHATTISGARH	6
11) MAHARASHTRA	28
12) MEGALAYA	2
13) ORISSA	8
14) PUNJAB	2
15) RAJASTHAN	1
16) SIKKIM	1
17) TAMIL NADU	15
18) UTTAR PRADESH, UTTARANCHAL	15
19) WEST BENGAL	1

ANDAMAN & NICOBAR ISLAND

Mumbai : Swamiji at the 500th and 452nd *yajnas*

Mumbai : Mahayajna by Swami Tejomayananda, December 1994.

Mumbai : Smt. Rajashri Birla on her way to inaugurate Swami Tejomayananda's *Yajna*

Rewa:Swamiji and Swami Tejomayanand at the temple

Palakkad:Swamiji with Swami Gnanananda Saraswathi and Prof. Vijayan

Chennai: Swamiji with Kamdar,
Batra and Moorjani from Mumbai

Lucknow: Kamla Bhargava accompanying
Swami Tejomayananda to the book stall

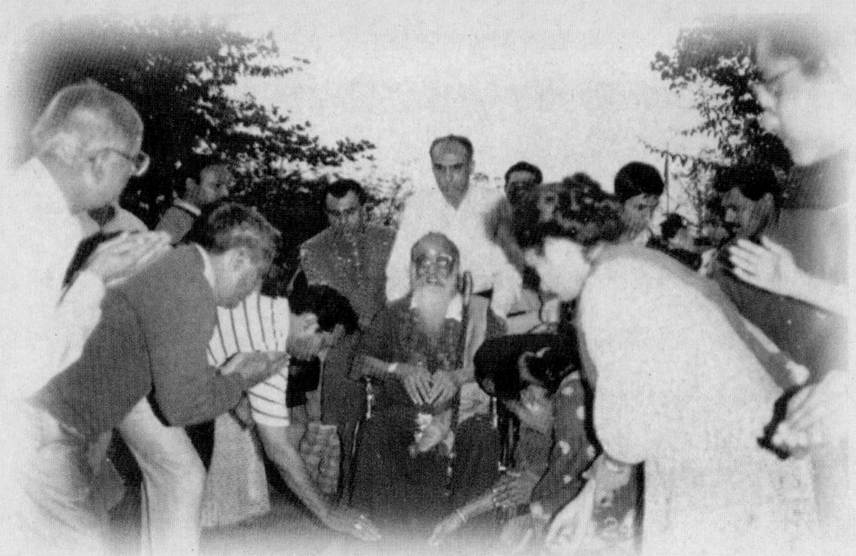

Ahmedabad: Swamiji's last visit.
President Arvind Mehta behind him

Kollengode:
Swamiji taken
in procession

Chennai: Swamiji with Mrs. Leela Nambiar, a loyal and ardent devotee

Rajupalem: Tulabhara of Swamini Saradapriyananda

Rajupalem: Honouring Smt. Annapurnamma with *pushpanjali* for her dedicated work in translating some of Swamiji's books into Telugu

Nagpur: Swami Purushottamananda delivering inaugural speech. Swamini Gayananda looks on

Veliyanad, CIF : Conference of scholars

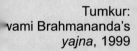

Tumkur:
vami Brahmananda's *yajna*, 1999

Port Blair:
Governor of Tamil Nadu Shri Bhishmanarain Singh with Swamiji in 1992

Bangalore: *Paduka - Pooja* of Swamiji
just before *Tulabhara* 1987

Bangalore: Gururaj Deshpande and Swami Brahmananda
walk towards the stage

Mumbai: “Drink with me!” B.M. Kamdar with Swamiji

Kolkata : Swamiji at Kalamandir, 1989.

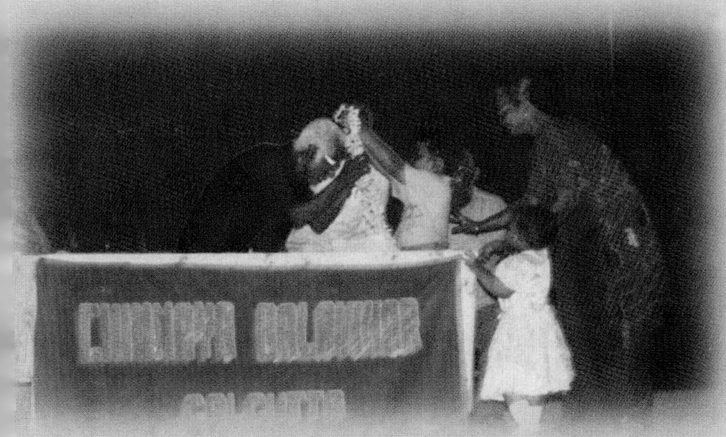

Kolkata : Swami Nityananda with Children

Ahmedabad: A Tulabhara

Delhi: Inauguration of Chimaya Centre of World Understanding; B.D. Kapur, Justice Venkatachalaiah, Swami Tejomayananda and Swami Jyotirmayananda on the dias

Cuttack :
One - Day *Satsang* with
Swami Subodhananda, 1999

Tezpur :
Swamini Purnananda
with the Chief Sevak
and Children.

Sultanpur: Vanaprastha Shivir 1998, Swami Shankarananda presides

Chas: Swami Nityananda with devotees and Br. Jaganmitra Chaitanya

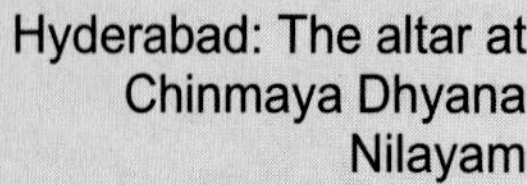

Hyderabad: The altar at Chinmaya Dhyana Nilayam

Kolhapur: Tulabhar present at the ritual Swami Tejomayana and Swami Purushottamanand in traditional gear

Geeta Swadhyaya, 1999 by Swami Viviktananda

Goa: Swamiji visits Margao – Vasantrao Dempo and D.N. Naik behind Swamiji

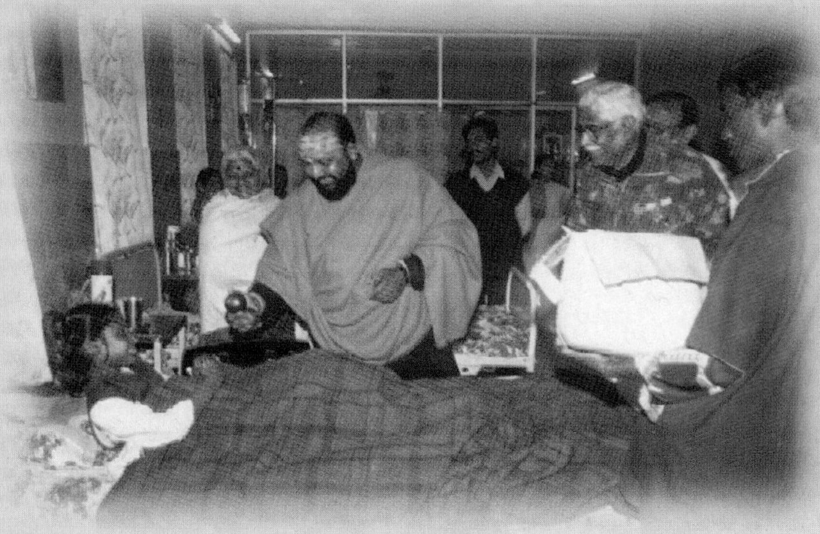

Jabalpur: Swami Subodhananda blesses the patie in M.J. Hospital

Kolhapur: Dakshineshwar Kailasnath Temple

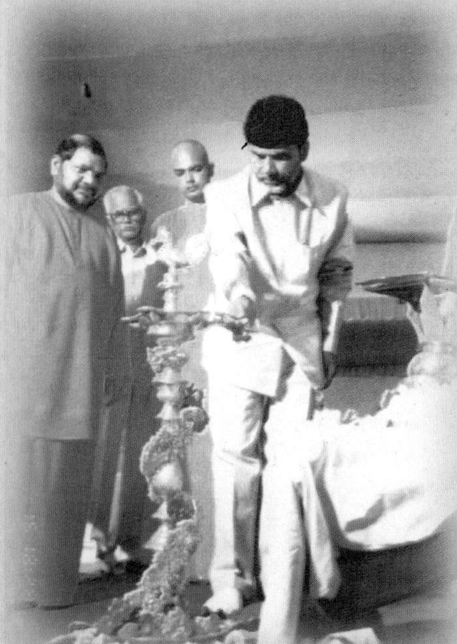

Hyderabad: Chief Minister Chandra Babu Naid inaugurates the Ramayana *yajna* of Swami Tejomayananda

Visakhapatnam: View of the Mission Centre

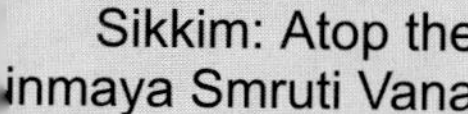

Sikkim: Atop the inmaya Smruti Vana

Meerut: Swami Shankarananda with Balavihar children

Vijayawada:
Swamiji with devotee
Mission members - 1

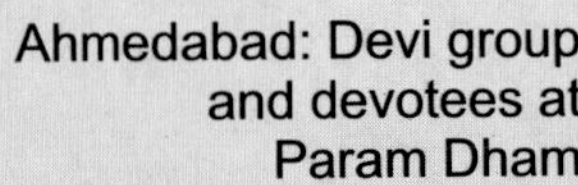

Ahmedabad: Devi group
and devotees at
Param Dham

Yavatmal, Mahara
The Mission centr

7

Moment of Silence

but the Music Goes On ...

From 1951 to 1970 Swami Chinmayananda was spinning around India and the world like a top. He was moving from *yajna-shala* to *yajnashala*, conducting *jnana-yajnas* all over the country. He was going on global tours of long duration, ranging from 90 to 180 days. He was writing copiously—books, commentaries on Vedanta texts, and articles for the Mission's journals. Above all he was running an organization that was growing at a dizzy speed. He was doing all this and more, single-handedly. The stress and strain told on his health. He was deprived of adequate rest and sleep. His intake of food was at irregular intervals. The writing on the wall was clear: sooner or later his health was going to be affected seriously.

Many devotees who were close to him were extremely concerned. A doctor devotee observed, "To Swamiji the body has become his slave because he has conquered his mind." He always believed that the best medicine for any physical or mental ailment was constant meditation.

It happened in 1970. He was participating in a symposium at Chennai. He collapsed on the stage and had to be carried away to hospital. The doctors declared that he was suffering from extreme fatigue. From then on, for the next twenty-three years, his health remained a matter of great concern. He would often declare that he wanted to slow down. He did try to do so occasionally by going on a retreat to Uttarakashi or to a clinic in Switzerland; but as soon as some signs of improvement showed, he would redouble his activities and make up for lost time.

Swamiji was conducting his 214th *yajna* at Mysore in March 1970. On the fifth day of the *yajna*, i.e. on March 21, he had a massive myocardial infarction. He was hospitalized and was advised complete rest for a few months. Devotees rushed to Mysore. Ram Batra brought the best cardiologist from Mumbai. In May 1970 he was moved, or rather Swamiji decided to move, to the Chinmaya Mission Hospital (CMH), Bangalore, for convalescence. The doctors and staff there felt that they were not equipped enough to take care of a cardiac patient. But they had no choice but to implement Swamiji's decision to shift to the CMH. Swamiji remarked jovially, "I inaugurated the out-patient ward of this hospital that day and now I am inaugurating the in-patient ward." Swami Chinmayananda was the first in-patient of the CMH, Bangalore. One of Swamiji's close devotees, a doctor by profession, has reported very interesting anecdotes relating to Swamiji's move to the hospital. A devotee of Swamiji from Chennai who was also a devotee of Sathya Sai Baba brought Baba to the hospital. Baba blessed Swamiji. He joined in the *keertans* and, at the request of Swamiji, led the *dhwanis* himself. Before being discharged from hospital, Swamiji gave away some of his personal belongings to the devotees who were attending on him—pen, clothes, books, etc. His doctors advised him to give up wearing the wooden *padukas* so he gave them away to the doctor-devotee Mrs. Susheela Purushottam.

In June 1970, Swamiji returned to Mumbai and was advised further rest. He stayed in a private apartment, surrounded by devotees who were all keen to serve him. He was busy correcting and editing the manuscripts of *Vivekachoodamani*. Letters were pouring in from devotees, imploring him to listen to doctors' advice and take rest. While he was touched by the concern shown by them, he felt the need to express his views through an open letter. He said, "I am obeying doctors in my way. Nobody can change it—except He who is the One-Doer-Supreme everywhere." In spite of his indifferent health Swamiji participated in the function at Kanyakumari for the opening of Swami Vivekananda's Rock Memorial. He said, "Such sacred functions do not take place every day."

In December 1970 Swamiji left for Switzerland along with a few of his devotees to undergo treatment at the world famous Heart Rehabilitation Center, of the Bercher Benner Klinik at Zurich. Since the winter weather was freezing, the doctors advised him to move to Las Palmas, Canary Islands, where the warm climate would help recover earlier by reducing his anginal pains. On January 3, 1971 Swamiji went to Las Palmas.

Swamiji reported spasms of anginal pain visiting more frequently and with greater intensity. In a message on the occasion of the Golden Jubilee of Swami Dayananda's *yajna* in February 1971, he said: "In my present health I cannot take up any more strenuous activities. The brahmacharis and brahmacharinis, who are now working in various pockets of the country are all growing up at different levels, burgeoning their individual beauty. The dedicated, dynamic nucleus of Chinmaya workers in the country will pull as a team under the benign guidance and direction of Swami Dayananda."

On March 31, 1971, Swamiji was admitted to the Klinik at Zurich as an in-patient. He was on a herbal diet, massages, and baths. He undertook a 3-day fast. The doctors were none too happy about it; they insisted that he should drink at least fruit juices at frequent intervals. In hospital Swamiji gave a series of talks on spirituality and ended with a 3-day session on meditation. The local Swiss people were drawn to him. One of the participants wrote on the *Gurudakshina* cover: "We have never heard anything like this before." The Director of the Klinik gave a detailed medical report on the condition of Swamiji's health. He also gave a letter of appeal to devotees in India: "I beg of you all to help me in protecting Swamiji from overwork."

On reaching India, Swamiji went to Uttarakashi. While taking rest as advised by his doctors, Swamiji was writing his commentary on *Ashtavakra Geeta*. He was cheerful and, when physically tired, he would rest. Four senior devotees from Mumbai—G. H. Muni, Nalinbhai Vissanji, Ajit Kapadia, and Srichand Krishnani—went to Uttarakashi for a few days to meet him. Apart from writing his commentary, he was also having *satsangs* in the mornings on *Vivekachoodamani*. After spending four months at Uttarakashi, Swamiji's health improved. He went to Zurich again in November 1971 for a check-up. This time the doctors observed that the cholesterol level was rather high. They advised him to cut down on white sugar and white flour. They had their own doubts if the patient would follow their advice. They were, however, happy to note the improvement in his health. They placed restriction on his movements, stating that he could do only one *yajna* a year in India and attend one or two international conferences outside

India. From March 1970 to April 1972 Swamiji did not conduct any *jnana-yajna*. In April 1972 he conducted a *yajna* in Mumbai on the eighteenth chapter of the *Bhagavad Geeta*. In the mornings he spoke on the *Brahma Sootras*.

Swamiji's health was causing concern. Repeated visits to the Klinik in Zurich and consultation with doctors were quite expensive affairs. Not wanting to burden the Mission, devotees raised the necessary wherewithal from among themselves and donated it for Swamiji's treatment in foreign countries.

In his New Year greetings to devotees Swamiji told them to plan for a vibrant 1972. He said: "I am still not fit for reentering the usual *yajna* work." In April 1972, he addressed the All-India Chinmaya Mission Workers' Conference. He said: "The one who was representing the word "Chinmaya" in the Chinmaya Mission is now retired, and he will not be able to take up as much of the active work as before. Swami Dayananda will shoulder the responsibilities." He told the Mission workers to write, in future, to Swami Dayananda, not to him, regarding schemes, programmes, etc. He knew his health was failing but then he was anxious to ensure that the Mission worked vibrantly. He was concerned that the Sandeepany Sadhanalaya at Mumbai had been lying idle for two years. He was keen to activate it. He resolved that the following three crucial events would take place in 1972—a new course for brahmacharis would start in August 1972, a short-duration two-month course for white-collar workers would be conducted in August/September 1972, and a zonal workers' conference would be held for fifteen days in December 1972. He succeeded in achieving all these three *sankalpas*.

After the *yajna* of 1972 at Mumbai, there was a gap of nearly a year before he took up such strenuous work again. In May 1973 he conducted the second National *Yajna* at Bangalore. Again there was a break. The next *yajna* was in April 1974 at Chikkamagalur in Karnataka State. Swamiji was making frequent global tours to satisfy the demands made by the devotees outside India. He also had his health checked up during those tours. On some occasions the *yajna* dates given to the organizers in India had to be modified or cancelled owing to unexpected illness.

In 1980, Swamiji's health took a turn for the worse. He conducted his first *yajna* at Chicago, Illinois. About this, Dr. Apparao Mukkamala of the Flint centre wrote on August 21, 1980: "It so happened that while Swamiji this year was conducting his *yajna*, we in Michigan noticed that not only his blood sugar was inexplicably working up and down, but doctors who were attending to the medical needs of Swamiji recognized an erratic behaviour of his heart pulse. This gave us a lot of silent anxiety. Swamiji laughed at it all the time." He added that after a team of doctors had carried out the tests, the results showed that the four arteries supplying blood to the heart had 80% blockages calling for immediate surgery. Swamiji was a high-risk patient: he had had a heart attack in 1970, he was a diabetic, he had progressive anginal pains, and his age was 60 plus. All these were risk factors. Doctors reported that it was nothing short of a miracle that Swamiji had survived long enough for his serious condition to be detected.

Devotees in the United States arranged for a bypass surgery for Swamiji by Dr. Denton Cooley at Houston, Texas. Swamiji asked Dr. Mukkamala to send an appeal on his behalf to his devotees and Mission centres all over the world to send their token contributions to meet his medical expenses in the United States. Devotees considered this an opportune moment for serving Swamiji. The funds required were collected in full. On the day of the operation, devotees conducted *poojas*, *japa* of *Maha-mrityunjayamantra* for Swamiji's speedy recovery and safe return to India.

On August 26, 1980, the bypass surgery was performed at St. Luke's Hospital in Houston, Texas, by Dr. Denton Cooley and his team. On the night prior to the operation Swami Dayananda visited Swamiji in the hospital. The surgery was successful. And after a period of rest and recuperation, Swamiji returned to India in December 1980.

What did Swamiji have to say about this major setback to his missionary activity? "But for this unexpected turn of events the Chinmaya Mission would not so easily have become established here in this great, growing city of Houston." This was almost a prophetic statement in that the Houston Centre is today one of the most dynamic centres of the Mission in the United States.

The team of doctors at the hospital took a photograph of Swamiji's heart with its triple bypass. Some of the doctors in India, who were close devotees, received notes on the operation and a copy of the photograph. The doctors have preserved the photograph as *prasad* from Swamiji. The general reaction of devotees all over the world was that Swamiji had no need of the body but that he had willingly submitted to enormous pain and suffering out of his great love for them.

In November 1980, after recuperation at the CMH, Bangalore, Swamiji announced that Swami Dayananda would be the next in command of the Chinmaya Mission. At that time Swami Dayananda was at Sandeepany (West) as Acharya of the course, which still had eighteen months to go for completion. Swamiji said that Swami Dayananda would visit India once in four months until the course was completed. Swamiji announced his decision to shift to Sidhbari for rest and also to serve the people in the interior villages of Himalaya. This, he said, was his mission for the present, in deference to the wishes expressed by his guru, Swami Tapovanam, in 1951. Swami Tapovanam had always wanted Swami Chinmayananda to serve the mountain people (*pahadis*) in the Himalaya. Swamiji also said that while at Sandeepany Himalaya he would train workers for doing *prachar* work in the Hindi belt of North India.

The Health Bulletin issued by the Ashram in February 1981 was encouraging. Swamiji was walking one mile each day. There were no more anginal pain and the post-operative pain had ceased. His only health problem was diabetes, which was being constantly monitored. In May 1981 Swamiji was well enough to undertake a foreign tour to the west coast of America and to Dubai. He was even scheduled to conduct a *yajna* at Manila on chapter three of the *Bhagavad Geeta*. Suddenly on June 6, after a hectic morning crowded with engagements, he fell unconscious. He was admitted to a hospital and the *yajna* ended a day earlier than it was scheduled to end. He was in hospital for six days before he was pronounced fit enough to travel. He was flown to San Francisco for further treatment and investigation. The itinerary that had been drawn up for Swamiji, was adhered to meticulously in spite of the indifferent health he was keeping. In Los Angeles, where he was to conduct a 9-day *yajna*, Swami Dayananda took the classes for two days on behalf of Swamiji.

The year 1981 was a year of great tragedy for the Chinmaya Movement, as Ram Batra, a most trusted devotee of Swamiji, passed away suddenly in August. He had been the Secretary of the Chinmaya Mission. He had carried out many important projects and programmes—Sandeepany Sadhanalaya Powai, Sandeepany West in Piercy, Tapovan Kuti at Uttarakashi,

Sandeepany Himalaya, and several major *yajnas* at Mumbai. He had planned and executed all these programmes so meticulously that Swamiji said he often created a better result than one had hoped for. Swamiji was in the United States when the news reached him. He wrote: "It is terrible. I have never felt so much loss. He is irreplaceable." Loss of such a devotee and administrator of the Movement told inevitably on his health.

The year 1982 witnessed another upheaval in the Chinmaya Movement. Swami Dayananda, the most senior Swami in the Chinmaya Mission, next only to Swami Chinmayananda, and the man who had been designated since 1980 as next in command in the Mission left the Mission for personal reasons. Along with him twenty-two senior brahmacharis too left the Mission. Swamiji was magnanimous: he blessed them all. However he had to work out the Mission's future all by himself. In spite of failing health he put his shoulder to the wheel once again.

Swamiji continued with his missionary work both in India and abroad. He undertook a global tour almost every year, many times more than two foreign tours in the same year. His health parameters were obviously declining, and declining more and more sharply, but with the support of external aids he undertook such tours. In a letter to one of his devotees, in 1991, he wrote: "My health is crumbling. It is being scaffolded with pills and oxygen pumps." Whenever he visited a centre to keep up his engagement, the organizers would be fully prepared with medical support and services to handle any emergency. After a serious setback to his health in 1991, Swamiji was forced to take complete rest for three months. However, from April 1992 onwards in spite of his frail health, he worked with amazing vigour. He conducted *yajnas*, camps, and no fewer than five marathon camps at

Sidhbari. He launched many new projects, agreed to *tulabharas* (from sheer compassion for his devotees), made global tours, addressed the United Nations, and made a university tour of United States. While visiting the universities from November 9 to December 13, 1992 by air and by road, he had two major setbacks—on November 11 and December 9—which he managed to pull through. Back at Mumbai, the last major engagement he had was to give *sannyasa-deeksha* to Br. Sudheer Chaitanya, now Swami Dheerananda, and brahmachari-*deeksha* to eighteen students of the Vedanta Course of 1991-1993. He then left on his global tour on June 10, 1993. His first halt was at Paris. No one thought then that it was his last day with body and spirit in his motherland, Bharat.

THE MAHASAMADHI ON AUGUST 3, 1993

After completing his spiritual camp at Washington, D.C., July 19-25, 1993, Swamiji was to go to California. Though not keeping fit he flew to San Diego on July 26. However, by the evening his condition deteriorated, and he was taken into the Intensive Care Unit of the Scripps Memorial Hospital. On July 28, Dr Shivley, under whose care Swamiji had been placed, found all his native arteries blocked. Of the three grafted arteries, two were fully blocked and one was 90 percent blocked. "His condition is not just bad; it's horrible." The choice was to leave him alone without invasive surgery or to do a bypass surgery. On July 29, he was transferred to the Sharp Memorial Hospital in the city for undergoing an emergency bypass surgery. The surgery was performed the same day, and bypasses were carried out successfully. The next two days his condition remained critical but stable. Devotees all over the world were praying for his quick recovery and were chanting the *Maha-mrityunjaya-mantra*. Many devotees in the United States flew to San Diego to see Swamiji. The hospital made special arrangements for the devotees to assemble for the prayers and also to have a *darshan* of Swamiji.

On August 1, 1993 Swami Chidananda of the Divine Life Society of Rishikesh called the hospital to inquire about the condition of Swamiji. The two had spent several years together in the Ananda Ashram, Rishikesh; they were *Gurubhais*. They had received *sannyas-deeksha* from Swami Shivananda the same year, 1949, Swami Chidananda in July and Swami Chinmayananda in February. They were close associates and had mutual respect and reverence. Hearing about the health condition of Swamiji, Swami Chidananda said: "He is beyond the body. He has dived into and merged in the Self." To explain the Vedantic statement in simple English, Swamiji had renounced his identification with the body and was in communion with the Highest Power. Prayers from all quarters continued. On August 2, Swamiji's condition continued to be critical. On the morning of August 3, he had internal bleeding. The situation was grim. By mid afternoon, his organs stopped functioning, his blood pressure began to fall, and the end came about 5.40 p.m. (Pacific Day Time). Swami Tejomayananda, the Acharya of Chinmaya Mission, San Jose, was by his side.

Swami Chinmayananda attained *maha-samadhi* on August 3, 1993. There was a moment of silence. The founder of the Chinmaya Mission, the tireless and illumined defender, teacher, and missionary of *Sanatana Dharma*, the dynamic person who had spearheaded the Hindu Renaissance Movement since the 1950s, the greatest contemporary exponent of the *Bhagavad Geeta* and the *Upanishads*, the master with a world-wide following—was no more in his physical form.

The news of his passing received wide coverage on All India Radio and on Doordarshan (India's official TV). Newspapers carried the news to every nook and corner of the country. Many articles on Swamiji appeared paying glowing tributes to him. "He was an unorthodox guru", some said. "He was a Genius of the spiritual world", others claimed. In countries outside India, newspapers and magazines that targeted an Indian audience, solemnly announced the loss of a great spiritual leader.

The mortal remains of Swamiji were brought back to Delhi on August 7. On the grounds of the Delhi Mission's office on Lodhi Road, a *shamiana* was specially erected to receive his body, which arrived from the airport in a flower-bedecked vehicle at noon. Thousands of devotees and members of the public filed past and paid their respects. Late on the night of August 7, a caravan of vehicles, with Swamiji's body in a decorated jeep, proceeded to Sidhbari, where devotees from India and all over the world had gathered to give a tearful farewell to their Master. By midday next day (August 8) the cortege entered the Sidhbari Ashram. The body was kept in the newly built Kamala Hall for *darshan* throughout the night. Early on the morning of August 9, the body was taken to the final resting-place – the rose garden behind Swamiji's *kutia*. Swami Purushottamananda performed the last *archana* and *arati*. The body was then lowered into the pit amidst vedic chants. It was thus a *bhoosamadhi* (burial) at Sidhbari. In the course of his funeral oration, Swami Tejomayananda said: "There can be nobody like Gurudev. Nobody can ever replace him. All of us have to work together to carry on the work he began." On August 19, the main *shodashi* (the rites to be performed on the sixteenth day) was done at Sidhbari. Swami Tejomayananda, Swami Purushottamananda, and Swami Subodhananda respectfully received venerable monks from many leading spiritual organizations such as the Divine Life Society at Rishikesh, the Ramakrishna Mission, Akhandananda Maharaj's Ashram at Vrindavan and other senior monks from the Himalaya. They served them with *bhiksha* and gave them traditional gifts like sandals, shawls and *kamandalus*, etc. Learned pundits from Delhi performed the rites in accordance with the *shastras*. It was a solemn function. There were similar *shodashi* rites performed for Swamiji at Uttarakashi, at the Sandeepany Sadhanalaya, Mumbai and at many other Mission centres in India and abroad. The function at Powai was especially charged with emotion; for after all, the Sandeepany Sadhanalaya at Powai was the dream place of Swami Chinmayananda, a Vedanta institute for which he had struggled day and night from 1954 to 1963.

THE SUCCESSION

The Trustees of the Central Chinmaya Mission Trust (CCMT) gave serious consideration to the choice of a successor to head the Mission. Eventually the mantle fell on Swami Tejomayananda, who was at that time just fortythree years old. All concerned unanimously accepted his name.

The announcement of Swami Tejomayananda as the next Head of the Chinmaya Mission was made on August 22, 1993 at a meeting of the Board of Trustees of the CCMT.

The resolution read: "The situation was reviewed by all the trustees. It was… unanimously resolved that H.H. Swami Tejomayananda be and is hereby appointed as the Chairman of the Central Chinmaya Mission Trust and the Spiritual Head of Chinmaya Mission centres all over the world with immediate effect." It was also resolved that Swami Purushottamananda be appointed as a trustee of the CCMT with immediate effect and that, in the absence of the Chairman of the Board of Trustees, Swami Purushottamananda would act as the Chairman.

Thus, within three weeks of the *maha-samadhi* of Swami Chinmayananda, the succession plan was announced and the hierarchy clearly defined. The dedication of the leaders of the Mission, their determination to carry on the work of Swami Chinmayananda without interruption, the truly spiritual approach of senior swamis not to be tempted to clamour for power and position – all these were the basic supporting factors, contributing to a smooth transition.

SWAMI TEJOMAYANANDA
A Brief Life Sketch

Sudhakar Kaitwade was a young lad of twenty years when, in 1970, he first came to Sandeepany Sadhanalaya at Mumbai. He was from Khargone (near Indore) in Madhya Pradesh. In fact originally, his family was from Maharashtra. Recalling how he happened to be drawn to the Chinmaya Mission, he said in the course of a press interview:

> When I was doing my second year B.Sc. I came cross some books by Swami Vivekananda, and I was impressed. After B.Sc. I enrolled for M. Sc. (Physics) at Bhopal. That year, in 1969, the 203rd *Geeta jnana-yajna* of Swami Chinmayananda, the first in Bhopal, was being held. I attended the *yajna* and was so impressed that I left college. A few months later, the Manager of the Sandeepany Sadhanalaya was at Bhopal, and I heard about the Vedanta course. I came to Mumbai to join the

course but Swami Chinmayananda fell ill and the course was postponed.

That is how Swami Tejomayananda was drawn to the Chinmaya Mission. On joining the Ashram, he was entrusted with the job of being a personal attendant for some time on Swamiji, who was recuperating from the heart attack he had suffered in March 1970. Sudhakar attended on Swamiji with devotion. He accompanied Swamiji to Uttarakashi when Swamiji went there for a retreat. In 1972 Sudhakar joined the Vedanta course at the Sandeepany Sadhanalaya, Mumbai, and studied under Swami Dayananda. On completion of the course in 1975 he received the brahmachari-*deeksha* by Swami Chinmayananda; he became Br. Vivek Chaitanya and was posted as Resident Acharya first at Bhopal and then at Kanpur (1976-80). He was next made the first Resident Acharya at Sandeepany Himalaya at Sidhbari, in 1981. He conducted the first course 1981-83; there were twentyone young people studying Vedanta in the Hindi medium. On October 21, 1983, Br. Vivek Chaitanya took orders: he received *sannyasa-deeksha* from Swami Chinmayananda who also gave him the name of Swami Tejomayananda. He was then posted to Mumbai as Acharya at the Sandeepany Sadhanalaya, Powai. He conducted two courses, 1984-86 and 1986-88. He trained fifty-seven students in all. In 1986 Swami Tejomayananda made his first trip to the United States. Jairam Jaisinghani, Manager of the Ashram at Powai, accompanied him. He met Swami Chinmayananda at Olivet, near Detroit, Michigan, where Swamiji was conducting the second international camp of the Chinmaya Mission. At the end of the camp, Swami Chinmayananda said to Swami Tejomayananda, "No more lectures. Go and see America." Swami Tejomayananda went on a 15-day conducted tour of important places in America.

Between June 1989 and August 1993 Swami Tejomayananda worked as Resident Acharya at San Jose, California.

Swami Chinmayananda met Swami Tejomayananda's mother and the rest of his family in India in March 1993. It is reported that Swamiji told his mother that Swami Tejomayananda would soon be returning to India. Was it a premonition?

From 1951 to 1993, through a period of forty-two years Swami Chinmayananda conducted over five hundred *Geeta jnana-yajnas*, the last one being the *yajna* at the spiritual retreat organized at Badri, the School of Vedantic Studies, Chicago, Illinois, from July 2 to July 9, 1993.

Recollecting his feelings on August 23, 1993 when he was chosen as the Spiritual Head of the Chinmaya Mission, Swami Tejomayananda says:

> The only way I can express my feelings is that I felt overwhelmed–overwhelmed with [the] highest emotions. Although Pujya Gurudev [Swami Chinmayananda] had indicated to me that I would be required to take up organizational work, I never imagined in my dream that it would happen so suddenly and in this manner. I always thought that he would remain and that he would guide me slowly. Therefore, I was overwhelmed by the loss of Gurudev's presence. I was overwhelmed with the enormous responsibility of leading such a worldwide organization. Overwhelmed with the attitude of all, senior swamis in particular, and all those that reposed their faith in me. At the same time I had a feeling of being blessed and privileged of holding such responsibility. I invoke the grace of Pujya Gurudev and that of the Lord. Let me declare that I owe my position and situation to them

BUT THE MUSIC GOES ON

From 1993 to 2000 the main thrust of the Mission was to fulfil the *sankalpas* that Swami Chinmayananda had made during his lifetime. Swami Tejomayananda and his team were determined to complete the major projects that were on the anvil. Swami Tejomayananda declared that he would follow in the footsteps of his guru and would conduct *jnana-yajnas* around the world every year. He had useful interaction with the Regional Heads in 1994 and 1995, which helped him in solving organizational problems. At these conferences he spelt out clearly the roles of the various organizational units–the CCMT, the Chinmaya Seva Trusts at different Mission centres, the Executive Committees etc. In 1994 there was a two-day conference of all swamis/swaminis, and brahmacharis/brahmacharinis of the Chinmaya Mission in India. This conference was held at the Adi Sankara Nilayam, Veliyanad, Kerala. There was a free and frank exchange of views between the Head of the Mission on the one hand and the other swamis and the field workers on the other.

In December 1994 Swami Tejomayananda conducted a *Geeta jnana mahayajna* at Mumbai. He gave his discourses in Hindi on the eighteen chapters of the *Geeta* in eighteen days. He covered eight of the ten major *Upanishads* at the morning sessions in English. This was his homage and humble offering to his guru. The *yajna* was a grand success.

The first anniversary, *Aradhana*, of Swami Chinmayananda was performed at Sidhbari with a solemn Vedic ceremony, together with an *Ekadashavara Rudrabhisheka*, and Vedic chanting. About five hundred devotees came, some of them from Hong Kong, Singapore, and the United States. Swami Chidananda, President of the Divine Life Society of Rishikesh was present. On August 3, 1994 he spoke of Swamiji in superlative terms and also of Swami Tapovan Maharaj whom he referred to as the Light of the Himalayas. He then placed a copy of *Unto Him* at the feet of Swamiji's picture. This book, compiled by Anjali Singh, is a publication brought out by the CCMT to mark the first anniversary of Swamiji's *maha-samadhi*. It contains seventy-seven colour pictures and seventy-seven quotations from Swamiji.

Some of the major projects initiated by Swami Chinmayananda have already been completed since his *maha-samadhi*. To name a few, Swami Tejomayananda laid tne foundation stone for the Chinmaya Heritage Centre at Chennai on August 31, 1994—a fitting memorial for Swamiji. The Chinmaya International Residential School (CIRS), Coimbatore, a school that provides an environment that would help integrate the best of both cultures—Eastern and Western—had been conceptualized by Swami Chinmayananda. His vision was transformed into action by his disciple, Swami Tejomayananda. Swami Chidananda, President of the Divine Life Society, inaugurated the school on June 6, 1996.

Another important achievement by way of fulfilling the guru's *sankalpa* was the completion of the Chinmaya Centre of World Understanding (CCWU) in New Delhi. Swamiji had already done the *Bhoomipooja* for it before his *maha-samadhi*. Swami Tejomayananda laid the foundation stone on February 12, 1994. The premises were inaugurated in May 1997.

Swami Tejomayananda inaugurated the Chinmaya Smriti, a centre for learning and imparting knowledge of Hindu Scriptures at Houston, Texas, in January 1994. This again was a project in which Swami Chinmayananda had taken a great deal of interest. He had done the *bhoomipooja* in 1992. The construction of the Omkareshwara Dhyana Mandir was completed at Chokkahalli

(Kolar), Karnataka. Swami Tejomayananda performed the *prarambhotsava*. He also unveiled the pictures of Swami Tapovan Maharaj and Swami Chinmayananda.

The Chinmaya International Foundation (CIF) at Adi Sankara Nilayam, Veliyanad, Kerala is a project conceived by Swami Chinmayananda in 1989. In 1992 Swamiji made a global tour and met professors of religion, Indology etc. and got them to chalk out a plan for structuring the CIF. Unfortunately he did not live to implement the suggestions they made. Picking up the threads from where Swamiji had left, Swami Tejomayananda has now succeeded in making the CIF a place of vibrant action.

Two larger-than-life statues of Swami Chinmayananda were installed. The first one is at the Sandeepany Sadhanalaya, Mumbai. Swami Chidananda of Divine Life Society, Rishikesh, unveiled it on February 12, 1995. Swami Tejomayananda installed and unveiled a statue of Swami Chinmayananda, 10.5 feet tall, at the Chinmaya Vidyalaya, Kasargode. On August 3, 1995, he installed a magnificent life-size statue of Swami Chinmayananda in the *siddhasana* posture at the *samadhi-sthal* at Sidhbari. The statue is made of five auspicious metals or *panchaloha*, and it is a veritable *mandir* (temple), with a *trikala pooja* being offered to the Guru daily. All in all it is a befitting offering to the Master.

Houston, Texas, is the first centre outside India, which has a life-size bronze statue of Swami Chinmayananda. Swami Tejomayananda unveiled this statue on January 14, 1996.

True to the spirit of patriotism that Swami Chinmayananda had inculcated in all his devotees there was an appeal to all Mission centres to send donations for the welfare of the victims of the Kargil war. And donations came in a flood. And in October 1998 Swami

Tejomayananda in his turn presented a cheque for Rs.63,00,000/- (Rupees sixty-three lacs) to the Prime Minister, A.B. Vajpayee as the Chinmaya Mission's contribution to the Army Central Welfare Fund.

The Chinmaya Movement, which has weathered many a storm in the past, came out strong and stable in the post-1993 period after the *maha-samadhi* of Swamiji. The determination and courage shown by the monastic members of the Mission is the most important single factor contributing to a smooth transition. Further, the unshakeable devotion of the disciples, and the love that the children and youth bear towards those who represent the Chinmaya Movement at the grass-roots level have helped absorb the shock created by the loss of the Master.

There was a moment of shock; a moment of silence, but it yielded place soon enough to soft, soothing music.

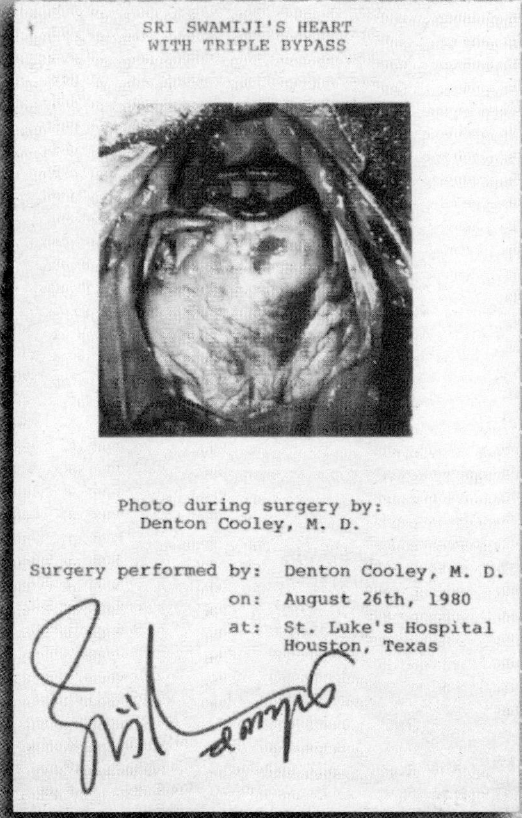
SRI SWAMIJI'S HEART
WITH TRIPLE BYPASS

Photo during surgery by:
Denton Cooley, M. D.

Surgery performed by: Denton Cooley, M. D.
on: August 26th, 1980
at: St. Luke's Hospital
Houston, Texas

Photo of Swamiji's heart, as Prasad –
after the by-pass surgery

Swamiji in Mahasamadhi state – Delhi, August 7, 1993

The Last Journey – the cortege winding its way to Sidhbari

Moving scenes of mourning disciples

Devotees attending Bhusamadhi – Sidhbari August 9, 1993

Samadhi Sthal at Sidhbari

Pratima at Samadhi Sthal

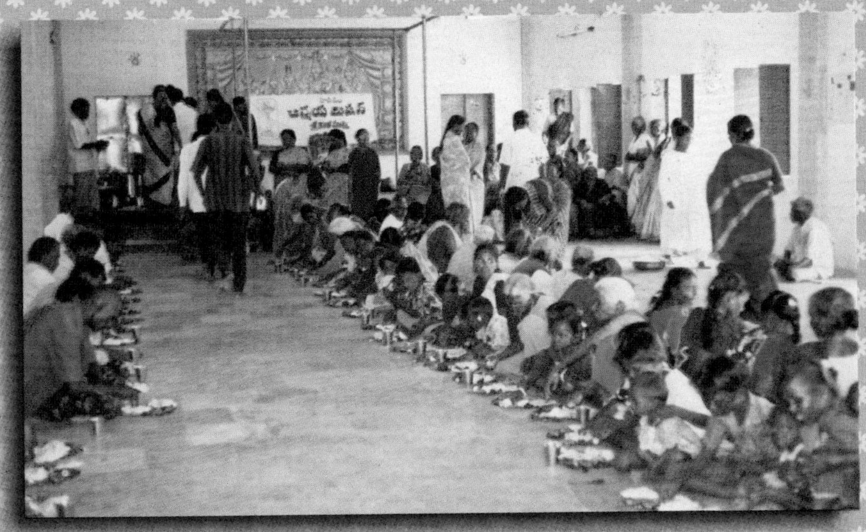

Prasad offered to devotees – First Anniversary of Mahasamadhi (A.P.)

Sudhakar comes to Sandeepany

Soon after *Sannyas Deeksha*,
Swami Tejomayananda

Indore: Swamiji visits the family of Swami Tejomayananda (March 1993).

Swami Tejomayananda with his Guru

Guru's Sankalpas fulfilled by Swami Tejomayananda

Chinmaya International Foundation (CIF)

Chinmaya Internationa Residential School (CIR

Chinmaya Centre of World Understanding (CCWU)

8

Touching The Lives of Millions

The Chinmaya Movement started as a crusade for spreading the message of the ancient scriptural texts of Hinduism. It branched out into various activities of selfless service. Swamiji ushered in many projects that were tailor-made to suit the needs of the people. Thanks to the efforts put in by inspired and dedicated workers, the projects had a perceptible impact on the social and moral fibre of the community at large. Globally, the Chinmaya Movement became synonymous with acquisition of knowledge of the scriptures, dissemination of a genuine concern for humanity, and selfless service.

SANDEEPANYS

Focusing on spread of scriptural knowledge, the Movement started with the founding of institutes for Vedantic studies. We have dealt with the topic of *Rishiputras* of Sandeepany elaborately in Chapter Four. The Mission has trained over 540 students in the Vedanta courses since 1963 in the various Sandeepanys. These brahmacharis and brahmacharinis have in turn entered the field and spread the knowledge of the Vedanta by their work of *prachar*, to multitudes of seekers. This has had a ripple effect of widening the circle of seekers worldwide.

GROUP ACTIVITIES

The spread of knowledge of the Vedanta has manifested itself in the form of many activities at the grass root level—*yajnas*, for instance, and the activities of Study groups, Yuva Kendras, Devi/bhajan groups, Vedic chanting/*Geeta* chanting groups, and, for the children, Balavihar groups. These form the backbone, as it were, of the Movement. Typically, all centres of the Mission provide the necessary facilities to conduct these programmes effectively. More details on Balavihars, Study groups, and Yuva Kendras are given at the end of this chapter. Devi groups and Bhajan groups provide an opportunity to women to join the Movement–taking part in *poojas*, bhajans, Study groups exclusively for women, etc. Vedic chanting groups are formed where the members are eager to learn the proper method of chanting the *mantras* of the Vedas. It is usually a group activity led by a person competent to teach. To supplement the skill of chanting *mantras* of the Vedas as also to learn the language, Sanskrit is also taught for the benefit of members wherever the necessary facilities are available. *Geeta* chanting, another activity, has gained popularity with members of all age groups. In recent years it has captured the attention of school children because of the annual competitions organized at the national level. Slogans like "Chant *Geeta*, Land Washington" are catchy and have inspired children to enter the contest. The number of children participating in the competitions has increased by leaps and bounds, making it a challenge for the centres of the

Mission to organize competitions at the district/State/national levels by the Mission centres concerned.

CHINMAYA VIDYALAYAS

"It all started as an experiment in the 1960s; it is even now an experiment and will perhaps always be", said Swami Chinmayananda. In the 1960s he identified children as the target audience for his goal of a cultural renaissance. Children had to be given value-based education. Swamiji used to say: "You can train a young plant to grow straight, but you cannot straighten a tree." Children are the architects of the future world and builders of the nation. We should adopt a methodical approach to foster their innate talents and tap their spiritual potential. Swamiji gave a clarion call to the workers of the Mission: "Catch them young." His deep love of children was the motivating force for the starting of Balavihars in the 1950s. This was followed by the opening of the first nursery school in 1965 at a place called Kollengode in Kerala, under the dynamic leadership of a retired Principal of a college, Pankajamma as she was affectionately called. In 1968, Swamiji ordained her into the monastic order as Swamini Vidyananda. She was the first Swamini of the Chinmaya Mission. The choice of Kollengode was natural and logical, as the Chinmaya Movement had enjoyed the patronage of the Kollengode royal family right from its inception. The Swamini took active interest in the implementation of the guidelines of the Education Department while incorporating Indian culture and history through story telling and celebrating numerous festivals. The aim was to create schools that would impart the latest secular education as well as inculcate moral values and the typically Hindu philosophy of life.

The sapling thus planted in Kollengode in 1965 grew into a mighty banyan tree before long. In the year 2001, after three and a half decades, there are 72 Chinmaya Vidyalayas in the country, including an international residential school at Coimbatore, a science degree college at Hardwar (Uttaranchal), five parallel colleges in Kerala, one Chinmaya Vidyapeeth at Ernakulam (providing degree courses in B. Com., foundation courses for C.A. and A.C.S.). Of these 72 Vidyalayas, 20 are Higher Secondary, 23 are Secondary schools and others are at different stages of growth. Most of the Vidyalayas are affiliated to the Central Board of Secondary Education (CBSE); a few, to the Indian Council of Secondary Education (ICSE), New Delhi. Others are affiliated to the respective State Boards. The Chinmaya International School is affiliated to CBSE as well as International Baccalaureate (IB), which is the basic level for admission to colleges in foreign countries. Student strength in the Vidyalayas is about 50,000, and in the colleges about 5000. The first Vidyalaya was opened at Kollengode in Kerala. The students of the Vidyalayas have shown conspicuous academic merit. In sports and extra curricular activities also they have acquitted themselves creditably. Many of the successful career professionals both in India and abroad, are proud of the fact that they are the products of some Chinmaya Vidyalaya or other.

CHINMAYA INTERNATIONAL RESIDENTIAL SCHOOL

It was Swami Chinmayananda who first conceived the idea of an international residential school. It was his disciple Swami Tejomayananda who realized it. This school has a unique fusion of the ancient and rich culture of the East with the creative and independent thinking of the West.

In June 1996 the Chinmaya International Residential School (CIRS) was opened at Coimbatore in Tamil Nadu. This was a dream come true, for Swami Chinmayananda's views on education had a global perspective. As Swamiji put it, "Education means the ability to see the whole world in unison working together–a macrocosmic vision".

The School offers two streams—one is prescribed by the CBSE, the other by the IB. (The latter is an organization based in Switzerland.) The response from the Indian community is encouraging. It is expected that more and more Indian families living abroad would take advantage of the education imparted in this School. Apart from aiming at academic excellence, the School imparts the eternal values of life that will help mould character into something strong and pure and enduring.

CHINMAYA VISION PROGRAMME (CVP)

"The purpose of education is to understand life, to know the Truth, and to qualify oneself to realize the goal." To fulfil this vision of Swami Chinmayananda, a comprehensive value-based educational programme known as the Chinmaya Vision Programme (CVP) is implicit in each and every Chinmaya Vidyalaya. Swami Tejomayananda launched this programme on May 21, 1996. It is a successful attempt to bring out an overall unfoldment at the physical, mental, intellectual, and spiritual levels of a child's personality. It aims at giving each child an exposure to Hindu culture, fosters in him a deep love for the nation, and gives him a universal outlook. The Educational Cell of the Central Chinmaya Mission Trust (CCMT) at Coimbatore, Tamil Nadu, is closely monitoring the implementation of the programme.

The motto of the Chinmaya Vidyalayas is "Keep Smiling". It keeps reminding the children that they should never get cowed down, come what may! They should face life's challenges cheerfully and with courage. Swami Chinmayananda's message is: "Be like a flower, give fragrance to all."

As an appendix to this chapter, we have given tabulated information on the Vidyalayas. Characteristic of the Vidyalayas are 1) their academic excellence 2) successful moulding of the character and outlook of the large student population—exceeding 50,000—as witness by the praise-worthy achievements of the students of the Vidyalayas and 3) the healthy teacher-student ratio that they sedulously maintained.

CHINMAYA INSTITUTE OF MANAGEMENT

Whether in management forums, in private and public companies, or in management institutes, Swami Chinmayananda was frequently invited to speak on holistic management. The Chinmaya Institute of Management (CIM) that he envisioned in the1980s is predicated on the natural nexus between the Vedanta and management. For about three years from 1980 onwards, a small team of dedicated workers at Bangalore researched and developed material and conducted seminars at companies. The result was the three-volume set of *Vedanta: The Science of Life* by K. V. K. Thampuran.

Swami Tejomayananda revived the CIM late in 1997. The institute is dedicated to offering management education and training with a holistic perspective that integrates spirituality, values and ethics into management. Located at Bangalore, the CIM has a variety of activities: Executive Development Workshops for corporations and colleges; seminars conducted by a world-class faculty; guest lectures; research; and publication of a journal Chinmaya Management Review with Indian and international contributors.

CIM functions under the broad umbrella of the Chinmaya Institute of Higher Learning (CIHL), which aims at research and imparts knowledge that applies values and Vedantic principles in several areas.

CHINMAYA INTERNATIONAL FOUNDATION

The Chinmaya International Foundation (CIF), an important limb of the Chinmaya Movement, came into being as a registered body with its headquarters at Veliyanad near Kochi on April 25, 1989. Officially inaugurated in February 1990, it is conceived as an international centre for research and studies in Sanskrit, the Vedanta and other Indological disciplines. It is a forum of seekers and scholars working together towards a deeper understanding of different world-views so as to discover and disseminate the underlying harmony of universal existence. The CIF is geared to function as a bridge between spirituality and science.

The site on which the CIF stands is believed to be the birthplace of Adi Shankaracharya. (It is his mother's home while Kaladi–the well-known town–is his father's place.) Swamiji said, "Let the CIF grow up as a National Institute of Hindu Culture gearing up to embrace the entire humanity in love and with great concern for their welfare."

Through research the CIF is expected to serve a large segment of people in the academic field and to endeavour, true to the vision of Swamiji, to bridge the communication gap between spirituality and science.

The CIF has been working for about ten years now. A very good infrastructure with a library of ten thousand books on Indological subjects, computer/internet facilities, and good accommodation beckons scholars and spiritual seekers alike to come and engage in research work or do *sadhana* at this site. In the year 2000, the Mahatma Gandhi University at Kottayam recognized it as a research centre. Several research projects are going on—as for example, a new translation of Adi Shankara's commentary on the *Brahmasootras*, a study of epigraphical writings in stone in Sanskrit in Kerala, etc. It has been offering a home-study course in Sanskrit from 1990 onwards. An eminent scholar, Dr. A. R. Iyengar, guides the academics as its Director. A. Balakrishnan (formerly of the Chinmaya family, Kuwait) worked very hard to build this fine facility for ten years. Reputed institutions like the Archaeological Survey of India and the National Council for Educational Research and Training have found the sprawling campus of the CIF ideal for holding their seminars.

It is a happy coincidence that it was founded in the centenary year of the birth of Swami Tapovan Maharaj.

BOOKS DIVISION (CCMT)

Availability of books at the appropriate time and in sufficient numbers is the prerequisite of the success of the efforts being made by the Mission for spreading knowledge. The experience gained in the initial years convinced Swamiji the relevant books should be readily available to those coming to attend his discourses. Books were also a must for the functioning of Study group.

The Chinmaya Publication Trust (Regd.), which was overseeing the publications of Swami Chinmayananda's books, was started in

March 1961. When the CCMT was formed in 1964, the Trustees of the Publication Trust at Chennai transferred their work to Swamiji. Swamiji in his turn gave this responsibility to the CCMT. Subsequently the entire work of the publications was shifted from Chennai to Mumbai.

Swamiji's books, especially his commentaries on *Bhagavad Geeta*, and the *Upanishads* generated great interest. There was a demand that the books be translated into Hindi and other regional languages. Swamiji's devotees brought out translations in Hindi, Marathi, Gujarati, and Telugu etc. With Swamiji's approval, regional committees were set up to ensure proper translations of the texts. The Hindi Publication Division of the CCMT, which was at Mandhana, Kanpur, under the guidance of Swami Tejomayananda and later, of Swami Shankarananda, did much to popularize the books in Hindi. In 1998, this division was transferred to Mumbai so as to ensure better co-ordination. The publication of Gujarati and Marathi translations, as also original books in English, was already being done at Mumbai. The regional committees have their headquarters in the corresponding States. Books are being published under the authority of CCMT; the copyrights are also being held by CCMT. Some publications have recently been translated into Bengali; more books are likely to be published in that language soon.

In October 1972, Swamiji's first book in a European language (other than English of course) was published. It was a translation of his commentary on the *Ishavasya Upanishad* into German by Urmila Ziechang. The Paris centre published a translation of Swamiji's *Bhagavad Geeta* into French (this translation was released by Swami Chinmayananda when he visited Paris in 1993, weeks before his *Maha-samadhi*). Brni. Sadhana Chaitanya translated *Art of Living* and *Know Thyself* into Polish.

By the year 2000 the Books Division had published about 550 titles in all in English, Hindi, Gujarati, Marathi, and other regional languages.

New publications are being added every month. Books written by Swamiji's disciples and the Acharyas of the Mission are also being published by the CCMT. More and more talks are being given by the Acharyas at educational institutions, management forums, etc., demonstrating the practical application of the Vedanta to life.

Centres in USA affiliated to the CCMT under the banner of Chinmaya Publications West have also undertaken publication of books according to local demand and interest.

Swami Tejomayananda appreciating the international standard and modern demands introduced professional management by inducting a long time mission Secretary of Rourkela, Orissa, K.C. Patnaik with his MBA Degree from USA and long experience in the management and administration in public sector and private sector to head the Books & Publications Division of CCMT as General Manager in July 1995. The Books Division has seen fast modernisation since then, adopting latest management skills and modern infrastructure. The sales outlets have expanded beyond Mission centres within India and export orders have consistently increased. The quality of printing has vastly improved and there are constant reviews and consistent attempts to upgrade the quality of publications keeping pace with international standards and demands. The CCMT is registered with the Federation of Publishers and Booksellers' Association in India and also has registration at International level with ISBN numbers for its publications.

The Audio Division at Bangalore and the Chinmaya Video Dham at Mumbai, as divisions of the CCMT, bring out audiocassettes and videocassettes, containing songs and discourses. They cover *Geeta* chanting, Vedic chanting and Bhajans by students, Acharyas, members of the Chinmaya Yuva Kendras, and other devotees. Some titles have been brought out in the form of CDs too with digital recording.

Thus the Books Division is doing its best to cater to the ever-growing demands from seekers and *pracharaks* for the supply of high quality books.

BALVIHAR MAGAZINE

Every child comes to earth
With the message that
God is not yet tired of man."

- Rabindranath Tagore

"We shall through the journal throw bridges of Love and understanding between children everywhere, and we shall learn to create a greater world out of what our parents have given us now", said Swami Chinmayananda in the inaugural issue of the *Balvihar*, the international children's magazine of the Chinmaya Mission, which he released in November 1969. Aruna Sheth was the first editor of the journal.

The growth of the *Balvihar* journal is like the growth of any child —full of ups and downs. Professional editors, artists and contributors ran the magazine published from Mumbai. It had a healthy response from readers and from members of the Mission. No wonder it received many popular advertisements and it was able to come out in several pages in colour.

Before long, however, there was a change in its fortunes. It changed hands frequently and passed into non-professional hands. Lack of coordination resulted in financial collapse in 1985-86. Swamiji offered two alternatives—either close down the magazine or start a children's section in *Tapovan Prasad*. The Mission centre at Chennai came to the rescue and revived the *Balvihar* by giving life-support. The magazine was published from Chennai for full nine years. The monthly circulation touched 9000 copies. Once again, however, it found itself in the midst of difficulties. Its editor resigned abruptly in August 1995. Swami Tejomayananda, the Head of the Mission worldwide, thereupon took the decision to transfer the editorial and publishing offices to Mumbai.

Since January 1996, the CCMT has published the magazine. Brni. Vividisa Chaitanya is the Chief Editor; Ms. Bharati Sukhtankar is editorial advisor. The magazine now enjoys a circulation of 20,000 and looks forward for support from professional contributors and advertisers. It hopes to continue to impart valuable nuggets on our cultural and spiritual traditions.

SOCIAL SERVICE

Let us now make a survey of the important projects at some of the centres. There are many more than are mentioned here, but we are not giving the entire list. Though some do not get mention, it does not mean their labour has been in vain. They have given immense happiness, peace and prosperity to the community.

CHINMAYARANYAM, ANDHRA PRADESH

"It was a sight for the gods to see. A village hardly with fifty families in it, all of them poor, labourers half-naked and even three-fourths naked. The lands were dry, men poor, and facilities nil." This was how Swamini Saradapriyananda, the founder of Chinmayaranyam, described the village when Swami Chinmayananda visited the place on February 8, 1982 for the *bhoomi-pooja* in Chinmayaranyam, Ellayapalle village, Kodur Taluk, Cuddappah District, Andhra Pradesh. Seventeen donors had given twenty-four acres of land to the Ashram run by the Chinmaya Mission, with Swamini Saradapriyananda as the Acharya. Swami Chinmayananda, sprinkling milk, turmeric water, sacred rice, and flowers worshipped Mother Earth and sanctified the land by his *tapas* and prayers. He narrated the story of the young man who worked upon a dry piece of land to convert it into a beautiful garden and illustrated how man had to offer only two per cent as his contribution to anything from Nature. The Lord would bless the man by doing the other 98 per cent. Swamiji proclaimed that this Ashram would be a new type of Ashram where the poor and needy would be served with love and affection. It would set an example to the whole country to show how village uplift had to be done. The plan was to have a forest around the Ashram. Its main activities would be cultivation and dairy farming. The Ashramites would live in thatched huts, studying and practising the lofty ideals of the *Upanishads* and other scriptures.

The village had two wells. One of these was dry, and the second looked as if it would go dry any moment. Against this background Swamiji was visualizing a forest around the Ashram. Many felt that it was all a pipe dream. Pointing with his walking stick to two banyan trees, standing on either side of the land, Swamiji said, "Dig along the line that connects the two trees. Water is sure to come." And, yes, water did spout forth from the well when it was dug.

Swamini Saradapriyananda, while writing about Swamiji's first visit to Ellayapalle, said:

Where he sits is a temple,
Where he treads is hallowed ground.

She was one of Swamiji's foremost disciples. She did him proud by her work for the uplift of the rural poor. The villagers just loved her. When she died on April 17, 2000, they wept for her, calling her "Amma". She had carved a special niche for herself in the Chinmaya Movement by her selfless service and unconditional love.

Chinmayaranyam at Ellayapalle concentrates on the spread of spiritual knowledge. It holds regular camps—*Jwala Sadas* in summer and *Geeta Sadas* on *Geeta Jayanti* Day. Many seekers of spiritual knowledge attend these camps. The summer camp coincides with the birthday of Swami Chinmayananda in May; and *Geeta Jayanti* is the birthday of Swami Tapovanam in December.

Social service at Chinmayaranyam, Ellayapalle is varied. True to its motto, ("Receive the Light of Knowledge, Bring out the heat of action"), the Ashram is ever busy with work for the poor and needy. There is an orphanage. Called *Satyakama Mandir* it started in October 1982, with two abandoned children. Now there are 109 children, both boys and girls. Eight of them are in college; and the rest go to school. A boy is employed in a Polytechnic. Harihar Schools were started in 1986 with twenty-six children. The children of the poor are educated in these schools from Grade 1 to Grade 7; they are each given a free mid-day meal and a glass of milk before they go home. The student strength of the school now is 119. There is a high school, which offers education from Grade 8 to Grade 10. At present it has thirty-nine students. In 1989, the boys and girls of the first batch were all given *Upanayana deeksha*.

With funds coming by way of donations from the United States, Chinmayaranyam built a hospital "Aapi Tana Hospital" in May 1990. There are a resident doctor and a nurse in this hospital. Medical and veterinary camps are held here, and patients/cattle are treated. *Hariseva* consists in feeding old and crippled villagers, who numbered 165 in the year 2000. These indigent villagers come daily to the Ashram for free lunch. Lunch is provided to the Ashramites only after the *Hariseva* is over. Chinmayaranyam has undertaken programmes for the afforestation of the hillocks around. The project gives employment to the villagers, who are engaged in planting and watering of the planted area. Chinmayaranyam also has a magneto-therapy clinic.

In 1997, Chinmayaranyam took up a project for intense rural reconstruction by adopting a village called Vadipalle, which has twenty-five houses. Food, clothing, shelter, and medical and educational needs of the local inhabitants were identified and catered to. There are plans to adopt two more villages in 2001. The Rural Reconstruction Project owes its success to a generous donation received from certain Mumbai devotees, K. B. Shroff and his sisters Vimala and Veena. The villagers have gratefully named the village Shroff Nagar, after the donor's family.

The Chinmayaranyam Project is an outstanding example of the way activities by the Chinmaya Family can change totally the economic and social history of a village. Many foreigners and other funding organizations are greatly impressed with the sincerity and dedication of the sevaks at Chinmayaranyam, and they have, therefore, made liberal donations.

Swamini Saradapriyananda has replicated the activities of Chinmayaranyam Ellayapalle, at Trikoota also, which is called "Chinmayaranyam–Trikoota". This centre is mainly used for conducting *Dharmaveera* courses. The Vedanta course is run at Ellayapalle in Telugu and English. This two-language course is run parallel and is very popular. So far nine Brahmacharis/ Brahmacharinis have done the course in English, and twenty-one in Telugu. All the trained workers are being gainfully utilized for *prachar* work and for the implementation of various projects.

There are three other Ashrams in the Chinmayaranyam complex–Chinmaya Sarada Tapovanam, Chinmaya Yoga Ashramam, and *Geeta* Ashramam. All the Ashrams are engaged in the work of explicating the spiritual texts to the seekers and providing facilities for meditation, *satsang* etc., to those engaged in *sadhana*.

PITAMAHA SADANS AND CENTRAL CHINMAYA VANAPRASTHA SANSTHAN

Projects under these two schemes aim at providing a quiet and serene life to senior citizens. There are what are called *Pitamaha Sadans* at Rewa, Mandhana (near Kanpur), Tamaraipakkam (near Chennai), Siruvani (Coimbatore), Ellayapalle (A. P.), Kolhapur (Maharashtra), Allahabad (U.P.), and Sidhbari (Himachal Pradesh). These places provide residential accommodation to senior citizens, food through community kitchens, medical care, etc., and aim at providing them with a home away from home. The inmates are encouraged to engage in spiritual pursuits–giving discourses, taking part in the activities of the Mission like Balavihar etc.

The Central Chinmaya Vanaprastha Sansthan (CCVS) is a scheme administered by the CCMT to give training to *vanaprasthis* as also to assist/train them to change from *grihasthashrama* to *vanaprasthashrama*. The implementation of the scheme at the grass-root level is the responsibility of the Chinmaya Vanaprastha

Sansthan (CVS). Training programmes are conducted from basic to advanced courses giving the participants inputs on scriptural texts, yoga, finance management etc. The aim is to help them withdraw increasingly from worldly life and progress towards a life of detachment and achieve the aim of getting liberation from the world of *samsara*.

CHINMAYA MISSION HOSPITAL

In 1960 a small but ardent group of devotees hired a room in a slum area in Murphy Town, Bangalore in order to run a bi-weekly clinic. This was the humble beginning of today's 200-bed Chinmaya Mission Hospital (CMH). When Swami Chinmayananda heard about the work being done by the devotees (to mention a few names: Dr. Sushila Purushottam, Ms. Kamala Reddy, Ms. Prafulla Iyengar, Ms. Dassanachar, Ms. Yogam), he was very happy and surprised. He gave them a cheque for Rs.500. He said, "Why not! This gives me the idea of starting a hospital." This is how the seed for the CMH was sown. Land was obtained, funds gathered, construction commenced; Swamiji consecrated the hospital in 1970. The bed strength was increased to fifty in 1979; the paediatric ward was commissioned with an additional thirteen beds in 1981. As the years rolled by and the need for more beds was felt, the facility expanded to a 100-bed hospital in 1993. While wondering where the funds came from for expansion, one can only recall Swamiji's words: "...and an organization needs funds and workers. The Chinmaya Mission has got workers but we are always in want of funds. But our faith in the goodness of our programmes is so powerful that we have never hesitated in launching programmes... Jagadeeswara always drove His messengers to reach us with the required funds at the most appropriate time. This has been our experience in the last forty years." On November 6, 1999, the CMH was declared open as a 200-bed hospital with the most modern equipment and facilities. The objective of the hospital is: "Immediate Humane Patient Care at Affordable Cost."

CHINMAYA INSTITUTE OF NURSING

The Chinmaya Institute of Nursing (CHIN) was started in 1986 with a view to providing trained nurses to the CMH in a very humble way, on the top floor of the Vijnana Mandir, which was lying vacant. To begin with, a two-year course for training Auxiliary Nursing Midwives was launched, with the approval of the Karnataka Nursing Council. In 1985 a retired Senior Nurse Superintendent joined as the Principal of CHIN. From 1983 to 1989, five batches of ten students each were trained as Auxiliary Nursing Midwives and sent to bigger hospitals for on-the-job training. Here they learnt specialized theatre work. The management of CHIN, thereafter, worked on a project to introduce a course for training Registered Nurses (R.N.), which required approval from the All India Nursing Council in Delhi. Having completed all the necessary formalities, the training course of Registered Nurses started in 1989. This is a three-year course after which a student can take up graduate and super-graduate courses. Swamiji's vision of starting a nursing institute as a sister discipline and providing services to the CMH became a reality in 1989. On an average, twenty students get trained at the institute each year. The nurses are angels of mercy and are constantly updating the treatment under the guidance of experienced doctors.

The motto of the institute is, "*Jana Seva is Janardana Seva*". It means, in other words, service to the people is service to the Lord.

The students were exposed to weekly classes on subjects like "Personality Development and Service" (Chapter Three of the *Bhagavad Geeta*). The yellow-robed monastic workers giving such talks were an attraction to those who came to CHIN to see the techniques of teaching at the institute!

CHINMAYA DIAGNOSTIC AND RESEARCH CENTRE

Located at Bansbaria, about seventy kilometres away from Kolkata, the Chinmaya Diagnostic and Research Centre (CDRC) caters to the patients of that area. These patients have otherwise to take the trouble of going all the way to the metropolis for diagnostic services. Sonography, E.C.G., X-Ray, and pathological services are also available.

CHINMAYA DIAGNOSTIC CENTRE AND CLINIC (CDCC)

This clinic in Chembur, Mumbai, is giving much needed medical services to the underprivileged in the neighbourhood. Dr. (Mrs.) Panjabi, an ardent devotee of Swamiji, started the clinic. The clinic is equipped with X-ray and Pathology Departments and functions under the direct supervision of CCMT.

CHINMAYA RURAL HEALTH CARE & TRAINING CENTRE (CRHTC)

The Chinmaya Rural Health Care and Training Centre ("The Centre"), a wing of the Chinmaya Tapovan Trust (CTT), Sidhbari, came into being in 1985. The project is an endeavour to provide the basic health services to remote villages. The project covers 278 villages in the Kangra District. The programme annually reaches about 20,000 people directly and approximately 15,00,000 of them indirectly, in the area. The overall aim is to initiate the process of empowerment of women in the area through comprehensive development. It seeks to increase women's capacity in effective participation in their own development. The training of women to assume grass-roots leadership and the upgrading of their skills of work are an integral part of its socio-economic, health, educational, and environmental programmes. The project has generated a great deal of participatory involvement of women in the project area as witness *mahila-mandals*, adolescent girls' groups, self-help groups, etc. Self-help groups are identified as micro-banking groups where the groups undertake a project, get bank finance, implement the project, and return the loan to the bank. The recovery of the loans so taken has been a hundred per cent success so far. The Centre has been able to reach out to as many as 4500 women and youth in these micro-enterprises. Activities that generate income include growing vegetables, traditional farming, the maintenance of dairies and poultry farms, bee keeping, the growing of mushrooms, bamboo products and food products etc.

It is a matter of pride that the National Bank for Agriculture and Rural Development (NABARD) identified CRHCT. Centre in 1998 as a mother NGO (non-government organization) for training of NGOs. The centre has already trained sixty-two NGOs.

The Centre's activities include twenty *Balwadies*, in twenty villages, with 400 children attending them daily. Its thrust on the rehabilitation of women seeking social justice and on environment and sanitation is an integral part of its approach to development. Many young volunteers from abroad have felt inspired to participate in its work. For some it has been a part of their academic preparation on outreach services at the grass roots.

Swami Chinmayananda was the source of inspiration for its dedicated and motivated workers.

The greatest legacy that the project has given to the simple women in the area is the unfoldment of their potential in many directions.

The credit for the achievement of the Centre goes, indisputably, to Dr. Kshama Metre, the 'Doctor Didi', who turned her back on a lucrative medical practice in Delhi and headed for the hills in 1985 to satisfy an inner urge. She donned the white of selfless social workers and joined the Chinmaya Ashram in Sidhbari. Since her arrival in the Kangra Valley, Himachal Pradesh, she has catalysed change by inspiring people, transforming them, and harnessing their energies. *The Week*, publication of the Malayala Manorama Group from Kottayam, India, awarded her the citation for "Woman of the Year" in 1993.

CHINMAYA SEVA CENTRE

Swami Chinmayananda conceived of the Chinmaya Seva Centre, Sidhbari, as an example of the Vedanta in action, and launched the project in 1992. Divorces, desertion of one's wife, etc., are common among the *Pahadi* (mountain people) in the region of the Kangra Valley. In almost all cases the women involved become easy targets for exploitation. The Chinmaya Seva Project was so designed as to enable such women to lead a life of self-respect and dignity by training them to pursue a vocation that they could easily learn and start earning. The Chinmaya Seva Centre has 3 sections—the sewing section, the weaving section and the carpet-making section.

The sewing section was started in 1992 with funds provided by NORAD (of the Norwegian Government). Selected candidates are offered stipends by way of an incentive. Coaching is by an expert designer. The response is encouraging. Various types of dresses for men, women, and children are sewn here. The trainees typically set up their own enterprises. A recent survey of the work showed that 30 to 40 per cent of them earn Rs.1000 to Rs.1500 per month as tailors.

The weaving section was started in 1996 with thirty looms. A variety of items of daily use like towels, bed sheets, woolen shawls, checked shirting, material for *salwar/kameez* (a set of costumes worn by women in India) are being made and devotees who come to the camps extend their patronage. A few ladies, after completing their training, have looms in their houses and continue weaving shawls/sheets etc. Rehabilitation of women in dire circumstances was (and is) the motive of the funding agency; income-generation was the aim of Swamiji. Both the objectives are achieved by this project.

The making of carpets commenced in January 1997, with some professional help from carpet manufacturers. The products from the looms are of good quality; the designs are attractive and what is more there is a ready market. A few of the women trained by the centre have set up looms in their own houses and have, with the help of leading manufacturers who supply material and designs, produced carpets. They are earning an income of Rs. 1000 to Rs. 2000 per month.

The funding agency NORAD is satisfied with the performance of the three sections and has kept up its aid. There are no fewer than a hundred women in the three sections. They are engaged in learning a vocation so as to become self-sufficient. The Centre has provided full employment to twelve people, most of them women.

CHINMAYA HUMAN RESEARCH AND DEVELOPMENT INSTITUTE

In November 1998, Swami Tejomayananda laid the foundation stone for the Chinmaya Human Research and Development Institute (CHRDI) in Ranipul in Sikkim. This institute, patterned on the rural welfare activity carried out at Sidhbari, is intended to serve the poor and needy people of the area. Empowerment of women and youth through training and education is one of the main goals. The institute focuses on the training of health workers and on the training of youth for self-employment skills. Income-generating schemes for women and saving schemes like micro banking are also to be implemented.

SEVA INC.

Swamiji founded this Washington-based organization around 1983. It offers educational scholarships (not necessarily scholarships for Vedantic education) and humanitarian contributions to charitable organizations. For instance, donations have been made to Mother Teresa's Mission. Various Chinmaya centres all over the world that require assistance in getting established have benefited through Seva Inc. A Board of Directors oversees the dispensing of funds to the various causes.

TEMPLES

The Chinmaya Movement has promoted temple culture even as it has sought to spread the knowledge of the scriptures. Meditation, *satsang* and prayers are strongly recommended as the main tools for the purification of the mind. To that end, it has built temples near to the Ashrams wherever possible. In some cases, it has taken over neglected temples at the request of the local community.

Sarve bhavantu sukhinah, Sarve santu niramayah
Sarve bhadrani pashyantu, ma kaschid duhkhabhag bhavet
May all be happy; may all be healthy;
May all see the good, and may none be sorrowful.

"What is in a temple?" asked a young devotee. Swamiji answered:

> Exactly what is in the udder of a cow? What is in the udder of the cow, please? Milk. Is it only in the udder of the cow? No, no. It is all over the body and it is the essence of the cow. It is the strength of the cow. It is the nutritive, final, end-result of a cow. Try to milk it in the ears. Take a pot and try to milk it in the tail. Everywhere you try; nowhere can you get milk, even though milk is everywhere. The only place you can get milk is the udder. Narayana is present everywhere. God is all-pervading, but if you want to contact him, run to the nearest temple.

Swami Tejomayananda says, in his book *Hindu Culture–An Introduction*,

> In the Hindu tradition, the temple was also meant for another purpose besides fulfilling the spiritual needs of a person. It was also a place for secular learning, for lectures, for the celebration of special festivals and for the dedication of music and arts. The temples were places where people could come together to share experiences of spiritual nature and those that were for the total cultural awakening and uplift of the people—just like our community centres today.

The Chinmaya centres worldwide have, therefore, built temples wherever possible. The main hall of the temple is for *satsangs* and for lectures by eminent Swamis/Swaminis and by Brahmacharis/ Brahmacharinis of the Chinmaya Mission. Besides devotees or *sevaks* give discourses in the temples. *Bhajan-sandhyas* organized by the Devi groups, or by the Yuva Kendras or by renowned artists are also held here.

The temples create an atmosphere of harmony, beauty, peace and serenity. Spiritual and cultural activity is organized so as to revive our ancient traditions and build a bridge, as it were, between different sects and communities.

The '*arati*' is performed at particular timings in the morning and evening. All the devotees present in the temple at that time, take part in it. The inmates of the centre chant Vedic hymns at dawn. Members of the Mission or the public can also join in the chanting provided they are trained to chant the hymns concerned in Vedic style.

Temple premises are kept scrupulously clean. A serene and peaceful environment is maintained so that devotees may benefit from the holy atmosphere.

The main temples of the Chinmaya Movement are listed in an annexure, together with details about the presiding deities concerned.

BALAVIHARS

"Love is to the human heart what sunshine is to the flowers." Being the visionary that he was, Swamiji saw that in the hi-tech urban civilization of today both sunshine and love are hard to come by. He, therefore, started the Balavihars. A group of ten to twenty-five children meet at a certain place every week and the children and the *sevaks/sevikas* learn the art of living in love, the Hindu way. The idea is to provide an environment where the personality of the child may blossom in a spontaneous way. Good conduct, emotional refinement, intellectual finesse and spiritual awareness are developed by mature *sevaks* through fun and play and through stories and bhajans. Sometimes it is through tears, but more often through smiles; sometimes through strictness, but mostly by persuasion, the children learn to be responsible, alert and sensitive members of society. Swamiji believed that just as the strength of a wall depended on the quality of each brick, so, the health of a society depended on the individuals. If the individuals are healthy, the society is healthy. His strategy for building a new society was to "Catch 'em young."

A typical Balavihar class starts with the chanting of "Om" three times, followed by the *Guru Stotram*. Then they sing a few bhajans and learn new ones. They have sessions in story telling, quiz etc. They end the class with the Balavihar anthem and finally they stand up to take the Mission pledge—nowadays in some centres, this is taken in the Sanskrit language. In most classes children get toffees at the end of the class.

The Balavihars have been the most popular and effective programmes in any Mission centre. The reasons are many—the programme is easy to organize, does not need elaborate infrastructure like hiring a venue or a sound system, *sevikas/sevaks* are enthusiastic to spend time with the children and, for conducting a Balavihar class, *sevaks* do not need to make elaborate textbook preparations. In fact there are many instances where a Balavihar has flourished to grow into a full-fledged Mission centre–for example, in Kolkata Balavihar started in 1969 and is still very active. The *sevika* who started the Balavihar in Kolkata went to New York on an assignment for a dance programme; she started a Balavihar in New York. There are many members of the Mission who, though not *sevikas*, are ready to help with Balavihar activities. In the West also, the grass-root level activity of Balavihar is most popular. The Chinmaya Mission centre in Houston is a case in point—it started with Balavihar activity where the parents were to become compulsorily members of the adult group for Vedanta classes. Today the centre is one of the most successful centres of the Chinmaya Mission. There are 250 families as members and 150 children in the Balavihar classes. The centre at Ann Arbor, Michigan, also started as a Balavihar class on Long Island N.Y., by Sarada and Kumar. Encouraged by Swamiji, they continued the Balavihar activity even when they moved to Ann Arbor. The classes were held in the basement of their house with a few children. It grew by leaps and bounds to hundred children and the venue changed to a nearby school. Today the centre is a full-fledged one with a lot of activity.

In Mumbai, Uncle Mani started Balavihar activity in 1965. In four years Mumbai had 2205 children divided into 63 classes with 58 *sevaks/sevikas*. Today in the fourteen areas in Mumbai there are more than 100 Balavihar classes. The children of Balavihar show a marked improvement in all their activities. They are happier, more stable and friendly. Because of the strong spiritual foundation some of the Balavihar children are today Swamis/ordained workers of the Mission.

The Balavihar activity of the Chinmaya Movement has touched the lives of thousands of children all over the world. As Swamiji would say, " Our children are our Future." Balavihar activity of the Mission ensures that the future of the Movement is bright and luminous.

CHINMAYA YUVA KENDRA

Youthfulness attracts the young and the old alike. The springboard of dynamism and cheerfulness in the form of Swami Chinmayananda attracted a large number of youth from his early days of missionary activity. But it was in early sixties when he went to institutions of higher education that youth started realizing the need to know more about the Vedanta.

The youth felt that they needed to be guided, moulded. They needed to be loved. The youth were searching for some master who could look into their problems. And the problems were aplenty. The youth lacked a sense of direction and purpose. Their view of life was narrow and self-hurting. They were unable to face their situations and felt frustrated. They took to various wrong habits and false notions. They were becoming escapists. They were also feeling lonely. They wanted to be loved but were never wanting to give love. Who could guide them in such situations? After each discourse by Swamiji they would meet him and ask so many questions on life and living that Swamiji felt something had to be done for them.

The Chinmaya Mission had started Balavihars for the kids going to school, Study groups for elders and Devi groups for ladies. How about the youth? Probably the time was not ripe so Swamiji went on encouraging elders to conduct teenagers' classes and give them some direction.

Finally, in 1975, after a 5-day camp for teenagers at Bangalore, Swamiji felt that the time had come for starting a Chinmaya Youth forum. This was renamed as Chinmaya Yuva Kendra as Swamiji felt that it should not be misunderstood as a political youth forum.

The news of starting of a Chinmaya Yuva Kendra (CHYK) spread in all directions like wildfire. Within a year such a Yuva Kendra started functioning in every major city. Br. Haridas Chaitanya who was a nuclear scientist in his *poorvashram*, was appointed as the General Secretary of the All India Yuva Kendra.

The first All India Youth Camp was organized in 1976 at Chennai. The Youth Camp held at Pune in the following year attracted large crowds from all over Maharashtra. Study groups for the young came up at a number of places like Bangalore, Coimbatore and Mumbai. At Chennai and Pune, the youth set about doing wonderful cultural programmes. In cities like Ernakulam, Hyderabad and Thiruvananthapuram they undertook projects of social service.

In 1979 a youth camp was organized at the Sandeepany Sadhanalaya, Mumbai. Youth from far-flung places like Kolkata and Assam also participated in good numbers. By this time the youth were organizing their classes and programmes. They organized lectures on various topics of interest themselves. They helped in organizing the *yajnas* with the help of the various disciples of Swamiji. They started taking Balavihar classes. Thanks to their enthusiasm the number of Balavihar classes increased manifold. In fact, they became a true pillar of the Chinmaya Movement.

It was in 1980 that the Chennai CHYK displayed their fantastic histrionic talents latent in its young members through a programme on the Ramayana, titled 'Kambar Tharum Katchi'. It was in fact a sound-and-light spectacle (son et lumiere). It was a runaway success. Several shows were performed and the Mission earned a good name as well as money, from them. The youth learnt many things—choreography, publicity, dramatics, event management etc. The Mumbai Yuva Kendra organized an M. S. Subbalakshmi Night, and collected over a lac of rupees. It handed over the money to Swamiji to buy a flat in a suburb of Mumbai for starting a small Mission centre. Taking a cue from Chennai, Pune organized a sound-and-light spectacle on its own account—'Samarth

Ramdas'. This show brought to life the upbringing and teachings of the great Swami Samarth Ramdas. More than fifty shows of both these sound-and-light programmes have been performed so far. "Kambar" was performed in Sri Lanka also.

In 1981 Swamiji gave a new idea to the Mumbai Chyks. And out of that new idea emerged what is now called the Chyk Soul Song Nite, an audio-visual presentation of devotionals supported by a lively orchestra and accompanied by appropriate slides. It literally brought ecstasy to one and all. Bangalore now excels in such programmes.

In 1983 another youth camp was organized at Tirunelveli. Here the All-India Chinmaya Yuva Kendra got its first President in Dr. Shrikant Jichkar, a young scholar from Nagpur who held a number of degrees to his credit and who was also the youngest Minister in the Maharashtra Cabinet.

In December 1983 the first International Spiritual Camp was organized at Mumbai. There was a torch march from Pune to Mumbai reflecting the journey of the Movement. More than a hundred youth took part in the march. Representatives of the Yuva Kendras from various centres participated in the discussions held during the camp. It was observed that in nineteen cities of India, the Yuva Kendra had a strong presence.

The Soul Song Nite by CHYK Kolkata, a cultural blitz by CHYK Vijayawada, relief work following the Latur earthquake by the Bangalore Chyks, Seva projects of the Chyks at Adoni and Chennai, and flood relief work by the Orissa Chyks deserve mention here.

In that eventful year Swamiji gave a new programme called CAM-TRA-CON i.e. CAMP-TRAINING-CONFERENCE. Parindra Kadakia was made the Secretary General of All India CHYK and was asked to coordinate that programme. It simply implied that not only spirituality should be taught but training be given in conducting CHYK classes, Balavihar classes, public speaking etc. Also the young had to be organized for meaningful discussions. All took up work to fulfil the great vision as given by Swamiji.

Given below are the year-wise events of the Chinmaya Yuva Kendra:

1984: First All India CHYK Conference was held at Coimbatore. H.N. Ramathirtha was made the President of AICHYK. CHYK worked hard for Hundi collection for the first ever Chinmaya Kumbh Mela that was to be held at Siruvani Ashram.

1985: The first ever Balavihar Camp with Swami Tejomayananda came off at Mumbai. Such camps came up before long all over India.

1986: The Yuva Kendra organized Temple visits and Cycle and Motor cycle yatras all over India. The Chinmaya Seva Camp was held at Chinmayaranyam.

1987: Swamiji's seventieth birthday celebrations were organized on a grand scale at the Shanmukhananda Hall in Mumbai. The Chyks performed Soul Song Nites. There was Hanuman Abhishek at Sidhbari with Chyks participating in large numbers from all over India.

1988: Regional camps were held all over India.

1989: New guidelines were laid down for the All India Chinmaya Yuva Kendra.

1991: The first National Youth Convention was held at Bangalore.

1993: There was a Chyk Camp at Sidhbari in the immediate presence of Swamiji.

At the moment there are seventy CHYK centres in India, and about ten abroad.

STUDY GROUPS

The Study group movement was conceived as a means of ensuring continued interest in the study of the scriptures. A Study group meets each week for an hour and a half at a place offered by some member of the group or other. The course of study is graded so as to make it easy for members to imbibe gradually the deeper suggestions available in the scriptures. A Study group follows three disciplines—first self-study, then enlightened discussion, and, finally, reflection on the knowledge gained in class. Swami Dayananda, one of the senior disciples of Swami Chinmayananda and a pioneer in Study group activity, once said: "Knowledge is acquired by inquiry. And knowledge acquired should be free from error, vagueness and doubt." He was a group *sevak* in the first Study group started by the Mission in Chennai in the 1950s.

In a manual prepared in 1965 and titled *Chinmaya Study Groups: How to Organize and Conduct*, Swami Chinmayananda compared the activity of Study groups to winnowing grain–separation of the chaff from the grain. He said: "In the breeze of discussions, in the wind of arguments, the chaff gets blown off and the true teachings in the clear depth become evident. This is discriminative knowledge". He added that the ground for the Study group was the opportunity for reflection. This kind of inquiry which removes "error, vagueness and doubt" and through which we come to own the knowledge is called *manana* or reflection; it is a process of purification through analysis.

Study group activities have been the backbone of the Chinmaya Movement. To quote Swami Dayananda again: "Study groups help you to provide opportunities for reflection." The *yajna-shala* is where the seeker listens to the teachings in the scriptures—this is called *shravana*. The Study group takes you to the next step in learning viz. reflection or manana. When the seeker of knowledge takes these two steps successfully, the third step is meditation which is single-pointed concentration. It is also called *nididhyasana*. Swami Chinmayananda advised, "Once you have gained discriminative knowledge, run away from the Study group. Apply it to your life and realize the State of Truth in yourself."

The core concept of Study group is the study of the scriptures by those who long to benefit from the perennial wisdom of the *rishis*. The method of study is to meet regularly at a common place and discuss a specific topic. When we meet in a Study group, the idea is primarily to practise reflection and also to cultivate the art of communicating knowledge to others. A Study group has the guidance of a trained *sevak*. In the formative years, when the concept of Study groups was first being implemented, there were orientation camps at the Sandeepany Sadhanalaya, Mumbai for Group *Sevaks*. Now, thanks to the availability of a large number of senior sevaks in the field, the training of new members is the responsibility of senior *sevaks* and Study group coordinators. Any member who has completed successfully the study of the first three books of the graded course–viz. *Kindle Life*, *Bhaja Govindam* and *Atma Bodha*–is eligible to be a *sevak*.

The Study group activity calls for regularity in attendance. Swami Chinmayananda used to insist on the group sevak maintaining an attendance register. He even used to check the attendance register maintained at some centres. If a member is found to be irregular, the group *sevak* takes the initiative and gets in touch with him or he writes a letter to him asking him to be regular. Members should not only to be regular but also come prepared with the topic allotted for discussion. Preparation helps crystallize thoughts, when there is any doubt the member concerned can get it cleared in the class. The group *sevak's* role is to act as a catalytic agent as also to ensure that there is meaningful discussion. He also helps in clearing the doubts of members and, where necessary, expands the ideas generated in class. For the group *sevak* it is a means of doing his *sadhana*.

A well-conducted class contributes to the self-development of a member by enhancing his powers of analytical thinking and inculcates the art of listening, patience, and reverence for others. It also provides fellowship. What is more, it strengthens his sense of belonging, as it were, to the same fraternity.

Giving guidance once to group *sevaks*, Swami Tejomayananda, the Head of the Chinmaya Mission worldwide, laid emphasis on commitment and said that it was the responsibility of each member of the Study group to make the discussion fruitful and interesting. On the basis of figures reported to the CCMT by over 150 centres in India, we can safely hazard the guess that there are over 900 Study groups which means that, with 10 members on an average in each Study group, the number of seekers who meet on a weekly basis would be over nine thousand. The Chinmaya Movement has to its credit the spiritual development of these people on an ongoing basis. Some choose to make an in-depth study of the Vedanta by joining the Vedanta course; others remain householders and continue to teach. They are encouraged to get more training and knowledge through attending *yajnas*, camps for *sevaks/sevikas*, Dharma Sevak courses etc. arranged by the Mission.

A Study group meeting starts with an invocation and ends with a *Shantipath*.

Swami Chinmayananda finalized the scheme of study of the texts for Study groups twenty-five years ago. Recently, Swami Tejomayananda revised the scheme taking into account the facts that new texts had been introduced and that there was some overlapping of texts in the adult and Yuva Kendra Study groups. He divided the graded study into two parts–Part I, called the "The Basic Scheme of Study" and Part II, called "The Advanced Scheme of Study". The scheme is meant to cater to (a) Adults, (b) Junior Chyks and (c) Senior Chyks.

A detailed tabulated scheme of study follows.

"Mere listening to my yajnas will not add to your beauty. These ideas are to be reflected upon deeply and digested slowly. This process is hastened only when you discuss what you have studied with others. Study groups constitute the heart of our Mission. The ideas gathered by you, when discussed with others, not only become deeply rooted in yourself, but as they become clearer in your own understanding, they also inspire those who listen to you. Thus, each student, while trying to strengthen his own understanding, can become an instrument for the spread of this knowledge. This process is the dynamic STUDY SCHEME followed in the Vedantic tradition. This is not a Chinmaya methodology, it is the most ancient Vedantic tradition of study."

- Swami Chinmayananda

ADULT STUDY GROUPS

Part-I: Basic Scheme of study

For Group Study	For Self Study	For Video Viewing
Kindle Life	Vedanta Through Letters	Vivekachoodamani
Bhaja Govindam	We Must	
Tattva Bodha	Sadhana Panchakam	
Manah Shodhanam	Purusha Sooktam	

Atma Bodha	Hymn to Badrinath	
Upadesa Saarah	Vishnu Sahasranama	
Narada Bhakti Sootra		
Meditation and Life		
Geeta, Introduction and Chapters 1 & 2		
Jnanasarah		
Kenopanishad		
Geeta, Chapters 3 - 6		
Dhyana Swaroopam		
Kaivalya Upanishad		
Geeta Chapters 7 - 9		
Ishavasya Upanishad		
Geeta, Chapters 10 - 12		
Bhakti Sudha		
Geeta Chapters 13 - 15		
Mundaka Upanishad		
Geeta Chapters 16 - 18		
Sat Darshana		

Part II: Advanced Study Scheme (to be taken up after completing Part-I)

Name of Book
Yoga Vasishtha Sara Samgraha
Advaita Makaranda
Aitareya Upanishad
Dakshinamoorthy Stotram
Kathopanishad
Prashnopanishad
Taittiriya Upanishad
Mandukya Upanishad

"Four factors, each as important as the other, make the learning process complete: 25% Guru's Blessings; 25% Self Study, 25% Group Study and 25% The Time Factor.

Every text has a central theme; it revolves round it. Look for this central theme first. Each verse should be taken up in the following sequence: First, the word meaning, then the translation of the entire verse, followed by the commentary, and, finally, the sum and substance of the verse."

- H. H. Swami Tejomayananda

CHYK STUDY GROUPS

For Senior Chyks	For Junior Chyks	For Self Study
Manual of Self Unfoldment	Art of Living	Hindu Culture
Art of Man Making	Hanuman Chalisa	
We Must	Art of God Symbolism	
Vibheeshana Geeta	I Love You	
Sadhana Panchakam	Game of Life	
Right Thinking		

Chinmaya Mission Motto

TO GIVE MAXIMUM HAPPINESS
TO MAXIMUM PEOPLE
FOR MAXIMUM TIME

Swami Akhandananda (Brindavan) is to the right of Swamiji

Following the footsteps of his Guru: patriotic offering to the Kargil warriors

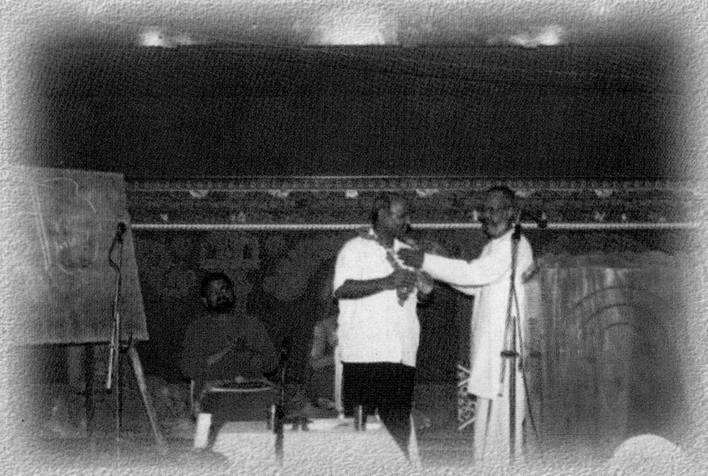

r. A Ramaswamy Iyengar, Director of CIF, honours Dr. K.K. Mishra, Director of Rashtriya Samskrita Sansthana of New Delhi at Adi Sankara Nilaya 1997

Mumbai: Jairam Jaisinghani, Manager of the Ashram, explaining a point to Swamiji

Chinmaya Vidyalaya, New Delhi: Principal Indira Bharadwaj and Swami Jyotirmayananda with the School's Students

Chinmaya Vidyal
Taliparamba, Ker

inmaya Vidyalaya,
Taylor's Road,
Chennai

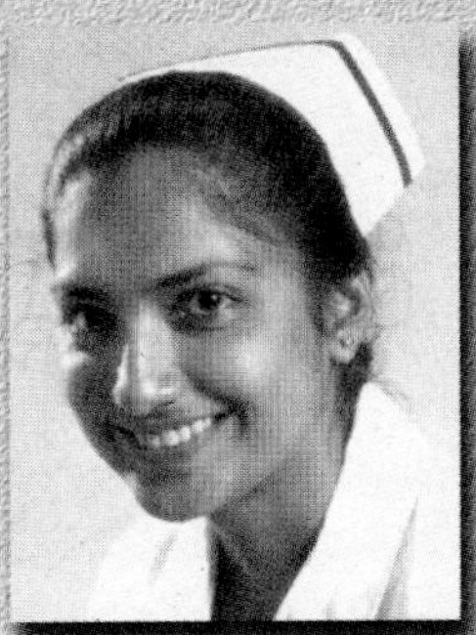

Service with a Smile:
Chinmaya Institute of
Nursing, Bangalore

Chinmaya Mission Hospital,
Bangalore: new Block

angalore: CMH
w Block opens,
Jovember 1999

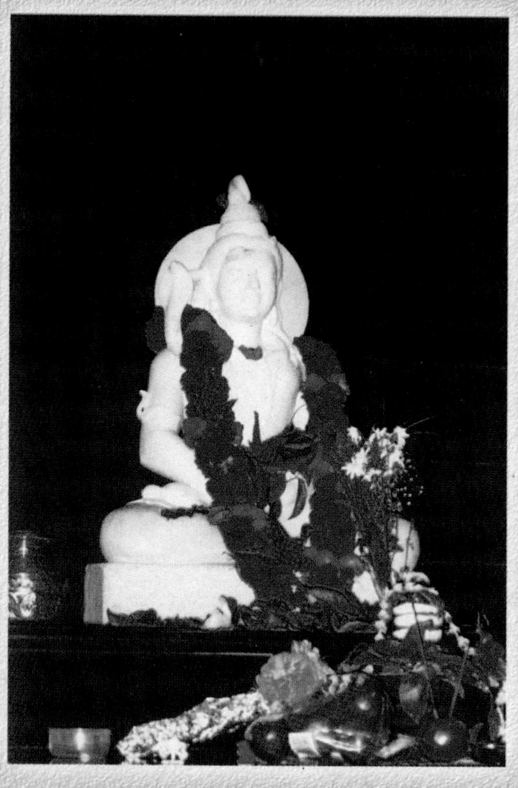

Lord Shiva at Kaivalya, Orlando

Lord Subrahmanya at
Kanhangard, Kerala

Lord Badri Narayana at Badri, Chicago

Lord Shiva at Tamarai pakkam

Deenabandhu Shri Krishna at Bangalore

d Aranyeshwara in Chinmayaranyam

Coimbatore : Ananda Nartana Vinayaka

Sidhbari: Microbanking Classes for village women

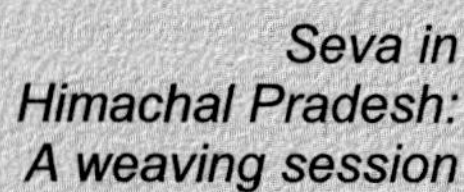

Seva in Himachal Pradesh: A weaving session

Balavihar: Children put up play on Dashavatar, Housto

Balavihar Children meet children of an orphanage, Parla khemundi

Children get ready for Geeta Chanting Competition, Rajapalayam

Chinmaya Yuvakendra: Students make a Pyramid

Chinmaya Yuvakendra: Sulini V. Nair (third from left) an Jayendran Sreenivasan (to her left) won th All India First Prize in the Culture Quiz, 2000

Chinmaya Vuvakendra: Youngsters in Orlando do Homa In the open

Matru Pujan in progre at Bhavanipatna, Orissa: Children worship their mothers

9

Reflections On The Movement

Knowledge is the gift that the Chinmaya Movement has made to one and all over the decades. It has brought fresh vigour to spiritual education. Shri Krishna says in the *Bhagavad Geeta* (IV:36), "You can cross the entire ocean of sin by the boat of knowledge alone." Spiritual ignorance is at the root of all misery in human life. The hundreds of mental complexes that psychology speaks of are the products of our spiritual illiteracy. When our bonds with God are weak, the ropes with which the world binds us to itself are strong. The closer we get to God, the brighter turns our life on earth. The lotus leaf does not get wet even though the plant may be rooted in water. A spiritually evolved person does not get entangled in worldly affairs although he or she may be called upon to handle numerous mundane responsibilities day after day.

Large numbers of people the world over, Hindus especially, and even institutions of learning look up to the Chinmaya Mission for answers to their needs in the area of Vedanta and spirituality. Over the years, the Mission has gained wide acceptance in intellectual circles as an organization they delivers goods. The Mission is now poised to face new challenges even as the responsibility of living up to its reputation weighs heavily upon it. Today the swamis of the Chinmaya fold are called upon to handle diverse issues, and the problems they produce, like changing social values, the stress of the Information Technology (I.T.) revolution, and inter-faith dialogues. As winds from different cultures blow more freely over new terrain, the generation that is coming up has more than one frame of reference in matters of ethics. They wonder if their moral compass shows a different true North than their parents' moral compass did. Do values really change over time? The Mission takes upon itself the hard task of convincing the younger generation of the eternal nature of the values of life. When advances in medicine, genetic engineering, etc. bring in new paradigms of study, teachers in the Mission have to take a stand on matters like abortion, euthanasia, human cloning, and mapping of human genome. Along with a grasp of Manu's laws, they have to know the new laws governing cyber space. On the whole, the Chinmaya Mission is geared to act as the custodian of *Sanatana Dharma* for generations to come. To anyone who reposes his faith in India's timeless spiritual traditions, the Mission dares to say, "If you have a problem, we have the solution."

THE MASTER'S LEGACY

Rome was not built in a day. Om is not reached in a day either. Tremendous inspiration, self-motivation, and love of the people made Swami Chinmayananda fashion this Chinmaya Movement. Our nation's cultural history will be incomplete without according a place to the contributions of the Chinmaya Mission and the numerous organizations flourishing under its umbrella. The universal message of the Vedanta is available more easily, to more people, in more places, and in more ways than ever before, thanks to Swamiji's liberal-minded propagation. Swami Akhandananda, a venerated saint of Brindavan, said once: "We make those who believe in God study the *Geeta*. Your Swamiji makes even those who are averse to God take the holy book in their hands." Men and women, the young and the old, the believers and the atheists–indeed a large number of categories of people find themselves drawn to the Chinmaya fold even as iron filings are drawn to a magnet. Many professionals regard spirituality as conveyed by Swamiji as making a great difference to them.

THE FESTIVE SEASON IS HERE

Swamiji created an excitement wherever he went. "It is like a joyous festival when this Swamiji comes to our city for his *Geeta* discourses", wrote a young student at the Indian Institute of Technology, Chennai to his mother in 1982. Before meeting Swamiji, he had felt an aversion to all that went by the name of religion. Now he found he belonged more to the Vedanta than anywhere else. An elderly brahmacharini at the Powai Ashram remarked once in 1985, "He is joy walking on two legs." The Asrham would get electrified whenever the master arrived there even on short visits. Vibrations of great, elevating energy were palpable whenever the *mahatma* was around. A charismatic leader, he made his presence felt in any gathering—formal or otherwise. With love in his heart and positive thoughts in his mind, vibrant, ever active, he made many hearts throb in resonance with his own.

A VISION COMES ALIVE

"Plan out your work, work out your plan!", said Swamiji, guiding youngsters on the secret of success. He demonstrated the appropriateness of this exhortation in his own life. He would go through the plan drawn up for a project in detail, discuss it with members of the committee concerned, and advise on the next course of action. If the "plan" was not implemented in time, he would show his displeasure. Very often his way of manifesting displeasure was anger, which, to use his own words, was "a tool that I carry always in my pocket." The pains he took to turn many a plan into a dream come true often made his devotees feel a variety of emotions. Some were surprised that a swami, rather than stay aloof from men, and from money and matters, should involve himself so intimately in designing buildings or other construction work, and in organizing marches or in addressing meetings. Some others, watching him work so hard, felt ashamed of themselves for being so slow in their work. Yet others, filled with love for the teacher, were filled with anxiety about his health. Identifying themselves with him, in their own hearts of course, they were alarmed at times and sympathetic at other times. The Guru meanwhile kept on working, burning his candle at both ends as it were. He was fond of saying, "Narayana likes the smell of sweat." In forty-two years, he turned out a tremendous lot of work, hard work, in the service of humanity. The legacy he left behind is unprecedented.

CHARITY BEGINS AT HOME

Sometimes the Chinmaya Movement is described as a Hindu spiritual organization. This surely has more than a grain of truth in it. The Vedanta has no walls. However, Swamiji saw clearly that the

Hindus were now as though they were a minority in their own country. To be sure, as a true saint, his goodwill embraced the entire humanity, but his work catered mainly to the Hindus; for they it was who needed most the education he was all set to impart. By God's will, Swamiji gave a boost to the morale of the Hindus. Having been ruled by foreign Powers for centuries, their psyche had suffered many a wound. More than a healing touch was needed. India as a nation, and the Hindus as representing the major faith in the country, require more Chinmayas to infuse into them the spirit of "We can, and we must." We must note that the essence of the Chinmaya Movement consists in a reawakening of the Hindus, in their self-development and in a value-based development of the human personality. Spiritual education aimed at making everybody a better human being is the main objective behind all its programmes. Religion is at best how the principles are packaged. Swamiji once pointed out, "Spirituality is one; religions are many." His Movement focussed on spirituality although, admittedly, a light, non-aggressive, non-fundamentalist Hindu format was employed. The doors of the Mission are open to all; there is no insistence on anybody changing his faith. Upon being asked, "Do you want to convert people to Hinduism?", Swamiji's witty answer was, "Yes, I want to convert Hindus into Hinduism!"

VEDANTA THE PANACEA

The perennial philosophy of the Vedanta is the foundation of the Chinmaya Movement. The truths of the *Upanishads* are the source of all solutions to the countless problems that arise in life. In fact the Vedanta can convert issues into non-issues. Swamiji often joked, "The Vedanta does not solve any of your problems...."

It dissolves them all!" While it might appear as though the Vedanta avoided the real issues of life, in fact, it does supreme justice to life's situations. When we think deeply, we find that the usual solutions over which we exult are hardly the answers to human conflicts. They are so superficial and temporary. The real cure lies in the human heart. A basic transformation and a total one–this alone can make a true difference. Otherwise it is all a change from tweedle-dom to tweedle-dee. "I, me, and mine" are a psychological construction rooted in ignorance. The Self, which is not a construction of thought, is ever pure and noble. The former by nature creates misery; and the latter, again by nature, is the endless source of happiness. The Vedanta teaches Self-knowledge. The *Upanishads*, synonymous with the Vedanta, declare, "You are that which the mind cannot know; the mind knows objects by the Light that you are." Again, "You are unborn, deathless, and without any change." Constant pondering over such pithy statements from the *Upanishads* with help from a competent teacher cannot but result in a different outlook on life. Our selfishness, our concern about our own tomorrow, our calculative ways of dealing with human relationships, our regrets over what life did not give us—these melt away in this outlook. We know how service leads to purity of mind; in the light of Self-knowledge, service emanates as the natural fragrance of a new vision.

HOPE FOR THE MASSES

There are times when some ill-informed critics charge the Chinmaya Mission with being elitist. On the contrary, the organization is most catholic in its approach; as we have just averred, its doors are .open to all. Perhaps one in a hundred programmes is an affair where one's purse, and not just one's heart, becomes the criterion for participation. For example, a couple of summer camps in a year are held in posh retreats. Five out of a hundred publications are expensive from the common man's point of view. A couple of schools, out of more than sixty, charge high fees (and provide very special facilities of course). The *Geeta jnana-yajnas*, the Study groups, the CHYK programmes, etc. are absolutely free; they are for everybody. Not the purse, but one's literacy and the intellectual level that one has attained may sometimes prove prohibitive. Water finds its own level; and people derive such benefits as they may according to their own mindsets. The work, which no doubt started in English, has spread to all the major Indian languages. The linguistic barrier is no longer there; it was taken down long ago. The Mission can boast of a large repertoire of skills and facilities that cater to a wide range of people—such as basic value-education, simple devotional programmes, humanitarian activities, and mind-boggling philosophical teachings. The schools, the hospitals, the temples, the publications, the Vijnana Mandirs and the *yajna-shalas*—all together—make it surely an "Everyman's Haven."

FOSTERING DYNAMISM

"*Karma jyayo hyakarmanah*—Action is better than inaction," says the *Geeta*. The hallmark of the Chinmaya Movement is vigorous activity. "Move on, move on," said the founder. These words have kept the inspired followers on their toes all along. In the Mission, those who work move up to higher responsibilities. Those who just talk run the risk of getting totally sidelined. It is speed of action, not grandeur of ideas, that matters. Hard, back-breaking work receives applause in the Chinmaya culture. *Karma* (action) receives the pride of place. Of course the teachings also focus on *jnana* (knowledge) and *bhakti* (devotion). In one of his addresses to a group of brahmacharis passing out of the Sandeepany Sadhanalaya, Mumbai, Swamiji said: "It is all right if you die while sweating it out in the villages, spreading the message of the *Geeta*." The present head, Swami Tejomayananda, says, "Think big, act wisely, and show results." An old saying in Sanskrit (*subhashita*) goes, "The ant that moves covers miles; even the mighty eagle Garuda [for all his famed celerity of movement] achieves nothing if he does not take the first step." (*Gacchan pipeeliko yaati yojanaanaam shataanyapi; agacchan vainateyo'pi padam-ekam na gacchati*). The Chinmaya ethos abhors sloth and exalts persistent efforts.

MAKING HEROES OF PEOPLE

Characteristic of a liberal enterprise, the Chinmaya Mission provides a platform to a speaker without any hindrance or restriction of any kind. Swamiji encouraged every member of a Study group to start and lead yet another group, if not conduct a *jnana-yajna*! Very often the disciples were hesitant. Once a brahmachari asked, "Swamiji, who am I to preach? What do I know after all?" The Guru replied: "Do not think you are preaching. You are doing loud thinking. It is *manana* so far as you are concerned." Often he added, in his own characteristic way, humorously, "It is their *prarabdha* to listen to you!" (*Prarabdha* typically means the result of some bad deed of a past life inexorably manifesting itself in the present life.) He told many a devotee, "Sit on the dais, close your eyes, think of the Lord, and the rest will happen." Many a devotee reminisces, "I just did that. Swamiji spoke through me." Brahmacharis and householders were not different in Swamiji's eyes. Swamiji loved them all equally. No wonder several of his followers from the latter camp blossomed forth as able, well-received spiritual teachers in their own right. P. G. Ananthanarayanan, lovingly called Uncle Mani, came from a background of banking and is respected in Chinmaya circles as a very able teacher of the scriptures, especially the Valmiki Ramayana. He was the Acharya at the Chinmaya Mission, Chicago, Illinois, for three years. In appreciation of his excellent work, Swami Chinmayananda once wrote to him: "Where were you moulded? Is there similar stuff available? Then order 1000 more. We need them immediately." He writes, while reflecting on Study groups, "We are the fortunate instruments representing a mighty cause, a unique institution, and a noble *paramparā*. Constant alertness, both on and off the field, is called for so that we do not become agents to tarnish the glorious image of the Renaissance Movement, so painstakingly built up at tremendous sacrifice by our Gurudev." He adds, in a recent message:

> Spiritual life is all-inclusive. It is not optional, part-time or a post-retirement occupation. It is a way of life, a life-style. Pujya Gurudev's *Maha-mantra* for us is: Learn, live, share. His advice is: Listen attentively, reflect deeply and practise slowly. His observation of one's progress in spiritual life is: The depth of a person's development is reflected on the surface of one's contacts. The essential values for *pracharaks* are gratitude, humility and forbearance. Bhakta Anjaneya is the ideal model for all *sadhaks*.

J. Vemaiah of Andhra Pradesh pleaded his inability when Swamiji asked him to conduct a *jnana-yajna*. The guru said: "Go, sit, and open your mouth. I will talk." The Master further assured him: "It is Krishna that speaks His *Geeta*, not you or I." Vemaiah thereafter conducted many *yajnas*. He says now: "I really experienced the Truth of his words!" H.N. Ramathirtha of Mysore is a rich, educated businessman. He heard Swamiji first at the age of eighteen. He recalls, "Swami Chinmayanandaji was a great visionary, a missionary and a living legend. His presence was inspiring and elevating. One look was enough to transform a person. Glory to Gurudev!" Ramathirtha has completed three hundred *yajnas* on the *Geeta* and other texts. Professor C.G. Vasudevan at Chennai taught English in a college. Swamiji's influence made him become a persuasive speaker on the Vedanta. He offers his tributes to the Master in poetic language: Parama Poojya H. H. Swami Chinmayananda is the blazing effulgence and conflagration from whom tremendous sparks are emanating endlessly, globally dispelling the darkness of ignorance. Chinmaya Jyoti is the unlit light that is ever and eternally shining and which can never be put out. It is our good fortune to have come in contact with the spiritual saga of this Fire, this plenitude which is ineffable and incomparable. It is this blazing glow that still sustains these sparks which continue to trail the blaze, shedding light into the dark hearts of millenniums past, present and future. Heartfelt *pranams* and gratitude to the Fire and the luminaries that have come out of this great Blaze.

CONTRIBUTION TO ART AND CULTURE

When the sun rises, the light nourishes all life, not the flowers alone. Swamiji showed keen interest in the talents of his devotees. Often, after his *Geeta* discourses, there would be a recital of classical music or a performance of Bharata Natyam. Often he took care to attend personally when some noted singer sang at a Mission centre. He stressed the significance of art in the spiritual development of a human being. He showered loving compliments on the performer. The tradition continues with Swami Tejomayananda, himself a gifted singer, encouraging music, dance, and other forms of art.

HOLD NARAYANA, LAKSHMI WILL FOLLOW

Swamiji came down from Uttarakashi with hardly a penny in his pocket. The Mission he built has now many properties around the world valued at many millions of dollars. The inflow of cash by way of donations, subscriptions etc. and the outflow in the form of expenditure on running programmes, maintaining facilities, etc. have multiplied a thousandfold over the past five decades. Yet the projects are forever on the increase; the Mission spends a lot of money to keep the show going. Apart from its regular activities, it has undertaken relief work whenever a tragedy has hit the nation. It has even gone around with a begging bowl to organize relief operations. The earthquake in Gujarat in 2001 promptly followed the Kargil crisis in 1999 and the Orissa cyclone in 2000. For both the usual and unexpected requirements, the raising of funds is a hard task. The founder always advised his followers: "Hold Narayana tightly; once He comes to you, Lakshmi will just follow." Narayana is the supreme God; Lakshmi is His consort and the goddess of wealth. Swamiji asked his people never to lose sight of the right priorities. Devotion to God comes before all else. Nothing else should be given more importance.

LEGACY OF HUMOUR

"I have been bypassed!", wrote Swamiji on a photograph of his, after a triple bypass surgery was performed on him in 1980. This was like the man who had three bullets in his body, and in the operation theatre, upon being asked if he had any known allergy, said, "Yes, I am very allergic to bullets; please remove them quickly!" Swamiji's sense of humour gave the whole Movement a distinct flavour. People often said, "Take some Vedanta, sprinkle some humour, there you have the Chinmaya recipe." However, the right proportion was always maintained. It never became a case of "a lot of humour and a sprinkling of Vedanta!" Once somebody said, "Swamiji, why do you take snuff?" The master replied, very wittily, "Ah, that is great; you have come up to my nose. Now go higher!" The humour, the dramatization, and a number of other communication skills made the Vedanta philosophy so delectable that his classes on the *Upanishads* attracted even very worldly-minded people. They would get some general idea of the profound thoughts and, at the least, go back with a sense of pride in their spiritual heritage. Swamiji wanted just that many a time. He exhorted his disciples, "Generate an awareness in the masses about the glory of Hinduism."

INTERNATIONAL SCENARIO

The Indian diaspora is a great, albeit recent, phenomenon of world history. Under British persuasion in colonial times and from self-motivation subsequently, the Indian people went to almost all the continents of the world, in search of work and settled down there. Today thus we have ethnic Indians as well as first-generation immigrants in many countries, all of them seeking to strengthen their bond with their motherland and her religion. Naturally, therefore the work of the Chinmaya Mission is welcomed and sustained mainly by the Indian population everywhere. Broadminded people with different backgrounds have also taken interest in the Chinmaya Mission and joined the Movement. Swamiji personally met and interacted with many foreigners. Some of them became his ardent admirers. He spoke at the United Nations. He is known today internationally. The spirituality of the Vedanta is universal; it does not necessarily require a Hindu background to appreciate it. It appeals to any rational thinker. Going well with developments in modern physics, mathematics, and other branches of knowledge, the pure Vedanta, which maintains that there is but One Truth and that everything else is a manifestation of it, is sure to be a winner internationally. While the Chinmaya Mission has succeeded to a certain extent in making its presence felt in the English-speaking countries, much needs to be done in countries where English is not spoken. Translations of some important Chinmaya books into French, Spanish and Portuguese have no doubt been made available. A few missionaries are also conveying the message of the Vedanta to small groups in languages other than English. Even then there is great scope for more work and for well-sustained efforts to reach more people. Time alone will tell if the work of Swami Chinmayananda would reach countries where the lingua franca is a language other than English.

RESEARCH

Spurred by the Chinmaya Mission's regular work, scholarly devotees have taken interest in doing research in the scriptures, in Sanskrit, and in other Indological subjects. Natural Language Processing (NLP) is an area where Brahmachari Vineet Chaitanya is working with great dedication at the Indian Institute of Information Technology, Hyderabad. Many devotees and swamis of the Mission are involved in this work being done in the area of Artificial Intelligence (AI). If computers, thanks to this work, can translate from English to Indian languages and vice versa, it will have great implications for the dissemination of the Indian heritage. A huge amount of literature is available in Sanskrit and other Indian languages. Many times an aspirant does not know the language of a given source book or an English translation is not available. This work at the Indian Institute of Information Technology is being supported partly by the Chinmaya International Foundation. The CIF aspires to promote research activity by Indian scholars and by scholars from foreign universities. While the regular work of the Mission focusses on spirituality and self-development, the research activity at the CIF can embrace the entire gamut of India's literary heritage. To cite a few examples, the *karma-kanda* of Vedas (ritualistic portion), the *Vedangas* (the six auxiliary limbs), the study of edicts and of ancient Sanskrit writings on stone, comparative religion, scientific insights into Indian literature, etc. are of interest to the research wing of the Mission.

SANSKRIT

Being a progressive organization devoted to the people, the Chinmaya Mission initially put stress on the content of the scriptural heritage rather than on the language in which this heritage is preserved. Now that the Movement has become stable, it is surely time to make significant contributions to the learning and propagation of Sanskrit. There is need to make more and more people feel comfortable with the original works rather than depend on translations. There is also the need to promote Sanskrit study for scriptural appreciation. Learned teachers of the Mission could work on providing vocabulary, grammar, and literary exercises to the common man, drawing abundantly from scriptural sources (rather than the works of Kalidasa or Bharavi). A knowledge of Sanskrit then familiarizes the student with the *Geeta* and the *Upanishads* right away. The Valmiki Ramayana is a very rich source of basics; it could also be used to familiarize oneself with all nuances of the divine language.

FORAY INTO MANAGEMENT

Swamiji said once, while addressing some executives at Ahmedabad, "Managers, manage yourselves." He spoke to the district conference of the Rotary Movement at Mumbai on "Service above self." His teachings are full of insights into the Science of Management, especially in the area of Human Resource Development. Noble motivation, practical ideas on achieving success, tips on leadership, secrets of time management, and, above all, the handling of emotions—are among the areas where the life and literature of Swami Chinmayananda have much to offer by way of guidance. His words came with great simplicity and force. Some of his quctable quotes are: "Plan out your work; work out your plan." "Let your mind be, where your hands are." "A successful man is he who uses the bricks that others throw at him to build a firm foundation." "Use your head while judging yourself; use your heart while judging others." While the Chinmaya Institute of Higher Learning (CIHL). and, under it, the Chinmaya Institute of Management (CIM) are set to bring the compelling truth of Vedanta to the area of Management, several swamis of the Mission are invited by the corporate world to conduct seminars and workshops for their executives. Value-based management with special emphasis on stress-reduction, leadership qualities, emotional intelligence, etc. is where spirituality enjoys common ground with the Science of Management.

The sky is the limit for good work. Service leads to one's own inner development. Serving others, purifying one's mind, improving one's vision of life, and living without yielding to the ego any more space than is necessary for the purpose of existence are the stages through which one passes in the course of one's soul's journey to the eternal truth. The aim of the Chinmaya Movement is to enable one and all to find the ultimate fulfilment of life.

Sidhbari : Pushpa Jaisinghani
Chinmaya Nursery School, Mumbai)
in the joyous company of Swamiji

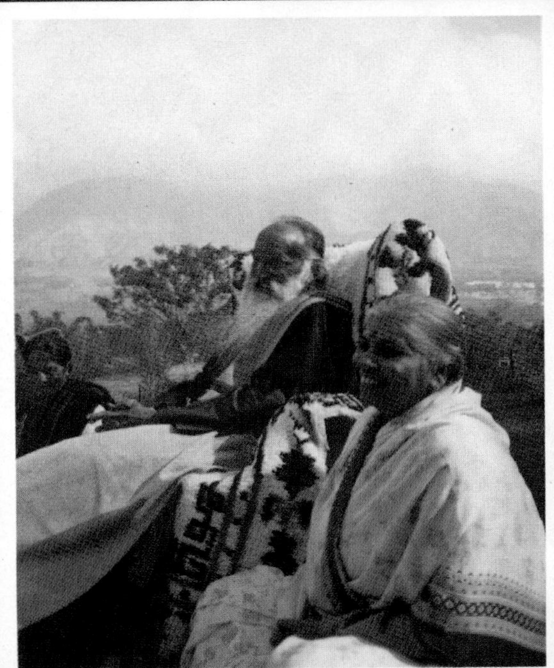

Kamala Chanrai (Mumbai)
with her son Laju

H.N. Ramathirtha

P.G. Ananthanarayan
'Uncle Mani'

Prof. C.G. Vasudevan

J. Vemaiah

Swami Chidananda (Muniji) and Shri Rameshbhai Ojha join Mission's Swamis in Kolkata

Sant Shri Morari Bapu graces a Mission Yajna in Ahmedabad

Swamiji Visits Bhagawan Swami Nityanar
in Vajreshwari near Mumbai

Jagadguru of Shringeri,
Shri Abhinava Vidya Tirtha,
visits the Deenabandhu
Devasthanam, Bangalore

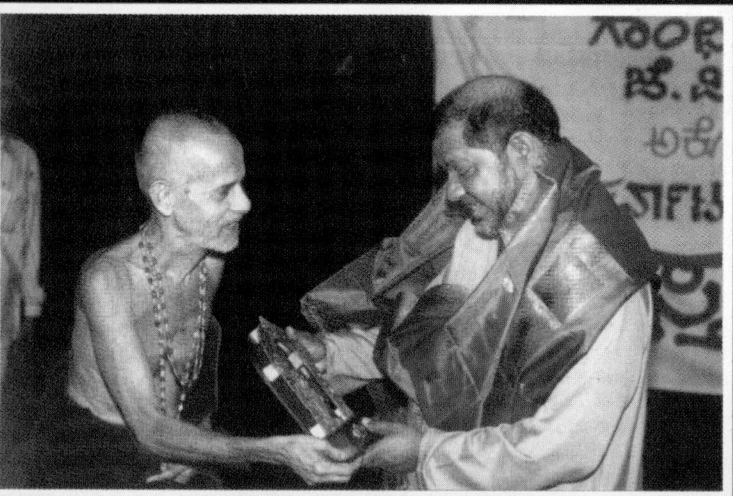

Swami Vishwesha Tirth
Pejawar Mutt presen
Memento to
Swami Tejomayanan
at Udupi, October 20

Orissa Super Cyclone 1999

Ravage

Devastation

Relief

Swami Mitrananda from Chennai inspecting the damage

Orissa Super Cyclone 1999

Relief

Supplying essential commodities to victims of cyclone

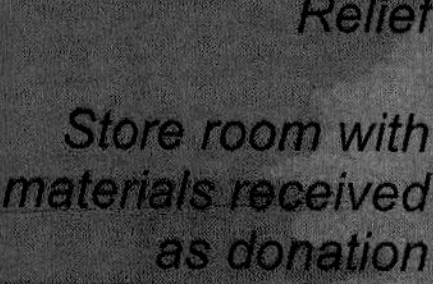

Relief

Store room with materials received as donation

Reconstruction

Houses constructed for the homeless

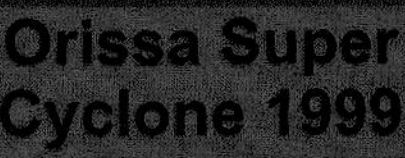

Orissa Super Cyclone 1999

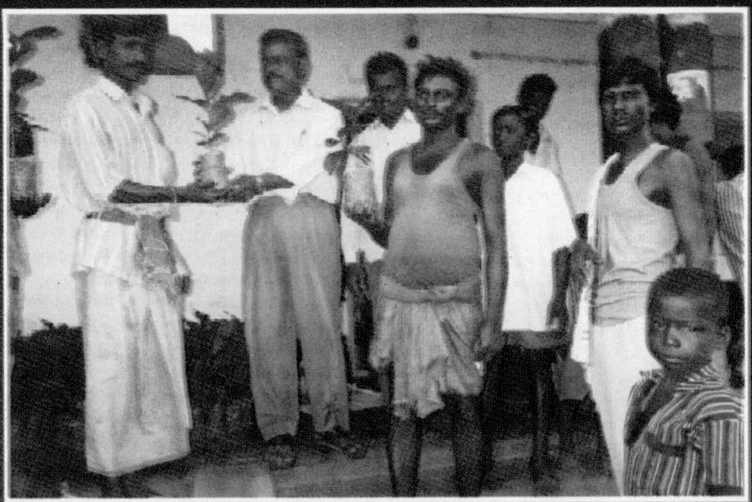

Environment-friendly - Chinmaya Mission distributes saplings for planting

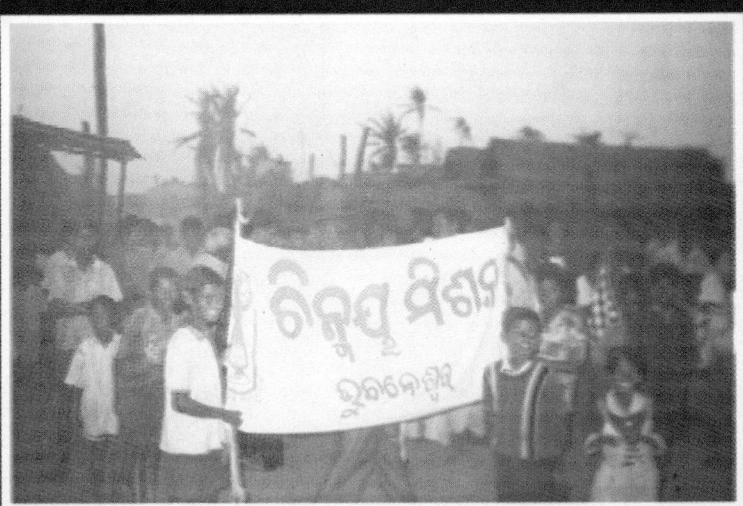

Chinmaya Mission relief action: A procession

' We seek thy grace and blessing
to keep us on the path of
Virtue, Courage and Wisdom'

Dawn Of The Revivalist Era

Five Stalwarts Of The Chinmaya Movement

It is difficult to explain why we have chosen only five out of the many stalwarts of the Chinmaya Movement—men and women who were steady and loyal to the Mission and its Master. Undoubtedly these people contributed a great deal to the making of the history and what better time, than the golden jubilee year, can we choose to remember them and their contribution with gratitude?

We are going back in time to the first *jnana-yajna* in 1951 when Swami Chinmayananda launched his Movement for the revival of Hinduism. In the initial years, people knew him only as a 'swami' from the Himalaya. At that time he needed the patronage and helping hand of local people who were prominent in the community. They were opinion makers who could draw more people to the Movement. With their undaunted support, he made a great impact on the people and the Chinmaya Movement set off to a glorious start.

It is not easy to select the persons who gave the Movement their unflinching support. Nor is it easy to restrict the number to five. All the same we have made a bold attempt to do this exercise with our apologies for not having been able to do a more exhaustive one. We restricted the field of choice of stalwarts to those who have left for their heavenly abode.

JAGDISH PRASAD OF DELHI

Jagdish Prasad's first meeting with Swami Chinmayananda happened during a *yajna* in 1956 in Bangalore where he was stationed at Managing Director of Indian Telephone Industries. In 1960, he came to Delhi as a member of the Postal and Telecommunications Board and also a member of the Union Public Service Commission. During his tenure in Delhi for five years he participated in work related to the Mission and arranged *yajnas*. From 1965 onwards, as General Manager with BHEL in Hardwar, he continued Chinmaya Mission work by organizing *yajnas* in the BHEL complex. In the late sixties he returned to Delhi and was the Chairman of Delton Cables till 1974. He resumed Mission work in Delhi.

Jagdish Prasad and his wife Shyama had some remarkable qualities. Their simple lifestyle, lack of ostentation, a sense of contentment and adherence to ethical values endeared them to Swamiji. Their interaction with people was without ego. Swamiji used to stay with them and whosoever went to see Swamiji were treated with warmth and hospitality.

Swamiji used to call Jagdish Prasad frequently to Mumbai to help in the Ashram's administrative work. This was during the period of construction of Sandeepany Sadhanalaya and the Jagadeeswara Temple in Mumbai. In 1974 Jagdish Prasad retired from service and joined Central Chinmaya Mission Trust (CCMT) at Mumbai as the General Manager. In 1979 he was made Managing Trustee of the Chinmaya Tapovan Trust at Sidhbari. In the 1980's Swamiji wanted to give *sannyas* to both Jagdish Prasad and his wife Shyama but their children and grandchildren did not approve of Swamiji's idea! The couple declined saying that they were not fit to receive the honour.

In 1986 Jagdish Prasad returned from Sidhbari and soon after, his wife passed away. This was a very hard hit on him after a lifetime of a sublime partnership. A lifetime of spiritual endeavour helped him through this period during which he stayed with his daughter, Urmila.

Once again he took up Mission work and helped Delhi Mission, as Trustee of the Delhi Sewa Trust, as Chairman of Chinmaya Degree College in Hardwar and Chairman of Chinmaya Vidyalaya in Vasant Vihar, Delhi. Towards the end of his active life he would attend all the meetings although he was not keeping well.

During his association with the Chinmaya Movement Jagdish Prasad always served Swami Chinmayananda as his right hand because he allowed his body, mind and intellect to become instruments for Swamiji to spread the message of the *rishis*.

Jagdish Prasad passed away on May 10, 1999, an active *karma yogi* till the very last.

B. M. KAMDAR OF MUMBAI

In 1957, Swami Chinmayananda was conducting a *yajna* on the terrace of K.C. College, Churchgate, Mumbai. A young couple, B. M. Kamdar and Mrs. Pushpa Kamdar came to hear his discourse as they had heard that an extraordinarily erudite young swami was speaking in English on the *Bhagavad Geeta.* When they heard Swamiji they were enthralled and sought a private audience with him. Swamiji was staying with Dewans at Warden Road. They met Swamiji and when Swamiji heard that Kamdar was an engineer and an architect, he exclaimed "Oh! You have a lot to do for me!" In course of time the bond between the Kamdars and Swamiji became stronger. Swamiji used to call Kamdar as "daddy" and Mrs. Kamdar as "amma".

In 1958, Swamiji entrusted to Kamdar the planning and designing of the various buildings in the Powai Ashram—the Vairagyalaya, Vivekalaya, Annakshetra, Sruti Mandir, Saraswathi Nilayam, Yashodalaya and a few buildings as quarters for the Ashram staff. In 1963 the construction of the Ashram was completed and during the construction, Swamiji used to occupy a room on the first floor of Vairagyalaya. Kamdar asked Swamiji for permission to donate a *kutia* in memory of his first wife, Shantibai Kamdar, for Swamiji's occupation. Swamiji agreed. Till this day the *kutia* is a place of pilgrimage to many of the devotees and the public, who make a special visit to offer their humble respects to Swamiji.

Kamdar was making frequent changes, while the *kutia* was being built, in his desire that it should be perfect and most comfortable for Swamiji. The guru was so amused one day, he said "Daddy, you are changing the plans of this *kutia* so many times that one day you will tell me to shorten my legs because I am too tall for these doors!"

In 1963, the first batch of brahmacharis of 11 students, carefully selected by Swamiji, joined Sandeepany Sadhanalaya. On January 6, the *upanayana* ceremony was performed and the *sankalpa* was made by Smt. and Shri Kamdar as god-parents of these students. A few of the outstanding students of this batch are Swami Purushottamananda, Swamini Gangananda and Swamini Saradapriyananda.

It is interesting to know that the two major Trusts in Mumbai, CCMT and Tara Cultural Trust (TCT) were formed out of suggestions made by Shri Kamdar to Swamiji.

The involvement of the Chinmaya Movement with the Vishwa Hindu Parishad (VHP) was also due to the close association of Kamdar with Guru Golvalkar who was supporting the Hindutva movement. Swami Chinmayananda was getting letters from foreign countries that the second-generation Indian immigrants had no exposure to Indian heritage. Guru Golvalkar also had similar views. With the far-reaching vision of the two Masters, the VHP was formed and its inaugural meeting was held in Sandeepany Sadhanalaya. The Rashtriya Seva Sangh (RSS), Master Tara Singh and K.M. Munshi also supported the VHP.

Kamdar presided over many meetings of the Chinmaya Mission and also headed *yajna* committees. He took active interest in the affairs of the Mission. He was a founder-trustee of CCMT. Those members who knew him closely fondly called him "Pappaji".

He passed away after a brief illness in Mumbai on February 10, 1979. Swamiji was abroad when he heard the sad news.

In 1981 at Sidhbari, in one of his reminiscent moods, gazing at the Himalayas, Swamiji suddenly burst out, "Just look at them!! Kamdar gone, Batra gone and this one (meaning himself) is still here."

RAM BATRA OF MUMBAI

There can be no fitting tribute to Ram Batra than reproducing relevant portions of the emotional outburst of Swami Chinmayananda when he wrote for a Souvenir in 1981.

It is difficult—hard, almost impossible, to express what I feel about Ram Batra and his sewa for the Chinmaya Mission during more than 20 years of pure energetic devoted work.

He had all the necessary qualities of a Missionary. He waited more than 4 years, attending the *yagnas* from the outer margins but watching the Swami and his work. Only

when he was convinced did he surrender to the way-of-life and the philosophy. I don't think in our mission, round the world, there is any other one student who had absorbed so much and lived the spirit of our philosophy so fully as Ram Batra did.

He applied what he had understood in all his varied fields of work...... there was an inner glow of the Karma Yoga. I had only to explain my vision–programme and plans. He WOULD elaborate and with intelligent plan work it all out, often creating a better result than what I expected.

It was a real blow to me when the news of his sudden departure reached me in the U.S.A. It was terrible. I never felt so much of loss ever. He is irreplaceable, our community can never fill up the vast vacuum he HAS created.

He has left us an ideal to emulate and live through. Cheerful always, a relaxed heart, bubbling with a subtle sense of humour, he was fully competent in all the varied fields he had worked.

Jai Jai Jagadeeswara,

- Swami Chinmayananda

Ram Batra was the Secretary of the Chinmaya Mission and was totally dedicated to the Mission for over 20 years. He was a close confidant of Swami Chinmayananda and was always at his beck and call. He concretized many a vision of Swamiji: Sandeepany Sadhanalaya, Tapovan Kuti, Sandeepany (West) and Sandeepany (Himalayas) etc. He made all the arrangements for the mega *yajnas* in Mumbai. He was generous to a fault—his office and its infrastructure were always at the disposal of the Mission. He was a well-known industrialist, owning a chain of reputed laundry outlets known as "Band Box" in Mumbai. The city adored him and made him its Sheriff in 1978. He was a man of great humility and referring to himself, he would say with humour, "I am only a dhobi". Swamiji and all those who came in contact with him loved him for his fine qualities of the head and the heart.

Ram Batra passed away on August 20, 1981.

N. V. RAMAKRISHNA REDDI OF BANGALORE

N.V.R. Reddi (NVR as he was popularly addressed) was one of the earliest disciples of Swami Chinmayananda. He was a great admirer of Swamiji and served him with *Ananyabhava* (one-pointed feeling). In 1953 he read in The Hindu, the daily newspaper, that a 'swami' was giving a talk. Presuming that the talk would be in Tamil, he did not go to the discourse. Years later, he went to listen to Swamiji's discourse in Madurai. He was greatly impressed. His sister, who lived in Hyderabad, was a great devotee of Swamiji. Reddi's pioneering work helped greatly in building up the Mission at the earlier stages. He was the President of the Mission in Bangalore for some time and was a Trustee of CCMT, Mumbai. He was a great source of support to the Chinmaya Movement, particularly in terms of raising funds. He piloted the scheme of setting up of the Chinmaya Mission Hospital and the Deenabandhu Devasthanam in Bangalore. He threw himself heart and soul into the publication of the Mission's journal *Tyagi.* Swami Chinmayananda affectionately blessed him as the 'Bhishma-pithamaha' of the Mission for all the pioneering work he had done. The chiselled stone pillars for a Temple sculptured during Reddy's father's time, ultimately found their destination in building up the monumental mantap at Shri Rama's temple at Sidhbari. Swamiji entrusted all his *guru-dakshina* from all over with Reddi, requesting him to round off all the money that came in trickles, which Reddi gladly did for his guru. He was very humble before Swamiji, a sincere devotee rendering his whole-hearted service in managing Swamiji's funds and in organizing *yajnas.* He spoke very little and implicitly obeyed Swamiji's orders. Swamiji in turn reciprocated with love and warmth towards him and his family. His wife Kamala Reddi and his daughter were also drawn towards Swamiji. For some years, Swamiji used to stay with them whenever he visited Bangalore. While remembering Reddi, one cannot forget that he had the greatest devotion for the Lord, equal to his guru. He used to attend all the *yajnas* of Swami Chinmayananda not only in Bangalore, but also in Mumbai, Sidhbari and other places.

Reddi thus was a sincere devotee of Swamiji, ever ready to take up responsibility for missionary work. He put in his best efforts to raise resources for the projects, which were close to the heart of Swamiji.

N.V. Ramakrishna Reddi passed away on March 30, 1990 in his 86th year.

JAMNADAS MOORJANI OF MUMBAI

Jamnadas H. Moorjani was a long-standing member of the Chinmaya Mission and a close devotee and confidant of Swami Chinmayananda and Swami Tejomayananda. Born on October 16, 1934 in Sind, he grew up and helped his father in his textile trading business in Mumbai.

Starting from a humble background, Jamnadas grew into an industrialist, who was respected in the textile community and outside. He made a name for himself as a person who stood for the good of the people who had reposed faith in him.

At an interview he had given to Swami Chidananda, just a few weeks before his demise, he reminisced on how he had been drawn to the Chinmaya Movement. A friend of his had chanced to drop in at his office and asked him to accompany him to listen to a lecture by a new Swamiji who had come to Mumbai. Though he was hard pressed for time, he attended the discourse. After that there was no looking back.

His wife and he reposed deep faith in Swamiji. When they did not have any issue for fifteen years after marriage, Swamiji assured them in a tone of certainty that they would have. Against contrary predictions from a couple of other sources, Vimla and Jamnadas had three brilliant children in due course of time.

Jamnadas hosted the first Study group in Mumbai at his residence in Padam, at Peddar Road. He stood with Swamiji all through the construction of the Jagadeeswara Temple. He traveled with Swamiji on some of his foreign tours like Malaysia. He stayed behind after the *yajna* to guide the new members on how to conduct a Study class etc. He enjoyed the confidence of Swamiji. After the *maha-samadhi* of Swami Chinmayananda, his ties with Swami Tejomayananda were just as strong. He was a founding Trustee of CCMT and a director on the Board of Chinmaya International Residential School at Coimbatore. He was involved in a lot of decision-making in a number of major projects not only in Mumbai but at several places in the country.

He observed in the interview that more professionals were being drawn nowadays to the Chinmaya Mission and, while they showed much interest in the subject, their understanding of the greatness of the Master was rather limited.

Jamnadas Moorjani attended the *Geeta Jayanti pooja* at the Powai Ashram on December 7, 2000. He passed away peacefully the same evening at his home.

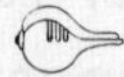

CHINMAYA VIDYALAYAS - TOUCHING THE LIVES OF MILLIONS

Sr. No.	State	Center Name	Attached to Chinmaya Mission	Year	Status	Number of Students	Number of Teachers	S/T Ratio	Affiliated
1.	Andhra Pradesh	Kundanbagh	Hyderabad	1993	Secondary	924	44	21	CBSE
2.	Andhra Pradesh	SVN Colony	Guntur	1982	Secondary	342	23	15	State Board
3.	Andhra Pradesh	Jyoti Nagar	NTPC	1994	Jr College	1800	54	33	State Board
4.	Andhra Pradesh	Chinmaya Aranyam	Ellayapalli	1986	Secondary	232	14	17	State Board
5.	Bihar	Gaya	Gaya	1994	Secondary	50	6	8	State Board
6.	Bihar	Jamshedpur	Jamshedpur	1979	Secondary	1258	40	31	State Board
7.	Himachal Pradesh	Nauni,Solan	Delhi	1992	Secondary	228	20	11	CBSE
8.	Karnataka	Jayalaxmipuram	Mysore	1975	Secondary	1356	42	32	State Board
9.	Karnataka	Hubli	Hubli	1990	Secondary	896	24	37	State Board
10.	Karnataka	St John's Road	Bangalore	1981	Secondary	971	35	28	State Board
11.	Karnataka	Kormangala	Bangalore	1995	Primary	505	19	27	State Board
12.	Karnataka	Kolar	Kolar	1977	Secondary	1250	51	25	State Board
13.	Kerala	Cannanore	Cannanore	1978	Secondary	2454	117	21	CBSE
14.	Kerala	Nellicode	Calicut	1969	Secondary	1496	60	25	State Board
				1988	State Govt.				
15.	Kerala	Vazathacaud	Trivandrum	1969	Secondary	1096	55	20	State Board
16.	Kerala	Kattakada	Trivandrum	1982	Secondary	437	27	16	State Board
17.	Kerala	Kollengode	Pallakkad	1965	Secondary	704	29	24	CBSE
18.	Kerala	Kunnampuram	Trivandrum	1980	Secondary	920	45	20	ICSE

19.	Kerala	Naruvamood	Trivandrum	1983	Secondary	276	24	11	State Board
20.	Kerala	Manacaud, Attukal	Trivandrum	1981	Secondary	1095	53	21	CBSE
21.	Kerala	Vaduthala	Cochin	1971	Secondary	2051	79	26	CBSE
22.	Kerala	Talliparamba	Talliparamba	1987	Nursery	119	4	30	
					Secondary	851	38	22	CBSE,Delhi
23.	Kerala	Thrissur	Thrissur	1979	Secondary	1383	58	24	CBSE
24.	Kerala	Manjeri	Calicut	1989	Secondary	195	18	11	CBSE
25.	Kerala	Tattamangalam	Pallakkad	1977	Secondary	762	34	22	CBSE
26.	Kerala	Mattancherry	Mattanchery	1995	Primary	179	11	16	
27.	Kerala	Pallavur	Pallakkad	1974	Secondary	1206	49	25	CBSE
28.	Kerala	Chandanathope	Kollam	1985	Middle Sch	300	16	19	not yet alloted
29.	Kerala	Payyanur	Kannur	1990	Secondary	340	19	18	
30.	Kerala	Kanhangad	Kannur	1978	Secondary	783	34	23	CBSE
31.	Kerala	Kasargod	Kasargod	1971	Secondary	1382	62	22	CBSE
32.	Kerala	Pallasena	Thrissur	1991	Primary	110	7	16	not recognised
33.	Kerala	Coyalmannam	Pallakkad	1985	Primary	150	8	19	not recognised
34.	Kerala	Moolavattom	Kottayam	1931	Secondary	1145	43	27	State Board
35.	Kerala	Pallakkad	Pallakkad	1976	College	838	25	34	Parellel College
36.	Kerala	Illickal	Kóttayam	1997	Secondary	349	24	15	CBSE
37.	Kerala	Nileshwar	Nileshwar	1983	Secondary	438	25	18	CBSE
38.	Kerala	Tripunithura	Tripunithura	1974	Secondary	1720	82	21	CBSE
39.	Madhya Pradesh	Satna	Satna	1977	Secondary	317	19	17	State Board

40.	Maharashtra	Tarapur	Boisar	1995	Middle Sch	710	22	32	State Board
41.	Maharashtra	Akola	Akola	1994	Nursery	22	2	11	State Board
42.	Orissa	NTPC	Deepshikha	1995	Middle Sch	242	12	20	State Board
43.	Orissa	Rourkela	Rourkela	1979	Secondary	1194	44	27	State Board
44.	Orissa	Therubali	CCMT	1980	Secondary	303	21	14	CBSE Delhi
45.	Tamil Nadu	Srirangam	Trichy	1982	Secondary	1178	50	24	State Board.
46.	Tamil Nadu	CIRS Coimbatore	Coimbatore	1996	Secondary	352	35	10	CBSE,Int. Baccalaureate
47.	Tamil Nadu	Tirunelveli	Tirunelveli	1974	Secondary	810	51	16	State Board.
48.	Tamil Nadu	Nagapattinam	Nagapattinam	1997	Primary	293	17	17	not recognised
49.	Tamil Nadu	Virugambakkam	Chennai	1978	Secondary	1230	62	20	CBSE
50.	Tamil Nadu	Salem	Salem	1995	Secondary	230	21	11	State Board.
51.	Tamil Nadu	Annanagar	Chennai	1990	Secondary	1243	58	21	CBSE
52.	Tamil Nadu	Vadavalli	Coimbatore	1971	Secondary	1459	63	23	State Board.
53.	Tamil Nadu	Thadagam Rd	Coimbatore	1971	Secondary	875	38	23	not recognised
54.	Tamil Nadu	Harrington Road	Chennai	1968	Secondary	1623	66	25	CBSE
55.	Tamil Nadu	Rajapalayam	Rajapalayam	1970	Secondary	903	45	20	State Board.
56.	Tamil Nadu	Trichy	CCMT,Mumbai	1982	Secondary	225	20	11	CBSE
57.	Uttar Pradesh	Haridwar	Haridwar	1989	Deg College	979	22	45	Charan Singh University
58.	Uttar Pradesh	Allahabad	Allahabad	1978	Midd. School	278	10	28	State Board
59.	Uttar Pradesh	Samesi	Lucknow	1991	Jr High School	425	9	47	
60.	Uttar Pradesh	Rai Bareilly	Delhi	1995	Secondary	592	26	23	CBSE
					T O T A L	48074	2131	22.6	

Chinmaya Vidyalayas

LIST OF ACHIEVMENTS

1.	Begumpet, Hyderabad	100% Results, Won prizes in English, GK, Quiz Competitions, I st Prize at National Group Song Competition conducted by Bharat Vikas Parishad.
2.	Guntur	Consistent Results, Prizes at District Science Fair.
3.	NTPC, Karimnagar	Consistent Results in X & XII
4.	Ellayapalli, Cuddapah	First Prize in Chant Geeta-Land Washington competition in 1991.
5.	Gaya	–
6.	Telco, Jamshedpur	Outstanding School Social Service Shield-Giants International.
7.	Nauni, Solan	School Team won the Second Prize in Tae Kwon Do Championship at Shimla, winning 4 Gold and 3 Bronze Medals.
8.	Jayalakshmipuram, Mysore	100% Results, participated in State Level Table-Tennis and Volleyball Competitions.
9.	Hubli, Karnataka	100% Results.
		The School has started Centres for Excellence for developing skills, Institute for Performing Arts for training in Instrumental and Vocal Music, 'Chetna'—a community service center for training poor women in nursing skills.

10.	St John's Cross Road, Bangalore	Sports Awards at State, Zonal, District Level Meets.
11.	Koramangala, Bangalore	Won Prizes in GK, Drawing, and IQ Competitions.
12.	Kolar	100% Results, won Prizes at Inter School Competitions.
13.	Cannanore	National Topper SSC Exam, Prizes won at District Level Youth Festival and CBSE Sports Meets.
14.	Nellicode Calicut	100 % Results
15.	Vazathacaud, Thiruananthapuram	Ranks secured at SSLC Exams, Won Prizes at Youth Festival, Geeta chanting Competitions.
16.	Kattakada, Thiruanathapuram	100% Results
17.	Kollengode	100% Results
18.	Kunnumpuram, T'puram	100 % Results, prizes won at Mathematics Olympiad, Quiz competitions.
19.	Naruvamood T'puram	–
20.	Manacaud, Attukal, T'puram	100% Results, prizes won at State Level CBSE Youth Festival, Literary, Poster competitions.
21.	Vaduthala,Cochin	100% Results, Special Teaching for Challenged Students, Scholarship from the K C Mahindra for Academic Excellence, under The Duke of Edinborough Award Scheme students have participated in exchange programmes to England, Chennai, Bangalore.
22.	Taliparamba, Kannur	100% Results. Prizes in Sports, Literary Competitions.
23.	Kolazhy, Thrissur	Won Prizes in Academics, Agricultural, Geeta Chanting, and Youth Festivals.

24.	Vetekodu, Pullanjeri,Calicut	–
25.	Tattamangalam, Kerala	Social Service activities
26.	Mattancherry, Kerala	Won Prizes in Cultural Competitions, Social Service Activities.
27.	Pallavur, Palakkad	Subject Toppers in Std X, XII CBSE EXAMS. Social Service Activities
28.	Chandanathope, Kollam.	One Student was admitted to the Sainik School, Kazhakootam, and Social Service activities
29.	Payyanur, Kannur	–
30.	Kanhangad	100 results.
31.	Kasaragod	100 Results. District Level Trophies and Medals won. Social Service activities.
32.	Pallassena, Pallakad	Social Service activities.
33.	CoyalMannan Palakkad	Social Service activities.
34.	Moolavattam, Kottayam	–
35.	Pallakad	First Prize in the Inter Collegiate Essay Competition.
36.	Thazhathangadi, Kottayam	100% Results, Participated in the Youth Festival, Debates, Quiz, and won Prizes.
37.	Nileshwar, Kasaragod	Participated in Painting, Quiz & Talent Search Examinations and won Prizes.
38.	Tripunithura	Bijukumar Bharatan of class X scored 492/500(98.4% in the All India Secondary School Examination held in March 2000.
39.	Satna MP	–
40.	Boisar, Maharashtra	Vision Certificate Award 99-2000, Championship in the Interschool Science Exhibition.
41.	Akola	–

42.	NTPC, Deepshika	–
43.	Rourkela	100% Results, Best School Trophy, Social Service Award, participated in Mathematics Olympaid.
44.	Therubali	Certificate of merit has been awarded to Master Jagajit Roy for excellent performance in Science Year-2000
45.	Srirangam, Trichy	–
46.	CIRS, Coimbatore.	100% Results in Class X Examination of CBSE for the Last Two Years.
		District Winners–Lawn Tennis, Football, Basket Ball, Badminton, Cricket.
47.	Tirunelveli	100% Results in SSC & Higher Secondary Examination and won Prizes in Statistics, Chemistry, Geography and Mathematics.
		Participated in GK Exams and won Scholarship.
		Two students selected for the U G Course in the USA based on their Performance n the Competitive Exams.
		Best Teacher Trophy.
48.	Nagapattinam	Won A Special Prize in Karate in District Karate Meet.
49.	Virugambakkam, Chennai	Karuna Club bagged the Rolling Trophy of The Indian Vegetarian Congress, participated in the Young Assembly of Greenways representing our country, Mandolin player toured USA and performed at Cultural Centers.
50.	Salem, TN	–

51.	Anna Nagar, Chennai	100% Results.
		Participated in Social Service activities
52.	Vadavalli, Coimbatore	Prizes in State Sports Meet, Best Teacher and Mathematics.
53.	Thadagam Road, Coimbatore	Social Service Activities.
54.	Harrington Road, Chennai	100% Results, Best Interact Club, participated in the National Athletic Meet and won the Individual Champion, won the 'Talk your way to London' Competition, participated in the National Children Painting Competition and won the II Prize.
		Best Teacher, Principal Awards.
55.	Rajapalayam	100% Results
56.	Ayyappa Nagar, Trichy	100% Results in X Board Examination for the 5th Year.
57.	Haridwar	95% to 100% Result
58.	Allahabad	–
59.	Samesi, Lucknow	–
60.	NTPC, Rae Bareli	100% Results

Temples—Altars of Worship

1. DEENABANDHU DEVASTHANAM, BANGALORE

Lord Krishna as a Kaliya Mardana is dancing on the seven-hooded serpent Kaliya. We can with constant and complete surrender to the Lord, crush and overcome all negative tendencies in us and in due course come to realize the Brahman.

2. SARVESHWARA DHYANA NILAYAM, TAMARAIPAKKAM

The 65 feet tall temple and *Satsang* Hall is designed in the form of a Shiva Linga. The rare Sphatika Linga is mounted on a special glass and Abhishekam is performed annually on Mahashivaratri day.

3. JAGADEESHWARA TEMPLE, MUMBAI

Shiva Leela is sculpted on the main arch of the temple. An inscription in Arabic is found on the entrance, which communicates the message, "Through Me you stand in the presence of the Lord of Universe."

4. RAM MANDIR, SIDHBARI

A *Maha-mastakabhishekam* of Lord Hanumanji, who is in the open on the campus, is performed every five years.

5. OMKARESHWAR TEMPLE, CHOKKAHALLI

Inside the temple is Lord Shiva. Outside in the open is the gigantic Chinmaya Ganapati. Through this unique art piece one is compelled to behold the Lord as the Living Entity in the 45 feet tall figure.

6. *ADI SHANKARA NILAYAM, VELIYANAD*

Adi Shankara Nilayam is synonymous today with Chinmaya International Foundation. The self-born Shasta (Lord Ayyappa) is the deity of Shri Adi Shankara's family.

7. *BHUVANESHWARI TEMPLE, THRISSUR*

Cochin Royal Family donated this 'Bhajan Madhom' to Swami Chinmayananda. The Divine Mother now blesses all.

8. *SHRI SUBRAHMANYA SWAMY TEMPLE, KANHANGAD*

This temple is very ancient and it is said that Lord Adi Subrahmanya underwent penance for years at this place to gather strength to slaughter Tarakasura.

9. *CHINMAYA DHYANA-NILAYAM, HYDERABAD*

Set at Kundanbagh, Begumpet, perched on top of a small hillock is the beautifully carved marble Murti of Lord Shiva, Lord of the Universe, the Creator, the Sustainer and the Destroyer.

10. *PARAM DHAM, AHMEDABAD*

The central Krishna Shrine has Lord Krishna playing the flute. Param Dham has a unique architectural style with three levels. It contains many *kutirs* and classes are held in the spacious open ground surrounding the temple.

11. *GNANA VINAYAKA TEMPLE, COIMBATORE*

This temple is situated at the Chinmaya Vidyalaya, Vadavalli, Coimbatore. The school children start their day invoking the blessings of Gnana Vinayaka.

12. SRI VARASIDDHI VINAYAKA TEMPLE, KOYAMBEDU

Chinmayagram Koyambedu was formed with the blessings of Pujya Gurudev. Koyambedu has a glorious significance. It is said that it is here in saint Valmiki's Ashram that Sita gave birth to Lava and Kusha.

13. DAKSHINESHWAR KAILASHNATH TEMPLE, KOLHAPUR

The Temple is situated in Chinmaya Ashram, Kolhapur. Swamiji suggested the name, as Kolhapur is famous as Dakshin Kashi. The deity is in the form of Shiva Linga made of black stone and adorned with Sphatika Linga.

14. VANKHANDESHWAR TEMPLE, MANDHANA

Housed in the verdant forest of the Pitamah Sadan, just outside Kanpur, the temple is ancient and draws a large number of villagers who have great faith in Lord Shiva.

15. SHRI RAGHUNATHJI TEMPLE, REWA

The Temple is built in the centre of the Pitamaha Sadan. Swamiji selected this area as it is close to Chitrakoot where Lord Rama spent twelve years of his *vanavasa*.

16. ARANYESHWARA TEMPLE, CHINMAYARANYAM

The impressive Shiva Linga in the complex of the sprawling Chinmayaranyam blesses the spiritual and social activities in the campus.

17. SHRI VISHVESHWARA SWAMY TEMPLE, TRIKOOTA

This Temple is situated in the Ashram. The Ashram also has a *Dhyana Mandir* of Pujya Swami Chinmayananda.

18. LORD SATYANARAYANA, SHIMOGA

The temple is situated on the site of the Chinmaya centre. It has a mural sculpted by the famous sculptor Kashinath at the entrance. The temple houses a satsang hall, which is constantly used for bhajans, discourses and *archanas*.

19. CHINMAYA GEETA MANDIR, TUMKUR

The Temple has the idol of Lord Krishna standing with flute in one hand and the 'Chinmudra' in the other. In the Temple premises, *yajnas* and other activities are held.

20. CHINMAYA RAMA MANDIR, MANDYA

The temple houses the mystical charming figures of Rama, Lakshmana, Sita and Hanuman. The serene surroundings with the marble flooring add to our contemplation of Lord Rama.

21. KEDAR TEMPLE, LANGHORNE

The idol of Lord Shiva wonderfully depicts Lord Shiva, who emerges from his meditative state after 1000 years in Samadhi. He has a bath and is now blessing the devotees.

22. RADHA KRISHNA TEMPLE, HOUSTON

The Temple is in the premises of Chinmaya Mission Houston (Chinmaya Prabha) and is the venue as Satsang and other activities of the mission.

23. SHIVA TEMPLE, SAN JOSE

The temple is part of the active centre, which has Balavihars, discourses, Vedic Chanting etc.

24. SHIVA TEMPLE, LOS ANGELES

Kasi symbolically indicates the brilliance and splendour of Consciousness that shines in the dawn of spiritual wisdom. Daily *poojas* are a notable feature of this shrine.

25. SHIVA TEMPLE, WASHINGTON D.C.

Kailas Niwas is the Ashram in Silver Spring, Maryland. Devotees worship an idol of Lord Shiva and a Shiva Linga here.

26. CHINMAYA SAKET, DALLAS/FORTWORTH

Housed in the vibrant Mission centre, Lord Rama and Mother Sita are in a sitting posture, which is not found at most places.

27. BADRI, CHICAGO

The majestic Lord Narayana, in a sitting posture, graces the large *satsang* hall. A number of spiritual, cultural activities are blessed by the Lord.

28. SHIVALAYA, TORONTO

The only temple/shrine built by Chinmaya Mission in the country of Canada. Lord Shiva is the resplendent deity.

29. CHINMAYA TAPOVAN, FLINT

Shri Krishna is the presiding deity here in this city of Michigan State. Housed in the Mission centre, the divine flute-bearer attracts devotees from far and wide.

30. SHIVA TEMPLE-KAIVALYA, ORLANDO

The Temple is part of the Ashram called "Kaivalya". Lord Shiva is its Deity in meditative state. Regular *pooja* and *arti* of Lord Shiva, Shiva Linga and Nandi are performed twice a day.

31. CHINMAYA AVANTIKA, ANN ARBOR, USA

This temple is dedicated to Lord Shiva in meditation, a Shiva *lingam* and Nandiji showering their blessings on the devotees.

Chinmaya Mission Temples

DEITY AND YEAR OF CONSECRATION

Sr. No.	Name of Temple	Location	Deity	Consecration Day
1.	Deenabandhu Devasthanam	Bangalore, Karnataka	Lord Krishna	March 24, 1978
2.	Sarveshwara Dhyana Nilayam	Tamaraipakam, Tamil Nadu	Lord Sarveshwara	October 15, 1989
3.	Jagadeeshwara Temple	Powai, Mumbai	Lord Jagadeeswara	November 10, 1968
4.	Ram Mandir	Sidhbari, Himachal Pradesh	Vanavasi Rama, Sita, Hanuman	October 10, 1982
5.	Shiva Temple	Chokkahalli, Karnataka	Lord Omkareshwara, Ganapati	November 20, 1994
6.	Adi Shankara Nilayam	Ernakulam, Kerala	Lord Ayyappa	Old temple taken over, 1989
7.	Neeranjali	Thrissur	Goddess Bhuvaneshwari	Old temple taken over, 1963
8.	Shri Subrahmanya Swamy Temple	Kanhangad, Kerala	Lord Subrahmanya	Donated in 1984
9.	Chinmaya Dhyana Nilayam	Hyderabad, Andhra Pradesh	Lord Shiva	February 14, 1999
10.	Param Dham	Ahmedabad, Gujarat	Lord Krishna–Venu Gopal	May 19, 1979
11.	Gnana Vinayaka Temple	Coimbatore, Tamil Nadu	Lord Ganesha	May 10, 1988
12.	Sri Varasiddhi Vinayaka Temple	Koyambedu	Lord Ganesha	1971, May 6, 1993.
13.	Shri Dakshineshwar Kailasnath	Kolhapur, Maharashtra	Lord Shiva	March 2, 1992

Sr. No.	Name of Temple	Location	Deity	Consecration Day
14.	Vankhandeshwar Temple	Mandhana, Kanpur	Lord Shiva	Ancient
15.	Shri Raghunathji Temple	Laxmanpur, Rewa, Madhya Pradesh	Lord Rama	April 6, 1984
16.	Aranyeshwara Temple	Chinmayaranyam, Andhra Pradesh	Lord Shiva	After 1982
17.	Shri Vishveshwara Swamy Temple	Chinmayaranyam, Trikoota, AP	Lord Vishveshwara	December 25, 1990
18.	Lord Satyanarayana	Shimoga, Karnataka.	Lord Satyanarayana	1991
19.	Chinmaya Geeta Mandir	Tumkur, Karnataka	Lord Krishna	February 26, 1994
20.	Chinmaya Rama Mandir	Mandya, Karnataka	Lord Rama	April 17, 1997
21.	Kedar Temple	Tri-State Center, USA	Lord Shiva	November 30, 1992
22.	Radha Krishna Temple	Houston ,USA	Lord Krishna and Radha	1994
23.	Shiva Temple	San Jose, USA	Lord Shiva(Meditative pose)	April 2, 1988.
24.	Siva Temple	Los Angeles, USA	Shiva Linga (Kasi)	February 19, 1997
25.	Shiva Temple	Washington, USA	Lord Shiva	July 1, 1989
26.	Chinmaya Saket	Dallas, TX, USA	Ram, Sita	December 31, 1999
27.	Badri	Chicago, IL, USA	Lord Badri Narayana	October 24, 1993
28.	Shivalaya	Toronto, Canada	Lord Shiva	July 12, 1998
29.	Chinmaya Tapovan	Flint, MI, USA	Shri Krishna	After 1990
30.	Shiva Temple	Orlando, USA	Lord Shiva	July 18, 1999
31.	Chinmaya Avantika	Ann Arbor, USA	Lord Shiva	July 29, 2000

Chinmaya Mission Foreign Centres

YEAR OF ESTABLISHMENT

Sr. No.	CITY	YEAR	COUNTRY
1.	MELBOURNE	1981	AUSTRALIA
2.	SYDNEY	1984	AUSTRALIA
3.	BAHRAIN	1971	BAHRAIN
4.	CALGARY	1972	CANADA
5.	OTTAWA	1977	CANADA
6.	TORONTO	1973	CANADA
7.	VANCOUVER	1972	CANADA
8.	HALTON REGION	1982	CANADA
9.	FRANCE	1992	EUROPE
10.	HONGKONG	1970	HONGKONG
11.	JAKARTA	1987	INDONESIA
12.	NAIROBI	1986	KENYA
13.	KUWAIT	1971	KUWAIT
14.	MAURITIUS	1977	MAURITIUS
15.	REUNION	1977	MAURITIUS
16.	KATHMANDU	1990	NEPAL
17.	NELSON	1994	NEW ZEALAND
18.	MANILA	1981	PHILIPPINES
19.	SINGAPORE	1968	SINGAPORE
20.	DURBAN	1979	SOUTH AFRICA

Sr. No.	CITY	YEAR	COUNTRY
21.	COLOMBO	1980	SRI LANKA
22.	MUSCAT	1984	SULTANATE OF OMAN
23.	DUBAI	1979	UAE
24.	MIDDLESEX	1986	UK
25.	ANN ARBOR	1994	USA
26.	AUSTIN	1996	USA
27.	BAKERSFIELD	1992	USA
28.	BOSTON	1991	USA
29.	BUFFALO	1994	USA
30.	CHICAGO	1979	USA
31.	DALLAS	1990	USA
32.	FLINT	1978	USA
33.	GRAND RAPIDS	1991	USA
34.	HOUSTON	1982	USA
35.	LOS ANGELES	1977	USA
36.	MIAMI	1989	USA
37.	MIDDLE GEORGIA	1994	USA
38.	NEW YORK	1965	USA
39.	ORLANDO	1990	USA
40.	PIERCY	1978	USA
41.	PITTSBURG	1974	USA
42.	SAN JOSE	1968	USA
43.	SEATTLE	1975	USA
44.	TRISTATE	1982	USA
45.	WASHINGTON	1978	USA
46.	TRINIDAD	1965	WEST INDIES

The Chinmaya Movement

30 Years and 50 Years—After The Start

	30 YEARS 1981	50 YEARS 2001
YAJNAS		
Swami Chinmayananda 1951-1981	323	
Swami Chinmayananda 1951-1993		515
Swami Tejomayananda 1993-2000		313
Total *Yagnas*	323	828
Chinmaya Mission Centres in India	83	198
Chinmaya Mission Centres Abroad	26	46
Total *Yagnas*	109	244
CHINMAYA VIDYALAYAS	43	73
Total Students	12, 438	48, 074
Total Teachers	514	2, 131
Teacher to Student Ratio	1: 25	1: 22.6
Chinmaya Mission Colleges	8	3
No. of Study Groups	427	931
No. of CHYK Groups	123	276
No. of Balavihar Groups	417	1094
No. of Mission Members	N.A.	30529
No. of Swamis	N.A.	40
No. of Swaminis	N.A.	25
No. of Brahmacharis	N.A.	92
No. of Brahmacharinis	N.A.	46

N.A. = not available

In 1966, Swamiji had taken stock of the growth of the Movement after 15 years. This was a pictorial representation of the major events in the first 15 years. Please see *Tapovan Prasad* of January 1967.

The statistics above is based on reports received from 150 centres out of the 198 in India.

The number of *yajnas* conducted by Swami Chinmayananda and by Swami Tejomayananda is based on the published itineraries.

The number of Vidyalayas is as per the 'address book' of CCMT. The statistics above, however, is based on the reports received from 60 Vidyalayas/colleges.

Early Birds

This book on the history of the Chinmaya Movement has been possible because of the reports and pictures we have received from the various Chinmaya Mission centres. I had made an appeal, at the Mission workers' conference in December 1998 to all, to submit a detailed report on the history of their centres. A standard format in which the history was to be submitted was also circulated. This format was uploaded on the Chinmaya Mission website for easy and instant access.

The response from the centres was somewhat slow. The 'Update' on the state of response was published in the *Tapovan Prasad* from time to time. Speed in submission picked up after publishing the 'Update' and with the constant follow-up by me. Among the 198 centres in India, 184 centres submitted their reports. All 46 foreign centres sent their reports.

We appreciate the response from all the centres. As a special token of appreciation I am disclosing the names of five centres (out of 184 centres which have submitted the report) from India and three (out of the forty-six foreign centres) who rank amongst the 'first'

Chinmaya Mission Centres in India – First Five

Name of Centre	Report received in
1. Chinchwad	July 1999
2. Mandya	October 1999

3. Dahanu & Bordi	October 1999
4. Rewa	October 1999
5. Kolhapur	October 1999

Chinmaya Mission Centres abroad – First Three

Name of Centre	Report received in
1. San Jose	July 1999
2. Houston	September 1999
3. Pittsburg	October 1999

Congratulations to the Acharyas, *Sevaks* and *Sevikas* at these centres.

- S. C.

Emblem of
Sandeepany Sadhanalaya

Emblem of
Chinmaya Mission

The Emblems

The different aspects of our activities are all represented in the chosen symbol of the Chinmaya Mission. The Sandeepany Sadhanalaya carries the emblem of "the books, the lamp and the bird". The books are three in number, representing the *Prasthanatraya*—the three great textbooks from which the entire Hinduism springs forth. They are the *Upanishad*, the *Brahmasootra* and the *Geeta*. To study the Scriptures in the light of moral and ethical contexts is to develop the discriminative power of the human intellect, which is conditionally symbolized by the 'sacred bird', the *Hamsa*. A Hindu tradition describes the *Hamsa* as a bird that can drink the milk alone from a mixture of milk and water. The human intellect with its discriminative power must be able to, in a spiritual seeker, discriminate the spirit and the matter, and must come to enjoy the spiritual essence in the world of names and forms.

The entire emblem is superimposed upon a fully opened lotus: the lotus is the national flower accepted by the immortal culture of Bharat: it represents the final goal, the super manhood.

When a seeker in the light of his just and moral life studies the scriptures he develops his discriminative faculty with the help of which he comes to experience the natural substratum of the world of endless changes of the play of finite experiences.

The Chinmaya Mission has for its emblem only the lamp and bird suggesting that the function of the Mission is to help people to developing their ethical values and in cultivating in them the discriminative power.

N.B. – This is an explanatory note published in 1967.

Chinmaya Mission Pledge

सर्वे वयं गोत्रमिव स्म एकं
प्रेमादरश्लक्ष्णगुणानुबद्धाः।

योद्धुं सदा चाखिलदुष्प्रवृत्तीः
सेनेव सिद्धा नियताश्च धीराः।

सेवापरित्यागमयायुषा च
प्रतिग्रहेभ्योऽधिकमेव दद्मः।

मनस्वितासद्गुणधैर्यमार्गे
यातुं प्रसादाय भजाम ईशम्।

प्रभो, कृपा ते च शुभाशिषोऽस्मद्-
द्वाराऽभितोऽस्मिन् जगति स्रवन्तु।

स्वदेशसेवैव च देवसेवा
सदेति भो विश्वसिमो दृढं च।

जनेषु भक्तिः परमात्मभक्तिः
इति स्वकार्याणि च सुष्ठु विद्मः।

तेषां प्रपूर्त्यै कृपया प्रभो नो
बलं च धैर्यं वितरोपयुक्तम्।।

ॐ तत् सत्

WE STAND as one family bound to each other with love and respect.

WE SERVE as an army courageous and disciplined ever ready to fight against all low tendencies and false values within and without us.

WE LIVE honestly the noble life of sacrifice and service producing more than what we consume and giving more than what we take.

WE SEEK the Lord's grace to keep us on the path of virtue, courage and wisdom.

May Thy grace and blessings flow through us to the world around us.

WE BELIEVE that the service of our country is the service of the Lord of Lords, and

Devotion to the people is the devotion to the Supreme Self.

WE KNOW our responsibilities; give us the ability and courage to fulfill them.

Om Tat Sat

CODE OF CONDUCT FOR MISSION MEMBERS

1. By thought, word and deed, every member of the Chinmaya Mission should try to live up to and fulfill the motto as well as the pledge of the Mission.
2. He should spare time daily to do meditation and scripture study.
3. Once a week, on any convenient day, he must offer worship at a nearby temple with the members of his family.
4. He should discover a life of harmony first at home. It is expected of him that he does not, on any account, create any domestic unhappiness.
5. If there are children at home, he will have at least once a week a *satsang* at home consisting mainly of members of the family wherein reading of *Itihasas*, like *Ramayana* and *Mahabharata* or *Puranas* like *Bhagavata*, in a language the children know, would form an important part.
6. When he meets another Mission member, he greets him with "Hari Om".
7. Daily offering of *pranams* to the elders in the house by the younger ones should be followed and inculcated by the Mission members.

Mission Statement

Chinmaya Mission

TO PROVIDE TO INDIVIDUALS

FROM ANY BACKGROUND,

THE WISDOM OF VEDANTA

AND

PRACTICAL MEANS FOR

SPIRITUAL GROWTH AND HAPPINESS

ENABLING THEM TO

BECOME POSITIVE CONTRIBUTORS

TO SOCIETY.

Chronological List of Major Events in The Chinmaya Movement

To trace the growth and spread of the Mission activities, a chronological list of major events is given here.

1951 First Geeta *Jnana-yajna* starts at Ganapati Temple, Rasthapeth, Pune.

1952 Swami Chinmayananda is on the Editorial Board of 'Call Divine' a publication by devotees of Bhagavan Ramana Maharshi in Mumbai.

1953 Chinmaya Mission is formed in Chennai on August 8.

1954 Four *yajnas* cover 144 days. The one in Delhi of 61days is organized by Ms. Sheila Puri, who later plays an important role in firmly establishing the Movement in the capital.

1955 *Tyagi* the first publication of the Chinmaya Mission is started in September.

Mobile *yajna* concept is introduced by Swamiji. The first *yajna* covers three localities in Chennai. Swamiji conducts *yajnas* in the three localities daily for 21 days moving around in a car.

1956 President of India, Babu Rajendra Prasad inaugurates the 23rd Yajna at Kashmere Gate, Delhi.

Hail Renaissance Volume-I is released, sponsored by Ms. Sheila Puri.

1957 Swami Tapovan Maharaj, guru of Swami Chinmayananda, attains *maha-samadhi* at Uttarakashi.

Swamiji starts writing his commentary on the *Bhagavad Geeta*.

1958 All India Conference of Chinmaya Workers at Chennai. Closed door meeting with workers where Swamiji emphasizes the need for morality and ethics of Mission workers.

First Devi Group is inaugurated by Swamiji at Chennai.

In March, the first issue of *Usha*, a monthly, is published from Hyderabad.

1959 The first Bala Mahotsav is held in Chennai by Swamiji to interact with children of the Balavihars and the sevaks/sevikas. The first issue of *Balvihar* magazine is released.

1960 Tara Cultural Trust is registered in Mumbai on January 19. The Trust is instituted to manage the affairs of Sandeepany Sadhanalaya, the Vedanta Institute at Powai.

The Akhila Bharatiya Chinmayi Devi Sammelan, ABCD, is held in Kollengode, Kerala to enable men to appreciate the role that women play in society and for the women to understand their responsibilities. Swamiji guides the entire proceedings.

Hail Renaissance Volume II is published in October giving a collection of articles by several devotees.

1961 The Chinmaya Publications Trust (Regd) is registered in March at Chennai. Swamiji hands over to the Trust fifty-nine of his books for publication.

Chinmaya Tapovanam, a retreat and meditation centre is inaugurated in Nagamalai Hills, Madurai. This is the first one of its kind—several such centres follow years later at Chinmayaranyam (A.P.), Rewa (M.P), Sarada Tapovanam (A.P), Chinmaya Yoga Ashram, Iruvaram (A.P.) and Uttarakashi.

1962 A landmark year to celebrate the 100th Geeta *Jnana-Yajna*. The *yajna* is conducted in Chennai and is organized by an all-women *yajna* committee.

In December, the Tara Cultural Trust commences publication of *Tapovan Prasad*, a monthly magazine. *Tyagi* and *Usha*, the other two publications ultimately merge with *Tapovan Prasad–Tyagi* in 1962 and *Usha* in 1963.

1963 Under a veil of sadness due to the Chinese aggression, the first Vedanta Institute, Sandeepany Sadhanalaya is inaugurated on January 9 at Powai, Mumbai.

Swami Sivananda of Divine Life Society, the *deeksha guru* of Swami Chinmayananda attains *maha-samadhi* in July. Swamiji with due respect to his guru, goes into deep *tapas* (*tapovrata*) for a year.

1964 Central Chinmaya Mission Trust (CCMT) is formed in July. It is the apex body for administration of the Chinmaya Mission with headquarters in Mumbai.

The All India Chinmaya Mission conference is held in July in Mumbai with B.M. Kamdar as President.

Swamiji administers the Mission Pledge to the delegates at the conclusion of the conference.

1965 Swamiji undertakes the first global tour accompanied by B.V. Reddy, an ardent devotee. The tour lasts from March to July and covers 39 cities spread over three continents. It paves the way for opening of Chinmaya Mission centres in foreign countries.

The first of its kind, a Diagonistic Centre is opened at Navjivan Colony, Chembur, Mumbai for rendering medical facilities to the poor and needy. The original promoter is Dr. Mrs. Panjabi and Dr. Mrs. Shyamala. Other diagnostic and research centres follow years later at Panvel (Maharashtra), Tamaraipakkam (Tamil Nadu), Bansbaria (Kolkata) and in other places.

Swamiji's appeal to devotees to rise up for a National cause leads to collection of gold of thirteen kilograms at the State Bank of India stall at the *Yajna-shala* during the 151st *yajna* at Mumbai.

The first meeting of the All-India Advisory Board of Chinmaya Mission is held at Tripunithura, Kerala.

1966 The first Geeta *jnana-yajna* on foreign soil at Kuala Lampur, Malaysia.

The first camp for training of teachers is held in Kollengode from May 8 to 22. The camp is a great success and is greatly appreciated by Swamiji.

1967 A review of the 15 years of the Chinmaya Movement is made in Tapovan Prasad issue of January, partly in text and partly in pictures. The caption is "Live Rightly, Dynamically and Vividly". The Movement has marched a long way.

The President Dr. S. Radhakrishnan inaugurates Swamiji's talk on 'Power and Morality' at Bharatiya Vidya Bhavan and the valedictory function is presided over by the Vice-President Dr. Zakir Hussain.

1968 The first woman to join the monastic order of the Chinmaya Mission is Swamini Vidyananda–called fondly Pankajamma–who is initiated as a *sannyasini* in February.

In May the publication of Tapovan Prasad is shifted from Mumbai to Chennai.

The first temple of Chinmaya Mission, Lord Jagadeeswara Temple at Powai, is consecrated on November 10.

1969 Swamiji introduces for the first time the concept of *Vichara yajna*. Once a month members gather together for one day and discuss a pre-determined topic–the aim is to promote co-operative thinking. The first event is held at Mumbai and the subject chosen is "Student Restlessness".

Hail Renaissance Volume III is published as a fund-raising project.

Swamiji gives, for the first time, *sannyas* to a Negro student–Dr. Baldwin George, a Trinidadian. He is given the name of Swami Bhaskarananda.

1970 Earlier in the year Swamiji collapses on the podium, at a seminar in Chennai and it is diagnosed as fatigue. In March while conducting a *yajna* at Mysore, Swamiji has a heart attack and is rushed to the hospital. This is the first serious setback to his health, which vexes him till his last days.

From March 1970 to April 1972, for 2 years, Swamiji does not conduct any Geeta *jnana-yajna.* He announces that he will henceforth conduct only one National *Yajna* per year.

Swamiji inaugurates Chinmaya Kala Mandir for Balavihar children to be run under the guidance of Smt. Kamala Chanrai.

Unable to take the strain of *yajnas* Swamiji plans to record 50 ten-minute talks on Chapter Five of the Bhagavad Geeta, which is to be broadcast by A.I.R.

In December, Swamiji goes to a world famous Heart Rehabilitation Centre in Switzerland for treatment.

Swamiji attends the opening of the Vivekananda Rock Memorial at Kanyakumari although he has been advised by his doctors to take rest. Swamiji says that such events are rare and one cannot afford to miss them.

1971 Swamiji makes a tour of the Middle East where his 'chalk talks' become very popular.

Swamiji completes his historic 190 days trip round the world visiting 10 countries and about 40 cities.

1972 At the Fourth All India Mission Workers' conference held in Mumbai a code of conduct for the Mission Members is evolved.

Swamiji announces that he will not be able to take up much of the active work and that Swami Dayananda will in future shoulder the responsibilities.

Sandeepany Sadhanalaya becomes active again after being on a low key for two years.

1973 Swamiji holds a spiritual camp at Sonoma, California where representatives of four major religions meet–Hinduism, Christianity, Buddhism and Sufism. Swamiji says about the camp, "It started as an experiment but ended as an experience."

At Kuwait, Swamiji conducts an All-Gulf spiritual camp, which is attended by 56 participants. The camp is a great success.

Chinmaya Study Group of Napa, California, the earlier book distribution centre, hands over the work to Chinmaya Books U.S.A., which again is in Napa. This is a non-profit organization. The money out of the sales is to be retained in the U.S.A for spiritual work outside India.

Swamiji's Radio talks are published serially in 80 periodicals.

1974 Swamiji inaugurates Chinmaya Vidyalaya at Chennai.

A Post Office opens in Sandeepany Sadhanalaya, as an extra-department non-delivery Post Office. While Swamiji cuts the tape, Ram Batra makes the first purchase of stamps from the Post Master General of Mumbai.

The third National *yajna* is held at Jamshedpur attended by over 5000 people. There is a *vichara yajna* for college students on the subject 'No sacrifice, no progress'.

1975 The *Kalasha prathista* and *Kumbhabhishekam* of Lord Jagdeeswara is performed in February. Swami Dayananda performs the *abhisheka* ceremony. The gate in front of the temple is a contribution from the Arab lands and the inscription reads "Through me you stand in the presence of the Lord of the Universe"

The Chinmaya Youth Forum is formed with headquarters in Bangalore. The name later changes to Chinmaya Yuva Kendra to avoid any attribute of a political nature to the forum.

Chinmaya Mission West (CMW), a counterpart of CCMT, in the U.S. is formed. Chinmaya Publication (West) is formed and its first publication is the *Manual of Self-Unfoldment*.

The second All India Chinmaya Vidyalaya conference is convened in Chennai. It is attended by 150 delegates from 24 centres. According to Ram Batra, the Trustee of CCMT, the purpose of the conference is to give direction to the work, which has started purely out of enthusiasm.

1976 Swamiji's New Year message–Do your job well. Live straight. Devotedly pray and serve. Results will come to you.

The Chinmaya Foundation of Education and Culture, a gift from the TTK family of Chennai, starts with the primary aim of providing comprehensive grounding in Hindu Philosophy to the public by way of lectures and classes.

Swamiji's 60th birthday is celebrated in Coimbatore. Many devotees come from all over the country to wish Swamiji.

Swamiji moves to Uttarakashi in July for a two-month retreat. He releases an announcement that nobody should disturb him in July/August during his retreat.

Due to infection in the liver Swamiji is on a long routine treatment and his engagements up to March 1977 are all cancelled. He leaves Uttarakashi in September and returns to Mumbai.

1977 First All India CHYK camp is held in Chennai in the presence of Swamiji and Swami Harinamananda.

Swamiji inaugurates a cultural centre called *Neeranjali* at Trichur.

1978 Swamiji declares the year as the "Year of my Sadhana." You may slip; get up! Forget to remember the fall. Refuse to recognize the slip!

At Sandeepany Sadhanalaya the *pratima* of Swami Tapovan Maharaj is unveiled.

Swami Dayananda at Chowpatty, Mumbai, conducts Geeta Maha-yajna of 18 Chapters in 18 days.

1979 The First Geeta *jnana-yajna* in Colombo, Sri Lanka is held in the month of June.

Param Dham, the Chinmaya Ashram at Ahmedabad is inaugurated in the presence of Swamiji in August.

Swami Dayananda inaugurates Sandeepany West, at Piercy. Forty-two students join the course.

B.M. Kamdar, President of the Chinmaya Mission, an active member and a great devotee passes away in February, a serious setback to the Mission.

1980 There are alarming signals on Swamiji's health front. The cardiac catheterization reveals that all the four main arteries have more than eighty percent blockage. Dr. Denton Cooley at Houston Texas. performs multiple by-pass surgery. All the programmes of Swamiji for three months are cancelled.

Swamiji hands over all CCMT work to Swami Dayananda.

1981 A sound-and-light programme, "*Kamban Tharum Katchi*," is staged at Chennai. It is a mammoth production presented by the Chennai Chyks. It has 80 scenes, with 350 boys and girls. Swamiji applauds the show, which goes for many repeat performances.

Sandeepany (Himalayas) is inaugurated in April 1981 in the midst of a galaxy of prominent persons with Br. Vivek Chaitanya (now Swami Tejomayananda) as the Acharya. For the first time, the medium of instruction is Hindi.

Ram Batra, the pillar of strength to the Chinmaya Movement, passes away in August. Swamiji is in the U.S.A and is grieved to hear the news.

Vivekachoodamani camps by Swamiji are held at Sidhbari in September–October during which time the Dalai Lama also visits the Ashram.

'Uncle Mani' joins CCMT as a coordinator for Balavihars, Study Groups etc.

1982 Swamiji declares this year as the 'Year of Contact". In his message to the Mission members he says, "It is now time that you start giving out to others what you have imbibed. It is a sacred duty. Our Upanishad *rishis* insist upon it. Study yourself and teach others."

Swami Dayananda, the senior most swami and second in command, resigns from the Chinmaya Mission. A few months later, 22 brahmacharis follow suit. In this context Swamiji says, "The policy of Chinmaya Mission has always been that we give every member all freedom so that he or she may do effective work for the greater programme of the Mission—spread of Vedanta."

1983 New year message from Swamiji – "Let us think BIG".

"Let us forgive all others and keep them in our care. Let us give up meanness and habits of thinking small."

Swamiji gives Sannyasa Deeksha to Br. Vivek Chaitanya, Br. Radhakrishnan Chaitanya and Brni. Yamuna Devi. Their new names are Swami Tejomayananda, Swami Jyotirmayananda and Swamini Gangananda.

The first International Spiritual Camp and Geeta jnana-yajna is held in Mumbai in December. There are 800 participants in the camp. The function starts with a Torch March. The torch is lit at the altar of the Ganapati temple in Pune and brought to the *yajna-shala* at Andheri, Mumbai.

First All-India CHYK Conference is held at Tirunelveli. Dr. Shrikant Jichkar, MLA, and a devotee, inaugurates the conference.

Swamiji introduces the concept of Matru Pooja, on Navami Day of Devi Pooja festival. In Indian culture the mother is adored and revered because she is the one who gives us more than what we can ever hope to give her back. Since then all the Balavihars observe this day as Mothers' Day.

Br. Sahaja Chaitanya takes a vow on May 9, in the presence of Swamiji, to do a *pada yatra* to meet one crore people, to collect one rupee per head, and to offer the amount collected as *Guru Dakshina* to Swamiji. The *pada yatra* is to begin on September 1 from Coimbatore and end in September the next year.

Prana Pratishta of the idols at the Shree Rama temple at Sidhbari is performed.

1984 Chinmaya Kumbhamela at Siruvani is organized under the inspiring guidance of Swami Sahajananda. A Homa and 'Villakku' (lamp) pooja are performed and Swamiji addresses a large gathering.

Swamiji visits the Andamans for the first time.

A rare crystal glass, *sphatika-linga* is installed at the temple in Sidhbari. It is a unique idol in India both in size and shape. The light passing through the crystal beams in all directions–declaring itself a *jyotir-linga*. It is gift to Swamiji from Bitche of France.

1985 Brni. Pavitra Chaitanya and Uma Jeyarasasingam organize a children's camp in California, which is well attended and has plenty of Balavihar activities.

Chinmaya Mission, Houston, presents a cheque of $10,001 to Swamiji for his work in India.

At Sandeepany Sadhanalaya, Mumbai, the Tapovan Auditorium, a mini open-air stadium built in a semi-circular shape accommodating over a thousand people is inaugurated by a devotee on March 10, in the presence of Swamiji.

1986 Chinmaya Institute of Nursing is inaugurated by Swami Brahmananda in Bangalore.

The Chinmaya Seva Trust, Kerala is formed in December 1986, for handling projects in Kerala, including training of Brahmacharis.

1987 For the first time a *tulabhara* of Swamiji is organized, by the Mission members of Bangalore, honouring him on his 70th birthday. It is *rajata tulabhara*, where Swamiji is weighed in silver.

The second international spiritual camp is held at Olivet College campus, Michigan in July. There are 500 delegates for this camp from all over the world.

Tapovan Prasad, the international monthly, lovingly called the Voice of Chinmaya Mission, celebrates its silver jubilee.

Swamiji holds a marathon camp of 46 days on the entire *Bhagavad Geeta* at Sidhbari. About 500 delegates from all over the country and overseas avail of this rare opportunity.

1988 Kerala Sandeepany is inaugurated on February 16 in Kasargod. This is the fourth in the series of Vedanta institutes opened by the Mission in India.

1989 The Third International Spiritual camp is held at Cochin with 150 foreign, 600 resident and 300 non-resident delegates. This is the biggest spiritual camp of the Mission. The goal of such a camp as explained by Swamiji is to give an opportunity to people all over the world to live together as in a *gurukula*.

Birth centenary of Swami Tapovan Maharaj is celebrated.

The Mahakumbha abhisheka of Sri Sarveswara Temple at Tamaraipakkam is performed on October 15. At this unique function devotees perform *abhisheka* with *shanku (conch)*. Swamiji is the first to give the *abhisheka* with a large silver conch on the *sphatika linga*.

1990 The Chinmaya International Foundation (CIF) acquires the ancestral maternal house of Adi Shankaracharya, reclaiming it to limelight by making it a centre for research and study. Swamiji formally inaugurates it as Adi Sankara Nilayam in May.

Chinmayaranyam, the ashram at Trikoota in Andhra Pradesh is hit by a cyclone on May 9. It has created havoc in the coastal region. There is severe damage to the Ashram property. All the *kutias* crumble down, but as the inmates are away, there is no loss of life.

The yearlong Nama Japa Sadhana by the active members of the Mulund centre comes to a conclusion on November 28. Swamiji is present on this occasion and releases the reprint of D.K. Rajguru's "Manual of Sanskrit Grammar", a book published in 1938.

At Chinmaya Sandeepany, Chokkahalli, Kolar, Swamiji gives his benedictory address for the Hari-Har school and the new *Kutia* project.

1991 Swamiji's New Year message…"It is wisdom to suffer adversities meekly with the comfort and consolation of the knowledge of their finite nature. Even this will pass away."

In March, Swamiji announces plans to have a two-month 'Dharma Sevak Lower' course for young people and a four-month 'Dharma Sevak Higher' course for elderly people.

The first ever nation-wide Geeta chanting competition sponsored by CIF, "Chant Geeta–Land Washington" is organized. It also synchronizes with the 4th International Spiritual Camp at Washington, USA on July 5 to 14. On January 4, Swamiji lays the foundation stone for the Easwar Kripa building in Adi Shankara Nilayam which is designed to house students.

Swamiji announces major organizational reforms in October, in order to gear up the Mission activities and to reduce his administrative work. He delegates powers to seven of the senior swamis. The Swamis are to shoulder the responsibility of looking after Mission centres in specified States.

Kalasha Prathista is performed above the extension hall at the Jagadeeswara Temple when two brass Kalashas are placed at the right places on the roof.

The devotees celebrate the 75th Birth year of Swamiji by *suvarna tulabhara* or weighing Swamiji in gold. The function is held on December 24, at Hotel Leela Kempinski, Mumbai. This also coincides with Swamiji's 500th Geeta *jnana- yajna*.

1992 At Adi Sankara Nilayam, the second phase of Easwar Krupa, is inaugurated.

From July to October 1992, for 72 days, Swamiji conducts a marathon camp on Vivekachoodamani at Sidhbari. On October 10, the ceremonial bath, *Abhisheka*, of Lord Hanuman is performed, attended by large numbers from all over the country and abroad.

Swamiji addresses the United Nations on December 2. He urges the U.N. to be a catalyst agency to bring about a healthy and essential change, to remove poverty, pestilence and misery among humankind.

1993 A year of major calamity for the Mission. Swami Chinmayananda attains *maha-samadhi* on August 3 at San Diego, California.

On August 23, the Board of Trustees of CCMT announces the appointment of Swami Tejomayananda as the Head of the Chinmaya Mission Worldwide.

1994 The Chinmaya Vidyalaya, Chennai celebrates its Silver Jubilee year.

The first anniversary of Swami Chinmayananda's *maha-samadhi* is observed at Sidhbari. Swami Chidananda of Divine Life Society participates. The book *Unto Him* is released on this occasion.

Swami Tejomayananda lays the foundation stone for the Chinmaya Heritage Centre at Chennai.

Swami Tejomayananda conducts a *maha-yajna* in Mumbai. He holds discourses on the 18 Chapters of the Geeta in 18 days and covers 8 major *Upanishads* in the morning sessions. This is his homage and humble offering to his Guru.

1995 Meeting of the Regional Heads of the Chinmaya Mission with Swami Tejomayananda is held. A two-day Conference with the Acharyas (Swamis/Swaminis, Brahmacharis/ Brahmacharinis) of the Mission follows.

Swami Chidananda of the Divine Life Society does the *Pratima Prathista* of Swami Chinmayananda at Powai, Mumbai on February 12. "Behind the veil, behold the visage."

On August 3, the *Pratima Pratistha* of Swamiji at Sidhbari is performed. *Mahabhisheka* follows this.

The first International Chinmaya Spiritual Family Camp in South East Asia is held in Jakarta in June.

Swami Tejomayananda visits Port Blair, Andamans for the first time in November 1995. Swami Viviktananda, who was the first Brahmachari at Port Blair in 1977, accompanies him.

1996 Swami Tejomayananda unveils a life-size bronze statue of Swamiji at Houston in January. This is the first centre outside India to have such a statue.

Swami Tejomayananda launches the Chinmaya Vision Programme (CVP) on May 21, which is very well accepted by the schools venturing into value-based teaching.

The devotees with solemn respect and regards to the guru celebrate Swami Purushottamananda's sixtieth birthday in May.

In April, Swami Tejomayananda inaugurates the Chinmaya Seva Centre at Singapore.

The dream project of an international residential school becomes a reality–Swami Chidananda of Divine Life Society inaugurates Chinmaya International Residential School (CIRS) on June 6.

Chinmaya Yuva Kendra (UK) has its first youth camp with Swami Swaroopananda.

North American Chinmaya Mission Workers' Conference is held at Houston, Texas, presided over by Swami Tejomayananda.

1997 Swami Tejomayananda appeals to devotees to send "*likhita japa*" for powerful invocation for the sanctity of the sacred place in Adi Sankara Nilayam, where there is a proposal to build a meditation shrine as homage to Swamiji. The hall is to be consecrated at the time of the 4th anniversary of his *maha-samadhi*.

Swami Tejomayananda inaugurates Chinmaya Centre for World Understanding (CCWU) in Delhi in May. Conceived 25 years ago by Swamiji, the attempt of this centre will be to lessen the human communication gap between Science and economic progress.

Devotees all over the country attend *Maha-Mastakabhisheka* of Veer Hanuman at Sidhbari, held every five years.

At Manila, Balavihar and Yuva Kendra activities are combined as a walkathon event in August led by Swami Swaroopananda.

1998 Swami Tejomayananda conducts a very successful *yajna* on *Ramayana* in Hindi, in November in Sikkim. The Government declares him as a state guest.

He lays the foundation stone for the Chinmaya Human Research And Development Institute at Chinmaya Nagar, Ranipool, Sikkim.

The Chinmaya Vidyalaya and the Chinmaya Vidyapeeth, Ernakulam conceive the scheme, "Home for the Homeless." During his visit Swami Tejomayananda hands over the key to a home to a *papad* seller.

In July, the long-standing dream of having a centre in Toronto is realized when Swami Tejomayananda inaugurates the "Chinmaya Shivalaya". Brni. Sadhana, resident Acharya welcomes the gathering.

All Acharyas' Conference is held in December at Coimbatore. In a three-day session, the Acharyas meet their Regional Heads and Swami Tejomayananda and discuss important issues. Swami Tejomayananda explains the manual, *The Guidelines*, with illustrations so that the Acharyas could function smoothly.

1999 On February 15, Swami Tejomayananda consecrates the Chinmaya Dhyana Nilayam, Hyderabad, which is a Shiva shrine cum meditation hall. Swamiji's *yajna* is inaugurated by the Chief Minister, Shri Chandra Babu Naidu.

Swami Tejomayananda presents a cheque for Rs. 63 lakhs to the Prime Minister, Shri A.B. Vajpayee, as donation to the Army Central Welfare fund for the welfare of the families of Kargil warriors.

Swami Tejomayananda inaugurates the new block of Chinmaya Mission Hospital at Bangalore. It is a 200-bed hospital with most modern equipment and skilled and dedicated medical personnel.

Swami Brahmananda through the Karnataka Chinmaya Seva Trust offers to the temple at Sidhbari, a rosewood *mantap* with sandalwood icons of Sri Rama, Lakshman, Sita and Hanuman.

Swami Tejomayananda conducts a Geeta *jnana-yajna* at Nairobi in August. Apart from the *yajna*, a tree planting function is held at the India House, the residence of High-Commissioner of India in Kenya.

2000 Swamini Saradapriyananda, affectionately known as "Amma," attains *maha-samadhi* on April 17 at Tirupati.

Her life's work is a beautiful garland offered at the feet of Guru and God.

The Chinmaya Yuva Kendra, Chennai, stages an English play, "Line of Control (LOC)" at Delhi in the presence of the three National Defence Chiefs. The play speaks of the fragmented human mind and it emphasizes that the boundaries based on caste, creed and colour are man-made. It is conceived, written and directed by Swami Mitrananda.

Swami Tejomayananda formally inaugurates the Chinmaya Mission Amritsar in March. He also releases the spiritual monthly newsletter, *Chinmaya Amrit*.

The third Chinmaya International Camp is held at Pokhara, Nepal. The response is over-whelming. There are 350 delegates from all over the world. "Transformation Through Leadership" is the theme of the camp.

Sandeepany Vidyamandir is inaugurated at Coimbatore on August 31, 2000. The Acharya of the course is Br. Samahita Chaitanya.

Swami Chidananda, Swamini Premananda and several hundreds of devotees go on a torch march on December 31 in Powai, Mumbai to herald the dawn of the Golden Jubilee year of the Chinmaya Movement.

Glossary

Acharya	Spiritual teacher—one who practises what he teaches
Advaita	Literally it means 'not two' or non-dual. *Advaita* Vedanta is one of the six schools of Hindu philosophy which asserts that Brahman alone exists and the world and the individual self are illusory appearances within it. Shri Shankaracharya was the greatest exponent of *Advaita* Vedanta.
Akhanda Nama	Loud, group chanting of the name of the Lord without a break, usually the whole day as a religious discipline
Arati	Lighting the camphor (or an oil lamp) and waving it before the Lord as worship.
Archana	Worship of the Lord with flowers etc. while chanting the names of the Lord.
Ashram	A stage of life. The four Ashrams or stages of life are Brahmacharya (life of a student), *Grihastha* (life of a

	householder), *Vanaprastha* (life of a recluse in a forest) and *Sannyas* (life of a renunciant). (2) a place where hermits and sages live.
Avabhrita Snana	A ritualistic bath taken at a holy river by the teacher and the taught on the conclusion of a *yajna* or after seven days of reading and studying a religious text like *Bhagawat* or *Ramayan*
Bala Mahotsava	A coming together of many Balavihars in one place for a day or two to share their talents and ideas with each other in an atmosphere of joyful discipline and loving togetherness. Apart from display of talents there are also games, chanting, quiz programmes etc.
Balavihar	Weekly classes for children to inculcate Hindu culture in them. The children are helped to develop their personality.
Balvihar	Chinmaya Mission's international children's magazine.
Balwadis	A children's group activity in the villages.
Bhajan Choir	A choir for singing Bhajans which prepares the singers for singing the community.

Bhajans	Devotional songs in praise of the Lord.
Bhakti Margis	The seekers who try to reach the Lord by the path of devotion (*Bhakti*) or Love.
Bhoomi-pooja	Invoking the blessing of the Lord on the land where a building is going to be built.
Bhoo-samadhi	Burial of (typically) a monk. When a *Sannyasi* (a renunciant spiritual seeker) drops the body, it is either thrown into the river (Ganga) or buried.
Brahmachari	One who has taken the vow of celibacy during his study of the scriptures at the feet of his Guru.
Brahman	The infinite reality, the substratum for the manifestation of the entire pluralistic world. Its nature is Existence (*sat*), Consciousness (*chit*) and Bliss (*ananda*)
Chalk Talks	The talks where, during his global tour to America, Swamiji used to take the help of black board and chalk to make the listeners understand the Vedanta clearly.
Chinmaya Mission West	The organizational wing of Chinmaya Mission, comprising the Mission Centres in the West (USA, Canada).

Dakshina	A pecuniary offering to a mendicant or a token of money offered to a priest.
Darshan	(1) a vision, a system of philosophy; one of the six systems, for example, that accept the authority of the Vedas. (2) Seeing and receiving blessings of the lord or guru.
Deeksha	The ritual by which a person takes the vows to become a Brahmachari or *Sannyasi*.
Deeksha Guru	The teacher who gives the prescribed robes to a disciple at a ceremony initiating him into a particular stage of life like a Brahmacharya or *Sannyas*.
Devi Groups	Study classes for ladies.
Dharma Sevak	A short course in Vedanta conducted in Sandeepany for preparing workers (*sevaks*) with the right attitude to preserve *Dharma* (ethical life). It is for about a month or two.
Digvijaya Tour	Going on a global tour to spread what one considers to be the Truth and bringing about a change in people's thinking.
Dhwani	Musical sound
Narayana	Lord Vishnu, the husband of Goddess Lakshmi.

Ghar Ghar Mein Geeta	A series of lectures on the *Geeta* where the venue changes from house to house.
Guru	A teacher; a spiritual teacher.
Gurubhai	A classmate; a person who studied under the same preceptor.
Guru kula	The ancient system of education in India where a spiritual teacher and the students lived together, in an atmosphere of love. While the students served the master, the teacher imparted the knowledge of various subjects as well as self-knowledge
Guru-Seva	Service to teacher.
Havan	A fire ritual accompanied by the chanting of the vedic *mantras* with oblations of *ghee*, milk or grain.
Hindu	The foreign invaders who entered India through the North Western passes named the people as Hindus to indicate that they lived on the banks of the river Sindhu (Indus).From the ancient times the country was called *Bharata Varsha* and the people *Bharateeyas*.
Hindu Renaissance	Revival of Hindú culture, after periods of stagnation, by great masters like

	Shankaracharya, Rajaram Mohan Roy, Swami Vivekananda and Swami Chinmayananda.
Jayanti Pooja	The *pooja* conducted on the birth date of a great soul.
Jnana Yajna	A series of discourses by the master on scriptural texts, where ignorance is "sacrificed" in the fire of knowledge.
Jwala Sadas	A spiritual camp/gathering during summer.
Kaivalya	(1) State of aloneness—the realization that I alone am everything; (2) The name of the Ashram in Orlando.
Kamandalu	A vessel, typically made of dried pumpkin (the skin gets hard and colour is also changed), which serves as a food vessel for spiritual mendicants.
Karma Yoga	Dedicated, selfless actions undertaken with the spirit of serving others.
Karma Yoga Veera	The title given by Swamiji to Dr. B. V. Reddy of Chennai for conceiving and executing his first global tour: "a brave warrior practising *Karma Yoga*."
Karya Alochana Sabha	The workers' conference where the Mission workers plan the future course of action and evaluate the work.

Kirtans	Musical rendering of the Glory of the Lord.
Kumbhmela	A festival where people gather in large numbers to receive spiritual energy. When the *Devas* and the *Asuras* were fighting for the Nectar (*amrita*), which came out of the Milky ocean when it was churned, 4 drops of it fell in Ujjain, Nasik, Haridwar and Allahabad. It is believed that during a particular combination of the constellations the nectar emerges as energy vibration in these places.
Kuti	The small unpretentious abode of a monk, which is often a thatched hut.
Lesson course	A postal Vedanta course conducted by the Central Chinmaya Mission Trust for the benefit of those who want to learn Vedanta on their own.
Maha-samadhi	The great dissolution in The Infinite; leaving the body by a great mahatma, spiritual leader.
Mahatma	A great soul
Mahila Mandal	A forum formed for uplifting deprived women in the villages, making them fearless and self-sufficient.
Mananam	The name of a publication produced by Chinmaya Mission West that is a collection of articles.

Mandala Yajnas	Area yajnas; a district is divided into *Mandalas* for the sake of conducting *yajnas*.
Mantra	Mystic sound, a formula capable of conferring knowledge of God.
Maruti	Name of the Ashram in Boston Chinmaya centre; a name of Hanuman.
Meru	(1) The bead that hangs at the bottom of a *japa mala*, consisting of 108 beads. The devotee chants God's name, turns a bead and, upon reaching the *Meru*, reverses the direction. (2) the North Pole.
Meru Vidhi	A tradition where one goes to the North Pole and returns.
Mohallas	Localities in a town or city.
Mutt	Hindu monastery or seminary. For example, *Bhagavan* Adi Shankara established four *Mutts* for preserving the Vedas and other sacred scriptures at Badrinath, Shringeri, Dwarka and Puri.
Nagara-sankeertan	Devotees going around a town, chanting God's names as they walk on the roads..
Nama-sankeertan	Chanting the holy names of God, in groups typically.

Navaratri	The nine days' festival, in which the mother Goddess is worshipped as Saraswathi, Lakshmi and Durga, three days each. It is celebrated all over the country, and is extra grand in West Bengal.
Nididhyasana	Meditation that follows listening to the truth of the scriptures from a guru and reflection upon it.
OM (*Aum*)	A mystic sound or symbol that represents the Highest Reality–Brahman. The sound represents the entire world while the silence between two utterances represents Brahman.
Pahadis	The indigenous people who live on the Himalayan mountains.
Panchadashi	A scriptural text written by Swami Vidyaranya of Shringeri Mutt. It has fifteen (*panchadasha*) chapters, hence the name.
Parivraja	Wandering; life of a wandering monk who renounces the world, lives on whatever he gets by chance, by the grace of the Lord.
Parna Kuti	A hut made up of leaves for the stay of the *Mahatmas*.
Pauranic	Pertaining to the *Puranas*—(see *puranas*).

Poorva-ashram — Previous Ashram or stage of life.

Prachar — Spreading the message of the scriptural texts by discourses, workshops and other means.

Pradhan — A manager.

Pranava — The primordial sound Om. The creation, according to the Hindu scriptures, started with the sound Om.

Prarambhotsav — The festive function where something (a temple, for example) is opened or begun.

Prasad — Food, usually sweets, offered to the Gods during a ritualistic worship. It is distributed among the participants as a consecrated offering along with ash, sandalwood paste or other items from the worship.

Pratah Smaranam — Name of a Spiritual Programme in Trinidad

Pratima — A statue

Puranas — Books of stories in which Vedantic ideas are objectified and dramatized in the lives of saints, kings, devotees and divine incarnations. There are eighteen *Puranas* attributed to Shri Veda Vyasa.

Rajasic	Predominant in the quality *rajas*. Mind has three modes (*gunas*): *Sattva* (harmony or brightness), *Rajas* (restless activity) and *Tamas* (inertia or torpor). When Rajo-guna predominates in a man, he is called Rajasic by temperament and greed, restlessness, activity and longing rise in him.
Renaissance	A revival of a culture brought about typically by a great man.
Rishi	A divinely inspired sage or seer who is a man of deep scriptural knowledge and direct experience of the Truth.
Sadas	A gathering for discussing a particular topic.
Sadhak	A spiritual aspirant or practitioner
Sadhana	The spiritual disciplines adopted by a *sadhaka* (seeker) to reach his spiritual goal (*sadhyam*).
Sadhu	A practitioner of spiritual values. Renouncing the attachment to the world, he lives a life of goodness, happy in whatever comes to him by chance.
Samadhi sthal	A place of worship where the body of a Mahatma is placed beneath.
Samsara	Worldly life characterized by constant change. Our likes and dislikes create joys and sorrows, causing great stress.

Sanatana Dharma	The perennial Hindu culture or *Dharma* that never perishes. For it is Truth itself.
Sandhya Vandana	The worship of the sun that a boy does after taking the sacred thread and the instruction in Gayatri Mantra. This is thrice a day—at dawn, mid-day and dusk—the *Sandhyas*.
Sannyas	The fourth stage of life, which is renunciation of all other pursuits for the sake of Self-knowledge. (See Ashram)
Sannyas Deeksha	Conferring on a seeker the ritual where a seeker is formally led to the highest stage viz. renunciation.
Satsang	(1) Association or nearness with the virtuous; therefore discussions with or time spent in the presence of spiritual masters. (2) being in communion with the essence of one's being (*sat*).
Satyam-eva-Jayate	Famous saying from *Mundakopanishad* which says that only Truth will win ultimately.
Self-unfoldment	The unveiling on one's own true nature—which is *Sat Chit Ananda*.
Shantipath	A chant for peace within and without.

Shishya	A spiritual student who has accepted a guru or a master as his teacher and observes spiritual disciplines.
Shlokas	Hindu scriptural verses.
Shlokathon	A collection of more than 250 Hindu scriptural *shlokas* (stanzas) divided into 15 sections compiled by Houston Chinmaya Mission Centre.
Shmashana Vahanam	A service for the poor, where arrangement is provided to take a dead body to the cremation ground.
Shodashi	The functions held on the sixteenth day after a Mahatma sheds his mortal coil. Many *Sadhus* (mendicants) are called, given food and also *Dakshina*.
Shruti	The scriptural revelations 'heard' by great saints and sages in moments of deep meditation.
Son et lumiere	A light and sound show.
Study Groups	A small gathering of people who come together once a week to study together a scriptural text by discussion and sharing of ideas.
Svayambhoo-Linga	A *linga* (of Shiva) that came on its own, not created by a human being. It symbolizes Brahman which is causeless and unborn.

Swami	(1) a master; (2) the title used by one who has taken the vows of renunciation.
Talk Fest	The 'feast of talks' conducted by Swamiji in America and other Western countries
Tapas	Austerities at the physical, mental and intellectual levels undertaken to purify the mind, which makes it, shine or blaze.
Tapovan	The Guru of Swami Chinmayananda.
Tapovanam	Forest of austerities
Tapovan Day	The birthday of Swami Tapovan Maharaj, the teacher of Swami Chinmayananda. It is the eleventh day of the bright fortnight of the *Margashirsha*, typically falling in December. It coincides with *Geeta Jayanti*.
Tapovrata	A vow of austerity taken by a disciple for one year where he shaves off his hair when his teacher, guru, passes away.
Upanayana	A ritualistic ceremony when a child belonging to any of the three upper castes in the Hindu hierarchy, is initiated into spiritual life by giving him

	the holy *Gayatri Mantra* and the sacred thread. The ceremony for the purpose of "bringing near or leading to" the Truth is performed by a priest and presided over by the father of the boy being initiated.
Upanishads	The philosophical section and culmination of each of the four Vedas which reveals the essential oneness between God and man. These treatises which are meant for the highest seekers are to be taught by an enlightened teacher to students of a humble and receptive attitude, "seated below" both mentally and physically. (*upa*=near; *ni*=below; *sad*=sit)
Vastra	Clothes with which body is covered.
Vijaya-dashami	The tenth day after the *Navaratri* (the nine days' festival when Devi is worshipped) celebrated as the day of victory.
Vijnana Nilayam	The place where weekly Vedanta classes are conducted
Vishwa Hindu Parishad	The Hindu organization to bring the Hindus of the world together.

Yajna	(1) the ritual of "fire sacrifice" where a performer invokes the blessings of The Highest by sacrificing various substance in the fire for the common good or personal well being. (2) any activity performed in the spirit of self-sacrifice and dynamic togetherness for the good of all.
Yajna Prasad	(1) The offering of food etc. which is offered to the deity during a ritual, which is shared by all present after the ritual is over. (2) the small book given to all the participants by the speaker, at the end of a discourse series.
Yajna-shala	The venue where a *Yajna* is conducted.
Yogi	A practitioner of the art and science of union with God.
Yuva Kendra	The youth wing (of Chinmaya Mission).

References

from Books, Journels, Interviews etc.

SOURCES OF DATA

The major source of data was the History reports submitted by Chinmaya Mission centres. 184 centres out of 198 in India have submitted their reports. All the 46 foreign centres (100%) also submitted their reports. This source was very reliable and comprehensive. The reports on a rough calculation ran over 2,500 pages of typed matter, which is now converted into 'soft' copies (floppies) and preserved in the Archives Section of CCMT.

Sr.No.	SUBJECT	AUTHOR / PUBLISHER
1.	HAIL RENAISANCE Vol. I	CHINMAYA MISSION DELHI
2.	HAIL RENAISANCE Vol. II	CCMT PUBLICATIONS
3.	HAIL RENAISANCE Vol. III	TARA CULTURAL TRUST
4.	HAIL RENAISANCE Vol. IV	CHINMAYA MISSION – CHENNAI
5.	TAPOVAN PRASAD-SILVER JUBILEE	CHINMAYA MISSION – CHENNAI
6.	SAMARPAN	CELEBRATION COMMITTEE, CHINMAYA MISSION.
7.	MEDITATION (Souvenir)	CCMT PUBLICATIONS
8.	500th GEETA GNANA YAGNA & 75th BIRTH YEAR CELEBRATIONS	CCMT PUBLICATIONS
9.	SANATANA SANDESH	CHINMAYA MISSION (KCST- B'LORE)
10.	THE WEEK (11th ANNIVERSARY SPECIAL ON KSHAMA METRE, SIDHBARI)	MANORAMA PUBLICATIONS
11.	VISION 2001(Souvenir)	CHINMAYA MISSION – PUNE
12.	CHINMAYA MISSION HOSPITAL	CHINMAYA MISSION – BANGALORE

13.	SWAMI CHINMAYANANDA (A LIFE OF INSPIRATION AND SERVICE)	RUDITE EMIR (1998)
14.	THE JOURNEY OF A MASTER (SWAMI CHINMAYANANDA)	NANCY PATCHEN (1989)
15.	AGELESS GURU (THE INSPIRATIONAL LIFE OF SWAMI CHINMAYANANDA)	RADHIKA KRISHNAKUMAR (1999)
16.	CHINMAYA YUVA KENDRA GUIDE LINES	CCMT PUBLICATIONS
17.	STUDY GROUP – GUIDE LINES	CCMT PUBLICATIONS
18.	BALA VIHAR – GUIDE LINES	CCMT PUBLICATIONS
19.	AN AUTOBIOGRAHICAL SKETCH OF SWAMI CHINMAYANANDA	BIRTH OF A KARAKA PURUSHA – TAPOVAN PRASAD 1997, MAY.
20.	SUVARNA TULABHARAM SOUVENIR & 75TH BIRTH YEAR CELEBRATIONS	500TH YAGNA COMMITTEE
21.	CHINMAYA ALAYA VAIBHAVAN	CHINMAYA MISSION (KCST- B'LORE)
22.	CHINMAYA SAMSMARANAM	CHINMAYA MISSION (KCST- B'LORE)

CHINMAYA MISSION PUBLICATIONS—JOURNALS

Sr.No.	JOURNALS
1.	TYAGI (Fortnightly) – September 1955-1963—All issues.
2.	USHA – May 1958-1963—All issues.
3.	TAPOVAN PRASAD – 38 years of monthly issues from December 1963-December 2000.

INTERVIEWS

Swamis / Swaminis:

- Swami Tejomayananda
- Swami Purushottamananda
- Swami Jyotirmayananda
- Swami Brahmananda
- Swami Subodhananda
- Swami Swaroopananda
- Swamini Gangananda
- Swamini Nishtananda
- Swamini Purnananda

TRUSTEES

Ms. Tara Sarup (TCT)
Jamnadas Moorjani (CCMT)
Narasimhulu Shetty (KCST)

DEVOTEES

M. Ct. Petachi, *Chennai*
V. Sethu, *Hoe & Co., Chennai*
S. Parthasarathi, *Kumudam, Chennai*
Kamala N.V.R. Reddy, *Bangalore*
Sushila Purushottam, *Bangalore*
Shakuntala Bindra, *New Delhi*
Janak Kapoor, *Noida*
K.C. Bhatia, *New Delhi*
Smt. Indira Bhardawaj, *Chinmaya Vidyalaya, New Delhi*
Shri Purushumal, *New Delhi*
Anjali Singh, *New Delhi*
Sita Juneja, *New Delhi*
Mrs. Pushpa Kamdar, *Mumbai*
Ms. Darshanaben Nanavaty, *Houston*
Shri. Madhukar V. Naidoo, *Pune*

FROM THE LIBRARIES

1) *Ramana Centenary Library, Tiruvanamallai* – ref. work on 'Call Divine'.
2) *Divine Life Society Library, Rishikesh* – for documentation on *sannyas deeksha* to Swami Chinmayananda.

Acknowledgements

This assignment owes its gratitude to many who have, in big and small ways, helped us. We place on record our thanks to -

Swami Tejomayananda	for having given us the honour to handle this prestigious project and for the continuous guidance given to our team.
Swami Purushottamananda] Swami Jyotirmayananda] Swami Brahmananda] Swami Swaroopananda] Swami Subodhananda]	for sharing their experiences and perceptions.
Swamini Samvidananda	for her informative article on Chinmaya Vidyalayas.
Swamini Purnananda	for facilitating the meeting with the old devotees of Delhi.
Swamini Niranjanananda	for compiling the glossary.
Swamini Seelananda	who, along with Swamini Saradapriyananda assisted the team to get reports from the Chinmaya Mission Centres in Andhra Pradesh.
Jamnadas Moorjani	for sharing with us many valuable experiences he had as the Secretary of Chinmaya Mission in the '60s and as a Trustee of CCMT.

Ms. Anjali Singh	for photographs of Swami Chinmayananda, and other useful photos for the book.
Mrs. Pushpa Kamdar	for her write-up on her husband, B. M. Kamdar.
Mrs. Sushila Purushottam	for sharing her personal compilation on the life of Swami Chinmayananda.
Mrs. N. V. R. Reddy	for sharing her memories of her association with Swamiji.
Dr. Mrs. Madhuriben Sheth	for her compilation on history of the Mumbai Chinmaya Mission.

All those who encouraged us by sending their donations specially for the History Book Project.

K. C. Patnaik, G. M., Book Division, CCMT	for his assistance in coordination with the printers.
A. S. Hebbar	for having patiently edited the book.
Ms. Usha Hemmady	for rendering her services for editing the book.
Somik Chowdhry and his team	for printing and bringing out an attractive book.
N. J. Joseph	for his co-operation in typesetting the entire book.
Creative Minds, Kottayam	for beautiful cover design.
To all	who have sent contribution on various subject.
To all people big and small	who have been in many ways helpful in completing this mammoth task, and

Last but not the least to the following persons who assisted us—Br. Nandagopal, Br. Shailesh Chaitanya, Br. Aniketh Chaitanya, Ms. Jayshri Bhagawat, P. Ramkumar, K.S. Rindani, Ms. Devna Kamath and Devang Joshi.

S. C.
R. R.

Index